THE CAMB1
ENGL

MW00779607

This newly commissioned series of essays by leading scholars is the first volume
to offer both an overview of the field and currently emerging critical views on the
history, form, and influence of English melodrama. Authoritative voices provide
an introduction to melodrama's early formal features such as tableaux and
music, and trace the development of the genre in the nineteenth century through
the texts and performances of its various subgenres, the theatres within which the
plays were performed, and the audiences who watched them. The historical
contexts of melodrama are considered through essays on topics including contemporary politics, class, gender, race, and empire. And the extensive influences
of melodrama are demonstrated through a wide-ranging assessment of its
ongoing and sometimes unexpected expressions – in psychoanalysis, in other
art forms (the novel, film, television, musical theatre), and in popular culture
generally – from the nineteenth to the twenty-first century.

**Carolyn Williams** is Professor in the Department of English at Rutgers University
in New Brunswick, New Jersey. She is the author of *Gilbert and Sullivan:
Gender, Genre, Parody* (2010) and *Transfigured World: Walter Pater's
Aesthetic Historicism* (1989), and is the co-editor (with Laurel Brake and
Lesley Higgins) of *Walter Pater: Transparencies of Desire* (2002).

*A complete list of books in the series is at the back of this book.*

# THE CAMBRIDGE
# COMPANION TO
# ENGLISH MELODRAMA

EDITED BY
## CAROLYN WILLIAMS
*Rutgers University*

# CAMBRIDGE
## UNIVERSITY PRESS

University Printing House, Cambridge CB2 8BS, United Kingdom

One Liberty Plaza, 20th Floor, New York, NY 10006, USA

477 Williamstown Road, Port Melbourne, VIC 3207, Australia

314–321, 3rd Floor, Plot 3, Splendor Forum, Jasola District Centre,
New Delhi – 110025, India

79 Anson Road, #06–04/06, Singapore 079906

Cambridge University Press is part of the University of Cambridge.

It furthers the University's mission by disseminating knowledge in the pursuit of
education, learning, and research at the highest international levels of excellence.

www.cambridge.org
Information on this title: www.cambridge.org/9781107095939
DOI: 10.1017/9781316155875

First published 2018

Printed in the United Kingdom by TJ International Ltd. Padstow Cornwall

A catalogue record for this publication is available from the British Library.

Library of Congress Cataloging-in-Publication Data
NAMES: Williams, Carolyn, 1950– editor.
TITLE: The Cambridge companion to English melodrama / edited by Carolyn Williams.
DESCRIPTION: Cambridge, United Kingdom ; New York, NY : Cambridge University Press,
[2018] | Includes bibliographical references.
IDENTIFIERS: LCCN 2018022346| ISBN 9781107095939 (hardback) | ISBN
9781107479593 (paperback)
SUBJECTS: LCSH: Melodrama, English – History and criticism.
CLASSIFICATION: LCC PR635.M45 C36 2018 | DDC 822/.052709–dc23
LC record available at https://lccn.loc.gov/2018022346

ISBN 978-1-107-09593-9 Hardback
ISBN 978-1-107-47959-3 Paperback

*For Sally Ledger*
*(1961–2009)*

# CONTENTS

# CONTENTS

# ILLUSTRATIONS

CONTRIBUTORS

Hayley Jayne Bradley lectures in Performance for Stage and Screen at Sheffield Hallam University. She has written on aspects of late nineteenth- and early twentieth-century popular British theatre, including collaborating dramatists and theatrical adaptation. She is currently researching her first monograph, *British and American Theatrical Artisans: The Professional Craft of the Late Nineteenth-Century Theatrical Entrepreneur.*

Peter Brooks is Sterling Professor of Comparative Literature Emeritus at Yale University, where he was Founding Director of the Whitney Humanities Center, and is currently Andrew W. Mellon Foundation Scholar in the University Center for Human Values and the Department of Comparative Literature at Princeton University. He is the author of several books, including *The Melodramatic Imagination* (1976), *Reading for the Plot* (1984), *Troubling Confessions: Speaking Guilt in Law and Literature* (2000), *Henry James Goes to Paris* (2007), and the recently published *Flaubert in the Ruins of Paris* (2017).

Matthew Buckley is Associate Professor in the Department of English at Rutgers University (New Brunswick) and a scholar of comparative drama whose recent work has focused on the early development of stage melodrama and the extended, multimedial, transcultural history of melodrama as a form. He is the author of *Tragedy Walks the Streets: The French Revolution in the Making of Modern Drama* (2006), as well as articles in *Modern Drama, Theatre Survey, Theatre Journal, Victorian Studies, Studies in Romanticism,* and elsewhere. He is also the editor of *Modern Drama*'s special issue on stage, film, and television melodrama (2012) and the Ashgate *Research Companion to Melodrama* (in development). He is the founder and director of the Melodrama Research Consortium (www.melodramaresearchconsortium.org), a global network of more than 150 scholars formed to foster collaborative research on the topic, and the Melodrama Database Project, an international effort to construct a digital database of melodrama's global history.

**Jim Davis** is Professor of Theatre Studies at the University of Warwick. His major research interest is in nineteenth-century British theatre, and his most recent books are *Comic Acting and Portraiture in Late-Georgian and Regency England* (Cambridge University Press, 2015) and *Theatre and Entertainment* (2016). He is the editor of *Victorian Pantomime: A Collection of Critical Essays* (2010) and *Lives of Shakespearian Actors: Edmund Kean* (2009). He is also co-author of a study of London theatre audiences in the nineteenth century, *Reflecting the Audience: London Theatregoing 1840–1880* (2001). He has published a wide range of book chapters and refereed articles in his research field. Current research projects include a two-volume edition of nineteenth-century dramatizations of Dickens (with Jacky Bratton), and a study of cultural exchange between Britain and Australia 1880–1960 (with Australian academic Veronica Kelly) titled *Anglo-Australian Cultural Exchange 1880–1960*.

**Jane M. Gaines** is Professor of Film at Columbia University and author of two award-winning books: *Contested Culture: The Image, the Voice, and the Law* (1991) and *Fire and Desire: Mixed Race Movies in the Silent Era* (2001), both of which received the Katherine Singer Kovacs Best Book award from the Society for Cinema and Media Studies. She received an Academy of Motion Picture Arts and Sciences Film Scholars grant for her forthcoming *Pink-Slipped: What Happened to Women in the Silent Film Industries?* and for work on the Women Film Pioneers digital archive published by Columbia University Libraries in 2013, research supported by a Radcliffe Institute for Advanced Study Fellowship. She has written articles on intellectual property and piracies, documentary theory and radicalism, feminism and film, early cinema, and critical race theory that have appeared in *Cinema Journal, Screen, Cultural Studies, Framework, Camera Obscura*, and *Women and Performance*. Most recently she has been working on a critique of the 'historical turn' in film and media studies.

**Michael Gamer** is Professor of English at the University of Pennsylvania. He is the author of *Romanticism, Self-Canonization, and the Business of Poetry* (Cambridge University Press, 2017) and *Romanticism and the Gothic: Genre, Reception, and Canon Formation* (Cambridge University Press, 2000), and Associate Editor of the journal *EIR: Essays in Romanticism*. With Jeffrey Cox, he co-edited *The Broadview Anthology of Romantic Period Drama* (2003).

**Christine Gledhill** has written numerous essays on feminist film criticism, film genre, melodrama, and British cinema – including her anthology, *Home Is Where the Heart Is: Studies in Melodrama and the Woman's Film* (1987) and her monograph, *Reframing British Cinema, 1918–1928: Between Restraint and Passion* (2003). She has also published on stardom, the film actress from stage to screen, and early British scriptwriter Lydia Hayward. She has recently co-edited (with Julia Knight) *Doing Women's Film History: Reframing Cinemas Past and Present* (2015) and most recently has been writing for and co-editing (with Linda Williams) the anthology *Melodrama Unbound: Across History, Media, and National Cultures*, published in 2018.

**Marty Gould** is Associate Professor of English at the University of South Florida. He is the author of *Nineteenth-Century Theatre and the Imperial Encounter* (2011). His essays on empire and the Victorian stage have appeared in *Modern Drama*, *Cahiers victoriens et édouardiens*, and *Victorian Review*.

**Juliet John** is Hildred Carlile Chair of English Literature and Head of English at Royal Holloway, University of London. She has published widely on Victorian literature and culture, and on popular culture more broadly. She has published two monographs on Dickens, *Dickens's Villains: Melodrama, Character and Popular Culture* (2001) and *Dickens and Mass Culture* (2010), the first of which was informed by her career-long interest in melodrama. Since then, on melodrama, she has published the essay 'Melodrama and Its Critics: An Essay in Memory of Sally Ledger' in the journal *19: Interdisciplinary Studies in the Long Nineteenth Century* (2009) and the entry on melodrama for *Oxford Bibliographies: Victorian Literature*, of which she is editor-in-chief. She is the editor, most recently, of *The Oxford Handbook of Victorian Literary Culture* (2016).

**David Mayer** is Emeritus Professor of Drama at the University of Manchester and studies British and American popular entertainment of the nineteenth and early twentieth century. Recent writings explore links between the Victorian stage and early motion pictures. He is co-founder of the Victorian and Edwardian Stage on Film Project, and a contributing member to the [D. W.] Griffith Project. Books include *Harlequin in His Element* (1968), *Henry Irving and The Bells* (1980), *Four Bars of 'Agit': Music for Victorian and Edwardian Melodrama* (1983), *Playing Out the Empire: Ben-Hur and Other Toga-Plays and Films* (1994), *Stagestruck Filmmaker: D. W. Griffith and the American Theatre* (2009), and *Bandits! or The Collapsing Bridge: An Early Film and a Late-Victorian Stage* (2015). In 2012 he received the Distinguished Scholar Award from the American Society for Theatre Research. A Guggenheim Fellow, he has also received research fellowships from Yale and Harvard Universities, the Harry Ransom Humanities Research Center, the Leverhulme Trust, and the British Academy.

**Rohan McWilliam** is Professor of Modern British History at Anglia Ruskin University in Cambridge and a former President of the British Association for Victorian Studies. He is the author of *The Tichborne Claimant: A Victorian Sensation* (2007) and co-editor of *The Victorian Studies Reader* (2007), *Labour and the Left in the 1980s* (2017), and *New Directions in Social and Cultural History* (2018). He has also written articles about Victorian melodrama, Elsa

Lanchester, Jonathan Miller, and Asa Briggs. Currently, he is at work on a history of the West End of London and is co-editing a volume about the Victorian publisher Edward Lloyd.

**Sarah Meer** is Senior Lecturer at the University of Cambridge and a Fellow of Selwyn College. Her first book, *Uncle Tom Mania*, dealt substantially with melodrama and minstrelsy on both sides of the Atlantic (2005). She is now working towards a book on Dion Boucicault, on whose drama she has published four articles. First, however, she must finish a book called *Cousins and Claimants: Transatlantic Notions, 1820–1920*. This also has a theatre chapter on Tom Taylor's comedy *Our American Cousin*.

**Ankhi Mukherjee** is Professor of English and World Literatures at the University of Oxford and a Fellow of Wadham College. Mukherjee's first book is *Aesthetic Hysteria: The Great Neurosis in Victorian Melodrama and Contemporary Fiction* (2007). Her second monograph, *What is a Classic? Postcolonial Rewriting and Invention of the Canon*, published in 2014, won the British Academy Rose Mary Crawshay Prize in English Literature in 2015. Mukherjee has published on a wide range of topics in *PMLA, MLQ, Contemporary Literature, Paragraph, Parallax*, and others, and has co-edited *A Concise Companion to Psychoanalysis, Literature, and Culture* (2014). She is at work on her third monograph, *Unseen City: The Psychic Life of the Poor in Mumbai, London, and New York*, and has just finished editing a collection of essays, *After Lacan*, to be published by Cambridge University Press in 2018.

**Katherine Newey** is Professor of Theatre History at the University of Exeter. She is a literary historian specializing in nineteenth-century British popular theatre and women's writing. She has published widely on melodrama, pantomime, the theatre of the nineteenth century, and Victorian women's writing, particularly playwriting. Her recent books include *Politics, Performance and Popular Culture: Theatre and Society in Nineteenth-Century Britain* (with Peter Yeandle and Jeffrey Richards; 2016), *John Ruskin and the Victorian Theatre* (with Jeffrey Richards; 2010), and *Women's Theatre Writing in Victorian Britain* (2005).

**Michael V. Pisani** is Mary Conover Mellon Professor of Music at Vassar College and the author of *Music for the Melodramatic Theatre in Nineteenth-Century London and New York* (2014). He has published several articles on the use of music in drama, both for the stage and for film. His article 'When the Music Surges: Nineteenth-Century Theatrical Precedents for Film Music Style and Placement' explores the little-known pre-history of film music in the traditions of stage melodrama. He has also published on musical exoticism. His *Imagining Native America in Music* (2005) won an ASCAP-Deems Taylor Award. His most recent work is a college textbook titled *The Principles of Music Creation and Interpretation*.

**George Taylor** is Honorary Research Fellow in Drama at the University of Manchester and author of *Players and Performances in the Victorian Theatre* (1989) and *The French Revolution and the London Stage* (2000). He has written research papers, chapters, and articles on Thomas Holcroft's *Tale of Mystery*, François Delsarte's acting theory and practice, anti-slave trade plays, and Beerbohm Tree's performance as Svengali. He also has research and production interests in Ancient Greek and Russian theatre.

**Sharon Aronofsky Weltman** is Davis Alumni Professor of English at Louisiana State University. Widely published on Victorian literature, theatre, and culture, her books include *Performing the Victorian: John Ruskin and Identity in Theater, Science, and Education* (2007) and *Ruskin's Mythic Queen: Gender Subversion in Victorian Culture* (1998), which was chosen as Outstanding Academic Book by *Choice* magazine in 1999. Now the North American editor of *Nineteenth-Century Theatre and Film* (NCTF), she previously guest-edited issues of *Nineteenth-Century Prose* (2008) and *NCTF* (2011). Her *NCTF* special issue is a scholarly edition of the 1847 melodrama *Sweeney Todd*. In 2014, she directed a National Endowment for the Humanities Summer Seminar: 'Performing Dickens: *Oliver Twist* and *Great Expectations* on Page, Stage, and Screen'. Her current book project is 'Victorians on Broadway: The Afterlife of Nineteenth-Century British Literature on the Broadway Musical Stage'.

**Carolyn Williams** is Professor of English at Rutgers University (New Brunswick). In addition to essays on Victorian novels, poetry, nonfiction prose, and theatre, she is the author of *Gilbert and Sullivan: Gender, Genre, Parody* (2010). Her earlier books are *Transfigured World: Walter Pater's Aesthetic Historicism* (1989) and the co-edited collection of essays (with Laurel Brake and Lesley Higgins), *Walter Pater: Transparencies of Desire* (2002). She is currently writing a book about Victorian melodrama, under the working title *The Aesthetics of Melodramatic Form*.

# ACKNOWLEDGEMENTS

Sally Ledger and I had planned to edit this volume together. Sally's brilliant and generous collaborative spirit was evident to everyone, and I was eagerly looking forward to the experience of working with her again. Her 2007 study, *Dickens and the Popular Radical Imagination* (Cambridge University Press), evaluated the role melodrama played in Dickens's formation. At the time of her death, she was working on affect and sentimentality in the Victorian period, work that would no doubt have further contributed to our understanding of melodrama. Together we planned this volume – which is dedicated to her with love, gratitude, and admiration – under the redwoods in beautiful Santa Cruz, California, where we both gained so much from participating in the lively intellectual exchange at the annual Dickens Universe, organized by the Dickens Project. Thanks always to the director of the Dickens Project, John O. Jordan.

For timely suggestions along the way, I would like to thank Linda Bree, Matt Buckley, David Mayer, and Sharon Aronofsky Weltman. Each of you will know how much you helped by answering emails immediately and solving particularly knotty problems with very good cheer. No one could ask for a more attentive editor than Linda Bree. Conversations with her began long ago, during the earliest planning stages, and have guided me throughout the process. Many thanks to her and to her editorial assistant at the press, Tim Mason. Thanks also to Dawn Wade and Puviarassy Kalieperumal. Finally, great thanks and praise are due to Lech Harris, whose editorial precision, acumen, and tact have contributed so much to this project in its final stages. He, too, has made this a better book.

# A NOTE ON CITATIONS OF PLAYS

In the text of these essays, quoted lines from plays are cited parenthetically by act and scene number, as in (3:2) for Act 3, scene 2. The theatre in which a play was first performed is usually not given in the text of these essays, but in most cases it can be found in the Chronology.

# CHRONOLOGY

| | |
|---|---|
| 1737 | Licensing Act restricts 'spoken drama' to the patent theatres: Covent Garden and Drury Lane. |
| 1766 | The Haymarket joins the list of patent theatres. |
| 1781 | Horace Walpole's *The Castle of Otranto* adapted to the stage as *The Count of Narbonne* (Covent Garden). |
| 1782 | The Surrey Theatre, London, opens as the Royal Circus. |
| 1794 | John Philip Kemble's *Macbeth* celebrates the reopening of Drury Lane Theatre. Opposite, at Covent Garden, is James Boaden's *Fontainville Forest*, an adaptation of Ann Radcliffe's *Romance of the Forest*. |
| 1797 | Charles Farley's *Raymond and Agnes*, an adaptation of Matthew Lewis's *The Monk* (Covent Garden). Later in the year, Lewis's own *The Castle Spectre* (Drury Lane). |
| 1798 | George Colman the Younger's extravagant afterpiece *Blue Beard* (Drury Lane). |
| 1799 | Richard Brinsley Sheridan's *Pizarro* (Drury Lane), an adaption of August von Kotzebue's *Die Spaniard in Peru*. |
| 1802 | Thomas Holcroft's *A Tale of Mystery* (Covent Garden), an adaptation of Pixerécourt's *Coelina; ou l'enfant du mystère* (Ambigu-Comique, Paris, 1800). |
| 1803–15 | Napoleonic Wars. |
| 1805 | Matthew Lewis, *Rugantino; or, The Bravo of Venice* (Covent Garden). |
| 1806 | Adelphi Theatre opens on the Strand, London. |
| 1806 | Theodore Hook, *Tékéli; or, The Siege of Montgatz* (Drury Lane). |
| 1809 | Old Price Riots, Covent Garden. |
| 1809 | Lyceum Theatre opens, initially as an opera house. |
| 1810 | William Barrymore, *The Blood-Red Knight; or, The Fatal Bridge* (Astley's Amphitheatre). |

| | |
|---|---|
| 1811–16 | Luddite disturbances. |
| 1813 | Isaac Pocock, *The Miller and His Men* (Covent Garden). |
| 1818 | The *Rob Roy* mania. |
| 1818 | Opening of Royal Coburg Theatre (later the Victoria). |
| 1818 | William Barrymore, *El Hyder* (Coburg). |
| 1820 | William Thomas Moncrieff, *The Lear of Private Life; or, Father and Daughter* (Coburg). |
| 1823 | The *Frankenstein* mania. |
| 1823 | William Thomas Moncrieff, *The Cataract of the Ganges; or, The Rajah's Daughter* (Drury Lane). |
| 1823 | Richard Brinsley Peake, *Presumption; or, The Fate of Frankenstein* (English Opera House). |
| 1827 | J. B. Buckstone, *Luke the Labourer; or, The Lost Son* (Adelphi). |
| 1827 | Edward Fitzball, *The Flying Dutchman; or, The Phantom Ship* (Adelphi). |
| 1828 | Edward Fitzball, *The Inchcape Bell; or, The Dumb Sailor Boy* (Surrey). |
| 1828 | Douglas Jerrold, *Fifteen Years of a Drunkard's Life* (Coburg). |
| 1829 | Douglas Jerrold, *Black-Ey'd Susan*, with T. P. Cooke as William (Surrey). |
| 1829 | Douglas Jerrold, *John Overy, the Miser of Southwark Ferry* (Surrey). |
| 1832 | Select Parliamentary Committee on Dramatic Literature. |
| 1832 | First Reform Act. |
| 1832 | John Walker, *The Factory Lad* (Surrey). |
| 1832 | Douglas Jerrold, *The Rent Day* (Drury Lane). |
| 1833 | Slavery Abolition Act. |
| 1835 | R. J. Raymond, *The Old Oak Tree* (Lyceum). |
| 1838 | *The Idiot of Heidelberg* (various authors and various London theatres). |
| 1838–9 | The *Oliver Twist / Jack Sheppard* mania. |
| 1838–57 | Chartist Movement. |
| 1839–46 | Anti-Corn Law League. |
| 1843 | Theatres Regulation Act. |
| 1844 | Charles Selby, *Satan in Paris; or, The Mysterious Stranger* (Adelphi), adapted from the French, *Satan; ou, Le Diable à Paris*. |
| 1844 | Edward Fitzball, *Home Again! or, The Lieutenant's Daughter* (Lyceum). |

1845    J. B. Buckstone, *The Green Bushes*, music by Alfred Mellon (Adelphi).

1846    Tom Parry, *Eugenia Claircille; or, The New Found Home* (Adelphi).

1847    Edward Stirling, *Lilly Dawson; or, A Poor Girl's Story* (Surrey).

1847    T. P. Taylor, *The Bottle* (City).

1848    Chartist demonstrations in Trafalgar Square and Kennington Common.

1852    Mark Lemon and Tom Taylor, *Slave Life: or, Uncle Tom's Cabin* (Adelphi).

1852    Dion Boucicault, *The Corsican Brothers*, with Charles Kean (Princess's).

1857–8    Indian Rebellion.

1858    Dion Boucicault, *Jessie Brown: or, the Relief of Lucknow* (Wallack's, New York); a revised version of *Jessie Brown*, titled *The Relief of Lucknow*, is staged in 1862 (Drury Lane).

1859    Dion Boucicault, *The Octoroon; or, Life in Louisiana* opens in New York (Winter Garden); it debuts in London in 1861 (Adelphi).

1860    Dion Boucicault, *The Colleen Bawn; or, The Brides of Garryowen* (Adelphi).

1863    Colin Hazlewood's adaptation of Mary Elizabeth Braddon's *Lady Audley's Secret* (Royal Victoria); multiple adaptations staged in London throughout the year.

1863    Metropolitan Line opens as the world's first underground railway.

1863    Tom Taylor, *The Ticket-of-Leave- Man* (Olympic).

1864    Dion Boucicault, *Arrah-na-Pogue; or, The Wicklow Wedding* (Old Theatre Royal, Dublin); with a revised version in 1865 (Princess's).

1865    Staplehurst Rail Crash.

1865    Charles Reade, *It is Never Too Late To Mend* (Princess's).

1865    Tom Taylor, *The Serf; or, Love Levels All* (Olympic).

1866    *The Black Crook*, music by Thomas Baker, book by Charles M. Barras (Niblo's Garden, New York).

1867    Second Reform Act.

1867    T. W. Robertson, *Caste* (Prince of Wales's).

1870    Married Women's Property Act.

1871    Leopold Lewis, *The Bells*, with Henry Irving as Mathias (Lyceum).

| | |
|---|---|
| 1874 | T. A. Palmer, *East Lynne* (Nottingham), adapted from Ellen Wood's novel of the same name (1860–1). |
| 1877 | Queen Victoria proclaimed Empress of India. |
| 1878 | W. S. Gilbert and Arthur Sullivan, *H. M. S. Pinafore; or, The Lass That Loved a Sailor* (Opera Comique). |
| 1879–96 | Augustus Harris is manager of Drury Lane. |
| 1881 | Richard D'Oyly Carte's Savoy Theatre entirely illuminated by electricity. |
| 1881 | George R. Sims, *The Lights o' London* (Princess's). |
| 1884 | Third Reform Act. |
| 1889 | Henry Arthur Jones, *The Middleman* (Shaftesbury). |
| 1889 | Robert Buchanan, *A Man's Shadow* (Haymarket), adapted from the French. |
| 1895 | Lumière Brothers *cinématographe* premiere program (Café Indien, Paris). |
| 1896 | Edison Co. Kinetoscope premiere program (Koster and Bial's Music Hall, New York). |
| 1898 | Lottie Blair Parker, *Way Down East* (Manhattan Theatre, New York). |
| 1898 | First 'moving staircase' (escalator) installed in Harrods, London. |
| 1899–1902 | Boer War. |
| 1900 | Arthur Shirley, *The Absent-Minded Beggar* (Princess's). |
| 1903 | Film release of *The Great Train Robbery* (dir. Edwin S. Porter). |
| 1903 | *Uncle Tom's Cabin* (dir. Edwin S. Porter), first silent film version of Harriet Beecher Stowe's 1852 novel. |
| 1908 | D. W. Griffith, theatre melodrama actor, becomes director at Biograph Co. |
| 1920 | *Way Down East* (dir./prod. D. W. Griffith, D. W. Griffith Productions). |
| 1927 | *Uncle Tom's Cabin* (dir. Harry A. Pollard, Universal Pictures), last silent film version. |
| 1927 | *Show Boat*, music Jerome Kern, book and lyrics Oscar Hammerstein (Ziegfeld, New York). |
| 1927–9 | US transition to sound motion pictures. |
| 1936 | *Show Boat*, film (dir. James Whale). |
| 1943 | *Oklahoma!*, music Richard Rodgers, book and lyrics Oscar Hammerstein (St James, New York). |
| 1960 | *Oliver!*, music, lyrics, book Lionel Bart (New Theatre). |

1972    Douglas Sirk Retrospective, Edinburgh Film Festival,
        Scotland.

1979    *Sweeney Todd: The Demon Barber of Fleet Street*, music and
        lyrics by Stephen Sondheim, book by Hugh Wheeler (Uris,
        New York); adaptation of *Sweeney Todd: The Demon Barber
        of Fleet Street*, a new melodrama by Christopher Bond
        (1973, Theatre Workshop, Stratford East, London) that was
        adapted from George Dibdin Pitt's 1847 *The String of Pearls,
        or, The Fiend of Fleet Street* (Britannia, Hoxton, London).

# I

CAROLYN WILLIAMS

# Introduction

Frank Rahill gave a good definition of melodrama fifty years ago:

> Melodrama is a form of dramatic composition in prose partaking of the nature of tragedy, comedy, pantomime, and spectacle, and intended for a popular audience. Primarily concerned with situation and plot, it calls upon mimed action extensively and employs a more or less fixed complement of stock characters, the most important of which are a suffering heroine or hero, a persecuting villain, and a benevolent comic. It is conventionally moral and humanitarian in point of view and sentimental and optimistic in temper, concluding its fable happily with virtue rewarded after many trials and vice punished. Characteristically it offers elaborate scenic accessories and miscellaneous divertissements and introduces music freely, typically to underscore dramatic effect.[1]

As a stage genre, melodrama developed from the 1770s onward all over Europe, in a welter of hybridization that includes musical, spectacular, theatrical, and dramatic genres. Good new work on this early history has been and is being done, some of which emphasizes melodrama's continuity with earlier genres rather than disruption, innovation, and generic change.[2] Most scholars, however, agree on the French Revolution as the catalyst of disruption and change that precipitated the form of melodrama best represented in the works of Charles Renée de Pixérécourt. The 'first' English melodrama is still usually said to be Thomas Holcroft's *A Tale of Mystery*, his sleek and powerful adaptation of Pixérécourt's *Coelina; ou l'enfant du mystère* (1800), presented as an afterpiece at Covent Garden in 1802. Though technically not the very first English melodrama, Holcroft's play does conveniently mark a historical epoch in English drama, as, in the subsequent decades, French melodrama was grafted onto native English stock. English melodrama became the dominant form of the genre – and began to spread. As Matthew Buckley puts it in the first essay of this volume, 'If melodrama arrived in England from France, it was from England, and through the forms developed there in its first four decades of growth, that it reached the world.'[3]

Not only was French melodrama grafted onto English stock during the first decades of the nineteenth century, but also during the eighteenth century, French melodrama had itself drawn on English sources in drama, theatre, and literature.[4] Thus the prehistory of English melodrama is complex and multidirectional, involving exchanges among German, French, and Italian sources that were themselves, to varying degrees and in different ways, inspired by or developed in relation to English models – such as English ballad opera, English forms of pantomime, bourgeois sentimental drama (and sentimentalism in general), and Gothic stories and drama.

## What This *Companion* Provides

This volume of essays opens with new work on the history of melodrama in England, where the genre reached its high-water mark in the nineteenth century. The first section of the volume, 'Histories of English Melodrama', explores the early history of English melodrama and then traces its evolution as a genre through its important early subgenres (Gothic, nautical, domestic), ending with a consideration of the theatres and audiences associated with melodrama. It is important to stress that these chapters overlap in important ways, for the unfolding history of English melodrama is not by any means as strictly sequential as the arrangement of these chapters might at first glance suggest. Matthew Buckley explains in the opening essay that the story of early English melodrama is expansive rather than sequential; each subgenre is not replaced by the next, but survives and changes along with new forms as they emerge.

Part II, 'Melodramatic Technique', focuses on form – on melodramatic music, melodramatic acting, and melodramatic spectacle. These techniques guided audiences to experience the rhythm of melodrama, whose temporality might be described as periods of suspenseful absorption pierced by suddenly intensified moments of shock, terror, or sentiment. There are reasons to believe that melodrama's rhythmic patterning of affective response is a particularly modern phenomenon. In his essay on *Jack Sheppard*, for example, Matthew Buckley explains that melodramatic shock derives from the 'political modernity' of the French Revolution and develops toward the 'perceptual modernity' of cinema and other mass media; and in 'Refugee Theatre' he argues that the repeated traumatic violence experienced in the wake of the French Revolution yielded a melodramatic form that 'rehearsed, reinforced, and catalyzed the continual trauma and psychological dislocation of modern life'. In this view – with which I agree – melodrama is characterized by a serial aesthetic of affective sensation and spectacular shock.[5] Other scholars and critics, too, have noticed that melodrama 'oscillates' between

absorption and sudden shock (represented aesthetically by shifts in specta-
torial attention), and that its 'emotional economy' is 'best figured as a series
of waves'.[6]

Part III of this volume examines melodrama in relation to cultural
discourses of gender, class, empire, and race. The most important point
to grasp in Part III is that melodrama does not simply reflect but actively
contributes to the emergence and development of these modern categories
of social and cultural analysis. Important works by Elaine Hadley and
Bruce A. McConachie have approached the effort to describe this relation
historically and theoretically. Not only the titles of their studies,
*Melodramatic Tactics* and *Melodramatic Formations*, but even the term
'melodramatic' (as opposed to 'melodrama') signals the fact that their
interest moves beyond the stage genre toward cultural extensions and
other expressions of it. To put this point another way: they historicize
the genre by seeing it within a larger cultural context. But both works show
the complexity of this relation. For McConachie, 'reading formation' means
reading without imagining that text and context are separable entities.[7] Like
Hadley and McConachie, Michael Hays and Anastasia Nikolopoulou set out
not only to place the emergence of the genre within its cultural context, but
also to insist that, in general, 'melodrama played an important role in the
cultural dynamics of the nineteenth century'.[8] Moreover, the categories of
cultural analysis treated here – gender, class, race, empire – are separable
from one another only heuristically; so these essays – like the essays in
Parts I and II – go together as an overlapping set.

Think briefly of gender as an example. With the rise of companionate
marriage – which predates melodrama – women felt more independent from
their families than before, but at the same time were less protected by family
constraints than they had been in the past; therefore, they were more subject
to certain dangers. Seduction melodrama attempts to think through this
social problem, and one can clearly see in these plays gender norms in the
long process of their formation. These plays look at the problem from
various angles, many blaming the woman for her moral and sexual lapse,
while others seem to defend the heroine against what is clearly a sexual
double standard. This ideological disparity in attitudes can exist within the
same play, leading some critics to argue that melodrama not only reinforces
gender conventions but also points the way toward greater freedom
from them.[9] Often the seducer is of a higher class – though 'class' is not
precisely the correct term, especially early on, since the language of class
and class-consciousness is itself in the process of formation. This is meant
simply as a very brief example to show the inextricable intersection of
these dimensions of social experience and analysis, a phenomenon amply

illustrated in the essays themselves. Melodrama portrays both femininity and masculinity in flux and under pressure from a changing world; in melodrama we can see these pressures writ large, even in the contradictions articulated in and between individual plays.

Finally, the volume expands – as melodrama itself does – in Part IV, which focuses on 'Extensions of Melodrama' into other genres, media, discourses, and social practices. The vast extension of melodrama begins near its very beginnings as a genre and continues today – in novels, films and other forms of moving pictures, in the musical, in psychoanalysis, and in forms of contemporary mass culture (including sport and reality TV). This is why Peter Brooks's famous formulation still holds true: melodrama is a 'central poetry' of modernity.[10] At this point, 'melodrama has been a dominant shaping force of modernity for over two hundred and fifty years. We live, still, within its aesthetic regime in the twenty-first century.'[11] Though focused specifically on English melodrama, then, the variety of perspectives represented in this volume will demonstrate why and how melodrama is still a 'central poetry' of modern life, along with how and why the term 'melodramatic' has come to mean so many different things in current usage. Melodrama is both a genre and a mode. This volume begins firmly with the genre and then moves toward various ways of conceiving the mode.

Thus, the organization of *The Cambridge Companion to English Melodrama* forms a large part of its argument. It aims to trace the historical development of the stage genre – along with a detailed examination of its formal techniques – and then to explore both its influence on cultural formations and categories of cultural analysis and also its extensions in, to, and as other genres and discourses.

## Scholarship on Melodrama: A Brief Overview

The turn to melodrama as a serious topic of study began about fifty years ago. Peter Brooks's *The Melodramatic Imagination: Balzac, Henry James, Melodrama, and the Mode of Excess* (1976) attracted a great deal of attention and is still highly (and rightly) influential today, not only for its argument that melodrama is 'the principal mode for uncovering, demonstrating and making operative the essential moral universe in a post-sacred era' but also for its discussions of melodrama's central role in realist fiction and psychoanalysis.[12] But Brooks's study concentrates mainly on French melodrama.

And in any case, by the time Brooks had published his seminal work, foundational work specifically on English melodrama had already been published by Michael Booth, whose *English Melodrama* (1965) has never yet been properly appreciated or digested. Nor has Frank Rahill's *The World of Melodrama* (1967) been given as much critical attention as it deserves. Both are still extremely useful.[13] In addition, Martin Meisel's *Realizations: Narrative, Pictorial, and Theatrical Arts in Nineteenth-Century England* (1983), which focuses on intermittent pictorial narration – as a narrative form – and analyzes formal links between melodrama, narrative painting, and illustrated novels, has become an indispensable work on English melodrama and its consideration as a stage genre.[14]

On melodrama more broadly construed, film theorists – and especially feminist film theorists – were publishing great work at least by the 1980s. Christine Gledhill's edition of essays, *Home is Where the Heart Is: Melodrama and the Woman's Film* (1987), with its broad representation of issues and its powerful introduction, might be taken as an exemplary collection. Historians of film and television have unquestionably continued to be a driving force in the development of work on melodrama – now extending to melodrama all over the world. The description and critique of melodrama that emerged in film studies has caused scholars of stage melodrama to see the nineteenth-century stage genre anew; to place melodrama at the centre rather than the margins of nineteenth-century culture; and to attend to a long view, not only of the origins of melodrama but also of what it later becomes. Essays by David Mayer and Jane M. Gaines in this volume show that early cinema offers the best body of evidence today for what melodramatic practice was like on the nineteenth-century stage. But the relationship has also been reciprocal, as film studies continues to profit from the study of stage melodrama too.[15]

Many important books on melodrama have been published recently; in fact it might well be said that the field has been exploding with good work. Two edited volumes of essays are exemplary for work in the 1990s: Jacky Bratton, Jim Cook, and Christine Gledhill's *Melodrama: Stage, Picture, Screen* (1994); and Hays and Nikolopoulou's *Melodrama: The Cultural Emergence of a Genre* (1996). The former regards melodrama as 'an agent of modernity', while the latter emphasizes the genre's historical specificity at the time of its emergence.[16] We might pause to note that in the first case, the emphasis falls on melodrama in its extensive sense and depends on the assumption that the definition of melodrama encompasses stage, picture, and screen. Peter Brooks's study also favours this extensive sense, as do the works of Bruce McConachie and Elaine Hadley, already mentioned, though their 'extensions' of melodrama are not limited to other genres and media, but involve melodrama's expression in other historical discourses: for Brooks, realist fiction and psychoanalysis; for McConachie, the rhetorics embodying 'the decline of one type of cultural hegemony and the gradual rise of another'; and for Hadley, social modes of 'theatricalized dissent'.[17] All of these approaches are as rigorously historical as the essays collected by Hays and Nicolopoulou, but in very different ways. What we can see is a developing understanding of the range of differences and overlaps between considering 'melodrama' (as a genre) and 'the melodramatic' (as a mode of expression in other genres, discourses, and practices).

Other important studies have positioned melodrama in relation to historical developments of other kinds. Jane Moody's *Illegitimate Theatre in London, 1770–1840* (2000), for example, helps us to see melodrama within the sprawling development of theatrical performances conditioned by the Licensing Act of 1737, which had restricted 'spoken drama' to the Patent Houses (Covent Garden and Drury Lane, and, later, the Haymarket). That Act had had the effect of relegating all other theatrical performances to an 'illegitimate' cultural realm which, however, expanded to become highly productive and innovative, developing many genres – including melodrama – that evaded the Act by incorporating dance, pantomime, banners and signs, song, and orchestral music in order to fly under the radar of the restrictions on 'spoken drama'. Moody's study aptly shows that the relaxation of these strictures in 1843 did as much harm as good to this burgeoning 'illegitimate' theatre culture, for it exposed all plays to the censorship of the Lord Chamberlain's Examiner of Plays.[18] Jim Davis and Victor Emeljanow's *Reflecting the Audience: London Theatregoing, 1840–1880* (2001) focuses in detail on the composition of audiences for seven representative theatres in four different areas of London, while Kate Newey's work on women playwrights – importantly focused, as melodrama was, on gender – expands our sense of who created melodramatic plays.[19]

Historical methodology in theatre research has been developing too. Important statements on methodology by Jacky Bratton and Tracy C. Davis tend to agree in recommending that melodrama should be seen within a larger catchment of performance histories in the period. Both emphasize the complexity of the context within which any interpretation of a play must emerge, including performance conventions and their histories; repetitions and revisions of common figures and tropes; and social forces outside the theatre. Bratton's *New Readings in Theatre History* (2003), for example, advocates approaching the field through the concept of 'intertheatricality', that 'web of mutual understanding between potential audiences and their players ... that spans a lifetime or more' and includes all sorts of sources of knowledge and knowingness. She proposes an 'intertheatrical reading' of the historical record.[20] Davis's emphasis on 'repertoire' likewise cuts across genre difference in order to take account of 'processes of iteration, revision, citation, and incorporation' that link one play with another.[21] Like Bratton's, her method would situate melodrama within a larger body of performances while also giving due credit to the forms and pleasures found specifically in the repetitive, citational, and 'generic' element of these plays.

Most recently, digital projects have exponentially improved our access to source materials. Spearheaded by Richard Pearson, the University of Worcester's *Victorian Plays Project* provides an archive of play texts from T. H. Lacy's *Acting Editions*, while the Royal Holloway project *Buried Treasures* – led by Jacky Bratton in collaboration with the British Library – provides over 2,000 plays submitted to the Lord Chamberlain between 1852 and 1863.[22] In 2003, Matthew Buckley at Rutgers University launched the Melodrama Research Consortium (MRC), with the aim of providing a platform for research networks, working groups, and a comprehensive database of nineteenth-century melodramas.[23]

Meanwhile important special issues of journals, as well as new books devoted to melodrama continue to emerge apace.[24]

The writers of the essays in this volume have been central to these developments in the study of melodrama. Therefore, this volume provides not only a wide-ranging introduction to the topic but also a good indication of the ongoing progress and future directions of research in the field – future directions in which the historical, the aesthetic, the formal, and the theoretical are productively intertwined.

## Notes

1. Frank Rahill, *The World of Melodrama* (University Park: Pennsylvania State University Press, 1967), xiv.
2. See Matthew Buckley, 'The Formation of Melodrama', in *The Oxford Handbook of the Georgian Theatre 1737–1832*, eds. Julia Swindells and David Francis Taylor (Oxford: Oxford University Press, 2014), 457–75.
3. Matthew Buckley, 'Early English Melodrama', 15.
4. See Rahill, *The World of Melodrama* (*passim*) for a good introduction to these interactions; and see Carolyn Williams, 'Melodrama', in *The New Cambridge History of Victorian Literature*, ed. Kate Flint (Cambridge: Cambridge University Press, 2012), 195–8.
5. Matthew Buckley, 'Sensations of Celebrity: *Jack Sheppard* and the Mass Audience', *Victorian Studies*, 44 (2002): 423–63; 'Refugee Theatre: Melodrama and Modernity's Loss', *Theatre Journal*, 61.2 (2009): 175–190, quoted passage on 355. See also Ben Singer, *Melodrama and Modernity: Early Sensational Cinema and Its Contexts* (New York: Columbia University Press, 2001).
6. Carolyn Williams, 'Moving Pictures: George Eliot and Melodrama', in *Compassion: The Culture and Politics of an Emotion*, ed. Lauren Berlant (New York: Routledge, 2004), 113; Juliet John, *Dickens's Villains: Melodrama, Character, and Popular Culture* (Oxford: Oxford University Press, 2003), 31.

7. Bruce A. McConachie, *Melodramatic Formations: American Theatre and Society, 1820–1870* (Iowa City: University of Iowa Press, 1992), xi; Elaine Hadley, *Melodramatic Tactics: Theatricalized Dissent in the English Marketplace, 1800–1885* (Stanford: Stanford University Press, 1995).

8. Michael Hays and Anastasia Nikolopoulou (eds.), *Melodrama: The Cultural Emergence of a Genre* (New York: St. Martin's Press, 1996), viii.

9. For example, see Léon Metayer, 'What the Heroine Taught, 1830–1870', in *Melodrama: The Cultural Emergence of a Genre*, eds. Michael Hays and Anastasia Nikolopoulou (New York: St. Martin's Press, 1996), 235–44.

10. Peter Brooks, 'Melodrama: A Central Poetry', in *The Melodramatic Imagination: Balzac, Henry James, Melodrama, and the Mode of Excess*, second edition (New Haven: Yale University Press, 1995 [1976]), 200. Brooks borrows 'central poetry' from Wallace Stevens.

11. Williams, 'Melodrama', 193.

12. Brooks, *The Melodramatic Imagination*, 15.

13. Michael Booth, *English Melodrama* (London: Herbert Jenkins, 1965); Rahill, *The World of Melodrama*. Other important work before Brooks includes George Rowell, *The Victorian Theatre, 1792–1914: A Survey* (Oxford: Oxford University Press, 1956) and Allardyce Nicoll, *A History of Early Nineteenth-Century Drama, 1800–1850*, 2 vols. (Cambridge: Cambridge University Press, 1959) [vol. 4 of Nicoll's *A History of English Drama*, second edition, 6 vols. (Cambridge: Cambridge University Press, 1952–59)].

14. Martin Meisel, *Realizations: Narrative, Pictorial and Theatrical Arts in Nineteenth-Century England* (Princeton: Princeton University Press, 1983).

15. Laura Mulvey, '"It Will Be a Magnificent Obsession": The Melodrama's Role in the Development of Contemporary Film Theory', in *Melodrama: Stage, Picture, Screen*, eds. Jacky Bratton, Jim Cook, Christine Gledhill (London: British Film Institute, 1994), 121–33; David Mayer, *Stagestruck Filmmaker: D. W. Griffith and the American Theatre* (Iowa City: University of Iowa Press, 2009).

16. Jacky Bratton, Jim Cook, and Christine Gledhill (eds.), *Melodrama: Stage, Picture, Screen*, 1; Michael Hays and Anastasia Nikolopoulou (eds.), *Melodrama: The Cultural Emergence of a Genre*.

17. McConachie, *Melodramatic Formations*, xii.

18. Jane Moody, *Illegitimate Theatre in London, 1770–1840* (Cambridge: Cambridge University Press, 2000).

19. Jim Davis and Victor Emeljanow, *Reflecting the Audience: London Theatregoing 1840–1880* (Iowa City: University of Iowa Press, 2001); Katherine Newey, *Women's Theatre Writing in Victorian Britain* (Cambridge: Cambridge University Press, 2005); see also Tracy C. Davis and Ellen Donkin (eds.), *Women and Playwriting in Nineteenth-Century Britain* (Cambridge: Cambridge University Press, 1999).

20. Jacky Bratton, *New Readings in Theatre History* (Cambridge: Cambridge University Press, 2003), 37–8.

21. Tracy C. Davis, 'Nineteenth-Century Repertoire', *Nineteenth-Century Theatre and Film*, 36 (2009): 7; and her Introduction to *The Broadview Anthology of Nineteenth-Century British Performance*, ed. Tracy C. Davis (Peterborough, Ontario: Broadview Press, 2012), 13–26.

22. Juliet John, 'Melodrama and its Criticism: An Essay in Memory of Sally Ledger', *19: Interdisciplinary Studies in the Long Nineteenth Century*, 8 (2009), http://doi .org/10.16995/ntn.496.
23. See https://melodramaresearchconsortium.org.
24. Matthew Buckley (ed.), *Modern Drama*, 55 (2012), special issue on melodrama; Marcie Frank (ed.), *Criticism*, 35 (2013), special issue on melodrama; Janice Norwood (ed.), *Nineteenth-Century Theatre and Film*, 42 (2015), special issue on 'Adaptation and the Stage in the Nineteenth Century'. Jonathan Goldberg, *Melodrama: An Aesthetics of Impossibility* (Durham: Duke University Press, 2016); *Melodrama Unbound*, eds. Christine Gledhill and Linda Williams (New York: Columbia University Press, 2018); and *The Melodramatic Moment, 1790–1820*, eds. Katherine Hambridge and Jonathan Hicks (Chicago: University of Chicago Press, 2018).

# I
# Histories of English Melodrama

# 2

MATTHEW BUCKLEY

# Early English Melodrama

On the evening of 13 November 1802, at Covent Garden theatre, a new dramatic genre, called 'melo-drama', was introduced into England from France. The occasion was the premiere of *A Tale of Mystery*, Thomas Holcroft's light, lean adaptation of Charles Renée de Pixérécourt's *Coelina*, the simple but electrifying 'melo-drame' that had triumphed in Paris in 1800, swept like wildfire across the provinces the following year, and was now, in translated, adapted form, spreading across Western Europe. Although other recent plays had catalyzed analogous crazes, the mania for *Coelina* was both far greater in intensity and different in kind, for it was driven not by the play's matter – which was incidental, confused, and clichéd – but by its *effect*. Audiences in Paris, throughout France, in London, and all across Europe were not merely entertained by the play: they were – in a manner that seemed strange, inexplicable, and unquestionably new – riveted by it, gripped and absorbed by it, moved and terrified by it, emotionally and sensationally *intoxicated* by it. The experience was thrilling, exhausting, and perfectly suited to an era that sought nothing so ardently as the excitation of emotion and sensation, and the collective expression of joy. By 1802, *Coelina*'s immense popularity in France had given rise to a rush of imitations and variations; and with these, melodrama had begun its explosive rise to dominance on the French stage. The play's impact in England – and elsewhere – was similarly rapid and equally decisive: within a decade, and for the next forty years, melodrama written strictly along Pixérécourtian lines would become the conventional standard and vital core of all commercial theatre in England, across Europe, and throughout the trans-Atlantic and European colonial world.

Yet, if melodrama came to England from France, it hardly arrived as an alien form, for its development had taken place all over Europe, and not least in England itself. Like most theatrical drama of its day, melodrama is a 'mixed', 'illegitimate' form, one among many hybrid products of a decades-long, increasingly cosmopolitan effort to lend new vitality to drama by mixing and condensing traditional genres and modes, extracting and combining their most emotional and sensational elements, and heightening and intensifying (through any available theatrical means) the drama's affective and sensory effects. It formed gradually, by formal and aesthetic accretion, and is built on and of – rather than against – its era's conventions. Musical, spectacular, theatrical, and dramatic works that anticipate melodrama appear all over Europe as early as the 1770s; by the 1780s, *all* of its constitutive elements – from its emphasis on action and emotion, its monopathic character types and polarized moral structures, and its sensational use of spectacle and action to its affective employment of pantomime and tableau, its formal fusion of romantic, tragic, and sentimental comic modes, and even its use of music to accompany action and shape feeling – are either well-established norms or popular trends. By the 1790s, drama that combines most of these elements dominated the Western European stage, and those plays that most closely matched Pixérécourt's formula – like those of August von Kotzebue and Matthew 'Monk' Lewis, for example – were already producing similar responses and comparable fads. *Coelina* is different from these, not in kind but by degree: it compresses, distils, synthetizes just a little bit more – and in so doing, crosses a threshold, prompting a reaction both novel and sought after for many years.

That this breakthrough should happen in France rather than England is, in fact, surprising. By any reasonable measure, it was in England – where the dramatic intermixture of genre and mode was freer, the affective culture of sentiment most deeply rooted, and spectacular and musically accompanied theatrical production most powerful and advanced – that such trends had begun. It was in England, too – after decades of mixed dramas by Richard Cumberland, James Boaden, Thomas Morton, George Colman, Charles Dibdin, Samuel Arnold, Lewis, and Holcroft himself, among others – that such trends had, by 1800, become most developed. Indeed, it is from English Gothic drama – following Kotzebue's influential German cue – that Pixérécourt borrows the final elements of melodrama's form: those moments of suspenseful horror and terrifying evil that he adds to the essentially comic proto-melodrama developed in France by Denis Diderot, Pierre-Augustin Beaumarchais, Michel-Jean Sedaine, Louis-Sébastien Mercier, and Jean-Pierre Florian.

England would continue to import French melodrama for decades to come, in a cross-channel trade that ran heavily one way, and powerfully shaped English melodrama's history. However, it would also graft the new formula, from the start, to England's native, proto-melodramatic traditions and from these develop its own national, and imperial, variations of the form – variations that, by 1840, introduced melodrama for the first time to cultures all over the globe. If melodrama arrived in England from France, it was from England, and through the forms developed there in its first four decades of growth, that it reached the world.

## Development and Growth

Traditionally, the development of early English melodrama has been framed as a progression of more or less stable subgenres or types that appeared in succession on the London stage, each rising into vogue and then falling gradually into obsolescence in a sequence that makes visible melodrama's gradual development of a more tempered and nuanced aesthetic, its steadily more realistic engagement with life, and its eventual evolution into the restrained, bourgeois social drama from which modern, realist theatre would emerge. That sequence, while variously articulated by different scholars, is simple and clear: it begins with the lurid Gothic melodrama that dominated the century's first years; moves through the less fanciful exotic, military, and historical melodrama of the aughts and the teens, the less grandiose domestic and nautical melodramas of the twenties, and the less romanticized distress and crime melodrama of the thirties; and ends in the modified Adelphi melodramas of the 1840s, in which the genre takes on the more refined, tamed sensibility – and more interior focus – that would form the basis of its second-generation, Victorian mode. This close, authorial, realist-inflected, and London-centred perspective has evident value: it illuminates the landmarks and the leading edge of early English melodrama's subgeneric development; highlights its rapid evolution into a dramatic vehicle for political, social, and personal concerns; and throws into sharp relief the progress of technical and artistic innovation on the most prominent stages of the era.

However, this view also ignores a great deal, and distorts as well as elides the history it describes. These successive varieties of the form did not, in fact, supplant each other in turn, even in London. Rather, they rolled in like a series of waves, with each new subgenre building and expanding upon the success of the last, in a process of continual formal and demographic extension and growth. All of melodrama's subgenres continued to be produced – even and especially in London – long after their first hits had faded; all found, there and elsewhere, new audiences and enthusiastic devotees; all experienced, in updated guises and modified form, periodically, even regularly, renewed waves of cachet. The formal history suggested by this broader view is very different: not that of a genre being progressively tempered and tamed, made more rational, realistic, and refined, but that of a form steadily expanding its register, multiplying its varieties, and broadening its range – from supernaturalist fantasy through legend, romance, and history to contemporary events, social performance, and psychological experience – until it offers a complete palette, a full, modal spectrum, in which everything from the collective nightmares of an era to the personal negotiation of emotional pain could be presented in melodramatic form. This wider history – the history we would expect of a phase shift – has evident value as well: it shows us, much better, the impetus that propelled melodrama's rise as a popular art and the basis of its gradual penetration and suffusion of narrative culture as a rhetoric and a mode, a discourse, and, eventually, a structure of feeling woven into modern cultural life.

I have tried here not to choose between these two histories, but to balance and relate them: that is, to describe both the close progression of subgenres at the leading edge of the London stage and the broad inundation of English culture by melodrama as a mode, and to show how these processes were intertwined.

### 1800–1820: Generic Expansion

The development of early English melodrama began with the brief fashion for Gothic melodrama at Drury Lane and Covent Garden, London's patent theatres, that marked the century's opening years. While vigorous at its outset, that vogue waned almost from the start, for Gothic melodrama was, in a formal sense, a brief reinvigoration of a Gothic tide that was by *Coelina*'s time nearly played out. Prepossessed with nightmarish fears of a dying feudal order, the Gothic had – like the German Romantic tragedy from which it emerged – reflected the anxieties of the late eighteenth century well, and at the onset of revolution the horrors of its castles, dungeons, and lordly demons seemed resonant, carrying both romantic force and epistemological weight. Even by 1800, in the aftermath of a decade of revolutionary war and the startling rise of Napoleon, such nightmares seemed, if not quite dated, very nearly so, and within just a few years, the most fashionable Gothic melodrama – shedding its oppressive ruins and spectral powers for picturesque cottages and menacing *banditti* – had evolved into a second Gothic type, one no less devoted to terror, but thrilled rather by the fear of lawless violence in an uncivilized world than by the horror of dungeons and the aristocracy's dead hand.

The arc of Gothic melodrama's development during its brief reign is perhaps best exemplified by the trajectory of Matthew 'Monk' Lewis's landmark plays, from the proto-melodramatic *Castle Spectre* of 1797, which catalyzed the

English and continental mania for Gothic drama; through *Rugantino* (1805), which registers even Lewis's quick, profitable turn from ghosts to adventurers; to *One O'Clock* (1811), which appeared at the English Opera House and marked the beginning of Gothic drama's displacement – or extension – to England's minor stage.

While the convenience and brevity of Gothic melodrama's vogue may make its inaugural role seem merely circumstantial, this initial Gothic phase was both necessary and integral to the genre's formation. More than merely providing Pixérécourt with a modish addition to his hybrid mix, Gothic drama provided the final, necessary pieces – even the keystones – of melodrama's affective mode. From sentimental comedy, French melodramatic drama had drawn humour, sympathy, and pathos, the affective elements of the comic; from pantomime and spectacle, it had appropriated situational drama's sensational elements of action, interest, and fearful suspense. From the Gothic, Pixérécourt drew finally, and most directly, on the affective elements of tragedy: terror, horror, and existential despair. Thus melodrama's villains gained their full dimension and depth, and its suffering victims and communities of sentiment their link to the divine. That the addition of tragedy's affective elements should have been the final, post-Revolutionary step in melodrama's formation makes sense, for those elements define not only the most extreme but the most elevated and legally restricted register of its affective spectrum – that dramatic register most closely linked to power and tradition, and most reliant, as well, on the resonance of circumstantial extremity and catastrophic historical change.

Melodramatic tragedy appeared before the French Revolution, as Friedrich Schiller's radical *Robbers* (1781) makes plain, and we find there the formal inversion of the tragic hero from which the popular melodramatic villain is made. However, it is with the radical Gothic wave that accompanied the Revolution – in Germany, England, and France – that 'popular tragedy' of this sort found its audience and matured. Only then did its elements become available as conventions that could be distilled and integrated as legible gestures and prompts in a larger, more heterogeneous melodramatic whole. Indeed, it is hard not to see the hardening of the Gothic into convention, and not simply its appearance and fashionable rise as a formal precondition of Pixérécourt's potpourri.

Although its vogue passed quickly, Gothic melodrama never faded long from view. In fact, it drove the first great expansion of non-patent melodrama at the Coburg and the Lyceum in the late teens, and rose into fashion again in the 1820s, when technical advances like coloured fire and gas gave its lurid visions new, if less naïve charm, and plays like James Robinson Planché's *Vampire* (1820), the several melodramatic adaptations of *Frankenstein* in 1823, the Adelphi's sensational *Valmondi* (1824), and the feverish *Freischütz* craze of 1824–5 modified its forms and figures to resonate with the renewed Gothic nightmares of the reactionary post-Napoleonic world.

As the initial appeal of Gothic melodrama waned at the patents, it was succeeded in vogue by exotic or 'grand romantic' melodrama, a clearly post-Revolutionary type that retained Gothic melodrama's fantastic situations, lurid violence, and picturesque appeal, but traded its dark European settings for exotic climes, heightened the romanticism of its action and the spectacular realization of its scenes, and thus tempered melodrama's terrors while heightening its thrills. This brighter, larger-scale, often operatic subgenre, a type well suited to both the expansive tenor of the early Napoleonic era and the grandiose spectacular capabilities of the English stage, was prefigured as early as 1798, with Colman's *Blue Beard*, but it exploded into prominence in 1803, with Frederic Reynolds's *The Caravan*, which delivered Drury Lane from its then-precarious financial state and catalyzed the subgenre's rise. Like Bonaparte, whose Mediterranean adventures provided its archetypal milieu, grand romantic melodrama gained prominence quickly in works like William Dimond's *Hero of the North* (1803), Theodore Hook's *Tékéli* (1806), and James Kenney's *Blind Boy* (1807); and its vogue marks the apogee of patent-house melodrama in England: the moment when melodrama's spectacular possibilities were first fully exploited by stages fitted to the task, and the moment, too, when the patent houses' dependence upon melodrama as a profit source became clear. However, its fashionable reign was short-lived. Even by 1808, the continuation of continental war, the onset of the Peninsular campaign, and prolonged fears of invasion from France made its romanticized adventures seem naïve, and by 1810 at the latest, when the loss by fire of both patent houses interrupted the production of such lavish works, the subgenre's moment had passed.

While it may seem, like the Gothic, to reflect little more than a shift in tastes or topical concerns, grand romantic melodrama marked as well a formal advance, and an expansion of melodrama's tenor and range. Exotic and fantastic though it was, grand romantic melodrama set its action in a secular frame and in settings drawn not from the Gothic imagination but from – however distant – the actual world: with it, melodrama's tone moved from dream to reverie, and stepped closer to life in a manner as decisive as it was slight.

Like Gothic melodrama, grand romantic melodrama did not disappear: it was rather revived in force with the reopening of the patent houses, and it enjoyed continuing popularity at Sadler's Wells, Astley's, the Surrey, and the Royalty. Like the Gothic, it rose back into fashion around 1820, when its production expanded to houses like the Lyceum, Coburg, and the Adelphi, and the patent theatres engaged in a brief, lavish revival that peaked in 1823 with William Moncrieff's triumphant *Cataract of the Ganges* (1823) – with which Drury Lane's finances were again saved.

Its successor, the military melodrama that dominated the early teens, set aside mythic and exotic motifs while retaining romantic characterization and heightening martial heroism and spectacular force. Melodramatic military drama had enjoyed growing popularity since the 1790s, when both the patent houses and the popular spectacle venues (Sadler's Wells, the Royal Circus, and Astley's Pavilion) began to offer dramatic restagings of the events of the Revolution; its heyday, however, accompanied Britain's conflict with France between 1808 and 1815, when martial hippodramas like *The Blood-Red Knight* (1810) played to packed crowds, and the Royalty and Sadler's Wells offered spectacular melodramatic stagings of the battles of St. Quentin, Badajoz, Telavera, Salamanca, Vittoria, and, of course, Waterloo.

Although it may seem crude and situational, military melodrama, too, marked important formal advances. To a degree that earlier English melodrama was not, it was both fundamentally nationalistic and fundamentally popular: for the first time, English melodrama featured common English heroes, and for the first time, too, its fashionable houses were not the patents, where demands for legitimate drama carried force, but the popular spectacle theatres, where such demands held no sway at all. Moreover, although highly romanticized, it was also far more realistic, taking as its distinctive aim not the enchanting creation of fantastic adventure but the vivid, at times punctilious, recreation of recent national-historical events. This turn from the overtly fictitious to the insistently real would shape melodrama's development for the next thirty years and begin the form's engagement with the serial narration of life. Finally, military melodrama, like Napoleonic warfare, from which it derived its action and prompt, inaugurated a shift in melodrama's representation of terror in modern life. Unlike the Gothic, which had enacted the seemingly epochal nightmare of feudalism's fall, or the grand romantic, which had staged the spectacle of extraordinary heroic adventure, military melodrama reproduced the repetitive trauma of sustained, ever-widening, ever-closer war – a context in which terror seemed no longer climactic or cataclysmic, but recurrent and increasingly frequent over time. In military melodrama, we find for the first time melodramatic structures that aim not at single but multiple, repeated points of crisis, and that organize action in a fundamentally serial form.

Military melodrama, like its precedents, would later rise to fashion many times. The first such wave occurs just after 1825, with melodramatic spectacles of the Burmese War (1826), the battle of Navarino (1827; 1828), and the storming of Seringapatam (1829). However, unlike prior subgenres, military melodrama did not enjoy *continued* popularity at all nor produce any works later revived – not for any lack of achievement, but because, like the news, its appeal was derived largely from its freshness in time. Its formal impact was, however, felt continuously thereafter: melodrama of all kinds would adopt its popular frame, its sensational realism, and its serial structure.

Although well suited to the climax of England's struggle against France, military melodrama became with peace sentimental in turn. Its successor was national-historical melodrama, a subgenre in which the unremitting violence of martial melodrama was set aside, and the fascination with national history turned from the patriotic reenactment of foreign battles to the sentimental recreation of Britain's past. As Gothic melodrama's rise and fall is exemplified by the passing fashion for Lewis's plays, that of national-historical melodrama is exemplified by the extended rage – at the patent houses, the spectacle houses, and the rising numbers of 'illegitimate' theatres, including the Coburg and especially the Adelphi – for dramatic adaptations of Scott's romances, beginning with *Lady of the Lake* (1810) and *Knight of Snowdoun* (1811), but really exploding only after Waterloo, with *Rob Roy* (1818), *Ivanhoe* (1820), and *Kenilworth* (1821), each of which prompted several separate productions amid a tide of Caledonian and Old England plays.

Like its precedents, national-historical melodrama marked both a topical shift and a formal advance. Although set in a picturesque, heroic, often spectacular past, its situations were credible and frequently ordinary, and they extended military melodrama's realism to the depiction of common, quotidian life. Its characteristic sources, crucially, were not actual current events, but literary reimaginings of a time before war and invocations of the shared history from which national culture arose. Although nationalist and thoroughly heroic, its conflicts focused on ethnic, religious, and class difference *within* the nation, and its figures of pathos – unlike earlier melodrama's victims of cataclysmic disruption or monstrous perfidy – were those wronged rather by custom, law, or prejudicial chance. Such shifts reflect not only a progressive domestication of melodrama's aesthetic, but its adaptation, too, to a changed theatrical landscape, and to the increasingly large, popular, and diverse audiences for which it was produced. In fact, it was with national-historical melodrama's emergence that the patent theatres finally ceded their position at the forefront of fashion to the rising 'illegitimate' stage.

Although it was superseded at the forefront of fashion by 1820, national-historical melodrama would retain and periodically regain popularity for many decades – and not merely as a pleasant diversion, but as a canonical romance of Britain and a foundation of popular national and cultural identity. More than any prior variety of melodrama, it would live and breathe by revival, and its production reflected this heightened opportunity and desire for reproducibility. Indeed, national-historical melodrama is the first variety of the form to have been routinely and immediately copied and adapted for multiple stages, and it drove the boost – crucial to the creation of the modern audience – from a market of singular productions to one of popular fads, in which many versions of a successful theme are produced in a variety of forms. Appropriately, its advent marked, more generally, melodrama's expansive metamorphosis into a generalized dramatic mode – a narrative aesthetic evident and operative not only on stage but in popular literature, music, and art, and one that plays upon such intermedial richness to reinforce and extend its appeal. Unsurprisingly, its first resurgence took place quickly, just on the heels of the Gothic and grand romantic revivals of the early 1820s, in the weaker Caledonian vogue that followed the premieres of *Woodstock* (1826) and *Peveril of the Peak* (1826).

Its successor in vogue, domestic melodrama, set aside such exploits as it set aside the national past, even if it by no means dispensed with picturesque historical romance, and shifted its focus to the common experiences of familial life. Notably, domestic melodrama brought female protagonists to the fore and endowed them with a heroic stature quite unlike anything seen in those types of melodrama it followed in fashion. Domestic melodrama first appeared in the century's opening decade, arguably with Kenney's *Ella Rosenberg* (1807), a grand romantic melodrama that limited its action to the interior of the home and placed a heroic woman at centre stage. However, it was anticipated by a great deal of early melodrama, and in many ways even *Coelina* may be offered as an example of the type. The growing appeal of domestic melodrama was evident even by 1815, when adaptations of Louis-Charles Caigniez's *Magpie and the Maid* (1815) flooded the London stage, and one finds, in George Soane's *Innkeeper's Daughter* (1817), Reynolds's *Father and his Children* (1817), and R. Phillips's *The Heroine* (1819), markers of its growth even at the height of the Scottian tide. However, domestic melodrama's heyday arrived as that tide began to ebb, in a powerful wave that included Moncrieff's *Lear of Private Life* (1820), John Howard Payne's immensely successful *Thérèse* (1821) and *Clari* (1823), John Baldwin Buckstone's celebrated *Luke the Labourer* (1826), and Douglas Jerrold's landmark *Ambrose Gwinett* (1828).

The formal advances of domestic melodrama were considerable. While still often set in romantic, pastoral milieux, it set aside, finally, those feudal ideas of society and identity that melodrama had retained from its pre-Revolutionary past. In it society was presented in precisely contemporary terms; its figures, crises, and fears were local and ordinary, if exaggerated in tone. Heroism was shifted toward far more modest, egalitarian figures, as something now rather conjoined to pathos and suffering than set as its saving anti-type, and something displayed more forcefully by emotional faith and loving action than by manly discipline and prowess at arms.

Like its audience, domestic melodrama was preoccupied not with adventure but its aftermath, not with war but the return home, and the struggle to reunite with family, regain friendship, and experience love. As this shift suggests, domestic melodrama was far more intimate and personal in tone than its predecessors, and far more concerned with emotional than sensational response. In a sense, it may be seen as the anti-type and structural complement to military melodrama, a reactive pendulum swing away from external spectacular/sensational appeals toward internal affective/emotional pull. In it were developed for the first time techniques of affective drama – from the use of mise-en-scène as an externalized image of emotional suffering and of pathetic tableaux as a structural core, to the programmatic integration of heart-wrenching, ear-worm musical themes (like *Clari's* 'Home Sweet Home') – that ground domestic melodrama even today. Appropriately, its leading houses were not the patents or the amphitheatres but the Coburg – which made its reputation on the form – and the Adelphi, new houses built to accommodate that swelling postwar population and better suited than the cavernous patents to successful production of such an affective form.

With domestic melodrama, one might say, the initial phase of English melodrama's historical development was completed. Formally, the basic techniques and methods of melodrama's two primary structural dimensions – the spectacular/sensational and the affective/emotional – had found their language and limits. In cultural terms, melodrama's integration as a national and social art had been achieved: it had become a drama not only of tragic nightmare, of historical myth, romantic adventure, and national military, political, and social struggle, but of contemporary, day-to-day existence, the waking experience of emotional relations, and the psychological negotiation of familial and personal life. Equally important, melodrama had come to be produced on every sort of stage, from the most elevated and professional to the lowest and most spontaneously social. It had become a form now interwoven, after two decades of growth and expansion, with the entire experience of an age, and from this decade forward began to function as a discourse of popular political and social expression, and as a mode shaping not only the arts but the tenor and conduct of life.

## 1820–1840: Repetition and Change

Subsequent varieties of English stage melodrama – and of melodrama generally – would rework, recombine, and advance the models provided by these earliest subgeneric varieties, but they would offer relatively little that was new in structure or technique. Instead, they revived, readapted, and remade these basic types, following the same ambit over and over, making melodrama ever tighter and ever stronger in a cyclical process of spectacular amplification, commercial expansion, and structural distillation that continues to the present day. Melodrama's formal history from 1820 forward, for this reason, takes on a different dynamic, in which progressive tonal expansion gives way to reiterative, overlapping waves of readaptation and intensification over time. New subgeneric types do emerge from this rolling tide, but the process is slow, and melodrama's history from 1820 on, and still today, is more strongly marked by repetitions of this basic cycle than by departures from its trend.

The first such repetition – outlined already in the subgeneric histories above – unfolds over the course of the 1820s, beginning with the neo-Gothic vogue that opens the decade and proceeding through the revived fashions for grand romantic, military, and national-historical melodrama that succeed it in turn. However, its origins lie in the late teens, with the introduction of gaslight to the theatre and the sudden expansion of melodrama's production to industrial scale. The use of gaslight, begun at Drury Lane, Covent Garden, and the Lyceum in 1817 and largely completed in the next decade, marks an epochal shift not unlike that which we associate with the arrival of film. Gas lighting was, of course, brighter than candles or oil lamps, and thus amplified visual effects, enabled less-histrionic expressivity, and expanded the tonal palette of the stage, but its impact had less to do with its increased intensity than with the radically new effects enabled by its capacity for centralized, dynamic control – from the sudden, isolate glare of explosion and the gradual, multihued lightshow of a picturesque dawn to the slow fade of the auditorium itself into immersive darkness. More than merely charging the theatre with brightness, gaslight amplified the entire spectacle – focusing attention, coaxing the slip into reverie, elevating sensation, and supercharging shock. Perhaps most significantly, it set the stage off much more clearly as an artificial space separate from the real, both enhancing and easing the willing suspension of disbelief. With its advent, theatregoing began to take on its modern ritualistic character: audiences are induced to calm and settle, to turn and hold their attention on the illuminated stage, and to immerse themselves, as unobserved observers, in its intensified display.

The additional force lent to melodrama by gaslight is hard to overstate: in its remediated mode, the lurid supernaturalism of the Gothic could be given fresh horror, the exotic locales of grand romance new picturesque excitement, the violence of martial spectacle revived shock, and the sentimental tales of the past re-enlivened, rosy charm. Melodrama was not simply altered by gas: like the Gothic monsters that its advent revived, it was thrillingly, and through devilish *techné*, brought back to life. That producers and audiences should have responded to gas by starting over, returning to melodrama's most sensational, credulity-straining subgenres and then moving once more, through its range, toward the real, should not surprise us at all.

Yet, if gaslight provided the means for melodrama's first generic revival, the driving force behind it was provided rather by the second watershed development of the late teens – the sudden expansion, starting in 1818, of the volume of melodrama offered each year on London's stage. Production of melodrama had without question been rising steadily, and increasingly quickly, from the start, and the theatres' reportorial reliance upon it had become ever greater and more widespread: by the advent of gas in 1817, Londoners could expect roughly two dozen melodramas each season – nearly four times as many as just ten years before – from a field that included not only the patents, the Haymarket, Sadler's Wells, Astley's, and the Royal Circus (now the Surrey), but the Royalty and the English Opera House (as the Lyceum was then known). In 1818, however, the Olympic, Adelphi, Regency, and Coburg all enter the fray, and the volume of melodramatic drama in London rose immediately to about five dozen productions per year. Many more of the new productions were quick copies of hits, and the expanded market followed and fuelled trends, but variety, too, increased sharply. Offerings of all of melodrama's types rose immediately from a smattering to a handful or more each year; in matters of taste, progressive fashion had to suddenly contend with jostling choice. Theatres began to carve out market positions more strongly, to lay competing claims to mastery of different types, and to press forward their development along independent lines. For the first time, popular plays moved from the minors to the patents. Canny revival of early, now 'classic' hits, a practice first exploited by the Surrey in the early teens, became pronounced, starting in 1819 with *The Bravo of Venice*, Philip Astley's resuscitation of Lewis's *Rugantino* (1805), itself the Gothic's first 'fad' drama and most memorable success; rising with Payne's *Adeline* (1822), a Drury Lane rewrite of Dibdin's then-ancient *Valentin and Orson* of 1804; and cresting with the Coburg's double revival in 1824 of both *Tékéli* (the salvation of Drury Lane in 1806) and *Tale of Mystery* itself, just as the neo-Gothic wave peaks. Such revivals would extend through the decade, accompanying each subsequent subgeneric revival in turn, and become standard practice, at the minors especially, to establish a new niche, attract aficionados, or offer a sentimental treat.

This first recycling of melodrama in the 1820s unfolded against a far broader, more forceful, and more heterogeneous tide than before, and its successive waves were proportionately smaller, more superficial, overlapping, and short-lived than the original vogues they recapitulate and succeed. Even the first wave, the neo-Gothic fashion sparked by Planché's hypnotic *Vampire* in 1820, lasted barely five years, was burlesqued even as it unfolded, and rose only momentarily above the surges of domestic and revived grand romantic melodrama between which it arrived; similarly, the late renewed vogue for Scott, while it arrived as if on cue by 1828, was in some ways less a fashion than a quick fad, bobbing up amid an ocean of melodrama of all kinds. The whole process took less than ten years, half the time of the first subgeneric 'roll', and by the decade's close, a third cycle had already begun, with yet another, smaller, quicker vogue for the Gothic at the patents and Lyceum (punctuated, appropriately, by the latter's 1829 revival of *The Vampire* – the second wave's foundational success, now a classic). Yet, this third roll was far weaker, for the new force provided by gaslight was now old, and revival itself had lost its fashionable thrill.

Gaslight and expansion drove melodrama through a cycle of renewal and revivification, but by the middle of the twenties, even, a third stage of melodrama's development had begun: a process, closely akin to that which shaped melodrama's emergence, of formal recombination and redistillation – though one in which the constituent materials were not, as in melodrama's originary synthesis, romantic tragedy, Gothic and bourgeois drama, boulevard romance, sentimental comedy, and pantomime, but melodrama's own subgeneric types, which had through revival and reproduction been reified as convention, and thus became available as gestural tropes in a more densely mixed and ironic melodramatic form.

This redistillation of melodrama began with nautical melodrama, which arose rapidly in the mid-1820s, as domestic melodrama's dreams of familial reunion and rustic social peace ceased to provide more than sentimental excitement to audiences then dealing with – and chafing against – the widespread displacement, poverty, and urban overcrowding that had followed the end of the war, the contraction of the economy, and the disenchanting transition to industrialism. By 1825, 'home', such as it was, was for many nothing at all like domestic melodrama's dream: rather, it – and the familial relations, communities, and traditions it exalted – seemed like sentimental dreams perhaps best escaped and forgotten, in both the theatre and life. Nautical melodrama played most directly to that desire, whisking its audience off to a world of adventure in which anything might be possible still. In it, all of the supernaturalism, grand romantic spectacle and action, and masculine, patriotic heroism of melodrama's foundational varieties was revived, and those appeals were set cheek-by-jowl with the contemporary populism, affective drama, and modest romance of their successors. English melodrama written along nautical themes appeared very early, of course, in the military melodrama that began to appear in the Revolutionary era at Sadler's Wells, the Royal Circus, and even the patent houses. However, its consolidation and heyday accompanied not naval war but the expansion and consolidation, in the mid- to late-twenties, of Britain's imperial presence, and the great wave of postwar emigration from its shores. Unlike all prior subgenres, nautical melodrama's rise and fall took place almost not at all on the patent stages: its privileged locations, rather, were the Coburg, the Surrey, and the Adelphi, a powerful indicator of the melodrama's by then thoroughly popular audience base; in fact, nautical melodrama's primary history – unlike that of any of its precedent forms – was played out on amateur stages all over the world.

Nautical melodrama's reign at the forefront of fashion in London was brief, beginning with Edward Fitzball's supernaturalistic *Flying Dutchman* (1827) and Gothic *Inchcape Bell* (1828), peaking in his romantic *Red Rover* (1829) and Jerrold's national-domestic *Black-Ey'd Susan* (1829), and then playing out into more closely contextualized and domesticated works like Jerrold's *Press-Gang* (1830) and John Haines's *My Poll and My Partner Joe* (1835), in a trajectory that itself recapitulated early melodrama's own steady movement from the Gothic to the domestic and from the imagined to the real. Like its precedents, nautical melodrama marked not only a topical shift but a formal advance, and in this instance not only a change in melodrama's theatrical milieu but a shift in the status of its appeals and its claims. In nautical melodrama, these all – from the shock horror of ghosts to the tears of the orphan, and including even the romance of sail in that nascent age of steam – arrive as pleasing reflexive 'bits', open to irony and even mockery, often inside the play, and frequently more sentimental, and even childishly, comically nostalgic than earnest in their plea. Melodrama had worked in similar veins before with great success; the Gothic, for example, closed in 1813 with Isaac Pocock's triumphant *The Miller and His Men,* in which the admixture of Gothic villainy and prosaic village life lends both the same sort of sentimental charm. Like that play, nautical melodrama would serve as a mainstay of toy theatre production, fuelling melodrama's entry into juvenile culture, and its works would quickly be adopted as beloved touchstones of mass cultural sentiment. They would also count among the most popular and widely produced melodramas of the early British empire and, as such,

26

indicate the indebtedness of global melodrama to this second-generation, slightly reflexive, and fundamentally English version of melodramatic form.

In England, however, nautical melodrama was fairly quickly superseded, for like the romantic forms from which it borrowed, and the escapist dreams on which it rode, it soon seemed naïve in a context overshadowed, by 1830 at the latest, by growing political crisis, severe economic inequality and distress, increasingly desperate resistance to industrialization, and emigration's rapid demystification of the world. Indeed, nautical melodrama's brief vogue, as well as its sentimental place in popular culture, might be best understood in the end as a reflection of the lingering desire to evade and postpone that recognition, and to suggest, in a kind of nostalgic romanticism, that freedom from everyday, actual modern life, and the correction of injustice within it, are still available in some other place – if one slowly recognized as largely sentimental, and, finally, unreal.

What succeeded nautical melodrama, in a surging tide that rises along-side the Reform crisis of 1832, poured in after the New Poor Law of 1834, and reached its threatening peak with the onset, in 1837, of the century's greatest depression, was a variety of melodrama – variously concerned with poverty, labour, urbanization, and crime – that one might call the melo-drama of economic distress. Here the situational displacement of all earlier types was firmly, if gradually, set aside, and melodrama turned its gaze, against a rising clamour of critical opposition and alarm, to the common suffering, economic exploitation, collective violence, and criminal adven-ture taking place in its audience's lives, and unfolding just outside the theatre's doors. Nautical melodrama had itself, as we've seen, turned by the thirties to more proximate experience and contemporary economic concerns, and domestic melodrama, too, stepped clearly and consistently closer to actuality. However, the final turn away from sentiment really began in 1832, with Jerrold's vividly realistic, ardent, plain-spoken *Rent Day* (1832), George Dibdin Pitt's *Drunkard's Doom* (1832; 1833), and John Walker's *Factory Lad* (1832), finding its fullest expression in the unstoppable deluge of finely rendered, luridly intensified crime melodrama that floods the stage as social pressure builds, starting with Benjamin Webster's *Paul Clifford* (1832), Moncrieff's popular *Eugene Aram* (1832), and Fitzball's *Jonathan Bradford* (1833). The Surrey, the Royal Pavilion, and the Coburg (after 1833 the Victoria, or the 'Bleedin' Vic') drove the market, but in 1835, Fitzball's *Note-Forger* and revival of *Paul Clifford* brought crime melodrama to the patents; and in 1838 and 1839, respectively – at the height of economic agony – *Oliver Twist* and *Jack Sheppard* sparked a craze so intense that new productions of the latter were prohibited, and both were condemned publicly as catalysts of crime.

Like its precedents, economic distress melodrama marked not only a situational shift but a formal advance, and one that, like nautical melodrama before it, may be seen as a further distillation of earlier forms: in this instance, however, the redistillation drew from precedent the thrilling arts of the spectacular real, and the emphasis on contemporaneity, terror, and shock, that nautical melodrama had softened and elided. Crime melodrama sets aside the Gothic's ghosts with raw scorn, but seizes upon and amplifies its horror and sensational gore; discards grand romantic melodrama's exotic locales as clap-trap, but embraces – and significantly advances – its bravura use of mise-en-scène; leaves military melodrama's battles and martial codes behind as obsolete, but appropriates and intensifies its serialized structure of shock and surprise, as well as its hot focus on the documentary rendering of actual and immediate events. In all of these ways, the development of distress melodrama adapted melodramatic form to the intensified and changed temporal character of urban existence. With it, revolutionary, romantic modernity was left behind, and perceptual, industrial modernity arrived.

Significantly, too, economic distress melodrama borrows from national-historical melodrama its appeals to popular history, but the popular history it invokes is now that of modern dislocation, poverty, labour unrest, and especially crime; and while it takes up domestic melodrama's setting, conflict, and pathos, it repudiates – or offers as a tragically misguided naïveté – that variety's rosy vision of familial, communal, and social trust and support, as well as its hope in the force of non-violent action and purely emotional appeal. It is, even in its lightest and most nostalgic vein, unarguably grim, enacting almost programmatically the collapse of familial structure, individual isolation in a hostile modern world, and the failure – and often forced abandonment – of traditional moral values; and is, at times, tragic rather than melodramatic in structure, though its operations remain melodramatic throughout. In distress melodrama, one might say, we find a return to the existential register of the Gothic – but in a common, contemporary world. Its thrills, as well as its terrors, derive in no small part from this yoking of melodrama's most and least fantastic, and most and least extreme, situations and actions: ordinary people, living ordinary lives, caught in nightmarish events, doing fearful things – the realm of the domestic, but now overlapping with its opposite pole, in a kind of popular tragedy that might be seen as Schiller's post-Romantic successor, and which finds its most extreme expression in Georg Büchner's *Woyzeck* (1837), the true-crime tragedy from which radical modern drama would spring. In distress melodrama, too, one finds Victorian sensation drama's seed, not least because in this type, for the first time, melodrama's seemingly fundamental moralism is, with its romanticism, set aside as a now inoperative, or even repressive, behavioural code.

For contemporaries, including not least Pixérécourt himself, the advent of crime melodrama in particular marked for these reasons the form's bitter fall into illegitimacy and degeneracy, and it was from this time that the term itself became not merely derogatory but condemnatory, and took on its lasting, fearful association with the discontented, impoverished, immoral mob, and with a nihilist, unhealthy frame of mind obsessed with, and addicted to, lurid, sensationalist thrills. There is some justification to such fears, for crime melodrama, to a degree that distinguishes it from all precedent types, marked a major step forward in melodrama's penetration of English culture as an intermedial, and not simply a theatrical, form, and it thus exercised commensurately greater force on its audience's lives. Rising with the tide of popular literature and the penny press, it added to the amplifications of gas those of print and extended melodrama's presence well beyond the stage and the event of performance. Its plots, figures, and actions were not only ripped from the headlines and the flood of cheap prints of criminals and crimes, but staged with those fresh in mind, as abundant paratexts, scenic prompts, and even gestural guides. The first great hits of the genre were drawn from Newgate tales – just then being published on an unprecedented scale – or coordinated with, or stolen from, the rising tide of illustrated crime novels, which were themselves written with such intermedial marketing in mind, and accompanied by images designed to be 'realized' on stage. Once underway, demand for popular crime melodramas was stoked not only by theatrical imitations but by printed portraits, ballads, and souvenirs. *Jack Sheppard* and *Oliver Twist* certainly reflect the suffering and discontent of their time, but their success was owed no less to their magnified impact, through these means, on the cultural life of their time. More than mere vogues, they produced participatory crazes, modern consumer fads that enabled the creative assertion, in a world of increasing anonymity and isolation, of personal identity, and a new sense of belonging in the public expression of a community of fans.

Yet, if recognition of this shift from mere vogues to hot crazes lends force to contemporary fears that melodrama had become a kind of mania or madness, and certainly indicates the greater degree to which melodramatic form, by this time, had worked its way into and come to mediate even day-to-day existence, it is from crime melodrama, really, that social melodrama, psychological melodrama, and also dramatic naturalism and realism will later emerge. With its forced abandonment of traditional social morality, crime melodrama – and distress melodrama generally – brings a more progressive, ethical code into view, and enables the extension of sympathetic melodramatic recognition to figures whose criminal actions and anti-social behaviour would traditionally exclude them from communal regard, deprive them of human dignity, human rights, and even life. To it we owe antiheroes of every modern sort, and melodrama has since employed distress melodrama's heightened, sensationalized verisimilitude and dark, critical view of moral judgment to lend heroic and sympathetic dimension to marginalized populations of every kind. If in domestic melodrama, then, we find the marker of melodrama's maturation as a genre, its achievement of a spectrum of forms expressive of the full range of experience and imagination, we find in distress melodrama the marker of that genre's maturation as a mode, available for use in any and all media, and expressive now of any and all actions and lives.

# 3

MICHAEL GAMER

# Gothic Melodrama

## Cataloguing 'Melodrama'

On 6 July 1793 George Colman the Younger, successful playwright and manager of the Haymarket Theatre, announced 'a Musical Drama' entitled 'The Mountaineers . . . in preparation'.[1] At the end of that month, he submitted the play's manuscript to the Licenser of Plays for authorization. Now housed in the Huntington Library, it is catalogued as 'The Mountaineers, Melodrama' – though, surprisingly, the word 'melodrama' occurs nowhere in its pages.[2] Instead, Colman's title page declares it 'A Play in Three Acts', likely to emphasize its similarity to two earlier hits, *The Battle of Hexham; A Play* (1789) and *The Surrender of Calais; A Play, in Three Acts* (1791). Looking over the manuscript in the late 1930s, Larpent cataloguer Dougald Macmillan likely chose the label 'melodrama' because he found Colman's play characteristic of the genre.[3] What is strange is that he apparently did so only for *The Mountaineers*, sticking closely to the title pages of other plays. Had *The Mountaineers* possessed no subtitle, the interpolation would be more understandable. As it is, the substitution of 'Melodrama' for 'Play' is provocative, carrying within it an implicit argument concerning melodrama's historical and geographical origins. Among other things, it reminds us that conferring genre can be as accidental as it is retrospective – that had Colman persisted with 'musical drama', for example, commentaries would likely have been different. At the very least, it invites a re-examination of melodrama's roots in English theatre, particularly the Gothic drama of the 1790s.

Within this account, *The Mountaineers* comprises a useful point of reference because it embodies long-standing divisions over the function and propriety of music in theatrical performance. Such divisions are captured, for example, in Colman's decision to advertise his drama ultimately as a 'play' rather than as a 'musical drama'.[4] They are epitomized, moreover, in the play's reception and early critical history. Elizabeth Inchbald, for example, chose to reprint *The Mountaineers* in her collection of standard English plays, *The British Theatre* (1808). She did so, however, not to praise the play as a whole but rather to extol 'the extraordinary talents of one performer', John Philip Kemble, whose performance as Octavian had captured the public imagination. Betrayed by the parents of his fiancé, Floranthe, and believing himself to have killed his rival, Octavian has retreated to a remote cave, inconsolable in remorse and sustained by the kindness of the nearby Goatherds. There he meets the fleeing Agnes and Sadi, and on learning their plight guides them over the mountain to shelter. In the play, this act of kindness eventually leads to his discovery that he is not a murderer: that his rival, in fact, has recovered from his wounds and married another woman. Reunited with Floranthe, Octavian manages in the ensuing action to rescue Bulcazin and convince him to sanction yet another union, between Bulcazin's daughter Zorayda and Virolet. What Inchbald chooses to remember, however, is not the final happiness of the couples but Colman's portrayals of Octavian's despair:

> — 'He is as a rock,
> 'Oppos'd to the rude sea that beats against it;
> 'Worn by the waves, yet still o'ertopping them
> 'In sullen majesty.'                               (3:2)[5]

Anticipating figures like Walter Scott's Marmion and Lord Byron's Manfred, such lines epitomize the dramatic tradition we now term 'Gothic'. Driven nearly to madness by guilt, Octavian is characterized by what he believes to be unforgivable deeds and by his own passions, which, like the sea beating on a rock, have permanently marked him while leaving the features of his younger self still visible. In this he recalls the title characters of John Home's *Douglas: A Tragedy* (1757) and Robert Jephson's *The Count of Narbonne: A Tragedy* (1781), themselves drawn from earlier Renaissance tragic figures.

*The Mountaineers*, however, is anything but a tragedy. Its primary plotlines involve three pairs of lovers, all of whom are ultimately successful. Its closing scene is resolutely happy and ends with a Grand Finale sung by the Goatherds. As with later melodramas, its primary vehicle is suspense heightened by music, which either sets or accompanies key scenes. Its mixture of comedy and tragedy arises in part from its source materials, two discrete stories from *Don Quixote* brought together by Colman's denouement and choral ending. Noting these two strands, Inchbald singled out Colman's Octavian for praise. At the same time, she called her readers' attention to his reliance on music to sustain his story and characters:

> The other characters, where this sublime one is not concerned, have music to uphold them – which tempts a parody on one of the most beautiful and nervous passages of the play:
>
> > 'Providence has slubber'd them in haste,
> > 'They are some of her unmeaning compositions
> > 'She manufactures, when she makes a gross.

'She'll form a million such – and all alike –
'Then turn them forth, asham'd of her own work,
'And give them songs.'[6]

In Colman's original text, the final line of this passage reads 'And set no mark upon them'. Inchbald's substitution of 'And give them songs' draws on this missing line even as she points to Colman's strategy of musically supplementing otherwise unoriginal characters. Octavian, after all, sings no songs. Music's presence for Inchbald thus signals deficiency, functioning as a crutch to support figures otherwise undistinguished or generic. The same could be said – and for two centuries, has been said – about Gothic melodrama.

As this essay shows, Gothic was the first language of melodrama, and many of melodrama's roots can be found in the music and sonic effects of late eighteenth-century Gothic plays. While not sharing Inchbald's views on the corrosive effects of music on the stage, my account of Gothic melodrama here explores music's function first within the vogue for the Gothic at the end of the eighteenth century. This combination of sonic experience and supernatural effect brought a radical new dimension to a London stage already in transition. From here the essay moves into the early nineteenth century, to a range of musical dramas that revelled in conspiracy, the supernatural, and the darker side of human motivation and consciousness.

### Gothic Origins: The Supernatural Onstage

Gothic's intimacy with the stage goes back at least to Horace Walpole, whose *The Castle of Otranto: A Gothic Story* (1764) and *The Mysterious Mother: A Tragedy* (1768) often open accounts of the rise of Gothic fiction and drama, respectively.[7] At first privately printed because of its incestuous subject matter, Walpole's tragedy was eventually published in 1781 because of a threatened piracy. While its publication raised eyebrows, it was the success in that same year of *The Count of Narbonne*, Robert Jephson's adaptation of *Otranto*, that placed Gothic fiction firmly on the stage for the next half-century. Performed twenty-one times at Covent Garden Theatre during its initial run, *The Count of Narbonne* proved the hit of the 1781–2 theatrical season and, like *The Mountaineers*, was reprinted in 1808 as part of Inchbald's collection of standard plays. It also brought about renewed interest in Walpole's original Gothic story, which saw a new edition after being fourteen years out of print. The suggestion here is one less of adaptation than symbiosis. Walpole's Gothic novel may have given rise to Jephson's Gothic play, but the adaptation in turn renewed its original, so much so that since 1781 *The Castle of Otranto* has never been out of print.

Still, *The Count of Narbonne* can hardly be called a full endorsement of Gothic aesthetics, let alone melodramatic ones. Focusing on the fall of Manfred's house to the superior claims of Theodore, Jephson's play eschewed the supernatural scenes and machinery of its original. His blank-verse adaptation features no hermit skeletons, no giant limbs in armor, no ghosts walking out of paintings. Gone also are Walpole's humorous touches and moments of absurd pathos. The action instead centres on the Count's attempts to retain power in the face of irresistible fate and powerful rivals. It is a striking departure from a source text, corroborating *The Count of Narbonne*'s pretensions to that reputedly highest and most pure of theatrical genres, tragedy.[8] It also suggests a strong taboo against representing the supernatural on stage, one memorably captured in Robert Lloyd's poem 'The Actor' (1760), which succinctly captures a critical consensus that continued to grow in the second half of the eighteenth century:

> But in stage-customs what offends me most
> Is the slip-door, and slowly-rising ghost.
> Tell me, nor count the question too severe,
> Why need the dismal powder'd forms appear?[9]

Echoed in publications like *The Drury Lane Journal* (1752) and *The Dramatic Censor* (1770),[10] such remonstrations were directed not just at new plays like *The Count of Narbonne* but also at high-profile productions of older plays in the repertory. Most famous among these is the April 1794 production of *Macbeth*, which omitted – to considerable critical approbation – representing Banquo's ghost on stage. In his role as theatre manager, Kemble had chosen this production to dedicate the newly renovated Drury Lane to Shakespeare's memory. With an audience capacity of over 3,600 people, the theatre was the largest in Europe, its interior designed to resemble a Gothic cathedral.[11] The demand for spectacle to fill such a space was formidable and unprecedented: while Kemble may have withheld Banquo's ghost as a nod to critics, this did not stop him from adding other Gothic effects conducive to Drury Lane's new architectural style and cavernous size. Among these were new sets, costumes, and music, including Matthew Locke's popular vocal arrangements for the play, reset to an original score by W. H. Ware.

Judging from accounts of the play, the results were mixed. While producing a grand spectacle, James Boaden recalled, 'the noble firmness and compactness of the action were dreadfully broken and attenuated by the vast crowds of witches and spirits that filled the stage, and thundered in the ear a music of dire potency. The auxiliary injured the principal, and Matthew Locke became the rival of his master.' His description at once foregrounds the critical difficulty of reconstructing any dramatic spectacle while also carrying a hint of allegory. In Boaden's chaotic recollection, melody and song threaten in their 'dire potency' to overwhelm the English stage, upsetting dramatic hierarchies and producing unwholesome rivalries between 'auxiliaries' and 'master[s]'.

Kemble's predicament was one faced by every theatre manager, that of filling the house. And now that house required fuller casts and more spectacular productions to people its vast stage. Still, as Scott's description suggests, the greater challenges arguably were aural. Kemble's additions to *Macbeth* may have had a strong visual component, but their primary effect was sonic. 'Mere speech, however masterly', Boaden noted, 'is weak upon the ear after the noise (call it harmony if you will) of a full orchestra, and perhaps fifty voices, with difficulty kept together in tolerable time and tune.'[12] This spectacle of fifty singing, dancing witches nicely captures the increasingly musical nature of the times, as blank-verse tragedy is transformed by movement and song into something else. For Boaden, the changes are prophetic and a denigration: Shakespeare supplanted by 'noise', individual performance by 'vast crowds', and 'mere speech' by a full orchestra and an unruly, even disorderly, chorus.

Written retrospectively and published in 1830, Boaden's criticisms are at least somewhat disingenuous. Arguably no dramatist of the eighteenth century more thoroughly cultivated the vogue for supernatural stage effect than he did. Kemble's decision to bar the ghost of Banquo, in fact, likely found part of its inspiration in Boaden's own success with *Fontainville Forest* (1794), an adaptation of Ann Radcliffe's *The Romance of the Forest* that premiered at Covent Garden in the same weeks as Kemble's *Macbeth* at Drury Lane.[13] Boaden's play had proven both popular and controversial thanks to his introduction of a ghost – a decision that went against Radcliffe's standard practice of supplying rational explanations for apparently supernatural events. In *The Romance of the Forest*'s original scene, Adeline awakens from a nightmare, hears what is identified at novel's end as the voice of a servant, and faints. She derives her 'supernatural' experience from her own imagination and heightened emotional state. The Adeline of *Fontainville Forest*, meanwhile, is visited by an actual spectre, in this case that of the same murdered Cavalier who has previously haunted her dreams. Her fainting dramatically closes the third act. Where Jephson had removed most of Walpole's marvels in *The Count of Narbonne*, Boaden chose, in the words of his own epilogue, not 'to give up the ghost',[14] providing neither empirical nor psychological extenuations for his stage spectre.

To create supernatural effects, Boaden took elaborate technical measures. Abandoning Covent Garden's stage armour, he instead dressed the panto-mime actor John Follet in a close-fitting costume that resembled armour but made no noise. The aim was to emphasize sublime effect and Shakespearean precedent by backlighting Follet behind a blue gauze screen. The result strongly resembled the lofty figure of Henry Fuseli's painting *Hamlet and the Ghost*, then on display at Thomas Boydell's Shakespeare Gallery. Follet's gigantic steps and expressive gestures had delighted audiences, who watched electrified as Adeline swooned. Predictably, the scene proved unpopular with reviewers, who vocally protested against it as a supernatural imposition.[15] Given their negative response to Boaden's *coup de théâtre*, Kemble's decision to bar the ghost of Banquo – in what otherwise promised the most elaborate and spectacular *Macbeth* of the century – seems a prudential move, smacking of marketing savvy and inter-theatrical rivalry. His decision invited Boaden, in turn, to emphasize the rivalry between the plays both on and off the stage. Tellingly, the title page of the print version of *Fontainville Forest* promi-nently features an epigraph from Act 3, scene 4 of *Macbeth*: 'It will have blood: they say, blood will have blood. / Stones have been known to move, and trees to speak.'

## Sonic Innovations

When cultural historians talk about the vogue for staging Gothic in the 1790s, they usually emphasize its penchant for visual effect: elaborate sets, scenes of violence, and striking tableaux.[16] These all are important to the genre. As the accounts of Inchbald and Boaden remind us, how-ever, such scenes also produced powerful *aural* effects through original music and choral arrangements. It is for this reason that he emphasizes not the sights of *Macbeth* but its sounds. Even the silent ghost scene in *Fontainville Forest* was designed to produce a sonic effect – in this case, among the audience:

> [Follet's] figure ... thus drest, and faintly visible behind the gauze or crape spread before the scene, the whisper of the house, as he was about to enter, – the breathless silence, while he floated along like a shadow, – proved to me, that I had achieved the great desideratum; and the often-renewed plaudits, when the curtain fell, told me that the audience "had enjoyed
> 'that sacred terror, that severe delight', for which alone it is excusable to overpass the ordinary limits of nature."[17]

Ever the showman, Boaden inserts a palpable, supernatural silence into a play otherwise filled with music to produce that most melodramatic of audience effects: hushed suspense succeeded by gasps of terror and wonder.

Even that most celebrated reviver of traditional comedy, Richard Brinsley Sheridan, mixed spectacle with spoken word, music, scene, and sound to great effect. The early years of Sheridan's career witnessed the triumph of *The Duenna* (1775), a comic opera premiering in the same year as *The Rivals* and considered by Byron as the best of the age. A quarter-century later, Sheridan would come out of dramatic retirement to stage *Pizarro* (1799), an adaptation of August von Kotzebue's *Die Spanier in Peru* written ostensibly to address the Drury Lane company's increasing financial woes. Presenting, in Daniel O'Quinn's words, 'an innovative integration of tragedy, spectacle and music', *Pizarro* was a huge hit, featuring elaborate costumes, an original score, and timely politics.[18] Premiering amidst French invasion scares and in the aftermath of the naval mutiny at Spithead, it deeply resonated with contemporary English audiences, who identified with Kemble's performance as Rolla, the Incan prince who must face an invading foe void of scruple. It also caused genuine controversy and discussion among reviewers, who, fascinated by its wartime allegory, were uncertain whether Sheridan's generic hybrid constituted an aesthetic triumph or a threat to dramaturgical legitimacy.

Part of what provoked such critical uncertainty was what we might call *Pizarro*'s questionable origins and associates. Like Inchbald's *Lover's Vows* (1798) a year earlier, *Pizarro* was a German-Austrian importation refitted for London audiences. Its composer, moreover, was Michael Kelly, the Irish tenor most famous – or notorious – for providing soundscapes for London theatres' increasingly supernatural offerings. In the previous eighteen months, Kelly had written the music for what are arguably the two most important Gothic plays of the eighteenth century: *Blue-Beard* and *The Castle Spectre*. These remarkable productions premiered at Drury Lane within weeks of one another during the winter months of the 1797–8 season. Both are remembered today for their spectacular sets and visual effects, and for the consternation they caused among dramatic reviewers, who saw in them heralds of the imminent decline of the British stage. What we are prone to forget – though audiences never did – is their music, which sought to arrest attention and intensify experience. For *The Castle Spectre*'s celebrated ghost scene – in which a Gothic oratory opens to reveal the ghost of Angela's mother, who advances first to bless and then to warn her daughter before retreating back to the oratory, which shuts again on her – Kelly wrote equally evocative music. Heralding the ghost's appearance is a guitar playing a lullaby, accompanied by an unseen woman's voice. This is succeeded by a dreary, slow march adapted from a chaconne of Niccolò Jomelli that builds as she advances, blesses, and retreats. A full 'Jubilate' chorus closes both the doors of the oratory and the scene. Kelly's composition proved so popular that he eventually published it as a separate piece: a rare instance of incidental music claiming notice equal to a play's overture and songs.[19] *Blue-Beard*, meanwhile, was famous for two scenes: its opening, which featured a huge, animated panorama showing the advance of Abomelique's party; and its final scene in the dreaded 'Blue Chamber', with its moving skeleton and bleeding walls. For both, Kelly provided powerful music to heighten suspense and affective impact, making them feel newly urgent to audiences of the national theatres. It is for this reason that Jeffrey Cox calls melodrama a genre 'built for speed ... a new deployment of existing theatrical practices that created a different kind of theatrical experience, a different relationship between the audience and the "reality" it watches on stage'.[20]

## Genre Crossings

Neither comedy nor tragedy, pantomime nor farce, melodrama's newness stemmed from its tendency to consume other genres into itself. Gothic melodramas were especially adept at these acts of conspicuous dramatic consumption, avidly borrowing from a myriad of sources to create highly wrought scenes of action and suspense.[21] Writing to William Wordsworth in January of 1798 after having read Matthew Lewis's *The Castle Spectre*, Samuel Coleridge called these scenes 'situations':

> The merit of the Castle Spectre consists wholly in its *situations*. These are all borrowed, and absolutely *pantomimical*; ... the play is a mere patchwork of plagiarisms – but they are very well worked up, & for stage effect make an excellent *whole*. There is a pretty little Ballad-song introduced – and Lewis, I think, has great & particular excellence in these compositions. ... This play struck me with utter hopelessness – it would be easy to produce these situations, but not in a play so forcibly.[22]

Coleridge's account nicely captures the impact of Gothic melodrama, its ability to thrill audiences and confound readers by transforming familiar materials into new and powerful experiences. Reading *The Castle Spectre* in the privacy of his own study, Coleridge discovers little of the magic supposedly thrilling London audiences. Instead, he finds only 'plagiarisms': '*situations*' both 'borrowed' and '*pantomimical*' that must move beyond the printed word to achieve their effect. What causes him to throw up his hands in mock despair, however, is the 'patchwork' nature of this new genre: what *The St James's Chronicle* termed its 'mingled nature, Operatic, Comical and Tragical',[23] and the *Monthly Review* simply presented as an unsolvable conundrum:

After having to read this – *What do you call it?* – a drama, it seems, it must be, we cannot but regret that an author, whose talents seem designed for better things, should condescend to make us stare at *Groves*, and *Suits of Armor*, and *Pedestals* with *Names*, … and, in short, whatever presented itself to his imagination.[24]

The review nicely captures a problem facing anyone trying to make sense of a new cultural form at its beginnings. Where audience members in the 1820s would recognize Lewis's play as a classic of that established genre, Gothic melodrama, the *Monthly* reviewer can only see a monstrous, heterogeneous mess: an assemblage of props produced by a playwright's overactive imagination.

What, then, finally made a Gothic play a 'melodrama'? We can begin to answer this question by surveying adaptations of another work by Lewis, *The Monk* (1796), which between 1797 and 1820 was transformed into a range of genres, from ballad and chapbook to 'ballet pantomime', 'drama with music', and melodrama.[25] Taken as a whole, these provide an illuminating snapshot of theatrical culture and of the early nineteenth-century culture industry more generally. The first, *Raymond and Agnes; or, The Castle of Lindenberg* (1797), was labelled by its author Charles Farley as 'A New Grand Ballet Pantomime of Action'. Here, the subtitles are telling. Dissatisfied with calling his play either a ballet or a pantomime, Farley chooses a hybrid, which he then bolsters with adjectives to foreground his play's novelty and the 'action' of Lewis's original.

In Lewis's novel, the story of Don Raymond de las Cisternas stands as an inset story within the main tale of the monk Ambrosio and his seduction into vice. In it, Raymond sets off on his travels under an assumed name to hide his illustrious parentage. While in Germany he meets and rescues Agnes from a gang of banditti who infest the forests there, and is invited by her grateful aunt and uncle, the Baroness and Baron of Lindenberg, for a lengthy visit. He and Agnes fall in love, but when Raymond seeks to tell the Baroness of their passion, the Baroness misunderstands his intentions and declares her own love for him. When informed of her mistake, she swears revenge on Raymond, banishes him from the house, and informs Agnes that she must take the veil. Without alternative, Agnes resolves to elope with Raymond. Taking advantage of the Baron and Baroness's superstition and a local legend, she disguises herself as the Bleeding Nun, a ghost appearing at the Castle of Lindenberg every fifth year on the fifth day of the fifth month. Her plan proceeds perfectly, except that the real Bleeding Nun appears first and goes off with the awaiting Raymond, who, mistaking her for Agnes on her first appearance, swears eternal love to her. Appearing five minutes later and finding no Raymond, Agnes returns to her chambers and a few days later is sent to a convent in Madrid. Raymond, meanwhile, is haunted nightly by the Bleeding Nun until he manages, with the help of the Wandering Jew, to exorcise her spirit and bury her remains. He then proceeds to Madrid to find the now cloistered Agnes, at which the point his story rejoins the main thread of the novel.

To extract the subplot of Don Raymond from Lewis's romance, Farley was forced to supply an altered ending. In it, the Bleeding Nun does not haunt Raymond; instead, she abjures him to protect Agnes even as Agnes is seized by the banditti again and is borne to a nearby cavern. In the climactic scene, Raymond surprises the banditti, kills their leader Baptiste, and rescues Agnes. The epilogue then accompanies the happy couple and a protecting band of Muleteers over the mountains to Spain where Raymond presents Agnes to his father, who blesses their marriage accompanied by a 'Glee of Muleteers' and a Fandango:

> Strike the Lute's enchanting Wires!
> Every chord the dance inspires!
> In the brisk Fandango meeting
> And with smiles each other greeting
> The Castinet shall time our Measure
> And the night dissolve in pleasure. (1:16)[26]

Borrowing from a range of plays including *The Mountaineers* and Schiller's *The Robbers*, Farley's *Raymond and Agnes* provided a model for later adaptations of Lewis's romance, most of which focused on the story of Don Raymond at the expense of that of Ambrosio.[27] Equally suggestive, however, are those aspects of the Raymond and Agnes story *not* adapted by Farley or his successors. The grisly comedy of dame Cunegonda's kidnapping in *The Monk*, for example, is nowhere to be found in the later adaptations, nor are the more gently comic scenes of Theodore learning Spanish or writing poetry. Gone also is Lewis's narrative frame, in which Raymond must inform the hotheaded Lorenzo of Agnes's pregnancy while preserving their friendship. What remains constant across decades of adaptations are the scenes of greatest suspense, always accompanied by a compelling score.

The most successful of these, W. H. Grosette's *Raymond and Agnes, or the Bleeding Nun of Lindenberg; an Interesting Melodrama*, premiered in June of 1811 at the Theatre Royal Norwich before transferring to the Theatre Royal Haymarket that September. It enjoyed later revivals at Covent Garden and the English Opera, and a printed version appeared around 1820. The differences between the original Norwich manuscript and the eventual print publication show a play, as it moved across four theatres, continually streamlining its suspense and action at the expense of comic interludes and character development. Thus, the manuscript features several scenes of exposition not present in the later version, including repartees on Cunegonda's vanity, extended dialogues between Baptiste and his fellow robbers, and two concluding scenes at the house of Don Felix, where Raymond presents Agnes to his father and their marriage is celebrated. Five songs regulate the pace of the action, and incidental music is reserved for entrances, exits, scenes of pantomimic action, and tableaux. The manuscript's stage directions for the two scenes with the Bleeding Nun are exemplary of its sonic ways and means:

> RAYMOND. HARK – *[The Clock strikes One – soft Musick heard. The Spectre comes from the Castle crosses the Stage and Exits – Raymond following in extasy supposing it Agnes – Re-Enter Theodore – musick ceases.]*  (2:5)

After Theodore shares his ghostly fears and makes a hasty exit, the scene then changes to:

> *[A Dreary Wood very Dark. Enter the Spectre followed by Raymond still supposing it Agnes. When she gets on the trap he attempts to Embrace her. She Vanishes – leaving the following 'Protect the Child of the Murder'd Agnes.'' Musick ceases.]*  (2:6)

Three London productions later, much has accelerated. The early scenes of back-story are gone, as are the exchanges developing Baptiste's character. The two separate scenes with the Bleeding Nun, meanwhile, appear in the print version without Theodore's comic monologue, in a single extended sequence to focus dramatic action and supernatural effect.

Similar logic governs the printed play's ending. Where Grosette's original manuscript had culminated with a pantomimed marriage ceremony in which 'the Space behind the Alter breaks away and discovers the Spirit of the Bleeding Nun blessing the Nuptials of her Child',[28] the later version deletes these final scenes altogether, ending instead with the climactic battle:

> *Music. – Enter* RAYMOND, THEODORE, *and* MARGUERETTE, *rushing in hastily,* L. – RAYMOND *saves* AGNES, *and attacks* ROBERT, *who falls wounded –* THEODORE *darts furiously on* CLAUDE, *and overcomes him –* JAQUES *is shot by* MARGUERETTE – RAYMOND *and* AGNES *embrace,* R. – *a loud crash is heard – the back of the cavern falls to pieces, and discovers the* BLEEDING NUN, *in a blue ethereal flame, invoking a blessing on them – she slowly ascends, still blessing them – tableau, and curtain.*

## THE BLEEDING NUN.

RAYMOND.      MARGUERETTE.

AGNES.                        JAQUES.

ROBERT.                    THEODORE.

CLAUDE.

R.            CURTAIN.            L. (2:7)

In a frenzy of sword thrusts and gunshots yielding to a final tableau, Grosette's revised ending rejects that most traditional of comic endings, marriage. The closing embrace of Raymond and Agnes may forecast their happy end, but the dramatic focus sits squarely with resolving suspense and overcoming danger so that antagonists, as they are overcome, are fixed into an orderly tableau as the curtain falls.

This tendency to streamline action over successive performances is probably inevitable in any chain of adaptation: with each new revival, extraneous material becomes less necessary, as audiences become familiar with a play. Still, with Gothic melodrama this appears especially the case – in part because its *coups de théâtre*, whether scenes of supernatural visitation or suspense, function as a kind of portable property. Comparing early and late versions of this play, we witness Gothic melodrama acquiring its key conventions, trying first one device and then another in search of what will thrill and satisfy audiences. Thus, we find Grosette's scene in the robbers' cave appearing in only slightly altered form in Isaac Pocock's *The Miller and His Men* (1813). Both turn on a hero infiltrating a lair of banditti to rescue an abducted woman. With *The Miller and His Men*, Pocock introduced two innovations: that of ending his play with the climatic battle, and ending that scene with a final explosion:

GRINDOFF. For that threat, be this your recompence!
LOTHAIR. And this my triumph! *(music.)*
[*Lothair ... throws himself before Claudine, and receives Grindoff's attack, the robber is wounded, and staggers back, sounds his bugle, and the Mill is crowded with banditti. Lothair, having caught Claudine in his arms, and previously thrown back the bridge upon his release from Grindoff, hurries across it, and as he is on it, cries, 'Now, Ravina, now, fire the train.' Ravina instantly sets fire to the fuze, the flash of which is seen to run down the side of the rock into the gully ... and the explosion immediately takes place. Kelmar rushing forward, catches Claudine in his arms, and the whole form a group as the curtain descends.]* (2:5)

Arguably the most popular melodrama of the Regency, *The Miller and His Men* drew its fame from its signature combination of suspense, action, and technical innovation. Audiences returned night after night to see Grindoff vanquished and his lair destroyed. Similarities to *Raymond and Agnes* or other plays were rendered inconsequential by Pocock's pyrotechnics. Their influence is made clearest in later versions of Grosette's *Raymond and Agnes*, which jettison the closing marriage scenes and end in similarly cataclysmic fashion: *'the back of the cavern falls to pieces, and discovers the BLEEDING NUN, in a blue ethereal flame'*.

These instances of sustained borrowing become more comprehensible when we recall the closed nature of Regency theatrical culture – which, even as it drew large audiences, relied on a fairly small group of writers, composers, producers, and leading actors to produce new melodramas at London's legitimate theatres. The character of Grindoff in *The Miller and His Men*, for example, was played by the same Charles Farley who adapted *The Monk* into *Raymond and Agnes* and starred as Francisco in Thomas Holcroft's *A Tale of Mystery* (1802), the first play in English to call itself a 'melo-drame'. *A Tale of Mystery*'s composer, John Busby, also produced music for Matthew Lewis's *Rugantino; or, The Bravo of Venice* (1805), a play directed by Farley. Put another way, it is significant that John Philip Kemble, facing mounting losses from several unrenumerative productions of Shakespeare at Covent Garden during the 1811–12 season, looked to established names rather than new ones to reverse his fortunes. First reviving *Blue-Beard* with the added novelty of live horses performing to Kelly's music, he next drew Lewis out of retirement to compose *Timour the Tartar: A Grand Romantic Melodrama* (1811), also featuring performing horses and with Farley in the starring role.

This tendency for Gothic melodramas to be staged by a fairly small group of playwrights and producers is even true of the final play this essay invokes, *Presumption; or the Fate of Frankenstein* (1823). Penned by Richard Brinsley Peake, it delighted *Frankenstein*'s author, Mary Shelley; became a standard play in nineteenth-century repertories; and fostered no fewer than three further adaptations, including James Whale's 1931 film. Peake may have been part of the new generation of playwrights expanding Gothic melodrama into London's minor theatres, but his roots were those of the dramatic establishment. His father serving as treasurer of Drury Lane Theatre, he wrote across a range of dramatic forms. *Presumption* – called in manuscript 'Frankenstein: A Melo-Dramatic Opera' – remains his best-remembered work: in part because it so uncannily anticipates later film versions of *Frankenstein*, and in part because it shows Gothic melodrama in such fully matured form. Drawing on three decades of innovation in

43

supernatural representation, it is one of the earliest plays to take advantage of new lighting technologies, darkening parts of the stage in key scenes to render Frankenstein's creation (represented in playbills simply as '—') more spectral. In portraying the creation as unable to speak, however, Peake looked most pointedly to the example of Thomas Holcroft, whose *Deaf and Dumb* (1801) and *A Tale of Mystery* portrayed sympathetic characters as expressive as they were mute; *Presumption*'s most affecting scenes occur in dumb show.[29] Played by the great pantomime actor Thomas Potter Cooke, the creation's combination of pathos and near-acrobatic physicality creates electrifying scenes, such as this one, which ends Act 2:

> MUSIC. *– Agatha recovers. – The Demon hangs over them, with fondness. Felix and Frankenstein suddenly enter.*
> FRANK. Misery! The Demon!
> FELIX. What horrid monster is this? – Agatha, my father is in danger?
> *The Demon retreats.*
> MUSIC.*– Felix discharges his gun and wounds the Demon, who writhes under the wound. – In desperation he pulls a burning branch from the fire – rushes at them – beholds Frankenstein – in agony of feeling dashes through the portico. Safie Enters to Agatha. – Hurried Music.*
>
> ### FINALE.
>
> > Tell us – tell us – what form was there?
> > (With anxious fear enquiring)
> > Saw you its Eye – the hideous glare
> > Terrific dread inspiring!
>
> *The Demon is seen climbing the outside of the Portico. He bursts through the thatch with burning brand.*
>
> > The fiend of Sin
> > With ghastly grin!
> > Behold the Cottage firing!
>
> *The Demon hangs to the Rafters, setting light to the thatch and Rafters, with malignant joy – as parts of the building fall – groups of gypsies appear on the bridge, and through the burning apertures – who join in the Chorus.* (2:5)

Encompassing some three decades of theatrical innovation and generic experimentation, the scene captures what Gothic melodrama became in the 1820s and beyond. It combines choral exposition and thrilling action, pantomime and score, metaphysical allegory and quasi-supernatural spectacle.

Above all, it is strikingly efficient, presenting in a single sequence a sympathetic being goaded into a vengeance that extends to the very fabric of human relations. As such, it provides a crucial bridge into Victorian theater and later domestic melodramas, not to mention the origins of the modern horror film.

## Notes

1. *Morning Herald*, 4463 (6 July 1793): 1; *Morning Chronicle*, 7516 (6 July 1793): 1.
2. Colman's play is Huntington Library Manuscript LA989.
3. Dougald Macmillan, *Catalogue of the Larpent Plays in the Huntington Library* (San Marino: Huntington Library Press, 1939), 164.
4. 'Play' appears in advertisements beginning in the second week of July of 1793.
5. George Colman, *The Mountaineers*, quoted in Inchbald, 'Remarks on *The Mountaineers*', *The British Theatre*, vol. 21 (London: Longman, Hurst, Rees, and Orme, 1808), 4.
6. Inchbald, 'Remarks on *The Mountaineers*', vol. 21, 4–5.
7. See Bertrand Evans, *Gothic Drama from Walpole to Shelley* (Berkeley and Los Angeles: University of California Press, 1947), reprinted in its entirety as part of Frederick Frank's compendious *The Origins of the Modern Study of Gothic Drama* (Lewiston: Edwin Mellen Press, 2006).
8. Walpole and Jephson engaged in an extended discussion on tragedy in February of 1775; see *Correspondence of Horace Walpole*, vol. 41, 296–7.
9. Robert Lloyd, 'The Actor' (1760), in *Works of the English Poets from Chaucer to Cowper*, ed. Alexander Chalmers, vol. 15 (London: J. Johnson, 1810), 78.
10. See *Drury Lane Journal* (London: Publick Register Office, 1752), quoted in *Shakespeare: The Critical Heritage*, ed. Brian Vickers, vol. 3 (London and Boston: Routledge and Kegan Paul, 1975), 463; and '*Macbeth*', *The Dramatic Censor*, vol. 1 (London: J. Bell, 1770), 79. For a contrasting view, see *The Thespian Magazine*, 3 (1794): 174–5.
11. See *Thespian Magazine*, 3 (1794): 127–8; and *European Magazine*, 25 (1794): 236.
12. James Boaden, *The Life of Mrs. Jordan*, vol. 1 (London: E. Bull, 1831), 260.
13. For a full account of this production, see Francesca Saggini, *The Gothic Novel and the Stage: Romantic Appropriations* (London: Pickering & Chatto, 2015), 75–84, 127–9, and 154–75.
14. James Boaden, *Fontainville Forest: A Play* (London: Hookham and Carpenter, 1794), 69.
15. See *Analytical Review*, 19 (1794): 187; *Monthly Review*, 2nd Series, 14 (1794): 352; *Thespian Magazine*, 3 (1794): 127–8; and *European Magazine*, 25 (1794): 236.
16. Here, see especially Paula Backscheider, *Spectacular Politics: Theatrical Power and Mass Culture in Early Modern England* (Baltimore and London: Johns Hopkins University Press, 1993); and Jacky Bratton, 'Romantic Melodrama', in *The Cambridge Companion to British Theatre 1730–1830*, eds. Jane Moody and Daniel O'Quinn (Cambridge: Cambridge University Press, 2007), 115–27.

17. James Boaden, *Memoirs of the Life of John Philip Kemble*, vol. 2 (London: Longman, Hurst, Rees, Orme, Brown, and Green, 1825), 115–19.
18. Daniel O'Quinn, '*Pizarro*'s Spectacular Dialectics: Sheridan's Bridge to the Cosmopolitical Future', in *Richard Brinsley Sheridan: The Impresario in Political and Cultural Context*, eds. Jack E. DeRochi and Daniel J. Ennis (Lewisburg, PA: Bucknell University Press, 2013), 191–233 (192).
19. *The Favorite Movement, performed . . . during the appearance of the Ghost in the Drama of the Castle Spectre* (London: Lavenu [1798]).
20. Jeffrey N. Cox, *Romanticism in the Shadow of War: Literary Culture in the Napoleonic War Years* (Cambridge: Cambridge University Press, 2014), 46.
21. On the explosion of melodramatic forms in the early nineteenth century, see Diego Saglia, 'The Gothic Stage', in *Romantic Gothic*, eds. Angela Wright and Dale Townsend (Edinburgh: Edinburgh University Press, 2016), 80.
22. Samuel Coleridge to William Wordsworth, 28 January 1798, *Collected Letters*, ed. Earl Leslie Griggs, vol. 1 (Oxford: Clarendon Press, 1956), 378.
23. *St. James Chronicle; or, British Evening-Post*, 6240 (1797): 4.
24. *Monthly Review*, 26 (1798): 96.
25. See Saggini, *The Gothic Novel and the Stage*, 9 and 279n121.
26. The British Library copy (shelf mark 161.i.50) of *Airs, Glees, and Chorusses in a New Grand Ballet Pantomime of Action, called Raymond and Agnes* (London: T. N. Longman, 1797) is imperfect, and so contains additional pages of manuscript appended to it. The quotation is from page 15 of that text.
27. The most notable exception is James Boaden's *Aurelio and Miranda* (Drury Lane, 1798), which failed after six nights.
28. H. W. Grosette, *Raymond and Agnes; or, The Bleeding Nun*, Huntington Library MS LA1597, Act 2, scene 7, page 53.
29. See Michael R. Booth, *English Melodrama* (London: Herbert Jenkins, 1965), 71; and Peter Brooks, 'The Text of Muteness', *New Literary History: A Journal of Theory and Interpretation*, 5 (1974): 549–64.

# 4

## ANKHI MUKHERJEE

# Nautical Melodrama

In Act 2, scene 3 of Douglas Jerrold's *Black-Ey'd Susan* (1829), the most popular nautical melodrama and one of the most frequently produced plays of the nineteenth century, St Domingo Billy, or Billy the Shark, makes a memorable, if all-too-brief, appearance. The episode in question marks a welcome respite between the high excitement of scene 2, where William, a returning sailor, has had to rescue his wife, the eponymous heroine, from the unwanted advances of Tom Hatchet, a smuggler, and the climactic section of scene 3, which sees William incriminating himself by unwittingly striking his superior officer, who is also in amorous pursuit of Susan. We find William chattering happily with Gnatbrain, who has been a reliable friend to Susan, and his fellow sailors. He introduces Susan to his shipmates, declaring that he would not relinquish 'command of this craft' even for promotion to the rank of 'Lord High Admiral' (2:3), and offers tobacco to Gnatbrain.

> *[Takes out box.]* Here, take a bit from St. Domingo Billy.
> GNATBRAIN. From what? [SAILORS *gather round* WILLIAM.]
> WILLIAM. From St. Domingo Billy! I see you are taken back –steering in a fog; well,
> I'll just put on my top-lights to direct your course.                    (2:3)

In the thick nautical jargon characteristic of melodramas of this subgenre, and using nautical metaphors, William spins a fetching yarn of the time when the fleet was stationed at St Domingo (also known as Saint-Domingue or Santo Domingo, depending on whether the portion of the Hispaniola island in question was controlled by French or Spanish powers). The crew liked 'new rum and dancing with the niggers', William says, and were known to swim ashore at night (2:3). To prevent these nightly proclivities, the admiral and the captains groomed a shark to patrol the waters. Billy, as the sailors liked to call him, would obligingly swim around the fleet, going from ship to ship 'for his biscuit and raw junk, just like a Christian' (2:3). The mutually advantageous relationship came to a precipitate end one day:

[O]ne morning, about eight bells, there was a black bumboat woman aboard, with a little piccaninny, not much longer than my hand; well, she sat just in the gangway, and there was Billy along side, with his three decks of grinders, ready for what might come, – well afore you could say about-ship, the little black baby jumped out of its mother's grappling, and fell into Billy's jaws, – the black woman gave a shriek that would have split the boatswain's whistle! Tom Gunnel ... snatched up a knife, overboard he jumps, dives under Billy, and in a minute the sea was as red as a marine. (2:3)

Gunnel, 'as fine a seaman as ever stept', guts the shark to find in its belly purloined treasures: watches; tobacco boxes that had been lost in the last ten years, including the one William was now offering to his mates; an admiral's hat and three pilots' telescopes. Sheryllynne Haggerty's study of business culture in the British Atlantic in this time period would suggest that tobacco, chewed or used as snuff, when not smoked, on British fleets such as those described by William, was imported from the Chesapeake colonies (Maryland and Virginia) and arrived at Norfolk to be re-exported to Europe, especially France. The use of a black baby (eventually a black corpse) in the maws of the tobacco-ingesting shark is not a trifling coincidence, nor should we overlook the fact that 'Billy' is an abbreviation of William, the honest British tar. Without feeling the need to make a trenchant political critique, Jerrold is referencing nineteenth-century empire; the scramble between France and Spain for the West Indies, as seen in the name, St Domingo, which summarily combines French and Spanish words; the centrality of black bodies in the ravenous trans-Atlantic commodity trade, which gobbles up black babies and tobacco alike; and, finally, the British sailor as not merely a scourge of the Napoleonic wars but a consumer of the global capitalist economy that was soon to become a corollary of colonial expansion.

Making a distinction between John Bull, the figure of domestic drama 'tied to hearth and land', and the Jack Tar, who has left the confines of home to rule the waves, Jeffrey Cox argues that it is the latter who most forcefully upholds traditional family values:

[T]he tar has gone out into the world, confronted the enemy, perhaps been shipwrecked or captured or sold into slavery. He has lived in proximity to the Other, and yet all he wants is a return to the same, thus validating, in a way that John Bull cannot, the British status quo.[1]

Cox's reference to the Atlantic economy of slavery in relation to the honest British tar of military melodrama reminds us again of the composite, often mutually cancelling, historical aspects of the figure, and the lability of representational strategies that enabled it to traverse the spectrum from perpetrator to victim, victor to the vanquished. The sailor heroes dominating the melodramatic stage in the 1820s and 1830s, their names 'positively smelling of salt water and courage', as Michael Booth puts it, fought 'wreckers, pirates, slavers, smugglers, and the French'.[2] They were also frequently represented as slaves to the state machinery. William Richardson, author of *Mariner of England*, an autobiographical account of his service in the Royal Navy in the late eighteenth century, writes,

> People may talk of negro slavery and the whip, but let them look nearer home, and see a poor sailor arrived from a long voyage ... when a press gang seizes him like a felon ... if he complains he is likely to be seized up and flogged with a cat, far more severe than the negro driver's whip, and if he deserts he is flogged round the fleet nearly to death.[3]

The brutalizing culture of conscription and impressment, and the violent disciplining of young sailors on board the king's ships alluded to by Richardson, are related to the upheavals of the Napoleonic Wars, which necessitated the mobilizing of a large wartime navy. It is intriguing, however, that despite the fact that impressment had been discontinued at the end of the Napoleonic Wars, nautical melodrama continued to represent it as a contemporary issue. John Storey provides two explanations for this. First, he views it 'as an example of melodrama's empty radicalism – moving safely past in historical time, attacking something that is no longer in existence'.[4] He qualifies this reading by stating that the treatment of impressment in a play such as John Thomas Haines's *My Poll and My Partner Joe; A Nautical Drama in Three Acts* (1835), when examined in the context of the clashes between the Chartists and the Anti-Corn Law League in Manchester, where the play was staged in 1841, could signify nautical melodrama's 'sustained *connotative* critique of a society seemingly without justice'.[5]

'Because England had become a naval power, the popular imagination was always easily captured by plays which depicted nautical characters and events', writes George D. Glenn of the period of the French Revolution and the Napoleonic Wars (1792–1815):

> Three categories of naval events provided opportunities for theatrical adaptation: the great naval battles between British and French fleets, land-based civilian celebrations commemorating British fleet victories, and battles between single British and enemy ships.[6]

Nautical docudramas of the kind Glenn describes usually represented a number of historical events and were hurried into production to air the timely dramatic content. With 'numerous scenic displays and a spectacular conclusion, [they] stimulated and reinforced patriotic sentiment in the audience'.[7] Thomas Dibdin's musical interlude *The Hermione; or,*

*Retaliation*, staged at Covent Garden on 5 April 1800, is based on the story of the frigate *Hermione*, which was stationed in the West Indies and was the scene of a mutiny in August 1797. The mutineers killed and dismembered the captain and his officers before surrendering the ship to Spanish-held territory. The subtitle of Dibdin's play, 'Retaliation', refers to the recovery of the *Hermione* on 25 October 1799 by Captain Edward Hamilton of HMS *Surprize*. Hamilton captured the *Hermione* through a cunning strategy whereby fifty of his crew members took on over 400 men aboard the *Hermione*, while the remaining men on boats cut the rogue ship's cables and took her in tow. Through the fierce fire of the shore batteries, *Hermione* was sailed into Kingston, where Sir Peter Parker, the admiral, commissioned her as the *Retaliation*. Dibdin's *The Hermione* focuses less on the mutiny than on a contestation of national definitions, with Englishness triumphing over Spanish and French nationalisms. Spanish troops are seen to perceive the mutiny as a robbery and the mutineers as 'renegade rascals'.[8] They vocalize their preference for the brave English over a villainous French officer (who bosses over them in heavily accented English). There is an interracial romantic interlude on shore between Sam Swig, a (non-mutineering) English sailor who has escaped from a Spanish prison, and Orora, 'a black girl'; there is also a near-rape of the English Captain's Lady by the Frenchman holding her hostage. The English boat appears, and both the *Hermione* and the Captain's Lady are saved from further violation in the nick of time.

The aquatic theatre of the first decade of the nineteenth century rowdily celebrated British maritime prowess and colonial expansion through spectacles such as *The Siege of Gibraltar* (1804), *The Siege, Storming, and Taking of Badajoz* (1812), *The Siege of Salamanca* (1812), and *The Battle of the Nile* (1815). The Licensing Act of 1737, which reserved spoken drama for Drury Lane and Covent Garden, gave rise to new genres of non-patent theatre in playhouses south of the Thames: musical dramas, equestrian acts, harlequinades, pantomime, burlettas, farces, spectacles, and nautical dramas. Sadler's Wells Theatre, which originated in 1683 as Sadler's Music House, specialized in nautical dramas and marine spectacles under the management of the resident playwright Charles Dibdin the Younger (brother of Thomas Dibdin, discussed above), who took over in 1804. Located at the New River Head in Islington, it took advantage of the plentiful water supply to create a water tank, which covered its entire stage and was reputed to hold 64,800 gallons. Dibdin launched the aquatic theatre in 1804, with a tank of water ninety feet long, twenty-four feet wide (narrowing to ten feet), and three feet deep. He also ordered the construction of a large number of ships, constructed on a scale of one inch to a foot of those in the navy, with the regular tiers and number of brass cannon (which were fired and recharged in action), and exact rigging.[9] In the aptly titled 'A Defence of Nineteenth-century English Drama', Michael Booth argues that despite its crudities, melodrama was not only thoroughly representative of its age but socially and politically more advanced than other forms of nineteenth-century theatre. While the naval entertainments discussed above were not identified as melodramas, Booth's observation about nautical melodrama as aiding wartime propaganda and self-aggrandizement holds true of these precursor forms:

> military and nautical melodrama fought the major land and sea battles of British history, and long before imperialism was a conscious political doctrine the Union Jack waved triumphantly over a battalion of militantly expansionist and imperialist melodramas.[10]

To this collective fantasy of the ideal British tar, or 'a sea-going John Bull', as Booth puts it,[11] nautical melodrama, unlike the jingoistic aqua dramas or the nautical docudramas before it, brought the abiding realities of poverty and compulsory conscription; the inequality between master and man; the uneasy moral distinctions between sailor, smuggler, and pirate; and the question of upward mobility (or the lack of it) – all contested in the microcosm of a ship of the Royal Navy.

Nautical melodrama, which had come into its own by the 1820s, was indebted also to the Gothic novel and continental playhouses. The theatre historian George Rowell points out that melodrama, the very word appearing almost simultaneously in France and Germany (to signify a passage of mime to music, in the first instance, and dialogue spoken to music between the sung passages of opera in the second), was a 'product of the Gothic extravaganza which gripped a Europe bored by the Age of Reason, and which found architectural and antiquarian as well as literary form'.[12]

> In the first thirty years of its life English melodrama remained resolutely exotic – a strange, brilliant plant blooming amongst the familiar flowers of Covent Garden or on Surrey side. Where these early melodramas reflected the English scene at all it was not a contemporary England, but a country lent enchantment by the period of the Crusades or the Armada. . . . When eventually the appeal of the Gothic ghosts and Bohemian bandits began to flag, even for this unexacting audience, the writers were forced to turn to their own world in their own day for further subjects.[13]

T. P. Cooke, tired of playing vampires and Frankensteins, is known to have urged the maverick playwright Edward Fitzball to give him a chance to play a sailor. Cooke's definitive role as the hero of nautical melodrama came in *The Pilot* (1825), Fitzball's loose adaptation of James Fenimore Cooper's novel *The Pilot: A Tale of the Sea* (1824), in which the American setting was changed to that of Britain during the American Revolution, and where the Yanks were the villains and the British the heroes. Cooke, who had served at sea in his youth, played Long Tom Coffin, coxswain and tar delight, and the nautical burletta was a national success. *Belgravia*, a London magazine edited by Mary Elizabeth Braddon, reported that *The Pilot*, first staged at the Adelphi, ran for 200 nights and that the managers cleared 7,000 pounds. T. P. Cooke was 'the most picturesque and high-souled of sailors, with a deep-toned passion for the sea, a love of its mystery and a defiance of its dangers'.[14] Fitzball's *The Pilot* and his wildly popular *The Flying Dutchman*, which followed in 1826, retained unmistakable Gothic elements. In *The Pilot*, Cooke's character is given a tormented interiority, albeit temporarily, in a scene wherein the roaring tempest outside, made immediate through the mechanical accoutrements of the production, is perceivable as a projection of Gothic dread. He gives an impassioned speech about his deep psychic connection to Ariel, the ship, the spectre of whose destruction threatens to drive him to insanity. 'It is as if he were the spirit of the navy rather than one of its men', observes Jacqueline Bratton.[15] Fitzball's *The Flying Dutchman* continues the supernatural theme in its portrayal of an undead sailor – the figure of Vanderdecken – entrapped in a ghost ship. Fitzball made use of special effects at the Adelphi theatre to create phantasmagoria around the ghost ship and its ghostly mariner: a lantern on tracks, which rear-projected the *Flying Dutchman* on an intervening gauze screen; gas footlights in a float that could be raised and lowered (to darken the stage); a devil's trap and a concealed panel on the stage, which aided Vanderdecken's mysterious comings and goings. The maritime and the Gothic coalesce powerfully in the figure of Vanderdecken, a symbol of accursed piracy (Vanderdecken is the dark double of the wholesome sailor Toby Varnish), the fear of plague that rises from the murky depths of the darkened sea, or a Faustian compact with the devil (in this instance Rockalda, Evil Spirit of the Deep).

Cooke, the stage sailor who was described by Robert Dyer as 'an amphibious animal ... [who] moves on the shore like a fish out of water',[16] facilitated the rise of both the most popular form of nautical melodrama and its playwright, Douglas Jerrold (1803–57). Robert William Elliston, the manager of the Surrey Theatre who was instrumental in making it one of the most successful of all minor theatres, had engaged the services of Cooke for eight nights, and, as Michael Slater writes in his magisterial *Douglas Jerrold*, he 'needed a new piece written to "showcase" the actor and his unique abilities'.[17] Jerrold wrote *Black Ey'd Susan; or, All in the Downs*, for Cooke in 1829, giving him the role of a lifetime. He stayed on at the Surrey for a lot longer than the initial eight weeks, re-engaged at twenty-five pounds per week. Cooke played Sweet William in *Black Ey'd Susan* over 800 times over the next thirty years, and was the inspiration for Herman Melville's *Billy Budd*. Douglas Jerrold, who was a midshipman for two years during the Napoleonic Wars, and who had also known grinding poverty as a struggling theatre manager in London, imbued nautical drama with a lived understanding of the plight of the poor and a searing vision of (and plea for) distributive justice. As Michael Slater observes, in *Black Ey'd Susan* 'there is no trace of the triumphal jingoism usually associated with nautical drama':

> In place of the swashbuckling British tar fighting any number of inferior foreigners (in *The Pilot* Tom Coffin defeats six Yankee soldiers armed only with his harpoon), he presents William as a devoted husband, returning eagerly to his Susan after three years' brave service in his nation's wars.[18]

In the five-page preface to an octavo edition of *Black Ey'd Susan*, published following the tremendous acclaim received by Jerrold's most successful play to date, the playwright pokes fun at 'the usual recipe for the composition of the tar of the theatre', which was to make him 'shiver his timbers', 'bless the king', and 'swear that one true-born Briton can lick "ten Frenchmen"'. His own aim, he writes, is to depict 'an English seaman' from 'observation made at an early period of life'.[19] *The Mutiny at the Nore* (1830) was also written as vehicle for T. P. Cooke, though not for the Surrey but for the Pavilion, Whitechapel, an East End playhouse, as Jerrold was keen to escape the clutches of the exploitative Elliston.[20] Despite the runaway success of *Black Ey'd Susan*, Douglas Jerrold had had no share in its profits, and had, in fact, landed in the King's Bench debtor's prison in 1830. Neither Elliston nor Cooke had offered any help to secure Jerrold's release. The *Mutiny* was, therefore, launched at the Royal Pavilion with Thomas Cobham as Richard Parker and John Farrell as Jack Adams. This personal history is not irrelevant in the discussion of a play about a mutiny that is historically attributed to 'the harshness of the sailors' lives and discontent about the alleged unequal distribution of prize-money', not simply the political radicalism and labour movements of its time.[21]

*The Mutiny at the Nore; or British Sailors in 1797*, was based on actual events but borrowed narrative elements from Frederick Marryat's nautical novel *The King's Own*, published earlier in 1830. The play has two protagonists, Jack Adams and Richard Parker, both sailors and leaders of different phases of the naval mutiny. As Jeffrey Cox points out, 'Jerrold includes the first mutiny at Spithead near Portsmouth to frame his account of the Nore mutiny, to present a "good" mutiny before taking on the more dangerous events at the Nore.'[22] Jack Adams, a loyal seaman who finds himself unwittingly at the head of the Spithead mutineers, is gradually co-opted as a mediator figure for the Admiralty, while Parker, who has suffered personally in the hands of a sadistic officer – Captain Arlington – is, to use an anachronistic but apt term, increasingly radicalized. The fraught exchanges between the two men, especially in the last scene of the second act on board the *Sandwich*, provide grist for the melodramatic mill. Here, we see the commander of the ship, Captain Arlington, refusing to release sailors who have been imprisoned on suspicion of mutinous intent, which proves extremely divisive for the ship's crew. As Richard Parker aims the forecastle guns on the captain and the marines, Jack Adams rushes in to snatch Parker's child, who is found sleeping in front of one of the guns. Arlington takes advantage of the confusion to snatch the child and orders the marines to shoot the sailors, who are, however, repulsed by this act of cruelty and refuse to obey orders. Parker's life on the lam allows for a tender, domestic interlude, but he is apprehended and precipitately hanged after he shoots Arlington in the ensuing struggle. Adams assumes guardianship of Parker's wife and child as the noose is tightened around the condemned sailor's neck. Parker drinks to the king's health before being executed.

*The Mutiny at the Nore* has much in common with the nautical plays (authored by Jerrold) which preceded it, especially *The Press-Gang* (1830) and *Black Ey'd Susan*, and these similarities shed light on the constitutive features of nautical melodrama in the 1820s and '30s. Arthur Bryght in *The Press-Gang*, played by T. P. Cooke, is press-ganged just after his marriage, just as William is forced by the rural labourer's poverty to leave his new wife to fight in the nation's wars for three years. Like Parker in *Mutiny*, Bryght flees the navy, is re-captured, and sentenced to flogging. Both Parker's wife Mary and William's wife Susan become the unhappy targets of their superior officers' lustful advances, and the husband in each case is sentenced to death for striking his officer. The parting scene between Richard and Mary Parker in *Mutiny at the Nore* captures the pathos of the farewell scene between William and Susan. *Black Ey'd Susan*, as well as *Mutiny at the Nore*, have a wide range of private citizens: some harmless rustics, others conniving informers, middlemen, and mercenaries. *Black Ey'd Susan* has pivotal civilian characters such as Doggrass, Susan's rapacious uncle and landlord, the smuggler Hatchet, good-hearted Gnatbrain, and the half-wit Jacob Twig. Similarly, the plot of *Mutiny* is propelled by the shenanigans of Timothy Bubble and his sidekick, Dicky Chicken. In *Black Ey'd Susan* as well as *Mutiny*, Jerrold excoriates the ill-gotten gains and easeful lives of men like

Doggrass and Bubble, in marked contrast with the poverty-stricken, socially adrift sailor-heroes. As Jack Adams tells Bubble of the men in his fleet:

> many a brave heart there has watched, fought, bled, for his country; has spent years upon the salt sea in storms and peril; has had the waves beating over him and the shots flying about him, whilst you, and such as you, have been scratching your sixpences together, taking your grog with the curtains drawn, the doors listed, your feet upon the fender, and your wife and children alongside of you. (1:1)

Arthur Bryght's flogging in *The Press-Gang* is averted at the last minute by a revelation by Archibald that Arthur is high-born, a peer of the realm. Victor Emeljanow refers to contemporary reviews in the *Times* and the *Examiner*, which clearly show that the irony of the ending, which revealed 'the double standards affecting the common man and the aristocrat', was not lost on the play's audience.[23] The double standards are evoked forcefully, and in multiple ways, in *Mutiny at the Nore*. The sailors, when rebuffed by the Captain for their insolence, point out that it was related to the very dauntlessness that saved 'Old England thro' many a tough gale': 'it was our boldness that kept the French from the shores, and the merchantsmen safe in the ports, – it was our boldness that saved everything that was British; and now we'll see if our "boldness" can't serve ourselves!' (1:1). When Jack Adams enjoins patience and calm on the quarter-deck of the *Sandwich* at the Nore, promising that the Admiralty will grant the sailors their due, Richard Parker, the leader of the mutineers, dispassionately points out the routine infringement of human rights aboard the ship, aided by a grotesque imbalance of power between the enslaved sailors and their tyrannical master, with his musket-wielding henchmen:

> Are we not hourly goaded, spurned, treated like dogs? Even this very morning, ten of the crew, as bold and honest tars as ever braved a storm or met a foe, have been placed in irons, are now below, with marines standing with loaded muskets over them; and what have these men committed? Why, the captain did not like their looks; he thought he saw mutiny gleaming in their eye, and swelling in their lip. (1:3)

D-G (the theatre critic George Daniel), author of the remarks appended to the play, praises its subject matter – 'a memorable epoch in the page of history' – and concedes that those who cannot attend a naval execution are allowed to 'have their soft sympathies excited' by witnessing this drama. He praises the horror-inducing 'paraphernalia of death' and the 'domestic agony' of the wife and the 'unconscious' infant, which provide a dramatic contrast to 'the stern group of executioners'.[24] 'To resist oppression is a duty that we owe to ourselves and to mankind', the reviewer muses,[25] but he is also ambivalent about the critique of social inequity mounted by the play. In fact, he seems to suggest that the proletariat's propensity to rise against their social betters should be disciplined, not facilitated:

> While thus we advocate resistance against tyranny, we would not entrust with the illiterate the means, or the degree. To resist lawful authority is the peculiar privilege of the vulgar, who forget that *their* station, however humble, in society, is upheld by its due maintenance; for gradations in fortune are natural to man, as in stature or intellect.[26]

In a similar vein, D.-G. cautions against any inappropriate political enfranchisement of the Jack Tar. While the sailor's honesty and patriotism are indubitable, he is no legislator, the reviewer argues:

> To hold councils, and appoint delegates, is as much out of his province, as to turn his guns against his liege lord exceeds the bounds of his duty. His petitions for redress must not fly from the cannon's mouth; nor must a whole fleet be held in mutiny to call attention to his complaints.[27]

Jerrold's attitude towards the naval mutiny, unlike that of the reviewer, seems unequivocal at first. 'We want more pay, better provisions, and less flogging, captain', says Jack Morris (1:1), and *Mutiny at the Nore* attacks directly 'the arbitrary nature of acts by offices, the poor pay and living conditions of the navy, and the savagery of its discipline', as Victor Emeljanow puts it.[28] Jerrold achieves this critique through the personal drama he creates between the sadistic Captain Arlington and the common sailor Richard Parker, and through the interpolation of a wife/child plotline. Arlington's animus is related to his foiled seduction of Parker's wife Mary in the past. He seeks revenge now by tormenting Mary, inflicting unjust punishments on Richard, and even threatening to kill their child. Richard Parker is framed for a theft he did not commit: he deserts the navy in utter vexation, but is apprehended and tried for desertion, his punishment settled at 500 lashes at the side of each ship in the fleet. George Daniel, in his remarks, points out that the incident of the stolen watch (which the Captain devises to frame Parker) and that of the flogging are both plot details with no historical basis, and that it was misleading to insert these fabrications:

> All this is allowable as fiction; but, unless the audience, which we doubt, can detect the interpolations, these mitigating circumstances, when put forth in connection with history, and aided by scenic effect, are likely to produce a wrong impression – to inspire horror at the sword of justice, when justice is mercy.[29]

For all its critique of social injustice through narrative embellishment, Jerrold's nautical melodrama shies away from its violent correction in a full-fledged people's uprising. Jack Adams, in *Mutiny*, a sailor 'who talks better than any lawyer', offers a viable alternative to both the oppressive authority of the top brass and the inarticulate agony of the sailor on the deck. 'My lads, I have fought too long for my king and country to go the course you are steering now', he tells the mutinous sailors, adding with bureaucratic flair that 'if you have wrongs, as mayhap you have, write to the Admiralty' (3:1). In the climactic scene, where Adams rescues Richard Parker's child from the muzzle of the gun Parker was about to fire, Adams points out to Parker that he wouldn't have seen the little boy had he remained on Parker's (rebellious) side when the battle lines were drawn. He offers Parker a new lease of life, demonstrating his mature understanding of (and compassion for) the widely reviled figure of the mutineer, although this moral ambivalence, which is his as well as the Victorian spectator's, does not prevent the tale's tragic denouement. Jack Adams is also the custodian of the future (and the junior Parker): Richard Parker is allowed his avenging fury, but he will not live to see his son made admiral one day, as Jack Adams promises will be the case.

In nautical melodrama, tragedy is usually averted through 'sudden and highly improbable resolutions', as Carolyn Williams puts it.[30] In *Black-Ey 'd Susan*, for example, William's backdated discharge papers from the navy are discovered on the (re-surfaced) corpse of Susan's uncle, whose unseemly excitement at the spectacle of William's court martial had made his boat lurch and capsize. These papers proved that William was no longer a sailor when he struck Captain Crosstree. As Carolyn Williams observes,

> [T]heir social relation is suddenly – and retroactively – transformed. This re-creation of social identity releases William from his crime, as well as from his service to the state; in place of hierarchy, it establishes equality; and it provides the platform for his upward mobility. But the 'sheer contingency' of this happy outcome must be keenly felt. Justice easily might *not* have been done.[31]

The happy ending of John Thomas Haines's *My Poll and My Partner Joe* is equally contingent and improbable. It is as if chance, which has wantonly determined the fates of the poor and the disenfranchised, can sometimes be counted on to absentmindedly rule in their favour. Founded on a popular song by the naval poet Charles Dibdin (father of Thomas and Charles the Younger), just as *Black Ey'd Susan* was named after a John Gay ballad, Haines's play is unique in the way it brings interlinked social issues – debt, impressment, slavery – to bear on the nautical romances spun by comic songs. It is unsurprising, of course, that its emancipatory vision of class and race remains underdeveloped. Despite showcasing the British sailor as the arch-enemy of the slave trade, and despite Harry referring to Brandon's captives as 'angels' and 'ebony gentlemen', these professed ideals are under-cut by the visual of Zinga and Zamba, the rescued African couple, lying prostrate at Harry's feet in gratitude. 'They know their place', Hazel Waters states, 'even if Harry is such a true Englishman that he refuses to see it.'[32]

Harry Halyard is press-ganged and prosecuted a few years later for an infraction he did not commit. As was the case with Sweet William and Richard Parker before him, even his captain, the instrument of military discipline, acknowledges that the errant sailor is one of the best seamen that ever trod a plank. Harry submits to the letter of the law, but the trial is interrupted when his ship encounters the slave vessel belonging to Black Brandon, a human trafficker who had pressed Harry into the navy. Harry redeems himself by taking the slaver's ship and fort, and the British standard is triumphantly hoisted to the tune of 'Rule Britannia'. In the third act, Harry returns home to find his 'Poll' – Mary – in a marriage of convenience with his friend Joe. By happy chance, Joe drops dead and Harry's homecoming (to Battersea) culminates in the estranged lovers' reunion.

*The Mutiny at the Nore* offers glimpses of a more sustainable vision of social change in an extraordinary scene where the much-abused Dicky Chicken finally stands up to his master, Bubble, cautioning the latter of the retribution for his unconscionable actions towards a poor sailor and his family:

> *Dic.* And then poor Richard Parker's ghost rises before you, and the captain's all over blood, and poor Mary Parker, in her grave clothes; and then they rush and whirl about you, and laugh, and point, and mock at you; you try to shout, but your voice dies in your throat, your veins swell like whip-cord in your forehead, your brain is turned to ice, terror shakes its soul from out of your body, and when daylight comes, the neighbours find you black and stiffened in your chair – then –                                          (3:2)

Timothy Bubble, late head clerk in his majesty's dockyard at Portsmouth, who had, indeed, directed the marines to Richard Parker's hideout (in Bubble's farm house), is shaken by this graphic depiction of his wrongdoings, and falls on his knees, begging for forgiveness. Similarly, Captain Crosstree, goes 'raving mad' at the prospect of William's impending court-martial and hanging, and is found 'shrieking and foaming' at the thought of his part in the honest sailor's downfall.[33] He is altogether more humble and contrite as he rushes on from the gangway, William's discharge papers in hand, in the final scene of *Black Ey'd Susan*. In *My Poll and My Partner Joe*, the class emanci-pation of Harry Halyard is justified by the racial emancipation of the 'black cattle' of Brandon's ship, the *Black Bet*, which Harry had facilitated (and will continue to facilitate).

A critical appraisal of Victorian nautical melodrama is perhaps not complete without a mention of Gilbert and Sullivan's parodies of the same in *H.M.S. Pinafore* (1878) and *The Pirates of Penzance* (1880). 'The radicalism of Jerrold's melodramas died away in the 1840s, and increasingly, after that, the figure of the British Tar became a tool of imperialist ideology', observes Carolyn Williams. 'Yet, *H.M.S. Pinafore* hints at the rise of a critical attitude toward Britain's imperial role',[34] just as the nautical melodramas of the '20s and '30s had subverted the very nationalist ideologies they helped crystallize. I have, in the course of this essay, tried to disabuse popular misconceptions about Victorian nautical melodrama as naive, self-referential, and apolitical. The anecdote of Billy the shark in Douglas Jerrold's *Black Ey'd Susan* shows a sophisticated understanding of the comic manipulability of the Jack Tar figure, 'a living ganglion of irreconcilable antagonisms', as *Pinafore*'s Ralph Rackstraw would call himself half a century later (Act 1). As a parody of a self-parodying and ludic cultural form, *H.M.S Pinafore* gives sincere utterance to nautical melodrama's nervous masculinity, its auto-ethnography, its reformist, if also conflicted, vision of class mobility and racial emancipation, its presentation of speciousness as style.

## Notes

1. Jeffrey N. Cox, 'The Ideological Tack of Nautical Melodrama', in *Melodrama: The Cultural Emergence of a Genre*, eds. Michael Hays and Anastasia Nikolopoulou (New York: St. Martin's Press, 1996), 178.
2. Michael Booth, *English Plays of the Nineteenth Century Volume 1: Drama 1800–1850* (Oxford: Clarendon Press, 1969), 154.
3. Glenn O'Hara, *Britain and the Sea: Since 1600* (Basingstoke: Palgrave Macmillan, 2010), 119.
4. John Storey, *Culture and Power in Cultural Studies: The Politics of Signification* (Edinburgh: Edinburgh University Press, 2010), 43.
5. Ibid., 43.
6. George D. Glenn, 'Nautical "Docudrama" in the Age of the Kembles', in *When They Weren't Doing Shakespeare: Essays on Nineteenth-Century British and American Theatre*, eds. Judith L. Fisher and Stephen Watt (Athens: University of Georgia Press, 1989), 137.
7. Ibid., 138.
8. Cited in Glenn, 'Nautical "Docudrama" in the Age of the Kembles', 147.
9. Donald Roy (ed.), *Romantic and Revolutionary Theatre 1789–1860* (Cambridge: Cambridge University Press, 2003).
10. Michael Booth, 'A Defence of Nineteenth-Century English Drama', *Educational Theatre Journal*, 26 (1974): 10.
11. Ibid., 10.

12. George Rowell, *Nineteenth Century Plays* (Oxford: Oxford University Press, 1972), 43.

13. Ibid., 46–47.

14. *Belgravia*, 10 (1870): 110.

15. J. S. Bratton, *Acts of Supremacy: The British Empire and the Stage, 1790–1930* (Manchester: Manchester University Press, 1991), 46.

16. *Nine Years of an Actor's Life*, cited in Michael Slater, *Douglas Jerrold: 1803–1857* (London: Duckworth, 2002), 66.

17. Ibid.

18. Ibid., 67.

19. Ibid., 71.

20. On the subversive affect of nautical melodrama in his most famous play, *Black Ey'd Susan*, as well as more on Jerrold's reinvention of nautical melodrama as a subgenre, see Ankhi Mukherjee, *Aesthetic Hysteria: The Great Neurosis in Victorian Melodrama and Contemporary Fiction* (New York: Routledge, 2007), 25–41.

21. Ibid., 77.

22. Cox, 'The Ideological Tack of Nautical Melodrama', 183.

23. Victor Emeljanow, *Victorian Popular Dramatists* (Boston: Twayne Publishers, 1987), 34.

24. Ibid., 7.

25. Ibid., 6.

26. Ibid., 5.

27. Ibid., 6.

28. Ibid., 35.

29. D-G, 'Remarks' to *The Mutiny at the Nore* (London: Cumberland's Minor Theatre, 1828), 8.

30. Carolyn Williams, *Gilbert and Sullivan: Gender, Genre, Parody* (New York: Columbia University Press, 2010), 100.

31. Ibid.

32. Hazel Waters, *Racism on the Victorian Stage: Representation of Slavery and the Black Character* (Cambridge: Cambridge University Press, 2007), 56.

33. *Nineteenth Century Plays*, 38.

34. Williams, *Gilbert and Sullivan*, 112.

# 5

CHRISTINE GLEDHILL

# Domestic Melodrama

Since melodrama is characterized by generic hybridity and familial relations are common across its subgenres, the designation 'domestic' identifies an orientation rather than a bounded form. This chapter begins with the nature of 'domestication', which, connoting an ordinariness in tension with the heightened and sensational, suggests, to adapt Carolyn Williams's term, an 'oscillation' in the history of English melodrama between domestication and melodramatization.[1] Thus the domestic novel and sentimental drama, emerging in the eighteenth century, were melodramatized by the infiltration of the Gothic in the later 1780s, in turn narrowing to closer domestic focus during the social upheavals of the 1820s and 1830s, to be further melodramatized through the sensation novel and drama of the 1860s, followed by yet another domestication in late Victorian 'society' dramas and so on into the twentieth century.

Over time, a gendered separation of private from public spheres had refocused the home – increasingly separated from communal labour – as the centre of social and psychological rootedness once supported by community relationships. Middle-class women became managers of the domestic sphere and creators of the now idealized space of 'home'. For working-class women – or the wayward and downwardly mobile – the public world of the city and factory, loosened from supervision of church and community, became increasingly fraught with predatory economic and sexualized dangers. The risk of slippage between such classed and gendered spheres provided both structures of feeling and plot materials to fuel melodrama's ambivalent swings between domestication and sensationalism.

## The Meaning of the Domestic

The new emphasis on the domestic, everyday life of home and community intertwined painting, fiction, and theatre.[2] Domestic genre painting, departing from an earlier emphasis on historical and religious subjects rendered on large canvases, responded to a growing middle-class market and was quickly circulated in inexpensive engravings, providing new subjects for the stage. As one key practitioner, Richard Redgrave, explained, 'It was soon found that pictures to suit the English taste must be pictures to live by; to hang on the walls of ... home.'[3] Similarly, as 'domestic' became an acknowledged descriptor of theatrical entertainment, D-G, prefacing J. B. Buckstone's *Luke the Labourer; Or, The Lost Son* (1826), argued that 'a subject to come home to the business and bosoms of men must needs be of a domestic nature'. Citing pressure to appease not classical gods but those seated in the upper galleries of Covent Garden and Drury Lane, D-G democratizes recognition: 'The truest sympathy is excited by characters and events that come under the general observation of mankind. The public have no relish for magnificent woe ... in blank verse.'[4] For the minor theatres, contesting the privileges of the patent houses, domestication promised a broadening class appeal.

Different plays are cited as progenitors of domestic melodrama. Douglas Jerrold is said by his son to have claimed its invention: 'A poor thing – but mine own.'[5] However, the play frequently named as 'first', W. T. Moncrieff's *The Lear of Private Life; Or, Father and Daughter* (1820), advertised its source as 'Mrs Opie's Popular and Pathetic Story of *Father And Daughter*', published in 1800. This in turn developed a central incident of Oliver Goldsmith's *The Vicar of Wakefield* (1766), which, in its focus on the felicities and trials of a country vicar and his family, was counted the 'first genuine novel of domestic life'.[6] From Goldsmith's picaresque novel, Amelia Opie developed those episodes dealing with the seduction of the Vicar's beloved daughter by the philandering scion of an aristocratic family. While Opie intensifies and moralizes Agnes's years of expiation – giving her an illegitimate child and grief-maddened father – she excoriates the unbending attitudes of local neighbours. As Robert Mack notes, the eighteenth-century cult of feeling entailed 'one's ... ability to empathize with the misfortunes of fictional others ... [as] a measure of strength of one's own "heart" and of the vigour of those moral principles that in turn dictate the behaviour of our lives'.[7]

Falling between Opie and Moncrieff is Marie-Thérèse Kemble's *Smiles and Tears; Or, The Widow's Stratagem* (1815), which incorporates Agnes's – here Cecile's – story into a French masquerade comedy. Lady Emily is reproved by her uncle for declaring Cecile's moral downfall 'interesting'. When he later admires Cecile's devotion to her demented father, Emily replies, 'And may I not call that creature *interesting?* But what were ... her father's *sensations* when he first beheld her?' (5:1, emphasis mine). This move from the moral through the interesting to the sensational is central to the perceptual and aesthetic oscillations that underpin the relation between the domestic and melodrama. Emily's desire to justify her use of 'interesting' registers a shift from the medieval legal or financial meaning of 'interest' to its signification within a newly emerging emotional economy, emphasizing identification with socially and morally different others.[8] As D-G argued of *Luke the Labourer*, 'without being a farmer's servant ... we cannot but commiserate with Luke'.[9]

However, as Peter Brooks suggests, a tension arises between the 'interesting' located in the everyday and the 'exciting'.[10] The latter emerged with the sensationalism of Gothic fiction and drama, which, along with the rise of melodramatic spectacle in the minor theatres, interrupts the line that runs between eighteenth-century sentimental morality and nineteenth-century domestic melodrama. 'Sensation', then, points in two directions: to the bodily thrills of spectre-haunted dungeons, forest or house fires, explosions or drownings on stage; and to extreme states of personal being, appealing to an audience's fascination with areas of life known to exist in some hidden form and vicariously sought in theatre. In a class-ingrained society, undergoing slow democratization, for whose newly emerging middle classes 'privacy' became a vital defensive boundary, theatre played a key role by acknowledging private experiences in public spaces.

In Opie's tale and Moncrieff's play, elision of 'interest' with emotional 'sensation' peaks traumatically when, while crossing storm-wracked woods, penniless Agnes, seeking to return home, encounters her father, who has escaped from an asylum and is searching for her grave. Fearing potential capture, her father threatens her with a cudgel. However, his bitter response to her plea to spare her baby underlines the pathos of their mutual situation: 'A child! Strangle it, kill it ... I had a child myself, but she is dead.' If derangement justifies her father's violence, Agnes is its appalled and guilt-stricken spectator. But her tears break through his turbulence as he feels another's sorrow: 'Tears! In tears, poor thing, poor thing. Don't cry, don't cry! ... Come, come, come, you will not leave me, will you?' (2:3). Across these transformations, increasing 'sensation' adds to 'interest' an emotional supplement, grounding empathy as means of social cohesion for a society based on economic individualism. How situations *feel* to the protagonist is what 'interests' – engages – the audience. Theatre bills emphasize the term's new emotional freight. *The Lear of Private Life* was advertised as a 'Premier Domestic Melo-Drama of Interest', while 'deeply interesting', 'powerfully interesting', 'of intense interest', 'of peculiar interest', and 'of powerful domestic interest' recur throughout nineteenth-century play advertising, suggesting a central affective significance.

CHRISTINE GLEDHILL

## Domesticating the Gothic

Michael Booth details the shifts through which the medieval accoutrements of the Gothic were gradually domesticated, focusing on 'the virtuous simplicity and humble poverty of the cottage in the woods rather than on the tyrant-ridden, ghost-haunted castle'.[11] Booth enumerates the types that populate these early plays: 'the old farmer, the seducing and evicting squire or landlord, the erring but repentant daughter, often exiled by her father's curse, the honest workman or peasant'.[12] Peter Brooks, in his influential account of French melodrama, finds in such figures 'primary psychic roles as father, mother, child', embodying 'emotional states and psychic relationships'.[13] Both Booth and Brooks capture a certain ritualistic core to melodrama's cast of characters. Brooks in particular avoids Booth's tendency towards caricature by endowing them with a kind of archetypal dignity. In familial duty, loyalty, and affection, ethical values are realized as individualized emotional identities. But, if Booth's focus on social typifications omits the idiosyncratic vernacular that rendered the 'ordinariness' of the domestic, Brooks's emphasis on psychic states leaves the protagonists of French melodrama deracinated from social experience. This needs rethinking for British domestic melodrama, not least because the plays are replete with supporting, sardonically class-aware characters, who pull the idealized emotions of the central protagonists back into a social circuit. The family is beset from without by socially recognizable oppressors – unprincipled squires, rack-renting landlords, profiteering employers, seducers – supported by their self-seeking banking, legal, and law-enforcing agents. Once villainy is rooted in recognizable social practices, such figures could command recognition through their resonance with the turbulent social upheavals of the period, including accelerating land closures, rapid industrialization and urbanization, along with the destruction of traditional work patterns and displacement of paternalistic welfare by the casualization and exploitation of labour. Thus, while melodramatization distils from domestic experience moments of intense desire or excruciating conflict, the choral commentary of subsidiary characters animates social discourses that underpin the protagonists' dilemmas. Nevertheless, Gothic traces infused the domestic with the sensation, mystery, and excitement that made it melodrama. If the castle disappeared, the country house or cottage lay near a murky wood, and, not far off, the town featured a courthouse, a gaol, and an asylum; and if ghosts and specters vanished, premonitions, memories, and dreams kept the warning presences of the dead close at hand.

Since the plays making up the corpus of domestic melodrama are now rarely performed and are available largely through second-hand circulation

64

or, more recently, online reprints, they are mainly known only through generalizing lists of character types and plot summaries of the kind offered by Michael Booth and Gilbert B. Cross – often, despite the writers' best and pioneering intentions, with amused condescension.[14] What follows seeks to realize, through select examples from the first half-century, key aspects of the dramatic experience generated as the domestic intersected with melodrama on the nineteenth-century stage.

## Home and Community

At the neuralgic centre of domestic melodrama's emotional landscape is the idea of 'home', which is often explicit in play titles: Edward Fitzball's *Home Again! Or, The Lieutenant's Daughter* (1844); Thomas Parry's *Eugenia Claircille; Or, The New Found Home* (1846). Home is both a physical space of familiar things and faces, and the psychological nub of personal identity: an iconography and dramatic crux. Within fast-consolidating capitalist social structures, home becomes 'the heart of a heartless' world: site of personal individuation but also rooted in past memories of childhood and community. Bearing such emotional freight, it is beset by real and nameless terrors. Ruthless social forces work through profiteering, vengeful, or power-seeking exploiters who threaten the home, both materially through appropriation or psychologically by tearing family members apart – sowing seeds of misrecognition, desertion, or betrayal – or leading breadwinners into dissolution and petty crime.

In early domestic melodrama, home is idealized as a humble cottage or modest country house, surrounded by a garden or pastoral landscape, like those pictured in nineteenth-century genre paintings as 'cottage picturesque'.[15] *Home Again!* opens in the sunny, flower- and birdsong-filled garden of Briary Cottage, where Lieutenant Leslie's two lively daughters, Alice and Sophy, chat over the gate with local lads. In *Luke the Labourer*, Farmer Wakefield, rescued from imprisonment for debt, looks round his cottage kitchen, crying, 'My warm, my comfortable fireside, do I again see thee. Oh, dame, dame! No man truly knows the blessings of his home but he who has been shut out from it' (1:2). At the centre of 'home' is the family, now the cohering unit of a socioeconomic organization that is rapidly undoing traditional hierarchical social relations. Familial relations are ordered by emotional bonds, rights, and duties, underpinned by Christian teaching, that moralize the family as economic unit, intertwining husband and wife, parents and children.

Home connects to the past, childhood, and ancestry through memories preserved in familiar household things. Douglas Jerrold, 'realizing' David Wilkie's two narrative paintings, 'The Rent Day' (1807) and 'Distraining for

Rent' (1815), in his Drury Lane hit, *The Rent Day* (1832), captures Martin Heywood's excruciation at the threatened loss of the farm that his family has worked for the last sixty years: 'My father's father grew grey under this roof . . . Here I was born, and here I will die . . . Leave the house! I almost love it like a living thing.' However, the monetizing logic of property relations controls events, as the bailiff Bullfrog, intoning his mantra, 'business is business', mechanically inventories the objects found in Wilkie's painting: 'One toasting-fork – one bird-cage – one baby's rattle' (1:5).

If home is the site of individual security, it is also nostalgically centred in communities of rural retainers, workpeople, or urban neighbours. While the minor theatres' initially legally enforced use of song and dance led many plays to open with celebratory choruses – harvest home (*Lear*); haymaking (*Eugenia Claircille*); vine feast (*Rose of Corbeille; Or, The Forest of Senart*, 1838); the (female) factory owner's birthday (*The Dumb Man of Manchester*, 1837) – the imaginary relation of home to community across these plays retains older paternalist structures of feeling embedded in relations between great house and villagers, now being broken by land closures and urbanization. When in *The Rent Day*, Martin suggests emigration, Rachel's reaction underlines the deeper meaning of place and community: 'But not our own fields, or our own sky, not the friends who love us, not the neighbours who respect us . . . Our children! They would die there. Die amongst strangers!' (1:3). When the estate manager Crumbs comes to dispossess them, it is the neighbours who rush to warn of his approach.

In contrast to rural nostalgia, home in urban melodramas is broken or reinvented by characters deracinated as they are drawn into the maelstrom of the city. As Bob Brierly in Tom Taylor's *The Ticket-of-Leave Man* (1863) advises young scapegrace Sam, 'Be steady – stick to work and home. It's an awful look out for a young chap adrift in this place, without them as sheet anchors' (3:1). London pulls those seeking adventure (*Ticket-of-Leave Man*); or escape from paternal prohibitions (*Lear*); or harassment by criminal or lusting pursuers (*Lilly Dawson: Or, A Poor Girl's Story*, 1847; *Eugenia Claircille; Home Again!*). The urban home often depends on women's capacity for survival and mutual support – as in *The Bottle* (1847) or *Ticket-of-Leave Man* – while memories, pictures, and photographs evoke nostalgia for past rural stability; Martha Willis (in Jerrold's 1831 play) treasures a painting of her childhood home, backed by the village church, as does Ruth in *The Bottle*, a picture she tries to withhold from the bailiff.

The allure of the city is double edged, casting a negative shadow back on rural life. *Lilly Dawson* opens in a desolate Cornish countryside, uninhabited except by a mill and the gothic Black Huntsman inn, run by the dysfunctional, shipwrecking Littlehans family. Luke Littlehans and his brother burn down the mill and subsequently murder its owner; the orphaned Lilly, their drudge, having stumbled upon the evidence, flees to London. The comedic vein of *Eugenia Claircille* plays London and the country against each other, while the play's ancillary villain, Hugh Matlock, returned from transportation, curses the myopia of rural beer-house conviviality:

> Fools! Drown your misery in noise! Forget if you can! The starving, homeless wretch crawls his way singing 'Happy Land!' Well, well! 'Happy Land' is a romance he may safely be allowed to revel in! ... I curse the past as I defy the future! (2:1)

Rural blight and London deracination threaten to undermine the Arcadian rhetoric of home and community that supports the utopian heart of domestic melodrama, in covert recognition of the negative forces at work in the new social dispensation.

## Fathers and Daughters – and Absent Mothers

The most exquisite of domestic ties binds father and daughter, facilitated by the absence or marginalization of the mother. Marriage choice threatens this relationship. In *Lear*, the paternalistic Squire Fitzarden worries about his daughter Agnes's attraction to Captain Alvanley, arguing that his 'idle' profession, with its 'habits of intemperance, expense and irregularity', means 'he cannot be either constant or domestic'. All Agnes can pose against domestic irregularity is 'unbounded love'. Father and daughter talk past each other, making contrary promises, her father ruefully commenting 'we are not used to differ, Agnes!' (1:2). Alvanley proves irresistible and elopement ensues. Father and daughter next meet in the snow-tossed wood. This scene of spectacular and coincidence-driven crisis ends in ultimate excruciation as the asylum keepers physically tear daughter from father, while rubbing in her guilt: 'Aye, aye, you may well weep! But your tears come a little too late, my fine lady' (2:3). At the play's end, however, it is Agnes's tearful question – 'Do you still love her then?' – that dissolves Fitzarden's threatened revenge into empathy: 'Thou weep'st, it would give thee pain? Then I'll not kill her' (3:3).

Repeated use of the father-daughter relationship suggests an undertow of incest, which in *Eugenia Claircille* colours the paternal relation of brother to his at first fatherless, then estranged, and now, dead sister. Her orphaned child, Eugenia, returns from Algeria to reclaim her mother's family, but disguised for safety's sake as a boy (played by the indomitable cross-dressing Madame Vestris). On hearing Eugenia's voice – so like his sister's – the dying Rugleigh is 'struck by a chord'. Merging brother, father, uncle in one

67

incestuous knot, he claims possession: 'Let me look on you – in you she still lives – mine – mine! [*they embrace*]' (1:3). Contrariwise, Douglas Jerrold's *John Overy: The Miser of Southwark Ferry* (1829) overturns familial desire by foregrounding its economic underside. Re-writing a medieval legend, Jerrold creates a miserly father, who regards his daughter Mary only as a drain on his hoarded fortune. Noting Baron Fitzgeffrey's attraction to her, he suggests: 'beauty is a marketable commodity, and 'twould be a pity to spoil merchandise by overkeeping'. Realizing his implication, Mary repudiates their relationship, hurling her dead mother's locket at his feet: 'Father! I disclaim you! . . . I cast thee off – my blood forgets its source, – master Overy, thou art a childless man.' For a brief moment, Overy finds a tear rising as she exits, but he kills the feeling: 'it is a libel on my heart' (2:1). When, later, Mary offers reconciliation, Overy brutally states the economics of paternity: 'No; I had a child, but I sold her – she is in my purse' (3:4). Perhaps this covert exposure of the bourgeois family pact is what led Moncrieff to find such episodes 'repulsive and unnatural'.[16]

Mary's talismanic locket and Eugenia's voice exemplify the tangential but vital role given to dead or absent mothers, who are often endowed with an unearthly power to warn or protect their children. In *The Dumb Man of Manchester* Jane, visiting her wrongly imprisoned dumb brother while holding back vital evidence that will betray her criminal husband, recognizes the ring given him by their dying mother: 'Oh, my mother! She calls to me from the depths of her grave to save my brother. Yes, Yes, my mother! I will reveal all!' (2:1).

## Villainy

Real economic and social dangers surrounding home mesh with fantasized threats. Debt, rent arrears, abduction by press-gang, imprisonment, prostitution, the workhouse constitute vulnerabilities through which corrupt agents of social regulation threaten familial bonds. Such intersections between public and private fuel fantasies which turn on unknown parentage, illegitimacy, and lost inheritances and are dramatized through engineered misrecognitions, mistaken perceptions, false claims, or hidden relationships. These often involve birth and marriage certificates, wills, and other legal documents, missing, purloined, or falsified. Dangers are also inherent in the family structure itself: parental ambition, incestuous identifications, sibling rivalry, paternal dysfunction (alcoholism, gambling), and female susceptibility to seduction or abduction.

Melodrama's villains, however, are neither moral abstractions nor mere social ciphers. Rather they embody the tension between the released entrepreneurial energy of the newly authorized individual and the inequalities and constraints of class and gender, now institutionalized around the family. It is his wife's death from starvation following his dismissal from Farmer Wakefield's employment that turns lackadaisical labourer Luke into a vengeful villain:

> I were then quite ruin'd. I felt alone in the world. I stood looking on her white face near an hour and did not move from the spot one inch; but when I *did* move, it were wi' my fist clenched in the air, while my tongue, all parched and dry, curs'd a curse, and swore that, if I had not my revenge, I wish'd I might fall as stiff and dead as she that lay before me. (1:2)

Social tensions are channeled as emotional forces. Earlier, defending his legal claims for payment against the now economically distressed Wakefield, Luke had justified vengeance as reversing class power: 'Ah, you may stare – poor Luke, who never owned an acre, measter of a stack o' wheat – you see some folk can get as well as other folk' (1:1). Now he tells Wakefield that his wife wouldn't let him apply to the Parish for help 'because she were a daughter of as good a man as you were then' (1:2).

This is not to suggest, however, that these plays set out to deliver explicit messages. They are commercial entertainments, attracting audiences through dramatic excitements. The reviewer who criticized Buckstone's failure to point up the moral lesson of Luke the Labourer's drunkenness as cause of his dismissal inadvertently suggests a dramatic appeal that lies elsewhere: 'a lesson of morality which [the author] here had the opportunity of reading to his auditors . . . he neglects for the sake of showing how far he could carry the love of revenge'.[17] Revenge is the high-octane emotion released through the villain. But melodrama's aesthetic thrills are not insignificant, their sensations exposing a psychic nerve or generating social perceptions beyond conventional moral articulation.

By definition, revenge is motivated, cathecting past events with current drives. Villainy seeks to compensate personal or social injury; to accumulate capital and gain power over others; or to relieve thwarted sexual desire. In *Home Again!* Lieutenant Leslie's assertion of class status in rejecting his landlord Dillon's desire for Alice is answered by a threat: 'Very well, sir – very well *Mister* Leslie. Your servant, *Miss* Leslie. Your father has just now ordered me out the house. Me, the man you find it impossible to love. Remember – I shall not forget' (3:3). The villain's sexual demand is often provoked by the heroine who stands in his way. Having cheated Eugenia of her inheritance, Bernard Langrel pursues her to London, now perversely desiring his victim: 'You are in my power – your fate hangs upon a thread – let me claim you as my wife!' (*Eugenia Claircille*, 3:3).

Economic, social, and sexual power flow into each other. If restoration of domestic harmony cannot defeat the social system, rarely does revenge or the ends of villainy bring satisfaction.

## Domestic Melodrama's Comedic Interface

A vernacular counterpoint is injected into dramatic crisis through the comic byplay of melodrama's supporting characters, their 'low' status licensing not only caustic commentary on the action's social stakes but, reflexively, on the rhetoric of melodrama itself.[18] In Thomas Holcroft's *A Tale of Mystery* (1802), Bonamo, arguing with his housekeeper Fiametta, asks, 'Have not I a right to do as I please in my own house?' To which she tartly responds: 'No, sir, you have no right to do wrong any where' (1:1).

In rural dramas, comic figures serve on the farm or in the manor house, their often amusingly troubled courtships offering reassurance about the possibility of home in the fluctuating world that threatens the main protagonists. In urban dramas, they appear as types like those documented by social investigators such as Henry Mayhew or melodramatist George Sims. The nosey neighbour, Kitty, whose comically tiresome truisms are sprinkled throughout *The Bottle*, nevertheless makes pointed commentary on working-class marriage: 'But as I told her, she is very foolish. Families will come, you know, Mrs. Thornley – short wages – children and bread and butter, all day long' (1:1).

In *Lilly Dawson*, Philip Ryland, ostensibly in London to solve the mystery of his father's murder, is sidetracked by the flirtatious back-chatting milliner, May Elliott, whom he tries to persuade to join him in Cornwall. She, however, has distinctly un-Arcadian notions of the countryside: 'I should die of the miserables. Get up at 4 o'clock, milk, plough, feed ducks, make hay and jog to market' (2:2). When he mentions his pity for Lilly, May's frank riposte asserts the primacy of material pleasures: 'Do you? I never pry into another's secrets, not I. All I want is attention – new clothes – to eat ices and go to Astley's' (3:2).

While enwrapping central protagonists in audience sympathy, this comic interface turns acerbic in the commentary of petty criminals, whose irony socializes villainy as the underhanded practices of business and officialdom: employers, estate managers, brokers, prison officers, and constabulary. In *The Bottle*, based on Cruikshank's serial engravings, a range of such types prey on the alcoholic Richard Thornley, his family, and his friends: from the petty thief and forger, Dogrose, who uses Thornley as his criminal pawn; to the recruiting sergeant who tricks Richard's loyal friend George Gray into taking the Queen's shilling; to Spike, who discourses on ways to get debtors to open the door; to the landlady who turns out George's rent-defaulting fiancée: 'I don't want no tears, because that performance won't bring the money' (2:3). This ritualized network of minor figures, each with a familiar mantra – Bullfrog's 'I must keep my books'; Kitty's 'I like to make everybody happy' – situates the 'private' dramas of the central protagonists within a wider social network.

## The Heroine; Or, When the Woman Weeps

One of the prevailing stereotypes of Victorian melodrama is the supposedly passive and suffering heroine, threatened by a monopathic villain with only one thing in mind. However, it is time to re-appraise this assumption. Possession of the moral high ground gives the heroine power within the dynamics of the drama, while by definition, the innocent under assault may not see through, still less use, the wiles of the unscrupulous. Assertion of moral rights and truth are acts of fearlessness and weapons in rhetorical combat. When Bernard Langrel, having purloined Eugenia's fortune and now pursuing her person, points out her 'dependent situation', she retorts 'humble though it be, this is still my home: I am mistress here – as such I request your departure' (*Eugenia Claircille*, 3:4). In *Home Again!*, Sophy, learning of the trap Dillon has set for her sister Alice, defiantly berates him: 'Oh, don't flash your eyes at me! I only wish I had a man's hand, I'd show you one woman's heart, at least, not to be intimidated by your fury' (2:3). Embodiment of strength in vulnerability testifies also to the power of the actress, as the 'Remarks' prefacing publication of Samuel Arnold's *The Woodman's Hut* (1814) acknowledge of Miss Kelly's exquisite acting, in the role of a young woman who takes on the baron's henchmen with flirtatious repartee, as she directs the chief villain to her bedroom – 'why not, one night is soon passed' – while organizing drugged wine for his soldiers (2:1).[19]

There comes a moment, however, in the heroine's drama that overpowers both strength and feeling, when the woman must weep or faint – a moment that a later age remembers with some amusement or contempt. In this respect, the dramatization of domestic relations involves a gendered division of emotional labour. While villains and heroes are volatile, succumbing to panic or derangement, it is the stoic endurance of the heroine, defending truth and resistant to corruption, whose eventual collapse registers conflicts inherent in patriarchy, making an overriding demand for empathy from other characters and audiences as emotional restitution. Heroines weep or faint not because they are weak or feeble but because they are sites of extremity – of anger, terror, pain. Following Lilly Dawson's escape to

London, Luke Littlehans tricks her into his lodgings and, locking her into a 'Dark – wretched garret', growls sadistically, 'I'll teach you a lesson you'll never forget … Remember what I say – submit quietly. You know me!' As Lilly mutters, 'Know you? Alas too well!', the force of misogyny surfaces, linked to the past in both the drama's back story and, perhaps, the history of heterosexuality: 'There's some hidden mystery in Luke's pursuing me thus … I am lost, lost!' And in this moment of extremity, Lilly weeps. 'Oh world, world! Why treat me so hardly?' (2:6).

The heroine of domestic melodrama bears the brunt of contradictory forces that intersect in its complex plotting. In *Lear*, Agnes has both 'resolved never to marry but to live single for the sake of my beloved father' *and* agreed to a midnight assignation (1:2). Oscillating between these demands, she may well weep. Significantly, however, when the domestic heroine is cast out into the world, she refuses dependency and takes up work: sewing, painting pictures, tutoring, singing as an entertainer.

## Marital Relations; Or, Gender Wars

Marriage – the happy end of comedy – is, in domestic melodrama, the beginning of crisis. The social gendering of domesticity, with middle-class women constructed as guardians of a moral equilibrium presumed not available to men, led to the investment of innocence and virtue in daughters and wives, while giving license to a masculinity imagined as rapacious, overpowering, and self-seeking. In *Home Again!* the marriage contract itself becomes a device of villainy. Having had Lieutenant Leslie imprisoned for rent arrears, Dillon tricks Alice into signing herself away: 'There lies the contract *[Putting it on table]*. Your father I learn is dangerously ill … Now, then, devoted daughter, shall your father perish of want or will you be mine?' Dillon will use Alice's legal bond to control the plot: 'Remember the contract. This day month expect me' (2:3). Here the gendered moral-emotional opposition is sexualized and monetized, infiltrating familial scenarios with a submerged sadistic – and when focused on daughters, covertly incestuous – frisson. Thus the contradictions of social gender offer material for drama that may set reverberating a domestic nerve.

In *Lear*, Moncrieff, following Mrs Opie, uses the double standard to create melodramatic shock. Agnes, hidden in Avanley's London lodgings, overhears not only his plan to marry an heiress but also that he has posted false reports of her father's remarriage, while withholding knowledge of his asylum confinement. Against her anger – 'Unhand me! Your touch is poison' – Alvanley delivers the arch-chauvinist's blow: 'What have you to complain of … Miss Sandford will possess my hand, my heart will still be yours.' Failing to understand the force of Agnes's outrage – 'I tell you we shall meet no more' – he insouciantly quips, 'Not till tomorrow ... this is our first quarrel, Agnes, and the quarrels of lovers are only the renewal of love' (2:1).

In a different social context, the hostile relationships of *Lilly Dawson*'s underclass characters enact the obverse of the idealized Victorian family:

CHARLOTTE: You'll break my tender heart you will.
HANS: It's too tough to break. It'll stretch like indy rubber – never break.
CHARLOTTE: I'll break your head in [*Raises a chair...*].                (2:3)

The drama's two lines of interaction – the sardonic sarcasms of the criminal family, and the comic repartee between the hopelessly romantic Philip and the back-chatting milliner May – work the tension between Victorian idealism and realities of class and gender experience. However, if Luke and his criminal partner Hans wield brute physical power, while Philip wants to play the romantic hero, the women have a down-to-earth understanding of the dynamics of masculinity and know what they want. Even the brutalized Lilly, recalling Philip's claim that 'liberty, freedom's a glorious, bright and happy thing', defiantly declares, 'I should like to know it. I will know it' (1:5).

The complexity of domestic melodrama lies in such intermeshing of ritualized emotions and contemporaneous socio-cultural discourses. Characters are caught in the cross-currents of plotting and rhetoric which they don't understand. However, it is misleading to call such figures monopathic, or lacking psychology – a conception based on the discursive conventions of novelistic interiority, rather than melodrama's recognition of emotions as material forces channelled by and into 'acculturated' lines of response.[20]

### The Knock at the Door; or, Melodramatizing Domestic Architecture

The iconography of the domestic features an interior space, where all is warm and safe. But the architecture of home makes windows and doors vulnerable interfaces with the outside, threatening the prying of spies or violent intrusion, while doors open to reveal the person the protagonist most dreads. In *Home Again!* doors open on cue to Dillon's threatening presence, while Wakefield's joyful homecoming in *Luke the Labourer* is immediately reversed, as a knock at the door reveals Luke, who has come to expedite further vengeance.

Using Victorian theatrical machinery, a living room could bring back the past. A magically realized dream sequence in *Lilly Dawson*, utilizing the opening and closing of sliding flats at the back of the set, reveals a series of dissolving scenes, as Lilly's traumatic history is projected behind her while she's in a restless sleep. Storm music supports the enactment of the shipwreck in which her baby-self clings to an Old Man, from whom she is snatched by the Littlehans wreckers. As the flats close, Lilly, dreaming in the foreground, mutters her refusal to become Luke's drudge. They re-open to reveal the Mill ruins, where Luke stands over the murdered Ryland. In a third scene, Lilly sees herself, hands clasped in prayer over Charlotte, whom Luke has stabbed, thinking she was Lilly. As she cries out, her dream projects forward to a fantasized tableau of a future she thinks she has no hope of obtaining:

> *Scene re-opens. Tableau. A country church* – Philip, Lilly, *surrounded by* Friends, *in the act of marrying.* Priest, &c. *This is painted on a flat. Bells ring joyously – expressive music.* Lilly *starts from a couch wildly, and falls on her knees)* Philip! Married! Those bells! Where – where am I? Is it a dream?

Her kindly rescuer, Winnie, agreeing it is, brings the sublimity of Lilly's dream-world down to earth: 'so do I when I eat pork chops' (3:3).

## Confronting the Past

There comes a moment in every play when the villain confronts his identity. *The Rent Day* concludes with the exposure of Robert Grantley's corrupt estate manager, Crumbs, who offers a chilling account of his lasting hatred provoked by Grantley senior's seduction of his wife and kept alive after the death of both by her portrait hanging in the Grantley mansion, in which he sees idealized love incarnating a devil:

> in the still night I have gazed on it, until I have thought the devil himself looked from its eyes, and smiled upon my purpose . . . Oh! I am an old man! – but there are injuries so cut within the heart, so burnt within the brain, that the heart and brain must live and die together. (2:4)

Consumed by a singular devastating emotion, Crumbs refuses Grantley's offer of pardon: 'Never. I scorn and spit at you.'

Luke Littlehans's past brings guilt to haunt him. Thinking he has killed Lilly, he flees back to Cornwall: 'I can't move a step without folks staring at me . . . A heavy leaden weight is at my heart . . . Sleeping or waking she is there – there, steeping my soul in blood and crime' (3:4). At his trial, he cleverly refutes each piece of evidence until the courtroom doors swing open to reveal Lilly herself. In a Gothic moment, imagining a phantom, Luke breaks: 'She lives – breathes – speaks! Who – who fell beneath my knife? Who was it?', and Lilly tells him, 'Your own sister!' (3:5). In bitter self-recognition, Luke confesses, seeing only death ahead. The dystopian family is eliminated and domestic melodrama's fantasized 'family romance' reinstated.

## Home and the World: Later Domestic Melodrama

The later nineteenth century saw a sedimentation of melodrama's hybridity, with increasingly consolidated plot structures and psychologized characteriza-tion, while the term 'melodrama' virtually disappeared from play advertising. 'And yet', regret many critics, plays categorized as 'well-made' or 'new drama' still turned on melodramatic devices and character oppositions.[21] Closer examination, however, suggests that the values of domestic melodrama – 'home', the 'interesting', the emotionalization of the social – not only persisted into 'modern' drama, but that its devices prepared the way.

While in mid-century, dramatic focus shifted from the 'poor and unfriended' to middle-class dilemmas of respectability and downward or upward mobility, villainy took on an increasingly institutional and eco-nomic rather than metaphysical force, embodied in figures such as the financier in *Ticket-of-Leave Man* (1863), the corn factor and prison officer in Charles Reade's *It Is Never Too Late To Mend* (1865), or the factory owner would-be politician and his publicity agent in Henry Arthur Jones's *The Middleman* (1889). The hidden processes and labyrinthine intercon-nections of an emerging capitalist order offered new forms of politicized villainy. Similarly, gender construction, so central to the domestic unit, generated new possibilities for dramatic conflict. Ideologies of true woman-hood, based in gender idealization, repression, and abasement, introduced a new form of sensation in mid-nineteenth-century fiction and drama, most familiarly in Mary Elizabeth Braddon's *Lady Audley's Secret* (1862, first dramatized 1863) and Mrs Henry Wood's *East Lynne* (1861, first drama-tized 1866). While Dion Boucicault claimed to have invented the theatrical 'sensation scene' in *The Colleen Bawn* (1860), ingeniously incorporating stage spectacle into an Irish mortgage-driven marriage drama, Braddon and Wood provided to their male theatrical adaptors sexualized sensations of moral shock, broken taboos, and heartrending pathos. True womanhood led the domestic in two directions, generating the powerful figure of the villainess – popularized at the turn of the century in Walter Melville's 'bad woman' melodramas, with titles such as *The Worst Woman in London* (1899), or *The Girl Who Took the Wrong Turning* (1906) – and, conver-sely, 'transvaluing' domestic virtue by demanding society itself become 'home'.[22]

Among melodrama's most important contributions to modern drama-turgy are those devices for which it is most derided: the aside, choric refrain, bold statements of identity (Peter Brooks's 'self-nomination') and stage blocking that facilitated overhearing or oversight of others' speech and gestures. Such mechanisms staged a reflexive mode of theatricality, revealing hidden feelings and meanings contrary to what is said. When, in Colin Hazlewood's *Lady Audley's Secret* (1863) – against Lucy Audley's warning, 'We may read faces but not hearts' – her elderly husband overconfidently asserts that *her* face is 'index to the mind', her wry aside exposes his illusory gender idealism: 'We may have two faces' (1:1).

The device of the overseen or overheard event activates the disastrous possibilities of misrecognition – when characters interpret what is seen through the ideological scripts of middle-class, paternalist culture within which they live. In T. A. Palmer's 1874 adaptation of *East Lynne*, Levison as seducer provokes the initially loyal Isabel's jealousy of her husband's child-hood friend, Barbara Hare, by directing her look towards their encounters and dropping manipulative hints: 'There, dear Isabel, will you believe your own eyes ... You see now why he could not accompany you – you see why he is so anxious for your retirement at Trouville' (1:4). The overseen event channels psychological impulses through discursive pathways into theatrical action. Isabel believes what she is prompted to see and acts accordingly.

Verbal masquerade and unmasking dramatize the discursive constructions of class, money, sex, and gender, making theatrically visible the hidden workings of patriarchal, capitalist, and imperial power through which the emotional drives of a modernizing society are routed. In *It Is Never Too Late To Mend*, Crawley, agent to business and property dealer John Meadows, sardonically identifies his master's weak spot, while explicitly laying out the gender debasement on which it rests: 'You love a woman! What are we coming to? A great man, an iron man, like you love such a small thing – compared to yourself – as a woman?' (1:1). Capital accumulation becomes a sexual hunger that drives Meadows into over-reaching and ultimate downfall. The entire plot of *The Colleen Bawn* not only depends on engineered misperception of appearances and manipulation of duplicitous signs, but also turns on the self-constructing power of colonial discourse in Irish peasant Eily's struggle to meet the expectations of her Anglo-Irish, upper-middle-class, secretly married husband, Hardress. As she tells her friends, 'I'm getting clane of the brogue, and learnin' to do nothing – I'm to be changed entirely' (1:3).

As dramas of mobilized emotions channelled through the sociocultural imaginaries in which writers, actors, theatrical producers, and protagonists were embedded, domestic melodrama developed a modern theatre that caught the reverberations of history intertwined in the psychosexual currents and social forces playing out through individual lives. In this respect, all contemporary drama calls on perceptions first staged by the strategies, tropes, and devices of nineteenth-century domestic melodrama.

## Notes

1. Carolyn Williams, 'Melodrama', in *The New Cambridge History of English Literature*, ed. Kate Flint (Cambridge: Cambridge University Press, 2012).
2. Martin Meisel, *Realizations: Narrative, Pictorial, and Theatrical Arts in Nineteenth-Century England* (Princeton: Princeton University Press, 1983).
3. Richard Redgrave, *A Century of Painters of the English School*, 2 vols. (London: Smith and Elder, 1866), 263.
4. D-G. [George Daniel], 'Remarks' to *Luke the Labourer; or, The Lost Son* (London: Cumberland's Minor Theatre, 1830), 5.
5. Blanchard Jerrold, *The Life and Remains of Douglas Jerrold* (Milton Keynes: Bibliobazaar/Open Source, 2010 [1869]), 79.
6. Robert L. Mack, 'Introduction', *The Vicar of Wakefield* (Oxford: Oxford University Press, 2006), ix.
7. Mack, 'Introduction', xxx.
8. See Raymond Williams, *Keywords* (London: Fontana, 1988), 171–3.
9. D-G, 'Remarks', 5.
10. Peter Brooks, *The Melodramatic Imagination: Balzac, James, Melodrama, and the Mode of Excess* (New Haven: Yale University Press, 1976), 64.
11. Michael Booth, *English Melodrama* (London: Herbert Jenkins, 1965), 76.
12. Booth, *English Melodrama*, 118.
13. Brooks, *Melodramatic Imagination*, 4, 42.
14. Gilbert B. Cross, *Next Week – East Lynne: Domestic Drama in Performance: 1820–1874* (London: Associated University Presses, 1977).
15. Meisel, *Realizations*, 144.
16. W. T. Moncrieff, 'Remarks' to *John Overy, the Miser of Southwark Ferry* (London: Richardson's Minor Drama), vi.
17. 'To the Wasp', unidentified cutting (1826), Enthoven Collection, Victoria and Albert Museum.
18. See Jacky Bratton, 'The Contending Discourses of Melodrama', in *Melodrama: Stage, Picture, Screen*, eds. Jacky Bratton, Jim Cook, and Christine Gledhill (London: British Film Institute, 1994).
19. 'Remarks' on *The Woodman's Hut: A Melo-dramatic Romance*, in W. Oxenberry, *The New English Drama* (London: John Miller, 1818).
20. See Deidre Pribram, 'Melodrama and the Aesthetics of Emotion', in *Melodrama Unbound*, eds. Christine Gledhill and Linda Williams (New York: Columbia University Press, 2018).
21. Booth, *English Melodrama*; Michael Hammet, ed., *Plays by Charles Reade* (Cambridge: Cambridge University Press, 1986).
22. See Elaine Aston and Ian Clarke, 'The Dangerous Woman of Melvillean Melodrama', *New Theatre Quarterly*, 12 (1996): 30–42, and E. Ann Kaplan, 'Mothering, Feminism and Representation', in *Home Is Where the Heart Is*, ed. Christine Gledhill (London: British Film Institute, 1987), 113–37.

# 6

JIM DAVIS

# Theatres and Their Audiences

Nineteenth-century melodrama is a difficult genre to define and categorize and this is also true of its audiences. Audiences varied, not only from theatre to theatre, but also over time at any individual theatre, and any attempt to hypothesize a generic audience for melodrama is doomed to failure. Many of the descriptions that do survive, such as those of Hazlitt, Dickens, or Thomas Earle, for example, not to mention endless accounts in newspapers and journals, are formulaic, often constructing audiences from a particular point of view. Yet nineteenth-century audiences also had agency: they were not passive spectators sitting in darkness, but active participants in a lit auditorium (for most of the nineteenth century) able to respond demonstratively to what was being performed before them. At times they may have been disorderly, but they also had the capacity to be attentive and engaged. Furthermore, while melodrama may have provided escapist entertainment for some, it also provided opportunities to come to terms with, and to negotiate the impact of, modernity, and it could be quite responsive to political and social concerns in its advocacy of social justice.

Audiences at specific theatres might comprise different social classes or predominantly consist of one particular class. The formulation of theatre space into box, pit, and gallery, later supplemented by the stalls and the dress circle, effectively segregated different classes from each other in individual theatres, a factor accentuated by the existence of separate entry points for different parts of the auditorium. While cheaper ticket prices outside the West End suggest that neighbourhood theatres offered greater access to working-class spectators, price differentials in the West End suggest that even theatres there were not merely the domain of more fashionable spectators. Moreover, theatres in the East End and south of the Thames (the latter known as transpontine theatres) attracted visitors from beyond their own neighbourhoods. Thus we should assume a degree of mobility among melodrama spectators, partly because some spectators

78

thought nothing of walking long distances to their theatre of choice and partly because, as the century progressed, spectators could take advantage of enhanced transport facilities.

Much that was written in the nineteenth century about melodrama audiences targets theatres in working-class neighbourhoods and gallery spectators. There are many references to rowdy behaviour, although volatility and inattention were normal features of audience behaviour in this period. It is quite likely that, as such accounts became increasingly formulaic, this aspect of audience behaviour was exaggerated: indeed, many such accounts are generated through Boxing Night descriptions of pantomime audiences, an occasion when unruliness, particularly in the gallery, often prevailed. Yet audiences could be self-disciplining and attentive, as Dickens implies in a description of the Royal Victoria audience:

> The gallery was of enormous dimensions; and overflowing with occupants. It required no close observation of the attentive faces, rising one above another, to the very door in the roof, and squeezed and jammed in, regardless of all discomforts, even there, to impress a stranger with a sense of its being highly desirable to lose no possible chance of effecting any mental improvement in that great audience.
>
> The company in the pit were not very clean or sweet-savoured, but there were some good-humoured young mechanics among them, with their wives. These were generally accompanied by 'the baby', insomuch that the pit was a perfect nursery . . . There were a good many cold fried soles in the pit, besides; and a variety of flat stone bottles, of all portable sizes.[1]

Dickens is of course 'constructing' his audience, in order to justify his defence of theatres as places offering not only amusement but also moral instruction to the people.

Throughout the nineteenth century most theatres in London and the provinces staged melodrama, and most regular theatregoers, whatever their background, would have attended performances of melodrama. Covent Garden was the first English theatre to stage a play designated a melodrama, Thomas Holcroft's *A Tale of Mystery* – a version of Charles Renée de Pixérécourt's *Coelina* (1800) – in 1802. Indeed, the Covent Garden and Drury Lane theatres were home to a large number of melodramas in the early nineteenth century, even though the genre also became strongly associated in London with neighbourhood theatres, such as the Surrey and Coburg (later Royal Victoria) theatres south of the river, and the Britannia, City of London, and Pavilion theatres to the east. Melodrama later held sway in the West End at such theatres as the Adelphi, Haymarket, Lyceum, and Drury Lane. Some of Dion Boucicault's earliest melodramas were staged by Charles Kean at the Princess's

Theatre in the 1850s, while Boucicault himself staged a series of his own sensation melodramas in the West End in the late 1850s and early 1860s. Henry Irving's first major success at the Lyceum Theatre, again in the West End, was as Mathias in *The Bells* in 1871, and Drury Lane's commercial success in the late nineteenth century was partially founded on a regular supply of sensational autumn melodramas. Provincial theatres also increasingly staged melodrama. In order to understand the diversity of melodrama as a genre it is important to know something of the theatres and actors for which these plays were specifically written, and also something of the audiences, wherever possible, for whom they were performed. To take as an example adaptations of Mary Elizabeth Braddon's novel *Lady Audley's Secret*, Colin Hazlewood's 1863 version for the Victoria and Britannia theatres in working-class districts of London is vastly different in tone from 'George Roberts's' version, written for the West End's St James's Theatre in the same year.[2] Audience reception of the two versions is likely to have been very different as well. Arguably, a full understanding of English melodrama is dependent on an understanding of the contexts in which individual melodramas were performed.

At the beginning of the nineteenth century, theatre in London was dominated by Covent Garden and Drury Lane, known as major theatres and licensed by patent to perform the legitimate drama. Both theatres had been rebuilt in the late eighteenth century to accommodate larger audiences of well over 3,000 in capacity, inevitably placing more emphasis on spectacle, heightened styles of acting, and narrative clarity, all of which fostered a taste for melodrama. In the meantime, pandering to the needs of a growing population, a number of minor theatres opened: these were not legally permitted to perform the legitimate drama, but gradually ignored the restrictions imposed upon them, performing both the legitimate drama and (often more lucratively) melodrama. Provincial theatres opening in the new industrial cities, such as Birmingham and Manchester, also recognized the economic potential of melodrama. For much of the century, particularly in the earlier years, theatres presented programmes lasting up to six hours or more. Thus an audience might see two or more melodramas in an evening, or a Shakespeare play followed by a melodrama, or a melodrama sandwiched between a comedy and a farce. Only in the months immediately after Christmas did the equally popular genre of pantomime usurp the place of melodrama as the central theatrical attraction.

By the 1830s there was such concern over the proliferation of minor theatres in London and the perceived 'decline' of the drama that Edward Bulwer Lytton chaired a Select Parliamentary Committee on Dramatic Literature in 1832. Many actors, authors, and managers bore testimony to the committee. Some, like Charles Kemble, believed that the patent theatres no longer attracted audiences: 'the people do not come, because there are minor theatres open where there is stronger excitement, and a coarser species of entertainment at a much cheaper rate'.[3] This obviously refers to melodramas, although spectacle was not crucial to a melodrama's success in Kemble's opinion, and the genre could just as easily be performed in a small as a large theatre: '[T]he most successful melodramas have been those which depended on strong excitement in the story or the incidents of the pieces, for without these all the splendour in the world will do nothing either in a large or a small theatre.'[4] Another witness, the actor Thomas Potter Cooke, argued that the minor theatres were the proper home of melodrama,[5] which was defined for the committee by Douglas Jerrold as 'a piece with what are called a great many telling situations', unlike the legitimate drama where the interest and the situation of the piece 'is rather mental than physical'.[6] George Bartley, stage manager at Covent Garden Theatre, saw melodrama as an inferior form of dramatic composition, regretting that its popularity at provincial theatres now deprived actors of the training and experience in the legitimate drama that they had previously acquired in the provinces.[7]

The Select Committee had little immediate impact, and it was not until 1843 that the London theatres were deregulated and given autonomy over what they performed, although now subject to censorship and inspection by the Lord Chamberlain's Office. In many of the newly licensed neighbourhood theatres melodrama was the standard fare, although the types of melodramas performed and the audiences who viewed them varied widely. Just before it became responsible for licensing all London theatres, the Lord Chamberlain's Office gathered short reports on neighbourhood audiences. The Surrey Theatre included '[s]ometimes nobility and gentry. Tradespeople. Mechanics in the gallery. Four women to one man in the Pit, the Husbands, Brothers being in the Gallery to save sixpence'.[8] In 1832 the Surrey manager, David Osbaldiston, told the Select Committee that the Surrey Theatre, which had a capacity of around 2,300, drew a respectable audience from all parts of town, although more from the theatre's vicinity than from the West End.[9] George Bolwell Davidge, manager of the Coburg Theatre, had also been at pains to convince the Select Committee that his theatre attracted a variegated audience: 'On Monday nights I conceive we have the working classes generally, and in the middle of the week we have the better classes, the play-going classes generally.'[10] However, the dramatist T. J. Serle told the committee that the Coburg drew audiences 'decidedly from its own neighbourhood',[11] while T. P. Cooke considered the Coburg audience 'almost restricted to that theatre' and very different in character from the Surrey Theatre's audience.[12] In 1843 the Lord Chamberlain's

Office report defined the theatre's (renamed the Royal Victoria in 1833) clientele as 'principally mechanics in the neighbourhood'.[13]

Theatres staging melodrama and the audiences they attracted varied considerably through the nineteenth century. Some of this was dependent on geographical location, although managerial policy, the presence of particular actors, and fluctuations in taste, fashion, and repertoire also had an influence. Old theatres closed, new theatres opened, and some theatres underwent numerous name changes during this period. While melodrama was a preeminent genre in many theatres, few theatres limited themselves solely to this form.

## The West End

Insofar as melodrama was an effective source of income for theatre managers, the genre continued to thrive in the West End, as well as in suburban and provincial playhouses. Improved transportation facilities enabled access to the West End from the outer suburbs and even the provinces as the century progressed, not to mention an increased presence of tourists from overseas. In the 1850s the management of Benjamin Webster and Céline Céleste at the Adelphi Theatre staged many melodramas, some of which, such as J. B. Buckstone's *The Green Bushes* (1845) and *The Flowers of the Forest* (1847), depended on Céleste's talent in non-speaking roles. In 1860 Dion Boucicault staged his sensation melodrama *The Colleen Bawn* at the Adelphi Theatre, audiences for which included Queen Victoria, who particularly enjoyed the scene in which Eily O'Connor was thrown into the water and almost drowned, prior to Boucicault himself – in the character of Myles na Coppoleen – taking a sensational 'header' in order to save her.[14] The last twenty years of the nineteenth century saw the Adelphi as one of the principal homes for West End melodrama, so much so that, according to George Rowell, 'An "Adelphi Melodrama" became a theatrical term recognized by the Victorian playgoer as promising an entertainment more stirring than subtle, more scenic than cerebral, and above all guaranteeing its public a heart-warming conclusion.'[15]

Boucicault's 'sensation' melodramas reaffirmed the centrality of spectacle in attracting audiences to melodrama. Special effects had been used in earlier plays, such as *The Corsican Brothers* (1852), which required the construction of a trap effect so that the ghost of Louis Dei Franchi could glide across the stage. Queen Victoria saw the play four times in eight weeks, writing that 'the effect of the ghost in the 1st act, with its wonderful management and entire noiselessness, was quite alarming', while both this and the tableau of the duel with which Act I concluded, were 'most impressive and creepy'.[16] However, the *Theatrical Journal* rebuked the monarch for her frequent attendance 'at this vulgar Victorian trash'.[17] A year earlier, the press had reprimanded the queen for clutching the curtains inside the royal box while watching a particularly tense scene in Boucicault's melodrama *Pauline* (1851) at the Princess's Theatre. In her own account of the performance she commented,

> I never saw anything more exciting. The Keans acted beautifully and she [Ellen Tree] acted really wonderfully in the most crucial and alarming moments, literally keeping one in a state of terror and suspense, so that one quite held one's breath, and was quite trembling when the play came to an end.[18]

Queen Victoria's enthusiasm for melodrama demonstrates that its appeal was wide, not just a foible of working-class audiences, although her attendance at theatres in London was strictly limited to the West End. Her presence at the Princess's helped draw upper- and middle-class spectators back to the theatre, although the gallery of the Princess's Theatre still attracted local inhabitants and working men and women.

Towards the end of the century, the Princess's Theatre was specifically a venue for middle-class melodrama, while spectacular melodrama was particularly associated with Drury Lane Theatre, especially after Augustus Harris's arrival as manager in 1879. Drury Lane provided the largest available seating capacity of any late-nineteenth-century London theatre and its autumn melodramas appealed to an audience who, in Harris's own words,

> demand a performance which must be, above all things, dramatic, full of life, novelty, and movement: treating, as a rule, of the age in which we live, dealing with characters they can sympathize with, and written in a language they can understand. It ... should appeal rather to the feelings of the public at large than the prejudice of a class.[19]

George Bernard Shaw complained in 1895 that Drury Lane melodramas always contained 'too much stuff which neither its patrons nor its authors would condescend to take seriously, and which is a mere superstition from the time when playgoers could be treated as a mere mob of gaping bumpkins',[20] although this rather generalized assumption is belied by the continuing success of these dramas well beyond the turn of the century, not to mention Shaw's own debt to them.

### East End Audiences

The Pavilion Theatre, Whitechapel, opened in the east end of London in 1826, and became a significant home for melodrama. Located close to the docks it often attracted sailors to its productions, many of which were nautical melodramas. The original theatre was 'very cramped, very hot, very crowded and very dirty, with the pungent odour compounded of orange peel and gas', while the sailors in the audience contributed to the aroma 'a further flavouring of Jamaica Rum and Cavendish tobacco'.[21] While many appreciated the difference between the stage sailor and the real item, the sailor (often performed by Harry Rignold or T. P. Cooke) was an iconic figure on the stages of the Pavilion and Surrey theatres. In 1858 the Pavilion Theatre was rebuilt (it had been destroyed by fire in 1856) and re-opened. Its capacity was almost 5,000 with accommodation for 2,000 in the pit, almost equalling Covent Garden in size, and with a large stage area of 70 by 80 feet. Careful attention had been paid to providing adequate ventilation and appropriate fireproofing.[22] According to Mayhew, the new theatre could stand comparison with several West End theatres, and he contested the common belief that such a theatre would be populated by 'a rough, noisy set of drunken thieves and prostitutes'. On approaching the theatre you might observe 'prostitutes standing outside in little gangs and knots, and you will also see them inside, but for the most part, they are accompanied by their men'.[23] Like many other theatres outside of the West End, the Pavilion attracted a varied and largely respectable audience. A commentator describing the Pavilion's audience in 1879 commented on the homogeneity of the spectators across all sections of the audience, and the tendency of 'females of a ripe age to deliver an audible running commentary on the action of the drama'.[24] Four years later the *Referee* described the Pavilion's audience in the pit:

> Here may be seen the bluff British tar; the swarthy foreign sailor ... the Semitic swell ... the rorty coster, a perfect blaze of pearly buttons artistically arranged in a suit of corduroy ... the sallow, callow youth in the shortest of jackets and the largest of collars; the sallow youth's sweetheart; the respectable tradesman accompanied by his wife, five children and a large bag of provisions and a bottle of enormous dimensions; a trio of artless maidens who giggle and weep in torrents.[25]

No wonder the *Referee* called this the most 'cosmopolitan' pit in Europe.

An evening in neighbourhood theatres often entailed the consumption of food and drink, as well as drama. At the Britannia Theatre, Hoxton, an impoverished working-class district in East London, spectators purchased 'sandwiches, saveloys, bread, ginger-beer and oranges', not to mention 'pies ... thick slices of bread plastered with jam, hunks of cheese, slabby sandwiches, fried fish, jellied eels'.[26] Beer and porter were also available, sometimes from attendants with barrels strapped to their waists. Melodrama was the mainstay of the theatre's repertory, provided by dramatists such as George Dibdin Pitt, William Seaman, and Colin Hazlewood, who were adept at meeting audience expectations. Their formula was straightforward:

Strange adventures by sea and land occupy the stage of 'The Britannia' and the incidents are frequently such as to keep crowded audiences in a state of breathless suspense. They follow the fortunes of some domestic heroine who is possibly, for the time, in the power of a villain; and the thwarting of his nefarious schemes and the ultimate triumph of persecuted beauty and innocence, eventually bring down the curtain amidst tremendous cheering.[27]

Britannia melodramas often reacted to social injustice, highlighting the exploitation of male and female labour (including seamstresses and artificial flower makers), poverty, the degradations of the workhouse, class inequality, the treatment of convicts, and the gulf between rich and poor, as well as highlighting the problems caused by seduction and desertion, drink, and gambling.[28] While good acting roles for favourite actors and spectacular effects drew audiences, the social aspects of some Britannia melodramas may have been informed by or even informed the attitudes of their spectators. Many accounts of Britannia audiences survive – they were lively and attentive, their loyalty reflected in the gifts they bestowed upon performers at the annual Britannia Festival, and in the theatre's large attendance figures.

Other East End theatres included the Effingham Theatre, the City of London, and the Standard, which all presented melodramas. Sometimes the clientele attracted were not very salubrious – often they were young, especially in the cheaper seats. A police report on the City of London theatre in 1845 describes the gallery audience for a performance of *Jack Sheppard* (n.d.):

The audience in this part of the house was composed of the youth of both sexes, whose ages varied from 11 to 18, and chiefly of the very lowest class of society, the majority of the males being without coats or jackets ... and some of the officers with me, saw several males the associates of thieves. – There were also between 40 & 50 young prostitutes, some apparently not more than 14 or 15 years old, and the language going forward among them was bad in the extreme.[29]

There are many accounts of youthful audiences frequenting the galleries of neighbourhood theatres, but only occasionally are audience members categorized as thieves and prostitutes, even in police reports. Plays about highwaymen such as Jack Sheppard regularly drew young audiences: when Frederick Wilton, the Britannia stage manager, revived *The Ride to York* (*Dick Turpin*) (n.d.) for his benefit, he was informed that a string of ragged, shoeless boys were queuing for admission to the gallery.[30] Yet the age range and even social background of audiences attracted to performances could vary, as they often did at the Pavilion and Standard theatres. Under the management of the Melville family at the end of the century, the Standard continued to attract mixed audiences for its subgenre of 'wicked women' melodramas, such as *The Worst Woman in London* (1899) and *The Girl Who Took the Wrong Turning* (1906). The *Daily Telegraph* published this announcement for a Melville play:

> Who wants a husband? Statistics show that ninety per cent of women, when they have reached a marriageable age, are only awaiting the first opportunity in order to get married; yet hundreds remain old maids. Perhaps husbands are scarce. Do you want to know why you do not get one? Go and see *Her Forbidden Marriage* at the Standard Theatre.[31]

An Italian, Mario Borsa, ascribes the popularity of such plays to the support of female audiences, 'who avail themselves of the liberty allowed them by custom, and the coldness of the English masculine temperament, to wander alone at night from one end of London to the other'.[32]

## South of the Thames: Surrey-side Audiences

Among the theatres presenting melodramas south of the Thames were the Surrey and Victoria theatres, and Astley's Amphitheatre (specializing in equestrian and military melodrama). The Victoria attracted predominantly neighbourhood audiences; the Surrey drew both local audiences and spectators from north of the Thames; and the specialized nature of Astley's entertainments drew an even broader audience. The Victoria's audiences were often the subject of journalistic accounts: Hazlitt, two years after the theatre had opened as the Coburg, described its audience in 1820 as 'Jew-boys, pickpockets, prostitutes and mountebanks',[33] while Dickens assumed that the local 'ragged boys' were enthusiastic half-price visitors to the theatre in 1838.[34] Henry Mayhew commented on the number of costermongers in the theatre's gallery in the early 1850s and the relative youth of its audience.[35] An account by John Hollingshead of a performance of *Oliver Twist* (n.d.) in the 1850s, in which Bill Sykes dragged Nancy across the stage by her hair before dashing her brains out, describes a gallery 'probably containing about fifteen hundred perspiring creatures, most of the men in shirt sleeves, and most of the women bare-headed, with coloured handkerchiefs round their shoulders'. At Nancy's death, 'a thousand enraged voices ... filled the theatre and deafened the audience'.[36] Even commentators such as Dickens and George Augustus Sala,[37] who argue for the moralistic effect of melodrama on such audiences, construct simple-minded, uncouth audiences as typifying this theatre. Situated in the insalubrious environment of the New Cut, the Victoria kept its prices low and seemingly attracted a working-class audience, although the more lurid accounts of its spectators tend towards exaggeration.

The Surrey Theatre drew a more varied clientele, although it was often in competition with the Coburg/Victoria. The theatre became particularly associated with nautical melodrama, particularly after the popularity of Douglas Jerrold's *Black Ey'd Susan* (1829), with T. P. Cooke as the sailor hero William. An 1841 playbill for *Poor Jack* and *My Poll and My Partner Joe* (1835) claimed the Surrey as 'THE FIRST NAUTICAL THEATRE IN EUROPE', although this reflected the broad appeal of nautical melodrama rather than a purely local absorption in nautical trades, for there is little demographic evidence to support the existence of a community involved in nautical activities in the vicinity of the Surrey Theatre.[38] That other types of melodrama were also played at the Surrey and could attract audiences from afar is indicated by Edward Fitzball, whose 1833 melodrama *Jonathan Bradford* included an innovative scene in which action took place in four rooms of a house simultaneously: Fitzball wrote that 400,000 spectators, not merely from the working and middle classes, but also 'some thousands of the highest order of intellect and society' witnessed this production.[39] Throughout much of the century the Surrey Theatre offered a varied repertoire, including melodrama, to a much wider range of spectators than those attracted to the Victoria – although in the 1870s, under William Holland's management, the fare became more popular. However, when critics refer to transpontine or Surrey-side melodrama indiscriminately, they are failing to differentiate effectively between the two theatres, their repertoires, and their audiences.

## Provincial Theatres and Audiences

Melodrama featured just as much in the provinces as it did in London. In the early years of the nineteenth century new melodramas were performed by companies based around circuits, moving from theatre to theatre within a specific area of the country. As some towns and cities became more prosperous, new theatres were built, whose repertoires, as with the London theatres, might depend on the district in which they were located. By the 1860s, touring companies were bringing plays to the provinces: Boucicault set up two touring companies, for instance, to perform *The Colleen Bawn* outside of London. Boucicault also saw the advantage of adapting scripts, where appropriate, for provincial performances. Thus, *The Poor of New York* (1857) became *The Poor of Liverpool* for its Liverpool premiere in 1864, also metamorphosing into *The Poor of Manchester, The Poor of Leeds,* and *The Streets of Dublin,* according to the performance's location. Sometimes an author would test out a new melodrama in the provinces before staging it in London. Local authors occasionally wrote melodramas for provincial theatres, often with localized settings, but in the main proven successes from London theatres predominated. By the end of the century major actors, such as Henry Irving, replete with their own touring companies, were appearing at venues throughout Britain.

Audiences in the provinces reflected, on a smaller scale, the composition and behaviour of London audiences. However, compared to London, a far greater proportion of the proletariat in industrial cities worked in factories, and sometimes local plays dealt with local issues. At the Sheffield Theatre Royal a melodrama by a local author, Joseph Fox, entitled *The Union Wheel* was staged in 1870. Based on recent industrial conflicts known as the 'outrages', the play was quite balanced in its depiction of the different parties involved, although the *Sheffield Independent* (18 April 1870) was concerned that the strong sentiments uttered by the union leader were 'loudly cheered by occupants of the gallery, while sentiments which went to the opposite effect met only with a very partial response'. Despite this, the local reception of the play was relatively mild compared with that of the national press, with *Punch* (7 May 1870) suggesting the drama should come to the attention of the Examiner of Plays, and others considering it an incitement to strikes and violence.[40]

During the nineteenth century Birmingham's population included not only factory workers but also a large number of artisans. In a short study of nineteenth-century Birmingham theatre audiences, Douglas A. Reid provides a useful insight into their behaviour and composition. According to a police report of 1840, the gallery audience at the Theatre Royal was predominantly youthful: out of 1,200 persons 'there were probably 600 girls and boys under 16 years of age, and 200 more from 16 to 20 years. The greater proportion were boys.' These were largely apprentices and other children employed in the factories. The adults in the gallery and in the pit were largely of the artisan class.[41] Yet the dangers of categorizing audiences were just as significant in Birmingham as they were in London. When *Jack Sheppard* was revived at the Theatre Royal in 1852 it apparently drew an atypical audience, largely to the pit and gallery, rather than the theatre's more regular spectators. Nevertheless, the gallery continued to draw youthful spectators, some of whom had a particular way of reserving seats for friends:

> A pal in front, if he had secured a seat for a chum coming in later, would save it till the arrival of the latter, who had no objection to being tossed or rolled over the heads of the audience until he was ultimately landed in his 'reserved seat'.[42]

Sometimes this could go wrong, as in 1873, when Thomas Millbanks, the thirteen-year-old son of a shoemaker 'made a "roll" from the top of the gallery over the heads of the audience to reach his companions who were seated in the front row'. Unfortunately, they failed to catch him and 'with headlong force, he cleared the boundary rail in the gallery and fell smash into the pit'.[43] Overall, according to Reid, theatre in Birmingham in the mid-nineteenth century was 'something of a social microcosm', with gentry and bourgeoisie in the boxes, artisans, shopkeepers, impecunious professionals and sometimes 'roughs' in the pit, and 'a youthful and predominantly working-class gallery audience' forming 'the largest and most separate section of the house'.[44]

Melodrama audiences attended a genre which aimed to extract emotional and visceral reactions, as witnessed in Queen Victoria's response to *Pauline*. Melodrama creates anxiety and empathy, terror and relief, while provoking tears, sweat, laughter, fainting fits, hysteria, and other physical responses. Bruce McConachie has argued for more emphasis on understanding spectator reaction and experience: in effect such an approach focuses less on who the audience were, and more on how they felt.[45] Erin Hurley has also emphasized the affective nature of melodrama, describing it as 'a kind of feeling-producing machine, formally engineered to elicit emotional response'.[46] There is a strong case for investigating this aspect of audience response to melodrama in more detail, drawing not only on the circumstances of performance but also on the historical data available, rather than on conjectural notions derived from the dramas themselves and their anticipated impact on audiences. Tiffany Watt Smith has developed a more nuanced approach, not only to audience engagement with nineteenth-century theatre, but also to the emotional performance of spectators.[47] Her discussion of the sensation drama, so-called of course because its aim is the extreme stimulation of spectators' sensory responses, considers the collusion between the spectator and melodrama's simulated terror as a deliberate contract through which spectators knowingly consume their own emotions.[48] Emotion is a significant aspect of audience behaviour, indicating engagement, attentiveness, response, and participation. Yet absorption and even emotional involvement in melodrama was countered, in some instances, by an awareness of its illusionistic nature, as when audiences hissed, booed, and cheered, much as they do in modern English pantomime.

Melodrama was also a medium that functioned as a form of cultural negotiation for its audiences, helping them to come to terms, in a period of rapid change and new technologies, with the impact of modernity and the anxieties this created. Many melodramas were set in the contemporary world, a world familiar to its spectators, and despite their excesses, exhibited a world that was identifiable and real. New inventions, new forms of transportation and contemporary architecture increasingly feature in the genre, providing not only a surface veneer of the real, but also contributing to an audience's sense of reality. In addition, J. S. Bratton has shown how English melodrama enabled negotiation with the impact of imperialism. Bratton highlights the role that the juxtaposition of comic with more serious scenes played in such negotiation, insofar as they might offer alternative perspectives on the same event. She also takes the Jack Tar as a pivotal figure in negotiating imperial and domestic ideology, not only through his embodiment of national identity but also through his inescapable implication of British imperialism, 'while at the same time accommodating doubts and tensions created by that role'.[49] Indeed, melodrama arguably enabled audiences to understand and engage with political and social issues, even if the narratives in which these negotiations occurred could be rather simplistic.

Because of melodrama's seemingly simplistic narratives and the rather clichéd ways in which pit and gallery audiences were depicted by contemporaries, there is sometimes a generalizing tendency to portray such audiences as simple-minded. Yet spectators were also individuals, they had agency, and their individual responses to melodrama may just as easily have been ironic or critical as escapist, active rather than passive. For most of the century, before the auditorium lights were dimmed, spectators could certainly choose to collude in an almost participatory theatrical experience, which was both thrilling and emotionally seductive. Yet while melodrama may have been fashioned to stimulate generic responses, we should be wary of assuming the existence of a generic audience for this type of entertainment.

# Notes

1. Charles Dickens, 'The Amusements of the People', Household Words, 30 March 1850, rpt. in *The Dent Uniform Edition of Dickens' Journalism, Vol. 2: 'The Amusements of the People' and Other Papers: Reports, Essays and Reviews 1834–51*, ed. Michael Slater (London: J. M. Dent, 1996), 182.
2. This was a pseudonym for Robert Walters, whose adaptation had Mary Braddon's full approval.
3. *Report from the Select Committee on Dramatic Literature: With the Minutes of Evidence* (London: House of Commons, 2 August 1832), 42, 627.
4. *Report from the Select Committee on Dramatic Literature*, 44, 603.
5. *Report from the Select Committee on Dramatic Literature*, 146, 2604.
6. *Report from the Select Committee on Dramatic Literature*, 15, 2843.
7. *Report from the Select Committee on Dramatic Literature*, 182, 3259.
8. LC7/5, Lord Chamberlain's Papers, Public Record Office.
9. *Report from the Select Committee on Dramatic Literature*, 95, 1597.
10. *Report from the Select Committee on Dramatic Literature*, 79, 1270.
11. *Report from the Select Committee on Dramatic Literature*, 122, 2133.
12. *Report from the Select Committee on Dramatic Literature*, 14, 2602.
13. LC7, Lord Chamberlain's Papers, Public Record Office.

14. Richard Schoch, *Queen Victoria and the Theatre of Her Age* (Basingstoke: Palgrave Macmillan, 2004), 155.
15. George Rowell, *William Terriss and Richard Prince: Two Players in an Adelphi Melodrama* (London: Society for Theatre Research, 1987), 5.
16. Quoted in Schoch, *Queen Victoria and the Theatre of Her Age*, 154.
17. *Theatrical Journal* (19 May 1852).
18. Quoted in Schoch, *Queen Victoria and the Theatre of Her Age*, 153–4.
19. *Fortnightly Review* 38 (1885): 635, quoted in 'Soldiers of the Queen: Drury Lane Imperialism', in *Melodrama: the Emergence of a Genre*, eds. Michael Hayes and Anastasia Nikolopoulou (New York: St. Martin's Press, 1996), 5.
20. Bernard Shaw, *Our Theatre in the Nineties*, Vol. 1 (London: Constable and Company Ltd., 1932), 207.
21. *East London Observer* (6 April 1861).
22. *Theatrical Journal* (3 November 1858).
23. Henry Mayhew, *London Labour and the London Poor*, Vol. 4 (1861–2, rpt. New York: Dover, 1967), 227.
24. *Saturday Musical Review* (29 March 1879): 196–7.
25. Quoted in A. E. Wilson, *East End Entertainment* (London: Arthur Barker Ltd., 1954), 89.
26. *Sketch* (24 June 1896); H. G. Hibbert, *Fifty Years of a Londoner's Life* (London: Grant Richards Ltd., 1916), 63–4.
27. Quoted in *Dramatic Notes* (London, n.d.), 74–5.
28. Jim Davis, 'The Gospel of Rags: Melodrama at the Britannia, 1863-74', *New Theatre Quarterly*, 7 (1991): 369–89.
29. LC7/6, Police Report, 22 July 1845, Lord Chamberlain's Papers, Public Record Office.
30. *The Britannia Diaries 1863–75: Selections from the Diaries of Frederick C. Wilton*, ed. Jim Davis (London: Society for Theatre Research, 1992), 161.
31. Mario Borsa, *The English Stage of Today*, trans. Selwyn Brinton (London: John Lane, 1908), 5.
32. Borsa, *The English Stage of Today*, 5.
33. William Hazlitt, 'The Minor Theatres', *London Magazine*, 1.3 (March 1820).
34. Charles Dickens, *Sketches by Boz*, second series (London: John Macrone, 1836), 23–4.
35. Henry Mayhew, *London Labour and the London Poor*, Vol. 1 (London: Griffin, Bohn and Company, 1861), 18.
36. John Hollingshead, *My Lifetime*, Vol. 1 (London: Sampson Low, 1895), 188–9.
37. George Augustus Sala, 'Nine o'Clock P.M. – Half Price in the New Cut', *Twice Round the Clock* (London: J. & R. Maxwell, 1859), 271.
38. Jim Davis and Victor Emeljanow, *Reflecting the Audience: London Theatregoing, 1840–1880* (Iowa City: University of Iowa Press, 2001), 4–5.
39. Edward Fitzball, *Thirty-Five Years of a Dramatic Author's Life*, Vol. 1 (London: Newby, 1839), 256.
40. John Russell Stephens, *The Censorship of English Drama, 1824–1901* (Cambridge: Cambridge University Press, 1980), 125. For a full account of *The Union Wheel* and its reception, see Hilary Wilson, *The Challenge of Nineteenth Century Theatre in Sheffield*, PhD Dissertation, University of Sheffield, 2013.

41. Douglas A. Reid, 'Popular Theatre in Victorian Birmingham', in *Performance and Politics in Popular Drama: Aspects of Popular Entertainment in Theatre, Film and Television*, eds. David Bradby, Louis James, and Bernard Sharratt (Cambridge: Cambridge University Press, 1980), 69–70.
42. Reid, 'Popular Theatre in Victorian Birmingham', 71.
43. Reid, 'Popular Theatre in Victorian Birmingham', 71.
44. Reid, 'Popular Theatre in Victorian Birmingham', 72.
45. Bruce McConachie, *Engaging Audiences: A Cognitive Approach to Spectating in the Theatre* (New York: Palgrave Macmillan, 2008).
46. Erin Hurley, *Theatre and Feeling* (Basingstoke: Palgrave Macmillan, 2010), 44.
47. Tiffany Watt Smith, *On Flinching: Theatricality and Scientific Looking from Darwin to Shell Shock* (Oxford: Oxford University Press, 2014), 8.
48. Watt Smith, *On Flinching*, 65.
49. J. S. Bratton, 'British Heroism and the Structure of Melodrama', in J. S. Bratton, Richard Allen Cave, Breandan Gregory, Heidi J. Holder, and Michael Pickering, *Acts of Supremacy: The British Empire and the Stage, 1790–1930* (Manchester: Manchester University Press, 1991), 59.

## II

# Melodramatic Technique

# 7

MICHAEL V. PISANI

# Melodramatic Music

## The 'Melo' in Melodrama

Many people today forget that the roots of *melodrame*, a compound French word first used in the last decades of the eighteenth century and later adopted into English, make clear that this describes a theatrical genre fused with music ('melody' being a common eighteenth-century translation for the Greek *melos*). The first 'melo-drames' were classical in nature, semi-staged scenic dramas for actors by the likes of Jean-Jacques Rousseau in France, Georg Benda in Germany, and Tomás de Iriarte in Spain. But by the turn of the nineteenth century, 'melodrama' had become the accepted English term for a musical-pantomimical action-drama, rather than the Greek revivalist experiment of instrumental music and the spoken word (or the Italian *melodramma*, which meant opera). Beginning first in London's major theatres – Covent Garden, Drury Lane – English melodrama established itself as a musical afterpiece to follow the performance of legitimate drama. It quickly moved to the many minor theatres, where as a mode or technique (rather than a genre, per se) it served as a way for these theatres to produce plays by circumventing licensing laws: that is, as long as the production maintained the semblance of a largely musical piece, rather than a spoken one. The popular theatre in England, as in France, meant drama and comedy aimed largely at the working and rising middle classes. The musical accompaniments, like the characters and situations onstage, were crafted to appeal to those audiences. Hence melodrama's stigma in over a hundred years of dramatic and musical scholarship.

If a melodrama originated in the royal theatres of London, Edinburgh, or Dublin, it is often possible to identify the source of the music. For these plays, the composer's name shows up on the playbills, and such music was sometimes even published. A good example is Charles Kemble's *The Hungarian Cottage, or The Brazen Bust* (1813). Even though the play itself was never printed, Henry Bishop's overture and 'action music', written for the first Covent Garden production, circulated almost immediately in a published piano score, which Kemble used again for his staging the following year at the Theatre Royal, Dublin.[1] For those who expect to chart the development of music in English-language melodrama through printed music, however, considerable frustration and confusion lie ahead, since the trail of music's connection to stage melodrama seems to fizzle out around 1820. The publication of piano scores – invaluable for English adaptations of Charles Renée de Pixérécourt melodramas like *A Tale of Mystery* (1802), *The Fortress* (1807), or *The Forest of Bondy* (1814) – trickles to a stop, even as the careers of famous melodramatists such as Edward Fitzball, Céline Céleste, George Davidge, John Buckstone, and Charles Selby were just taking off. This is why we need to sift carefully through the available evidence to learn more about the actual music that this second generation of melodramatists used for their productions at the Adelphi, the Coburg, the Surrey, and elsewhere across the English-speaking theatre world.

For the hundreds of melodramas produced in the 1820s, '30s, and '40s in regional theatres across the British Isles and America, the music (other than any songs associated with the play) often remained anonymous and may have been as much an assemblage of various musical sources – chosen by the author or acting manager – as original bits provided by orchestra leaders. One theory is that the music director of a theatre would compile the necessary *hurries, agitatos, plaintives,* and other requested characteristic and action pieces into a set of parts for his small orchestra, which he then led in performances, usually from the violin-leader book. A sample can be seen here, from a violin part to the opening of *The Idiot of Heidelberg* (1839), a true-crime drama based on the mysterious captivity and death of Kaspar Hauser a few years before (Figure 7.1).

*Melos* items such as this were ordered numerically as they occurred in the play (no. 1, no. 2, etc.), and it was more common than not that dialogue and visual cues were added to all the parts, since the musicians in most theatres of the time could easily observe the actors onstage.

## Music and Staging

Given the scarcity of such manuscript sources, however, clues can be found in the directions sprinkled liberally throughout nineteenth-century published play scripts, where it is obvious that authors and adaptors of melodramas thought not only visually, in terms of their characters' actions and positions onstage, but also aurally, in the sense that music as well as dialogue and sound effects formed a part of the dramatic ethos.

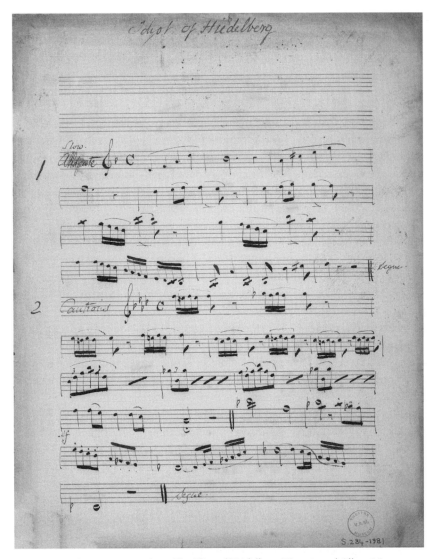

Figure 7.1 Anonymous music to *The Idiot of Heidelberg*. Victoria and Albert Museum, London. S.284–1981. ©Victoria and Albert Museum, London. (The Victoria and Albert record identifies this music as originating from the Surrey Theatre, even though that 1838 production was titled *Gaspard Hauser*. The title on this music matches that of the playbills for Andrew Ducrow's 1839 adaptation at Astley's.)

Take, for example, John Buckstone's domestic melodrama *Luke the Labourer* (1826), when resentful hired hand Luke confronts Farmer Wakefield and his family:

WAKEFIELD. Stand off, Dame. Clara, be you quiet. Let me come at him.

[**Music.** *Wakefield seizes Luke, but is grappled in return by the throat. Luke dashes him on the ground and rushes out of the cottage with a loud laugh. Clara screams and Dame Wakefield sinks senseless in the chair. Clara is endeavouring to raise her father and the scene closes.*]        (1:2)

The action here calls for some kind of *agitato,* a stormy musical cue. Because there is no dialogue, the theatre band – perhaps eight to twelve musicians – could play out to their hearts' content until the rowdy stage business came to an end. Perhaps it does not matter precisely what the music for this might have been; any sort of prolonged minor-mode flurry would seem to fit this situation just fine, as long as it matched the fierce tone of this confrontation. Of course, an excerpt borrowed from some classical or operatic repertoire could be plugged in, as it sometimes was, but with that would come the risk that the music's familiarity could prove distracting to the audience. Critics rarely commented on the melodramatic music anyway, at least until later in the century, when it became more ordinary practice to incorporate familiar classical pieces, mostly for their prestige value. We might conclude, then, that for these early decades of melodrama, generic mood music, appropriately chosen and placed, varied from theatre to theatre. Maybe that's why it's so surprising to learn that Samuel French made band parts for *Luke the Labourer* available for performance rental as late as the 1860s – along with other widely performed melodramas such as *Cataract of the Ganges* (1823) and *Robert Macaire* (1834). For two shillings sixpence a month, amateur theatrical groups could stage these melodramas with music specifically allocated by the publishers.[2] Similarly, Thomas Baker in New York advertised parts 'for large or small bands' to melodramas such as *The Green Bushes* (1845), *The Colleen Bawn* (1860), and *Jeanie Deans* (1860).[3] The presumption that every regional orchestra leader would automatically apply his or her own selections accounts for the ephemeral reputation that most melodramatic music has earned.

Since melodrama itself is often viewed as an inferior theatrical form, we can see that there were indeed qualitative differences between melodramas, not just in the dialogue and situations, but in the way music received just as much care as staging, sets, costumes, and lighting. *The Mysterious Stranger* (1844), adapted for the Adelphi by Charles Selby from a French original, 'was performed with so much skill as to keep the audience in a constant state of excitement'.[4] In the drama, Henry, a successful young gentleman, is visited by the devil. 'Tremulous music' is of course required, but not to depict the devil, who isn't really a devil after all, but to alert audiences to Henry's unease with the intruder. 'Satan' (acted by Céline Céleste) is actually a young lover, who – in clever disguise – plays on the coincidence that some years earlier, in the pit of despair, Henry had claimed he would sell his soul to the devil if only he had some luck; only to discover the very next day that a distant relative had died and left him a great deal of money. The audience is at first unaware that Satan is not who he appears to be, and is therefore caught up in Henry's vexation. At the end of Act 1, scene 2, Henry laughingly boasts to his friend Vanille, 'that's right, we'll have a jolly night'; meanwhile, 'Satan' appears at the door, stage center, having overheard him.

SATAN. Devilish jolly, ha! ha! ha!

HENRY. (*seeing him and laughing faintly.*) Yes – yes – yes – (*seriously*) very– very – very jolly – ha! ha! ha! [*Goes off right with Count Vanille, who has not observed Satan. Tremulous music in orches- tra, piano – Satan goes to the table, and strikes it with his hand – a chord – Crequet (Henry's valet) puts his head under the table- cloth, dreadfully alarmed – Satan motions to him to come out and follow him.*]

CREQUET. (*speaking through the music*) Oh, dear! I'm wanted – yes, yes, your serene highness – no, no, – yes, sir, – I – I – I'm coming – your most awful – I didn't mean to trouble you, I only wanted to know if – yes, yes, most infernal – I'm coming – I'm coming! [*Exit trembling, follow-ing Satan*]

SCENE III. – *The Ante-Chamber – same as scene I. Music continues. Enter Satan, right, beckoning Crequet, who enters in great alarm.*

Here we see no less than four instructions for music in this short passage of business and dialogue. The published play requests a characteristic *tremolo misterioso* for the devil, interrupted by a sharp chord coordinated with a stage gesture (often called a 'stinger' chord), and then 'trembling' music to continue under dialogue and through the scene change. The string tre- molo – that central resonance in the melodramatic imagination – serves a dual purpose: to accentuate Henry's discomfort with the stranger and to exaggerate the cowardice of the shivering valet. We also encounter a request for 'speaking through the music', a technique which – as any actor or orchestra leader who has performed musical theatre knows – requires clear projection and delicate shading in dynamics. Today it is natural to think of music playing *under* dialogue, where the actors carry on and it is the orches- tra director's responsibility to keep the musicians quiet enough. But 'through dialogue' was more common in the nineteenth century, implying that the actor finds and situates his or her voice *within* the musical sounds, and that the music might be arranged or orchestrated in such a way to allow space for the range or colours of the actor's voice to predominate.[5] (Strings alone were typically the most flexible in supporting the spoken voice, although the

99

inclusion of such things as a solo clarinet or cello for thematic reminiscence was not unusual.) Even though we know that the music for *The Mysterious Stranger* was by Alfred Mellon, we have no way to verify its effect in the dramatic sequence above, since it has disappeared. Still, Selby took great pains in the published version of his play to show music's precise placement and to identify its changing functions.

The cues for music that we see in printed versions of melodramas almost always reflect the play well into its run: in other words, after the trial-and-errors of any stage business with melodramatic music were already worked out. The manuscript of Selby's *Mysterious Stranger*, sent for licensing to the Lord Chamberlain a month before the premiere, and before the play went into rehearsal, did not have these musical instructions.[6] In this case, the one responsible for placing the music may have been Benjamin Webster, who staged the play. Regardless, music's role in the enactment of a scene remained as much a part of what constituted the final text of the play as the dialogue. For *The Mysterious Stranger*, the text – prepared 'from the [Adelphi] prompter's copy' – was quickly made available on both sides of the Atlantic, in London by the National Acting Drama Office and in New York by Samuel French. For those wishing to produce this play, specifications were clear for where and how music was supposed to occur, along with useful hints as to mood and dynamics. Learning how to interpret these instructions now, almost two centuries later, is a crucial step towards understanding nineteenth-century melodrama.

## Music and Character

Rather than allowing music to be haphazardly and indiscriminately placed, the best of the melodramatic authors and producers conceived and integrated it as part of the dramatic structure. Moreover, it was almost never a tenet of melodramatists such as George Colman, Edward Fitzball, John Howard Payne, Douglas Jerrold, John Buckstone, Louisa Medina, James Planché, George Almar, or others of this generation, that 'cheerful music' would always accompany the entrance of the heroine and overly obvious 'creepy music' would accompany the entrance of the villain, despite what one reads in twentieth-century histories. Such practice was, and remains today, founded upon the burlesque of genuine melodramas, which, given their immense popularity, were widely parodied in vaudeville and the music halls. *Melos*, as used by professional nineteenth-century practitioners of melodrama, though of course in essential ways still archetypal, was often far more strategic.

Let's take one of many such examples: R. J. Raymond's *The Old Oak Tree*, first produced in 1835 at the English Opera House (Lyceum). It featured the inimitable, deep-voiced O. Smith as Mouchard, 'a most villainous and sinister-looking spy as could be desired' (so observed *The Spectator*).[7] We can rely on the publication by J. Duncombe and Co., a standard purveyor of play texts, who advertised 'the only edition correctly marked by permission from the prompter's book'.[8] The edition specifies a total of twenty music cues, some with a tempo or dynamic. But there is no music for Smith's first appearances as Mouchard, nor does the music indicated to accompany his next entrance with Griffon the jailor have anything to do with villainy, but rather with a prisoner's distress over a carrier pigeon that Mouchard has intercepted and shot. Only in Act 2, scene 5 – well on towards the end of the play – when Mouchard enters alone to approach the old tree in which he's hidden a stash of money, is there music specified to accompany his furtive movements. 'Villain's music' is here the *pièce de resistance*: accompanying Mouchard in both dialogue and stage business, it is brought in not to mark the character for the audience – who by now knows exactly who he is and what he's up to – but to heighten the suspense surrounding discovery of this secretive act. For as soon as Mouchard hears approaching footsteps, the orchestra is instructed to change to 'hurried music', as the scene (and the play) rushes towards its dénouement.

Of course, the strategic effectiveness of melodramatic music depended greatly on the taste, skill, and dramatic sensitivities of the music director, which could vary widely in theatres of the time. The music for the original *Old Oak Tree* was devised and led by a young George Macfarren. (It appears to be lost, and is not listed among his works in the *New Grove Dictionary of Music*.) *The Spectator* observed that the play included 'a great deal of effective melodramatic music'.[9] Since theatre critics notoriously disregarded the music in most notices throughout the nineteenth century, the occasional offhand acknowledgement, whether praise or criticism, serves to demonstrate that music was involved far more than it was usually noticed. The best melodramatic music, so it would seem, worked quietly but essentially in the background, providing mood, characterization, and reinforcing dramatic structure.

What's more, some of the techniques of musical characterization described above can now be corroborated. Music used by the third generation of English melodramatists – W. Leman Rede, Edward Stirling, Mark Lemon, Dion Boucicault, Charles Reade, Edmund Falconer, William E. Suter, Wilkie Collins, Watts Philips, Tom Taylor, John Oxenford, Henry Leslie – is gradually beginning to turn up as libraries undertake to process long-ago acquired collections of items relating to these nineteenth-century playwrights and actor-managers, who often held on to manuscript orchestra music along with the prompt copies of their melodramas.

## Interpretive Functions of Melodramatic Music

In the absence of surviving music, however, we rely on the instructions in thousands of published play scripts and prompt copies of plays, prepared by melodramatic authors (and actor-managers) who conceived of music as an essential part of the construction and business of the play. And yet for the dozens – if not hundreds – of theatres in English-speaking countries that took up a play after its initial premiere, these instructions still needed to be translated into actual music, either by the actor-manager, the prompter, or the orchestra leader. Orchestra leaders could hardly be expected to read every play before rehearsal, so the intermediary between prompter and music director was a document called the 'music plot'. It specified the text or visual cue for music to begin, as well as some hint as to the character and function of the music (and sometimes even whether the music of an earlier cue should be repeated).

Such a music plot is to be found for Tom Taylor's *The Serf, or Love Levels All* (1865). Taylor's play was based on several older 'resentment against tyranny' melodramas, with additional effects in line with the new 'sensation drama', in vogue in the 1860s. It was first staged at the Olympic in London; Thomas Hailes Lacy published the play text. Reviews of the original production are many and widely divergent, but one reviewer asserted that its sensational elements would be better suited to one of the transpontine theatres (i.e., a 'melodramatic house' south of the Thames). History records that it only ran a few nights at the Olympic. What a thorough perusal of regional newspapers tells us, however, is that over the next decade several prominent British and American melodramatic actors – Charles Wyndam, Henry Neville, and Edwin Adams – included the play on their tours, where, outside London or New York, the public's taste for such melodramas was still very strong. Indeed, this music plot was associated with a production of Lawrence Barrett in Cincinnati, Ohio in 1865, and serves as a good example of how instructions for music circulated from the principal urban theatres to the provinces and beyond.

*The Serf's* complicated plot begins in Paris, where Ivan, a young Russian artist, falls in love with the Countess Marguerite de Mauléon while painting her portrait. Ivan is actually a serf, sent to France for training by his master. The time is prior to Alexander's decree of freedom for Russia's serfs, and the Countess, initially warm towards Ivan, reacts with revulsion when she learns of his rank and servitude. At the death of his master, Ivan must return to Russia, where he falls under the hand of Karateff, a cruel overlord he grows to resent and who has Ivan publically whipped for his insubordination. It turns out that Marguerite is the niece of the French ambassador to

Russia, who accepts a post in St Petersburg. She goes with him, now hoping to come to Ivan's aid. Meanwhile, Khor, Ivan's father, has been mounting an insurrection of Karateff's serfs. He reveals to his son the stocks of gunpowder stored in the vaults of Karateff's chateau and explains that, on a pre-arranged signal, a slow-burning fuse is planned to ignite an explosion. But when Ivan learns that the Countess Marguerite has unexpectedly arrived at the chateau, he puts his life in danger to intercept the signal. In the ensuing skirmish, Khor is mortally wounded. Before he dies, he confesses that Ivan is not his real son, but stolen from the former lord of the chateau whom he killed. Ivan is therefore free to marry the Countess, and the two of them promise to liberate the serfs.

Figure 7.2 shows the music cues for the climax and dénouement of Act 3 as they appear in the music plot, with text cues from the actors prompting the unnumbered music cues.

It is apparent here that the language the melodramatic director or promp-ter used to communicate to his orchestra leader consisted of the same style topics that were already plentiful earlier in the century. 'Hurry' – quick minor-mode music – is stipulated where there is clearly a stage struggle, a 'hurried tremolo' is called upon to build suspense, and 'plaintive' is the standard moniker for slow and mournful music. 'No. 2' refers to the second item on the music plot (not shown here), where it is described as 'Peculiar Characteristic Music until Khor is on.' Perhaps 'peculiar' is a metonym for something Russian-sounding, but clearly it served as a kind of theme for Ivan's father. The tune is played not only upon his first entry but is requested no less than seven times throughout the plot. Perhaps as the only specifically recurring music it is even meant to be symbolic somehow of the insurgency.

| [Text cue] | [Instructions to Orchestra Leader] |
|---|---|
| ' . . . I'll look no more' | Music until 'Father' – then chord |
| ' . . . we'll be here again' | Music until Khor exits – No. 2 |
| ' . . . Lord over Serf' | Hurry *piano* until "Stand off ruffian" – then chord |
| ' . . . No harm in promising' | Music until Ivan is off with Mauléon |
| ' . . . Marguerite gone' | Music until Khor is on – No. 2 |
| ' . . . as I do now' | Hurried tremolo till pistol shot |
| ' . . . pity to the Serf' | Plaintive music *piano* until Khor's death |

Figure 7.2 Excerpt from a handwritten music plot to Lawrence Barrett's touring production of *The Serf*. TS 3609.584, Harvard Theatre Collection, Houghton Library, Harvard University. Column titles by the author. (This plot is in the same folder as copies of the actors' parts and a playbill from Pike's Opera House, Cincinnati, OH.)

It was *not* the music used for Khor's death, however. There the need for poignant strains superseded the 'peculiar' music previously associated with this character. Finally, the stinger effect of a 'chord'– both times underlined in the music plot – serves as an important structural marker. This 'chord of dramatic reversal', as I call it, exerts a crucial and pivotal function, and its application is carefully reserved. The entire third act includes only two such requests, the first when Ivan decides to halt the explosion and the second when he confronts Karateff over Marguerite's intercession.

## Eight Types of Music Cues

Next, we turn to a wildly successful late-century melodrama, George R. Sims's *The Lights o' London* (1881). The promptbooks for Wilson Barrett's first production at the Princess's specify forty-three music cues, not including the original overture. Using these cues, as well as corroborating evidence in a surviving violin-conductor part, also from the Princess's, we can determine how music helped shape this famous crime drama.[10]

A wealthy country squire has a son, Harold Armytage, several years estranged because of his spendthrift ways and his elopement with Bess, a girl of the servant class. Harold returns destitute with his wife, repenting and hoping for forgiveness. He hears rumors that his angry father has changed his will, leaving the house, jewels, and fortune to a nephew. The duplicitous nephew, Clifford Armytage, plans upon the old squire's death to acquire the house and set up Hetty Preene, his scheming fiancé, and her doting father Seth. But Clifford and Seth are both impatient, and together plot to rob and murder the squire and place the blame on Harold. Disguised as the down-and-out son, Seth Preene steals into the house, observes the squire at his safe, and in attacking him accidentally causes him to fall through the pane-glass window and onto the lawn below, while he makes off with the contents of the safe. The old man, mortally wounded from the glass and the fall, dies thinking it was his impecunious son. What neither son nor nephew knows is that the squire, secretly forgiving of his son's estrangement, has had the will changed back again. But the will and the jewels have now disappeared, and Harold is arrested. Three years later, he escapes from prison and manages to reach his wife, now in London, and has teamed up with a family of traveling actors (the comedic and heartwarming Jarvises), all the while thwarting the efforts of Clifford, the police, and a private detective hot on his trail. (And this is just partway into the second of five acts!) After the unfolding of several inter-related subplots involving the acting troupe, Hetty and Clifford's disintegrating relationship, and the closing in of the private detective, two twists of fate occur when Harold, still a hunted escapee, saves Seth Preene's life and when Hetty decides to turn on Clifford, implicating him in the crime. These episodes unfold against a series of spectacular scenes at the boat slips in Regents Park and the bustling Borough Market in Southwark.

The music cues, of varying lengths, were dispersed as follows: ten in Act 1, nine in Act 2, eight in Act 3, eleven in Act 4, and four in Act 5. Many of the cues were simply mood-setters to open a scene. A 'lively' opened the first act on the Armytage estate, and an *andante* opened Act 2, scene 2 on a snowy moonlit road, which led into Jarvis's song 'On a Starry Night'. Nine cues over the course of the play were used to bring characters on or send them off. Not all characters, though, strode on to music. There was music for the initial entrances of Bess, of Harold, and of Clifford and Hetty, with the *melos* in each case serving to alert the audience to some aspect of character. Some characters were revealed already at scene opening, such as Mr and Mrs Jarvis and the private detective, and they had no specific introductory music. Some music entered on a character's last line to round out the emotion of the scene and usher him or her out, for example after Bess's touching scene with 'Shakespeare' (the young Jarvis prodigy). Here, the music welled up after her last line, played through her exit, and ended just as Mrs Jarvis returned. Three cues provided emotional underscoring for key dialogue sequences: for Harold's tender expression of gratitude to the Jarvises at the end of Act 2; for Harold's reunion with Bess at the Jarvises' in Act 3, and the couple's subsequent declaration of love; and for Harold and Bess's scene of distress, wandering the backstreets of London and Bess's delirium in Act 4. Of course, several of the cues were important 'action' hurries. Music accompanying action – and decidedly climactic action – occurred at or near the end of a scene: for example, for Preene's attack and struggle with the Squire, his fall, and the gathering crowd of spectators in Act 1; for the arrival of the detective and police during the Jarvises' rehearsal, and the ensuing struggle to snag the disguised Harold in Act 3; and for Clifford's fight with Preene on the bridge, the old man's fall into the water, and Harold leaping in to rescue him in Act 4.

There is one important advantage to using the actual orchestra parts to determine the function of the music cues (when such parts survive, that is): while published texts might have music specified for some event or action, only the manuscript parts, and sometimes the promptbook, will indicate how long this music continued (for example, 'play until . . . '). In some cases, music at the end of a scene carried through the change and into the opening of the next scene; which was also the case in *The Mysterious Stranger,* as we saw earlier. There are six such bridge cues specified in *Lights o' London*: to cover the scene change from Preene's lodge to the snowy road in Act 2; to cover the change from the police station to the Jarvis flat in Act 3; and to close out the scene in shady St John's Wood, where Clifford has set up Hetty as his mistress in richly furnished apartments, changing to the workhouse in Act 4, and so forth. The last of these actually begins as a long action cue – the confrontation between Clifford and Harold at the Jarvises'. It continues into the fight at the window and the rooftops outside, and covers the change back to the police station.

Taken together, we can conclude that the forty-three music cues in *Lights o' London* were of eight different types: 1) act or scene opener, 2) character entrance music, 3) character exit music, 4) accompaniment to a song or dance, 5) dialogue underscore (or music for actors to speak through), 6) action music, 7) a combination of dialogue and action, and 8) scene-bridging music. Most of these are associated with *movement* as much as mood: movement of actors and movement of curtains, drops, and scenery. It appears that music's indispensable role in this dramatic partnership – even as late as the 1880s – continued to affirm melodrama's indebtedness to the traditions of pantomime.

## Music Placement in Later Melodramatic Practice

Our final melodrama examines the unifying device of a strategically placed melody. Playwright Robert Buchanan turned a rather overwrought French courtroom drama into *A Man's Shadow* (1889), which J. M. Barrie called 'the *edition de luxe* of melodrama'.[11] It was given a lavish production at the Haymarket by Herbert Beerbohm Tree and his wife Ellen that ran for 205 performances. It was immediately taken up all over Great Britain and North America. Tree himself revived it in 1898 for Her Majesty's Theatre, where his music director, Raymond Roze, enlarged the orchestra but used essentially the same music.

Tree was part of a fourth and fifth generation of melodramatists, some of whom lived into the twentieth century, and whose performances are captured in part on film or recordings. This generation – including playwrights Augustin Daly, Andrew Halliday, W. G. Wills, Buchanan, J. Comyns Carr, Henry Arthur Jones, David Belasco, and actor-managers Sara Lane, Charles Calvert, Henry Irving, Wilson Barrett, Richard Mansfield, George Alexander, Steele MacKaye, William Seymour, and Sarah Bernhardt – linked music with more elaborate stage design and lighting, and more spectacular production values.

The melodramatic conceit of *A Man's Shadow* is the classic premise of the innocent man who resembles a guilty man and is falsely incriminated. Prior to the opening of the play, Lucien Laroque, a young businessman, and Raymond de Noirville, an attorney, served alongside one another in the Franco-Prussian

War. After Lucien saved Raymond's life, the two became intimate friends. The play opens shortly after the war, where we see the men returning to their separate lives. Lucien discovers that Raymond's wife, Julie, is a woman with whom he had earlier had an affair. Julie secretly tries to rekindle the old affection, but Lucien, now married and with a young daughter, will have none of it. Learning that Lucien's business is now failing and that he faces bankruptcy, Julie devises a way to help him. At this point, events of the war come back to haunt them. A former spy, Luversan, whom Lucien and Raymond entrapped during their time in the military – and whom they believed to have been killed in a fire – returns for revenge. He pays a visit to the Noirville home to settle with Raymond, but encounters his wife instead. So closely does he resemble Lucien that Julie mistakenly entrusts a man she thinks is her former beloved with a letter and a packet of money in the hopes of saving him from financial ruin. Luversan decides he will make the most of this delicious misunderstanding. He shadows Lucien Laroque, who, in the meantime, has come up with the cash to pay his banker. The blackmailer overhears their transaction, then moves forward with his plan when the banker is alone. From a window across the way, the little Laroque girl watches with horror as she sees a man who appears to be her father murder the banker and steal his money. Within a day, Lucien is shocked to discover the cash in his mail along with a letter apparently from Julie (actually, a copy). After burning the letter, Lucien turns to Raymond for legal help. Thus the hapless attorney, in the process of defending a friend, will end up implicating his wife.

Music in the production was all the more effective for its infrequent placement. Onstage music consisted of a small band in the Act 2 hotel scene, and an organ in the church. The surviving melodramatic parts for the orchestra contain only eleven music cues.[12] These consist of six distinct character pieces: one 'polka', three that fit the category of 'slow music', one '*pizzicato* misterioso', and a tense *tremolo*. Four of these were repeated a second or third time in other scenes, but not without dramatic relevance.

The pivotal jury trial takes place in Act 3. As Lucien reveals during his testimony, a letter accompanied the packet of money left in his box; but he refuses to say from whom, and his admission that he destroyed the evidence causes an outburst. The revelation deeply vexes Raymond Noirville, attorney for his defence, until a recess in the trial, when his clerk hands him a packet. He opens it, recognizes the tone and handwriting of the enclosed letter as his wife's, and, trembling, begins to read out loud, at which point music is instructed to begin. The *Lento* for this under-dialogue sequence (no. 9) was first heard when Lucien visited Raymond to divulge his financial failures. It was clearly intended to be linked with their intimacy, since in the earlier scene, the lyrical music ceased when Julie interrupted them. The sentimental melody, reminiscent of

Figure 7.3 Transcription from the orchestra parts to *A Man's Shadow,* 'No. 2', composer unknown. Sir Herbert Beerbohm Tree Theatre Music Collection. Boston Public Library.

French opera, is played by the first violins while the other strings provide a sustained accompaniment (Figure 7.3). When this same music returns later, played under Raymond's long Act 3 aside, here is how it happens:[13]

> NOIRVILLE. (opens the letter and reads) 'Enclosed is a document which may be useful to you in your defense. It established the identity of the person who sent at least a portion of that money.' Ah! (opens enclosure) What's this, in the handwriting of my wife. [*M U S I C*] 'My best loved Lucien, once more I appeal to you to let me help you.' No, no! 'To let me help you. Unknown to my husband I have money at my command. Take it for the sake of her who was once and is forever yours. For the sake of the past! For the sake of the love I still bear you! Yours till death, Julie de Noirville.' (aloud) My God, is it possible? Lucien – Julie – the wife I adored – the friend I cherished!

Ah, now I understand the reason of her agitation in his presence, – his words – 'He could not look me in the face without
a blush of shame.' And I am here to defend him, the man who has
destroyed my honour. And the proof of his guilt to me is the proof
of his innocence of the crime of which he is accused! Great
Heaven, direct me how to act. (staggers back) If when I am called
upon to speak in his defense, I but utter my wife's name – he is
saved – but I am disgraced forever. [*Music ends.*]

USHER. Take your places, gentleman. (Re-enter President and the jury.)

Here we have an excellent example of how dialogue and melodramatic
music could be expertly paced and modulated. The actor needed to deliver
his aside in a manner clearly audible to the audience, and yet the poignant
theme also needed to be heard and recognized, without its sentimentality
overwhelming the actor's gradual realization of this shocking reversal of fate.

Perhaps it is unreasonable to expect that audiences would have made
a connection between the music under this speech and its earlier appearance,
in Lucien's revelation of financial failure to his friend. After all, the best
melodramatic music worked below the conscious radar, so to speak. But a first-
class 'melodramatic manager' like Tree understood the cumulative intensity of
delaying music throughout a tense scene, even in places where melodramatic
traditions might require music to be employed; for example, at Lucien's sensational admission of destroying evidence, or for the emotional testimony of his
young daughter as an eyewitness. Music's absence during these psychologically
charged sequences meant that when it finally *did* enter, it was much more
powerful. Tree, and the best melodramatic managers, knew that too much
affective music could lull audiences into complacency. Yet, used sparingly, as
during Lucien's reading of the letter, music – 'even melodramatic music' – could
serve to emotionalize and humanize a character caught in the web of deception.

Countless instances abound throughout the nineteenth century to show
that the system of scaling down the melodramatic music was mishandled,
with sometimes the same three or four *andantes* and *hurries* recycled end-
lessly throughout the play. But in the best theatres, and under the experienced
eye of skilled actor-managers, the evidence is indisputable that melodramatic
music was carefully placed, timed, rehearsed, and executed.

In the case of certain subgenres of melodrama, however, melodramatic
practice could indeed allow for a genuine full-blown musical accompaniment. For heavy dialogue dramas like A Man's Shadow, Tree built tension with very little music. Yet the orchestra barely paused during his and
Sydney Grundy's version of Dumas's Three Musketeers (1898). Action
melodramas or swashbucklers traditionally required almost constant

music, as can be seen in Charles Fechter's *The Duke's Motto* (1863). Surviving parts to this costume melodrama, set in the late seventeenth century, contain seventy-three music cues.[14] Some of these expanded the 'combination of dialogue and action' type, mentioned above, to shape entire scenes – like the infant kidnapping in the prologue – that were acted out to music in a continuous underscore. Similarly, Henry Leslie and Nicholas Rowe's *The Orange Girl* (1864) and Edmund Falconer's *Eileen Oge* (1871) both used uninterrupted music to engage the audience emotionally in the progress of an attempted murder.[15] Such through-composed climactic episodes or sensation scenes resemble sound film scores of the 1930s and '40s, rather than the piecemeal numbers we are led to expect from a music plot like that for *The Serf*.

In short, there was indeed in nineteenth-century English-language melo-drama a common musical practice, within which ambitious actors, man-agers, and orchestra leaders often strove to make the form more dramatically compelling, using affective music to a greater or lesser degree in accordance with the melodramatic subgenre. The parallels, in the range of actual prac-tice, between the nineteenth-century stage and the use of music in twentieth-century cinema – especially sound film – are unmistakable.

## Notes

1. J. C. Greene, *Theatre in Dublin, 1745–1820: A Calendar of Performances*, vol. 6 (Bethlehem, PA: Lehigh Books, 2011), 4016.
2. 'Music of Burlesques, Operas, and Dramas to Loan', from *A Catalogue of Plays and Dramatic Works Especially Adapted for Amateurs* (London and New York: Samuel French, n.d. [ca. 1860s]), 22–3.
3. *New York Clipper* (9 July 1864): 103.
4. *The Theatrical Observer* (30 October 1844): 349.
5. See F. Wallerstein, 'Music at the Play', *Era*, 2011 (8 April 1877).
6. Lord Chamberlain Manuscripts at the British Library, Add. Ms. 42978. Now available in the series 'British Theatre, Music, and Literature: High and Popular Culture', in *Nineteenth Century Collections Online*.
7. *The Spectator* (29 August 1835): 10.
8. R(ichard) J(ohn) Raymond, *The Old Oak Tree* (London: J. Duncombe, 1835), title page.
9. *The Spectator* (29 August 1835): 10.
10. An incomplete set of parts for Michael Connelly's music to *The Lights 'o London* from the original production can be found in the George R. Sims Collection at the Rylands Library, University of Manchester.
11. 'What the Pit Says. A Man's Shadow at the Haymarket', *Time*, 2 (1889): 423–6.
12. This discussion is based on Carl Armbruster's 1889 Haymarket parts along with Raymond Roze's revisions for the 1897 revival at Her Majesty's Theatre.

The parts reside in the Sir Herbert Beerbohm Tree Music Collection at the Boston Public Library.

13. The spoken text and stage directions are from the unpublished typescript promptbook to *A Man's Shadow* in the Theatre Collection, University of Bristol.

14. William Montgomery's music to *The Duke's Motto*, as adapted for Lawrence Barrett's American touring productions, is at the Houghton Library, Harvard University, with copies in both the Lawrence Barrett Collection as well as the Boston Theatre Collection of Music Manuscripts.

15. Anonymously composed music to *The Orange Girl*, originally written for the Surrey Theatre, now forms part of the Drury Lane Theatre Collection, British Library. W. C. Levey's orchestra parts for *Eileen Oge* are in the Boston Theatre Collection of Music Manuscripts, Houghton Library, Harvard University.

# 8

## GEORGE TAYLOR

# Melodramatic Acting

For decades, British melodrama was disparaged as self-indulgent spectacle with shallow characterization and clichéd situations, but in 1967, Hugh Hunt's Abbey Theatre production of Boucicault's *The Shaughraun* (1874) marked a critical reassessment. Professor Hunt had seen Stephen Joseph's 1965 student production at Manchester University. Joseph was inspired by Eric Bentley's *Life of the Drama,* which had been published the previous year and which described melodrama as 'the quintessence' of Aristotle's catharsis through pity and terror. However, because its resolutions were generally unrealistic – a last-minute rescue, revelation, or repentance – Bentley characterized the genre as childish: 'Melodrama . . . is not mature. It is imaginative but it is not intelligent.'[1]

Peter Brooks, whose 1976 *The Melodramatic Imagination* defined melodrama as a Manichaean struggle between good and evil, subsequently claimed that it 'constantly reminds us of the psychoanalytic concept of "acting out": the use of the body itself, its actions, gestures . . . to represent meanings that . . . are somehow under the bar of repression'.[2] While Bentley described melodrama's extravagant feelings as dreamlike or neurotic, Brooks likened it to 'Freud's structure of pathogenetic trauma . . . a drama of pure psychic signs – called Father, Daughter, Protector, Persecutor, Judge, Duty, Obedience, Justice', and suggested that, as it lacked ambiguity, melodrama must 'be pursued on the plane of expression and representation. We must attend to melodramatic rhetoric'.[3]

Recent commentators have chosen to interpret that rhetoric as one of metaphor, by which the plays reflect – consciously or unconsciously – sociopolitical issues like class conflict, imperialism, and gender identity. However, nineteenth-century critics concentrated on the *emotional* impact of narrative, spectacle, and, above all, expressive acting.[4] Thus, to appreciate the original performance conventions, the psychological structure of melodrama may be more usefully studied than the politics of the plays.

When performing the archetypes of hero, villain, or victim, actors tended towards stereotypical representation rather than individualized characterization. They had been specifically employed to embody the 'stock characters' of the company: first and second leads, heavy character, low comedian, soubrette, walking lady or gentleman. The dramatic functions of their roles were distinguished by immediately legible emblems as formulaic as the black and white hats of classic Westerns. The hero was tall and fair, the villain dark and swarthy, the heroine fragile and lachrymose, the adventuress voluptuous and red-haired. Despite employing a limited range of emblems to personify their characters, the actors' expression of elemental emotions had to be explicit, intense, and infectious. If, as Bentley argued, Naturalism's authenticity of context and ambiguity of motivation brought 'maturity' to the drama of the later nineteenth century, it also brought a retreat from the explicit nature of melodramatic acting.

Edward Gordon Craig, in an appreciation of his mentor Henry Irving, complained that actors in drawing-room drama masked everything with 'realistic' reticence:

> The villain of the play comes on to the stage smiling: he is quite alone; and though he remains alone for five minutes, he does not tell us that he is 'the villain' – has not dared to let any tell-tale look escape him; he has failed to explain anything to us. It is called realism – it is no such thing: it is mere incompetence – an incapacity to understand that *everything* has to be clearly explained to the spectators, and little or no thought paid to whether the other characters on the stage over-hear or see.[5]

In the 1890s, Craig had played in *The Bells* as a customer at the inn, not overhearing or seeing that anything was amiss with the landlord, Mathias, as he remembers the approaching sleigh bells of the victim he murdered years before. Craig described this moment in great detail. It started with the 'realistic' business of buckling his shoes, but then

> His two long hands stretched down over the buckles. We suddenly saw these fingers stop their work ... the hands, still motionless and dead, were seen to be coming up the side of the leg ... the whole torso was gradually, and by an almost imperceptible movement, drawing up and back ... Puzzled, motionless ... he glides up to a standing position ... with one arm slightly raised, with sensitive hand speaking of far-off apprehended sounds ... 'Don't you – don't you hear the sound of sledge-bells on the road?' ... Suddenly he staggers and shivers from his toes to his neck; his jaws begin to chatter; the hair on his forehead, falling over, writhes as though it were a nest of little snakes.[6]

Thus Craig explains how, although Irving used unusual and original means to convey emotion, he was fulfilling the actor's task of telling us everything – even though by the final curtain no other characters suspected Mathias's guilty secret. In a melodrama like *The Bells*, the audience needed to recognize the inner feelings of the character, and for this the actor employed all 'the symbols of his art'.

George Henry Lewes coined this phrase, describing Charles Macready twenty years before *The Bells*. Macready studied his role minutely and emotionally identified with the character, but then

> sought by the means of *the symbols of his art* to express what the character felt; he did not stand outside his character and try to express its emotions by the symbols which had been employed for other characters by other actors.[7]

Macready and Irving were artists at the head of their profession, performing the classics or plays specially written for them. No wonder their 'symbols', or emblems, were original as well as communicative. No wonder, either, that most actors playing stock melodramas tended to employ the 'stock' symbols – appearances, gestures, business, and tones of voice – of their stock emotions. But where did these symbolic conventions originate, and what precisely did they convey?

In *Realizations* (1983) Martin Meisel demonstrates that nineteenth-century drama was directly related to visual art and illustrations from journals and novels. As well as specific pictures being 'realized' in scenic tableaux, he also suggests that visual conventions were unconsciously adopted on stage 'in the iconography of character':

> External marks – such as a man's fur collar and cigar or a woman's full bosom – came to signal not merely moral qualities, but predictable functions of plot and situation. In the iconography of emotion, interior experience was conveyed through a conventionalized language of facial expression, pose, and gesture, sometimes remote from the gestures of contemporary life.[8]

Such visual perception and representation had become increasingly significant since the mid-eighteenth century. Meisel cites the theatricality of Hogarth's genre paintings and his portraits of David Garrick, quoting the painter's remark that a foreigner ignorant of spoken language could understand a play from 'the lines of the movements belonging to each character'.[9] This reflection was to become a cliché of nineteenth-century acting manuals: 'for gesture should be to the deaf what speech is to the blind'.[10] In eighteenth-century France, the genre paintings of Greuze and the dramas of Diderot, a great theorist of acting, provided mutual inspiration. French performers were much influenced by the physically expressive Commedia dell'Arte, as performed in Paris from the mid-seventeenth century at the Comédie Italienne. Because, until the 1789 Revolution, spoken drama was the restricted privilege of the Royal Theatres, the visual conventions of the Commedia were adopted by performers in the popular mime and musical theatre of the fairs and boulevards.[11] The *ballets d'action* created by Jean-Georges Noverre for the Opéra similarly incorporated pictorial references: stage pictures were frozen in tableau; a dancer held a moment of stillness in a sculptural attitude.

However, the importance of visual stimulus went further than such pictorial moments. Emotions themselves, as defined by Descartes in 1649 as the 'Passions of the Soul', and illustrated in taxonomies of expression by Lebrun and Dubos, were explained as physical reflexes responding to sensory perception.[12] This physiological relationship between stimulus and response was central to David Garrick's transformation of acting techniques in the later eighteenth century. Joseph Roach's *The Player's Passion* (1985) examines how the philosophy, science, and psychology of an age affected the ways in which actors chose to express themselves. Many of these concepts have passed into the language, but without their original literal meanings: 'vital spark', 'melancholy humour', 'ruling passion', 'magnetic personality', 'instinctive reaction', 'unconscious motivation'. All these phrases, when first coined, related to specific philosophical or scientific theories. Roach's insight was that 'the central issues of psychology and physiology, by whatever names they are known, are not remote abstractions to the performer, but literally matters of flesh and blood'.[13]

In reference to the eighteenth century, having cited the physical expressiveness of the castrati opera singer Nicolini, who, like Noverre's dancers, adopted statuesque poses and attitudes, Roach argues that the key gesture of Garrick's performances was the 'start' – the instantaneous reaction to a momentary perception – as in Hogarth's picture of Richard III awaking in terror, or Hamlet seeing his father's ghost. For Roach, Garrick's starts demonstrated precisely Descartes's 'animal spirits' circulating along the nerves, as in a kind of hydraulic system – pressure at one point causing an automatic reaction in another, and the more shocking the perception the more violent the nervous/physical response[14]:

> Garrick turns sharply and at the same moment staggers back two or three paces with his knees giving way under him; his hat falls to the ground and both arms, especially the left, are stretched out nearly to full length with the hands as high as the head, the right arm more bent and the hand lower, and the fingers apart; his mouth open: thus he stands rooted to the spot, with legs apart, but no loss of dignity.[15]

This technique of starting was common far into the nineteenth century: the sudden reaction to an object of terror or of salvation – 'Horror! What form is this?'; or, 'Hark – the torrent is rushing down on us. See! See! Assistance is at hand!' – followed by a moment of stillness held in an attitude of emotional expression: '*The group stand amazed. Music.*'[16] It was the technique of Edmund Kean in the classics, and of T. P. Cooke in nautical drama. Their stance – knees bent, arms raised to greet or to deflect – is not only that of Garrick's Hamlet but of the two-dimensional printed figures of the juvenile drama, like a fencer ready to thrust or parry, or a tennis player awaiting a serve. Roach relates these mechanical reactions to Julian de la Mettrie's Cartesian *L'homme machine* (1747), and to hydraulic and musical automata.[17]

From the mid-eighteenth century – the period when the melodrama was invented – there was a flush of books and essays analyzing the art of acting, both theoretical and practical: in France, Sainte-Albine's *Le Comédien* (1749), and Diderot's *Entretiens sur Le fils naturel* (1757) and *Rameau's Nephew* (1761–2; revised 1773–4)[18]; in Germany, Lessing's *Hamburgische Dramaturgie* (1769), and J. J. Engel's *Ideen zu einer Mimik* (1786); in Italy, Gaspare Angiolini's *Letter to Monsieur Noverre* (1773); and in England, Aaron Hill's *Essay on Acting* (1753), John Hill's *The Actor* (1755), John Walker's *Elements of Elocution* (1781), and Henry Siddon's translation of Engel, *Practical Illustrations of Rhetorical Gesture and Action* (1822). These works provided detailed descriptions of how individual passions should be portrayed: some authors claiming these were natural expressions, others acknowledging models drawn from the visual arts. Several repeated earlier examples verbatim, as in William Scott's *Lessons in Elocution* (1814), which reproduces Aaron Hill's descriptions written sixty years before:

> *Grief,* sudden and violent, expresses itself by beating the head; grovelling on the ground, tearing of garments, hair and flesh; screaming aloud, weeping, stamping with the feet ...
>
> *Melancholy,* or fixed grief, is gloomy, sedentary, motionless. The lower jaw falls, the lips pale, the eyes are cast down, half shut, eyelids swelled and red or livid, tears trickling silent and unwiped ...
>
> *Fear,* violent and sudden, opens very wide the eyes and mouth; shortens the nose; draws down the eyebrows; gives the countenance an air of wildness; covers it with a deadly paleness; draws back the elbows parallel with the sides; lifts up the open hands, the fingers together, to the height of the breast, so that the palms face the dreadful object, as shields opposed against it. One foot is drawn back behind the other, so that the body seems shrinking from the danger, and putting itself in a posture for flight.[19]

Similar descriptions reappear more than sixty years later in *The Actor's Art* (1888) by Gustave Garcia, who taught acting at the Royal Academy and

Guildhall School of Music into the twentieth century. Although he provides more explanation of *why* we feel the emotions, they are still considered as specific passions and their expression is just as extreme:

> *Fear,* This sentiment is the result of a shock received by our nervous system, caused by the consciousness of danger. It affects our mental faculties to such a degree that we lose all control over ourselves; our countenance, our actions and attitudes, all combine in reflecting the disordered state of our mind . . . we tremble from head to foot, our breathing becomes spasmodic, our hearts beat rapidly.[20]

The late eighteenth century saw several new scientific – or pseudo-scientific – theories concerning the expression of emotions, based on Cartesian passions. Johann Casper Lavater (1778) expounded the theory of physiognomy: that facial expressions reveal both underlying personality and temporary emotion. He wrote that 'Virtue makes beauty; vice makes ugliness.'[21] His work was translated as *Essays on Physiognomy* (1789) by Thomas Holcroft, who was to bring Pixérécourt's melodrama to the English stage. Franz Joseph Gall proposed a correspondence between physical appearance and moral character in his theory of phrenology, arguing that as character and mental faculties are products of the brain and that the shape of the brain determines that of the skull, so character can be read in the bumps of the head. His theory was popularized in England by Scottish physician George Combe's *The Constitution of Man* (1828), and can be recognized in many of Dickens's character descriptions. The correspondence between appearance and moral standing was not just a literary conceit, but fundamental to the psychological science of the nineteenth century. It was also an essential aspect of Victorian social class attitudes, based on exclusivity and respectability: not only that behaviour, dress, and speech should be 'proper to one's station', but also that the white middle class display a racial and cultural superiority over their Jewish, Irish, and black counterparts. These 'us and them' stereotypes seemed to the Victorians to be validated by a scientific correspondence. The stereotypes and their associations – Irish = stupid; poverty = lazy; vulgarity = immorality; ignorance = viciousness – seem clearly prejudicial to us today. However, it was not just the upper class looking down on the lower, but also a reverse prejudice against snobs, swells, and all who 'behaved above their station'.

The theory of scientific correspondences contributed to Sir Charles Bell's *Anatomy and Expression, as connected with the Fine Arts* (1804), which brought science and aesthetics together under the principle that 'the muscles are the soul in action'. Noting how the eyes roll upwards in sleep, death, and trace-like ecstasy, he argued,

> Although we are taught ... that the Almighty is everywhere, yet, under the influence of this position of the eye, we seek Him on high ... See, then how this property of our bodily frame has influenced our opinions and belief; our conceptions of the Deity – our religious observances – our poetry and our daily habits ... It is curious that our expression appears to *precede* the intellectual operation ... the expression is in fact the spontaneous operation and classification of the muscles which await the development of the faculties to accompany them.[22]

In this, Bell is revising Descartes's process of perception/feeling/reaction and anticipating the celebrated proposal of William James in 1890 that 'the bodily changes follow *directly* the perception of the exciting fact, and our feeling of the same changes as they occur *is* the emotion'.[23] Mel Gordon has found it 'surprising' that James 'shied away from any formalized theory or system, believing that while certain patterns of muscular activity elicited certain emotional states, each of these states varied with the individual body, and were, therefore, infinite and unclassifiable'.[24] There was no such resistance to systematization in the period of Enlightenment: indeed, from Descartes to Darwin philosophers and scientists, not to mention acting instructors, all sought to propound 'universal truths'.

Given this scientific recognition of a correspondence between appearance and character, action and emotion, it is not surprising that actors adopted a highly physical style of performance. They may not have studied the physiology of nervous reactions, but were well aware of 'starts' and 'transitions' – the sudden recognition or the gradual realization – and of 'held attitudes' representing intense feelings. As Robert Elliston advised the provincial actress he was performing with:

> When he leaves you, do you, even after your father comes on, remain for a moment or two fixed, as a statue representing *horror*, then recovering shriek out '*He* was here – *he!*' ... after this, pause an instant – '*No, no, my eyes deceive me*' – quick – half belief, half doubt – I am deceived if you don't make a great line of this.[25]

Not only should the actress represent the heightened emotion in a static attitude, but she should also signal her confused thought process: 'half belief, half doubt'. And by making a 'great line' of it, she will have made what actors referred to as a 'point', a telling effect that would strike the audience with such power that they reward it with a round of applause.

Actors felt there was nothing shameful in setting up such a 'clap-trap'. It was part of their task, for not only should they impersonate intense feeling extravagantly, but they had to make spectators share their feelings of shock, horror, and fear. This process was at the heart of Diderot's as yet unpublished *Paradox*: in order to move the audience, the actor should remain unmoved.

He has rehearsed every note of his passion. He has learnt before a mirror every particle of his despair . . . You will see him weep at the word, at the syllable, he has chosen, not a second sooner or later. The broken voice, the half-uttered words . . . the trembling limbs, the fainting, the bursts of fury – all this is pure mimicry.[26]

He was describing the art of the finest French tragedians and referring to his observation of David Garrick in Paris. Jobbing actors playing a swiftly changing repertory of stock melodramas would certainly welcome such plainly mechanistic instructions. Their score of physical and verbal effects was determined by what theatrical experience, and their observations of other actors, had taught them would 'tell'.

Communicating to an audience the emotions of the moment was the essence of melodrama. Actors were not concerned with nuances of social behaviour, nor with the subtleties of unconscious motivation. Their virtuosity was to play each moment to the full, identifying the character by the emotions they felt in that moment. It was this principle that the Realists rejected. In antithesis to the reification of identity and of the moment, the naturalistic dramatists were vitally concerned with change and transformation.[27] Spectators could not judge how well actors had performed such parts until the curtain fell.

In musical performance, a virtuoso can thrill an audience with attack, phrasing, and tone, while not necessarily communicating the intellectual structure of a sonata as a whole. So, just as sophisticated concertgoers do not applaud after each movement of a symphony, spectators of Ibsen or Chekhov await the full unfolding of an interpretation before reaching a critical appreciation. In contrast, each phrase, speech or attitude of the melodrama actor prompted applause, for it was the experience of the moment that thrilled rather than the intellectual coherence of the whole.

Although the art of such performance has been lost to our literary theatre, it may still be found in music theatre. Indeed, several stage melodramas survive as opera libretti. From its origins, and of its nature, melodrama exploited the emotional immediacy of music. Early *melodrames* such as Rousseau's *Pygmalion* (1770), Georg Benda's *Ariadne auf Naxos* (1775), J. F. von Goez's *Lenardo und Blandine* (1779), and G. M. Lewis's *The Captive* (CG. 1803) alternated speech and music, the performers holding their expressive attitudes during the musical passages.[28] Later plays adopted the practice of speaking over music when the rhythm, tone, and intensity was influenced by the accompaniment. Charles Reade described how music director Edwin Ellis used

to watch the stage with one eye and the orchestra with another, and so accompany with vigilant delicacy a mixed scene of action and dialogue; to do which the music must be full when the actor works in silence, but subdued promptly as often as the actor speaks . . . he did not habitually run to the poor resource of a 'hurry' or a nonsense 'tremolo', but loved to find an appropriate melody, or a rational sequence of chords, or a motivated strain, that raised the scene or enforced the dialogue.[29]

Frederick Corder observed, when discussing musical recitation – an art form in its own right, in concert hall or drawing room:

The higher tones of the voice require to be constantly employed, especially in the case of a male reciter; the lower inflections grating too harshly against the musical notes. Yet there must be no suggestion of 'chanting' or 'sing-song', but only great clearness and purity of utterance – never any colloquial or ordinary quality except when the music ceases.[30]

Given this interaction of music and drama, it is not surprising that perhaps the best guide to melodrama acting is opera coach and philosopher François Delsarte, who died shortly after the Commune in Paris in 1872: the same year that Darwin published *The Expression of Emotion in Man & in Animals,* the century's most thorough scientific analysis of the subject. Unfortunately, although Delsarte is said to have taught several famous actors and singers, none recorded working with him and he never published his theories. We must rely mainly on elaborations of his system by American disciples as 'Delsartism', a particular form of physical and spiritual self-improvement.[31]

Delsarte himself rejected the mind/body dualism of Descartes for a triad of mind, body, and soul, attributing his theory to Swedenborg's Law of Correspondence: 'The human body, with all its parts and functions, is elaborated from the Soul, its faculties and powers; and therefore corresponds to it in every particular of structure, form and use.'[32] He proposed *correspondences* between separate parts of the body and the three interior activities: the vital, mental, and moral. The limbs are the agents of vital forces, the head the seat of mental activity, and the torso experiences the emotions of spiritual/moral excitation. Each of these 'zones' was further subdivided: the nose and mask react to physical perceptions, the mouth communicates ideas, and the eyes are the 'windows of the soul'; arms perform vital tasks, hand gestures illustrate intellectual argument, and the shoulders respond with tension or relaxation to emotional intensity; the gut contracts in physical pain, the chest expands with intellectual pride, and the heart responds to emotions of desire or revulsion. Delsarte applied this analysis to the physical expressivity of stance and gesture, and this, I suggest, helps explain certain theatrical clichés: gestures to the brow, to the heart or to the gut; wringing hands, hunching shoulders, quaking knees, and slapping the thigh.

In addition to these correspondences, Delsarte propounded Laws of Motion, each having particular expressive qualities: strength and velocity could be tentative or intense, with an extension beyond the hand – towards the beloved or feared, or even to heaven. He analyzed a stance, or the direction of a gesture, as being outward and open (eccentric), inward and secret (concentric) or poised (normal). The opposition or interplay between these qualities could express contradictory emotions or motives – deception or hypocrisy in a villain, moral misgivings in a lover, or comical timidity in a braggart. Rhythm and motion could convey transitory moods and thoughts flitting through the mind, betraying themselves in furtive glance, trembling hand, or awkward stiffness.

These were all techniques that could signal to the audience whilst being ignored by the others on the stage, like the drinkers in Mathias's inn. In plays cruder than *The Bells*, the villain could contrast his suave approach to the innocent victim with a leer to the audience, or even an aside: 'Little does she know!' The low comedian bravely confronting the wicked squire might turn out front with an expression of panic, the persecuted heroine direct her appeal to heaven towards the gallery, and the resolute hero declare his patriotic sentiments to the stalls. Thus a mastery of the 'qualities' defined by Delsarte could communicate complex and contradictory feeling, thoughts and attitudes through a skilful combination of stance, gesture, facial expression, and vocal intonation – some addressed to other players on the stage, and some directed to the audience. American actor and director Steele Mackaye was probably the most theatrically influential of Delsarte's disciples; as Edwin Forrest declared, 'In fifteen minutes [Mackaye] has given me a deeper insight into the philosophy of my own art than I myself had learnt in fifty years of study.'[33]

Of course, melodrama was not a static genre, and performance techniques changed over time, with different styles of theatre design and dramatic writing.[34] Large gestures that worked before painted backcloths were excessive in a box-set filled with furniture, as introduced by Madam Vestris at the Olympic in the 1830s,[35] thus telling 'business' replaced purely physical expression. Tom Robertson wrote with reference to his comedy *Caste* (1867), 'It seems a simple thing for a young lady to hand a young gentleman a cup of tea, but all depends on the manner.'[36] But even when business replaced gesticulation it was often just a greater originality in choosing the 'symbols of their art', as Lewes had called them. The 'gentlemanly' melodramas of the mid-nineteenth century were still primarily concerned with communicating the emotion of the characters so as to stir the emotion of the audience, though the acting technique was apparently more restrained, as in Lewes's account of Charles Kean in Boucicault's *The Corsican Brothers* (1852):

[He] plays the two brothers; and you must see him before you will believe how well and *quietly* he plays them; preserving a gentlemanly demeanour, a drawing-groom manner very difficult to assume on the stage, if one may judge from its rarity, which intensifies the passion of the part, and gives it a terrible reality ... the Bois de Boulogne itself has scarcely seen a duel more real and more exciting. Kean's dogged, quiet, terrible walk after Wigan, with the fragment of broken sword in his relentless grasp, I shall never forget.[37]

Boucicault also refined some of the stereotypes of earlier melodrama. His villains were more genteel in their manners, though their villainy was always immediately apparent, and his Irishmen were more nuanced than the Teagues and Paddies that dated back to the Restoration. The amiable rogues he wrote for himself to play (Myles-na-Coppaleen in *The Colleen Bawn* [1860], Shaun in *Arrah-na-Pogue* [1864] and Conn in *The Shaughraun* [1875]) combined wit, craft, and generosity, and his heroines had a robust intelligence seldom found in traditional lachrymose victims. Nevertheless, there is no doubting that his plays were still melodramas, and their perfor-mers fulfilled the genre's requirement of expressive clarity, though with a more restrained technique.

This shift in style could be attributed to the greater detail and accuracy of the plays' settings – the drawing-rooms Lewes refers to, the teacups of Robertsonian comedy, the antiquarianism of period plays – which led to a more painterly composition of stage pictures.[38] However, in the 'sensation scenes' of the Adelphi or Drury Lane under Augustus Harris, extravagance was still needed to compete with fires, floods, and train crashes. In neo-Gothic psychological dramas of the 1890s the 'super-natural' star, Henry Irving or Beerbohm Tree, could 'indulge in over-acting', while the supporting cast played in a more restrained style.

Yet the principle of communicating emotionally with the audience remained central to performance, as Craig vividly described at Irving's first entrance in *The Bells* (1871):

The hurricane of applause ... was no interruption. [It was] part and parcel of the whole, as right as rain. It was a torrent while it lasted. Power responded to power ... though Irving endured and did not accept the applause, he deliber-ately called it out of the spectators. It was necessary *to them* – not to him; it was something they had to experience ... or rather [be] released from.[39]

Simon Shepherd compares a moment of television melodrama from John Thaw acting Inspector Morse (1992) with a 'pause of mutual agitation' by Eugenia in William Dimond's *The Foundling of the Forest* (1809). When confronted by the man who once tried to kill her, but has now repented, she holds a motionless attitude, while he kneels before her. When Morse learns that a woman he once loved is involved in his current investigation he turns his head away, looking into the distance. In both instances the action freezes on a gesture:

> The fact that Morse's neck muscles have instant meaning shows how well learnt is the cultural message for which Eugenia's body was developing the vocabulary ... the acting of early melodrama required the body to be able to show not so much transparent emotional expressivity as the processes of coming to knowledge, of recognition and realisation.[40]

In other words, the 'start' does not have to be as violent as those of Garrick, Kean or Irving, but it needs to communicate to the audience a character's inner process. It is an exercise in physical semiology, with a transmitter and a receiver. The decline of melodramatic acting was not caused by Naturalistic dramas as such, but by the implicit convention that actors in these plays are *apparently* unaware of the audience's presence. In 1881, Andre Antoine saw actors turn their backs on the audience in a Saxe-Meiningen production, and he introduced the practice when producing the drama of Zola at le Théâtre Libre. This in turn inspired Strindberg to suggest in the preface to *Miss Julie* (1888) that turning away from the 'fourth wall' of the proscenium gave the impression of watching real life.[41] Stanislavski's actors improvised études, re-enacting their own experiences to 'bring life' to the characters of Chekhov, and developed 'circles of attention' to achieve 'public solitude' – performing as if the audience was not watching them at all. It was part of Stanislavski's conscious policy of removing all 'mechanical clichés' from acting.[42] And, of course, by 'cliché' he meant all the codified expressions that Lewes had called 'the symbols of the actor's art': the essential language in which melodrama had been acted for over a century.

## Notes

1. Eric Bentley, *The Life of the Drama* (New York: Atheneum, 1964), 215.
2. Peter Brooks, 'Melodrama, Body, Revolution', in *Melodrama: Stage, Picture, Screen*, eds. Jacky Bratton, Jim Cook, and Christine Gledhill (London: BFI Publishing, 1994), 19.
3. Peter Brooks, *The Melodramatic Imagination: Balzac, Henry James, Melodrama, and the Mode of Excess* (New Haven: Yale University Press, 1976), 35–6.
4. Even the champions of 'new drama', Archer and Shaw, focused their criticism on the acting as much as on the message of the drama.
5. E. G. Craig, *Henry Irving* (London: Dent, 1930), 61.
6. Ibid., 58–60.
7. G. H. Lewes, *On Actors and the Art of Acting* (London: Smith, Elder, & Co., 1875), 43.

8. Martin Meisel, *Realizations: Narrative, Pictorial, and Theatrical Arts in Nineteenth-Century England* (Princeton: Princeton University Press, 1983), 5.
9. William Hogarth, *The Analysis of Beauty: Written with a View of Fixing the Fluctuating Ideas of Taste* (London: John Reeves, 1753), 161.
10. Henry Neville, 'Gesture', in *Voice, Speech and Gesture: a Practical Handbook to the Elocutionary Art* (London: C. W. Deacon & Co., 1897), 111. See also Ben Brewster and Lea Jacobs, 'Pictorial Acting in the Theatre', in *Theatre to Cinema: Stage Pictorialism and the Early Feature Film* (Oxford: Oxford University Press, 1997), 85–98.
11. Michèle Root-Bernstein, *Boulevard Theatre and Revolution in Eighteenth-Century Paris* (Ann Arbor: Michigan University Press, 1984), 94–105.
12. Charles Le Brun, *Méthode pour apprendre à dessiner les passions* (Amsterdam: 1698) (translated into English in 1734); Jean-Baptiste Dubos, *Réflexions critiques sur la poésie et sur la peinture* (Paris: 1719) (translated into English in 1758).
13. Joseph Roach, *The Player's Passion: Studies in the Science of Acting* (Cranbury and New York: Associated University Presses, 1985), 16.
14. Ibid., 58; for Descartes's theory of 'animal spirits', see 62–6.
15. Georg Christoph Lichtenberg, *Visit to England as Described in his Letters and Diaries*, trans. Margaret L. Mare and W. H. Quarrel (Oxford: Clarendon Press, 1938), 10.
16. Matthew Lewis, *The Castle Spectre* (London: 1798), Act 3 scene 2; Edward Fitzball, *The Flying Dutchman; or The Phantom Ship* (London: 1827), Act 3 scene 4; Issac Pocock, *The Miller and his Men* (London: 1813), Act 2 scene 1.
17. Roach, *The Player's Passion*, 60.
18. Diderot's essay, *Le paradox sur le comédien* (1773) was not translated into English until 1883: see William Archer, *Masks or Faces? A Study in the Psychology of Acting* (Longmans: London, 1888).
19. William Scott, *Lessons in Elocution* (London: 1814), 32–3. The description of 'Fear' reproduces almost exactly Garrick's start.
20. Gustave Garcia, *The Actor's Art: A Practical Treatise on Stage Declamation, Public Speaking and Deportment, for the Use of Artists, Students and Amateurs*, second edition (London: Simpkin, Marshall & Co, 1888), 160–1.
21. Johann Caspar Lavater, *Essays on Physiognomy: Designed to Promote the Knowledge and the Love of Mankind*, trans. Thomas Holcroft (London: Robinson, 1789), 57.
22. Charles Bell, *The Anatomy and Philosophy of Expression, as Connected with the Fine Arts*, third edition (London: 1844), 190–8.
23. William James, *The Principles of Psychology*, 2 vols. (London: 1890).
24. Mel Gordon, 'Meyerhold's Biomechanics', in *Acting (Re)Considered*, ed. Phillip B. Zarrilli (London: Routlege, 1995), 89.
25. Elliston correspondence, 22 May 18[29], Harvard Theatre Collection, *Autographs*, I, A-F.
26. Denis Diderot, *The Paradox of Acting*, trans. W. H. Pollock, in *The Paradox of Acting & Masks or Faces?: Two Classics of the Art of Acting* (New York: Hill and Wang, 1957), 19.
27. See George Taylor, 'François Delsarte: A Codification of Nineteenth-Century Acting', *Theatre Research International*, 24 (1999): 79.

28. Thomas Betzwieser, 'Gesture, Composition and Performance in Eighteenth-Century German Melodrama', in *The Melodramatic Moment*, eds. Jonathan Hicks and Katherine Hambridge (Chicago: University of Chicago).

29. Charles Reade, 'A Dramatic Musician', *The Era*, rpt. in *Readiana* (London: 1880), 29.

30. Frederick Corder, 'Recitation with Music', in *Voice, Speech and Gesture*, ed. R. D. Blackman, new edition (London: Deacon and Co, 1897), 214.

31. Nancy Lee Chalfa Ruyter, *The Cultivation of Body and Mind in Nineteenth-Century American Delsartism* (Westport: Greenwood Press, 1999); Genevieve Stebbins, *The Delsarte System of Expression* (New York: E. S. Warner, 1885); Carrie J. Preston, *Modernism's Mythic Pose: Gender, Genre, Solo Performance* (Oxford: Oxford University Press, 2011), 60, lists Macready, Rachel, and Jenny Lind as pupils.

32. Moses True Brown, *The Synthetic Philosophy of Expression, as applied to the Arts of Reasoning, Oratory, and Personation* (Boston and New York: Houghton Mifflin, 1886), 50.

33. Percy Mackaye, *Epoch, the Life of Steele Mackaye* (New York: Boni & Liveright, 1927), 149; for D. W. Griffith's film actors trained in 'Delsarte', see Preston, *Modernism's Mythic Pose*, 87–90.

34. See George Taylor, *Players and Performances in the Victorian Theatre* (Manchester: Manchester University Press, 1989), chapters 7 and 9.

35. William Worthen Appleton, *Madame Vestris and the London Stage* (New York: Columbia University Press, 1974).

36. Maynard Savin, *Thomas William Robertson, His Plays and Stagecraft* (Providence: Brown University Press, 1950), 86.

37. G. H. Lewes, *The Leader* (28 February 1852).

38. Meisel, *Realizations*, 373ff.

39. Craig, *Henry Irving*, 54.

40. Simon Shepherd, 'Pauses of Mutual Agitation', in *Melodrama: Stage, Picture, Screen*, eds. Bratton, Cook, and Gledhill, 26–7.

41. Claude Schumacher, *Naturalism and Symbolism in European Theatre, 1850–1918* (Cambridge: Cambridge University Press, 1996), 80.

42. Konstantin Stanislavski, *An Actor Prepares*, trans. Elizabeth Reynolds Hapgood (New York: Theatre Arts Inc., 1937), 23–4.

# 9

HAYLEY JAYNE BRADLEY

# Stagecraft, Spectacle, and Sensation

> Over the scene, over the scene
> Cast a strong lime-light of blue or of green,
> Over the scene, over the scene,
> Cast a light coloured and strong.
> Thither march, march, march
> Your characters, whether
> Alone or together,
> Let them march, march, march
> To a doom that seems hopelessly wrong.
> Then, on to the scene, on to the scene,
> Bring your hero by some means to make all serene;
> Then sing, ho! For the scene, ho! For the scene,
> That keeps a piece running so long![1]

*Fun*'s take on the sensation scene derisively, albeit humorously, signals the perceived constituents of spectacle: the trajectory of action towards a climactic episode; the emphasis on 'the scene' as the ultimate priority – and, in later verses, the outlay of money and risk of debt in order to create it; the relegation of 'the play', and perceived sacrifice of literary merit and intellect, in favour of 'the scene'; and the capability of 'the scene' to secure a long run, for a sensation drama would succeed if the spectacle were 'sensational, stirring and strong'. These remarks in *Fun* show contemporary discourse around the sensation scene and its place within popular culture as a topic of interest and contemplation.[2]

Striking, impressive, and large-scale, spectacle – a feat of nineteenth-century stagecraft – offered an audience a visual feast and, although Aristotle considered it 'the least artistic' component for drama, in the mid to late 1800s it became an art form unto itself, demonstrating skill and craftsmanship from conceptualization to execution.[3] For Augustus Harris, whose own autumn dramas for Drury Lane would play a defining role in the genre, 'spectacular theatre must be ... the trysting-place of all the arts', combining perseverance, pluck, and cooperation in order to create this 'labour of love'.[4] Not merely the outcome of large expense and little else (as many critics argued), nor the creation of a single brain, spectacle was the 'result of the efforts of an army of workers – talented, trained, and proficient in their respective arts'.[5] As such, the sensation scene was the product of a judicious selection of subject, story-plotting, scenery variations, the even distribution of sequences (action, humour, display), and finally the music. All the while, its creators needed to remain mindful of the need to appeal to 'passing fancy and fashion', as well as the 'educated and refined classes' of the audience, in tandem with 'the more humble and unsophisticated patrons'.[6]

For Michael Booth, spectacle in melodrama functioned to 'imitate social and urban life on a size and scale appropriate to the magnitude of human emotion and the conflict between good and evil at the heart of its being, and to express in striking visual terms the sensationalism inherent in its nature'.[7] More recently, Bernard Beckerman has proposed that while 'spectacle is often realised mainly in visual terms, the visual terms do not alone make the spectacle', concluding that spectacle exists 'between extraordinary actuality and fascinating illusion'.[8] The mimetic quality of spectacle and the drive for realism in presenting modern life on stage, I would argue, combines in the sensation scene with a temporal proximity to reality – specifically focusing on topical issues and disasters – which ultimately sought to effect a physical response in the audience. What Baz Kershaw has described as the 'WOW! Factor' – i.e., 'excessive reactions' – was in part based on spectacles' ability to touch on 'highly sensitive spots in the changing nature of the human psyche by dealing directly with extremities of power: gods, monarchy, regicide, terrorism, catastrophe, apocalypse now'.[9] But also, the capacity of spectacles to bring static illustrations of real scenes to life, often 'founded on a fatal incident', with immediacy and contiguity.[10]

If spectacle was a perfect stage picture, then the sensation scene united the pictorial element with mechanical ingenuity to create a theatrical scene which would excite, thrill, and enthral audiences, and was ultimately designed to 'make the audience sit up and gasp'.[11] Combining melodrama and realism, from the early 1860s through to the 1910s, sensation drama went from an emerging style to a dominant form – continuing as a still popular, residual genre well into the new century. Initially exploding into popularity, sensation dramas thrived and endured; and while many, such as George Moore, George Bernard Shaw, and Max Beerbohm, worried that it would usurp the stage, others – Dion Boucicault and Cecil Raleigh – capitalized on the public demand, constantly striving to outdo their competitors, as well as their own previous efforts, and to continually offer novelty.

More than pleasure in the visual, the sensation scene contained 'something apart from acting which relying on scenic aid' intended to illicit a more complete sensory experience by 'causing that kind of emotion amongst spectators which has become accepted as "Sensation"'.[12] As Amy E. Hughes has observed, 'audiences actively sought the bodily sensations – the thrills and chills' of sensation drama so that, I would argue, rather than merely passively witnessing spectacle, the audience left the theatre 'feeling' they had experienced it.[13]

In March 1882, *The Times* remarked on 'the introduction of a new word into theatrical vocabulary' – the sensation scene, so called because 'the interest of the audience is violently concentrated on one particular scene, which thus stands in strong relief to the rest of the action'.[14] *The Times* attributed this new phrase to Boucicault's recent drama, wherein the 'the famous header' in the water cave was 'so conspicuous an incident' as to warrant the phrase.[15] Premiering in 1861, *The Colleen Bawn*'s sensation scene 'went on from first to last in the midst of an intense and almost painful silence' wherein the 'excitement of the spectators was protracted to the utmost pitch of intensity'.[16]

In order to save his foster brother from ruin, Danny Mann takes Eily O'Connor to a water cave to abandon her to the lake of Killarney. As Eily struggles, Danny is accidentally shot by Myles (who has mistaken him for an otter), tumbles from the rocks into the water, and is washed downstream to crawl home, confess murder to Father Tom (believing Eily dead), and die from his injuries. Meanwhile Myles – searching for the wounded otter – discovers and saves Eily from a watery grave, returning her home in the nick of time to stop her husband, Hardress Corrigan, now believing himself a widower, from marrying Ann Chute. Such was the design of the water cave that audiences 'almost fancied' they were 'looking at real rocks and real water', lending the sensation scene 'all the appearance of reality'.[17] With one play, Boucicault had established the term 'sensation scene', but it was to be a phrase and a genre that would be beloved and decried in almost equal measure.

While Boucicault has been widely acknowledged as the premiere 'sensation playwright', he himself challenged the usage and meaning of the 'sensational'.[18] In a letter to the editor of *The Times* in 1882, Boucicault, while acknowledging his role in bringing the term 'sensation' into use, 'beg[s] pardon for it' as a 'bad word'.[19] In his opinion, the term 'sensation' depreciated the drama by implying that the value of the play relied on 'one trick effect' and that this was the prime feature of the drama, as well as the only stimulus: whereas he is swift to point out that the water cave scene was in fact an 'after-thought'. If, however, 'a drama having sustaining power in its plot and in its development of character is to be called "sensation" because its scenic realisation is made as perfect as possible', then Boucicault credits Charles Kean's 1857 *Macbeth* (for the appearance of Banquo's ghost) and William Macready's 1838 *The Tempest* (for the shipwreck) as earlier examples of sensation scenes.[20]

Boucicault's exchange with *The Times* raises several central issues: firstly, the paradox that those involved in the play wanted the production to be recognized for all its components and not only for the sensation scene; however, by its very nature as 'the symbol of the piece', this scene would invite the greatest discussion. Secondly, it raised the issue of construction, and the concomitant division of sensation dramas into two classes: those in which the sensation scene comes first, and the plot is only a thin thread to enable the sensation scene; and those in which the drama comes first, and the sensation scene is a vital component to its development. Determining the category to which each sensation drama belonged – and, crucially, the relative probability or improbability of the sensation scene – was often the discourse of the press. While both classes could be deemed 'manufactured melodrama', motives and logic separate the two and were often scrutinized in order to distinguish so-called good melodrama from bad. In the case of *The Colleen Bawn*, Danny's reason for taking Eily to the water cave is as clear as the water itself – to drown her and see his family profit from her death (a tenable rationale). Plausible motives such as Danny's, in combination with originality, actuality, and humanity, along with a relevant and credible sensation scene, formed the essential components for 'good' spectacular melodrama (though Max Beerbohm would argue to the contrary). Public demand for such plays induced 'furious competition amongst their concoctors' and the pressure not only to invent but also to innovate, to make imaginative use of scientific and technological advancements in order to deliver utmost realism, resulted in a range of situations, spanning sea, land, and air.[21]

A visual and visceral encounter – ranging from hot air balloons to shipwrecks, horse races to train engines, cave-ins to earthquakes, with heroines, heroes, and villains dangling from mountain precipices, lying across railway lines, and clinging to revolving mill sails – sensation scenes were the dramatic and emotional climax of the drama, both the subject of speculation pre-opening night and the topic of discussion thereafter: the anticipation and suspense began long before the curtain rose. During a time when 'most of those who go to theatre lead humdrum lives . . . [audiences] like to be startled', sensation scenes shocked, surprised, and stunned spectators with their hair-breadth escapes, perilous near misses, feats of engineering (the heroine's rescue was now as much the job of the stage carpenter as it was of the hero), and more particularly, their ability to offer more than illusion – to offer realism.[22] While

*The Era* divided 'sensations' into those mainly appealing to the eye or to the mind, a more subtle, sophisticated spectrum of spectacle is needed in order to acknowledge sensation scenes that appealed to eye *and* mind, as well as affecting bodily sensations. In order to do so, I propose four broad categories for the 'situation' and manner of stagecraft within the sensation scene – courtroom/trial, equine business, nature, and the machine – the latter two of which form my focus in this brief chapter. This is not to say that each category is exclusive: areas of overlap proliferate and, indeed, as the century wore on, most sensation dramas sought to combine these elements and to present multiple spectacles – even one per act, rather than one per play. Nevertheless, these categories are useful as a means of charting how sensation scenes drew from the incidents and anxieties of contemporary life to become full of actualities, using the stage as a mimic world.

While the courtroom/trial scene has been the most documented of the four categories, it also stands apart from the other three in terms of the kind of 'sensation' felt by the audience: even when the character's life (and indeed soul) may be at risk, the trial scene lacks the sense of immediate physical danger of the others. A trial, as in Boucicault's *Janet Pride* (1855) and *The Trial of Effie Deans* (1864), offers the dramatic tension and peril of a sensation scene, and may even incorporate spectacle, as in Leopold Davis Lewis's *The Bells* (1871). But sensation scenes involving nature, the machine, or the horse involve a heightened dynamism, as they pit 'man' in direct physical conflict with these forces – in a contest of power and often a struggle for survival. As with the courtroom situation, however, all sensation scenes serve as a mechanism for justice and plot development.

'Nature' includes natural disasters, as these sensation scenes feature the forces of nature at their most deadly: earthquakes, floods (and all varieties of 'water' scenes), fires, cave-ins, quarries – as in *Peep O'Day* (1862) – and avalanches. More than pictorial representations of these events, the sensation scene sought to recreate them, producing actuality through illusion, using the vivid realism of the scenery and mounting. In 1883, W. G. Wills and Henry Herman's *Claudian* opened at the Lyceum, three years before the theatre would be completely equipped with electricity, and subsequently set the bar for the onstage earthquake. In Act 2, as Claudian's palace crumbled about him, the 'audience remained spell-bound', terror-stricken at the sight of such destruction and awed by a 'realism unequalled in the records of scenic art'.[23] However, the earthquake in *Claudian* took place against a painted backdrop of antiquity, and thus was still far removed, by time and location, from the everyday life of the playgoer – whereas in Paul Merritt and Augustus Harris's *Pleasure* (1887) at Drury Lane, the contemporaneity of the earthquake scene, set on the French Riviera, was all the closer to home.

In the mid to late nineteenth century, an earthquake was a sight that London audiences would likely have seen illustrated in newspapers but not witnessed firsthand; the staged version was as close as they would get to viewing such an event. As Joslin McKinney has noted, 'the unruliness of sceneographic spectacle is found in the way it makes a direct appeal to the body of the individual spectator and at the same time communicated images and ideas that spectators hold in common'.[24] The earthquake was one such 'common' image, offering a highly topical choice of sensation scene: between 1860 and 1911 there were high-profile earthquakes throughout Europe, the USA, and in outreaches of the British Empire, from Australia and New Zealand to India. In the build-up to the earthquake scene, audiences were already astounded by the 'Battle of Flowers' at Nice, a scene which was 'truthful . . . life-like' and afforded 'many thousands of English eyes that can never have a chance of gazing upon the original' an opportunity to experience the sight of it.[25] However, the height of sensation was still to come, with an earthquake 'more impressive' than *Claudian*: for where the Lyceum's earthquake was a 'purely imaginative affair', Drury Lane's 'was the clever imitation of a recent and terrible reality'.[26]

Jack Lovel, the gullible undergrad – once penniless, now titled and wealthy, but still the dupe of other's machinations – turns against his lover Jessie Newland, believing her to be unfaithful. He asks for heaven's judgement on his actions in disowning her and their unborn child:

> JACK: Bah! Too late! And yet I could almost believe in her innocence – no, I am a fool! It's my old love for her that rises in my heart and pleads for her. She has asked for justice – she has got it – and if I am wronging her, may heaven punish me as I deserve.
>
> CRASH – *All darkness*
> JACK: What's that? Is this indeed the answer of Heaven? Is she really innocent? Am I indeed guilty?
>
> CRASH – *Earthquake – fall of House, Jack buried beneath debris.*    (5:1)

Heaven's punishment is swift: with 'a tremendous clap of thunder . . . the walls of the room begin to totter, the ceiling falls in, and Jack lies buried beneath the earthquake' (5:1). Jack is later rescued from the rubble and all ends happily, with misunderstandings resolved and a marriage in Act 7, but in depicting such a 'catastrophe' as the 'convulsion of nature' in a 'modern and civilised city', Merritt and Harris staged a recent earthquake.[27] Only seven months earlier, the Mediterranean coast of southern France had been rocked by a 6.0 earthquake, killing more than 2,000 people and laying waste to properties along the Riviera (Figure 9.1).

Escalating the thrill of the sensation, then, was a temporal proximity to the situation itself – something the audience knew to be real and recent in the world

Figure 9.1 An illustration of the 1887 earthquake in Nice – moments before a tidal wave also struck the promenade. 'The Earthquake at Nice: Panic of the Carnival Pleasure- Seekers', *The Penny Illustrated Paper and Illustrated Times*, 5 March 1887, Issue 1344

outside the theatre, brought to life on the stage. Similarly, in 1911 *The Hope* (with its multiple sensation scenes, including a ball in Delhi and a Derby Race at Epsom) featured an earthquake in which the audience sat 'petrified with fear, clutching each other in darkness like early Christian martyrs just before the hour of the lions' supper (Figure 9.2). The whole theatre seem[ed] one great bead of perspiration'.[28]

In 1905, 1907, and 1908, earthquakes had taken lives across Italy, the worst of which, in Messina, killed between 75,000 and 200,000 people and damaged 91 per cent of the structures in the town.[29] Only a few months before *The Hope* premiered, a further earthquake hit Vernia (creating a fissure 24 feet by 33 miles long), and one month into the run, another struck Caponia. The topical nature of the sensation scene, set in Massiglia, made for a 'frightfully thrilling' situation in which the 'tottering house burst into flame', and a 'whole city came down in the midst of thundering noises, clouds of steam and dust and a red sea of fire'.[30] The earthquake forces a confession from Olive (as in *Pleasure*, mighty nature brings all to a head), and as the walls are falling in around them, she names the guilty party (Hector Grant), while the innocence of the hero (Lord Harold Norchester) is revealed:

OLIVE: I can't bear it – I'll speak! Father – Brenda! Forgive me! The man's
   name – in the face of death – it was – Sir Hector Grant.   (3:2)

Figure 9.2 The publicity postcard for Dance's touring production showing how the sensation scene (from advertising through to performance) sought to directly echo actual events. (Postcard for *The Hope*, author's own collection)

133

But melodrama heroes 'do not die when all the world and an earthquake are against them', so Harold guides the group to the roof, proclaiming it 'our only chance!' (3:2).[31] After this, the horse race – in which real horses galloped towards the audience – was regarded as a disappointment, eclipsed by the tangible fear evoked by the earlier 'sensation'.

While fire formed one component of the earthquake situation, it featured in several other sensation dramas as a solo effect – among them, *The Streets of London* (1864), *The Red Scarf* (1869), *Mabel's Life; or A Bitter Bargain* (1872), and *The World* (1880) – and particularly as an act of arson, favoured by Boucicault in *The Octoroon* (1859) and *The Poor of New York* (1864). Similarly, an ongoing fascination with water (in affinity with nautical melodrama) spawned sensation scenes with rivers; bridges; shipwrecks, including 'headers' and falls, as in *After Dark* (1868); locks, as in *Queen's Evidence* (1876) and *The White Heather* (1897); and even frozen water, as in *The Orange Girl* (1864); an iceberg in *The Sea of Ice* (1865); and floods, as in *The Flood Tide* (1903). Audience enthusiasm for a sensation scene featuring a ship was a nineteenth-century constant – pre- and post-Harris's *The Armada* (1888) – and ships sailing the water, sinking below it, and sunk at the bottom peppered the period, in *Formosa* (1869), *The Scuttled Ship* (1877), *A Sailor and His Lass* (1883), *The White Heather* (1897), and *The Best of Luck* (1916).

While some productions used lights and mirrors to suggest water, as in Louis N. Parker and G. R. Sims's *The Great Day* (1919), many were keen to advertise their use of real water. In Augustin Daly's *Under the Gaslight* (1867), the heroine, Laura Courtland, is 'hurled headforemost into the real water' in Act 2, where 'at imminent peril of drowning' she sinks out of sight four times before she is rescued by her sweetheart Ray.[32] Though the effect cost £200, it was outdone in the subsequent act when Laura rescues Snorkey from the path of an oncoming locomotive. In W. B. Donne's *Ashore and Afloat* (1864) the use of real water was deployed to escalate the tension in an already frightening disaster scene. Ruth, stranded down a mine by the villain, searches through the darkness for the hero, Newton – worried 'lest every step may bring [her] nearer to what [she] is dread to meet – his lifeless body!' – but water bursts into the mine, leaving her 'without a chance of life' (3:1). As the water continues to rise, she finds Newton and together they ascend the rope. Here again, the sensation scene bore close affinity to recent history; in 1862, the Hartley Colliery disaster resulted in the deaths of 204 men, many of whom died of suffocation. There are two direct echoes between the real events and Donne's depiction: a falling beam and asphyxiation. Ruth's own words must have offered a haunting reminder of recent events: 'I can hardly breathe ... the earth creates a living grave' (3:1). To the audience, a time lapse of barely two years must have felt like only a moment, as the 'sensation' of the scene itself sought to directly connect to living memory and bring to dramatic motion the illustrations many present would have viewed in the press.

*Ashore and Afloat* was not the only drama to depict the dangers of a working mine – *Lost in London* (1867) and *Dead Man's Point* (1871) would make similar use of mines as a part of the action and continued to echo current disasters as they were performed over the years: Barnsley in 1866, Pelsall in 1872, Haydock in 1878, Cornwall in 1883, Rhonda in 1885, Thornhill in 1893, and Westhoughton in 1910.

From below-ground disasters to above-ground alpine passes: Boucicault's *Pauvrette; or, Under the Snow* (1858), Mary Elizabeth Braddon's *Genevieve; or, The Missing Witness* (1874), and Cecil Raleigh and Henry Hamilton's *Hearts are Trumps* (1899) and *The Marriages of Mayfair* (1908) all featured avalanches for their sensation scenes, most often with the villain falling to his death. The use of hydraulic and electric bridges was key to most sensation scenes: raised and tilted they could create the illusion of a mountain slope, locks, sinking ships, avalanches, and earthquakes. Having seen the successful stage adaptations of her earlier novel, *Lady Audley's Secret* (1862), Mary Elizabeth Braddon penned her four-act play *Genevieve* in 1874, only a year after the obliteration of an entire Swiss town, Oberfest, by an avalanche – an event she would utilize for her sensation scene, which takes place on 'The Devil's Bridge', suspended midway between flies and stage to suggest alpine height:

> The villain draws his successful rival by a subterfuge, and there he throws him headlong from a dizzy height into a chasm which seems only measured by the extent of the stage, and as this sensation was crowned by another, which embraced a real falling avalanche, smothering a chalet which contained the only living witness of the foul deed, and the rescue from the chasm of the favoured lover, the enthusiasm of the audience rose to even a higher pitch.[33]

By the time of Raleigh and Hamilton's *Hearts are Trumps* in 1899, a succession of avalanches had struck the United States, Canada, and Iceland. In the early months of the same year, lives were lost in avalanches in Aspen and multiple incidents in Switzerland – including the death of Welsh climber Owen Glynne Jones on Dent Blanche. What audiences read about in the newspapers, the sensation scene staged, and the dialogue often explicitly acknowledged this origin of the dramatist's inspiration:

KOLNITZ: I was only reading about an accident.
GILLESPIE: In Switzerland? Yes – it's their accident season. Always the
same story – somebody goes where they oughtn't to go – without
a guide – and with a fatal result – really, the insurance companies
ought to make tourists pay double.                              (2:1)

While *The Graphic* featured images of the avalanches, and magic lantern slides depicted static moments of the events, British audiences could themselves bear witness to a 'stupendous ... thundering, crashing, smashing, snow-showering avalanche' at Drury Lane.[34] After a build-up of four spectacular scenes ('The Hall at Oak Dene'; 'The Botanical Gardens'; 'The Royal Academy', wherein actual paintings from the recent exhibition were reproduced for the set; and 'The "Frivolity" Music Hall', which was regarded as 'dividing honours' with the avalanche scene), the heroine Dora is led by Kolnitz to a pass in Switzerland, where he plans to push her over the precipice and claim her life insurance policy of £10,000. As Dora 'slides inch by inch towards the dreadful chasm ... the ladies in the theatre utter little screams'.[35] His plans are foiled by his repentant co-conspirator, who cuts the rope, thus saving Dora and sacrificing his own life. As the avalanche approaches, Dora is further saved from its path by her heroic fiancé, Rev. John Thorold, and they escape just as the wave of snow sweeps Kolnitz over the apex.

A similar escape is featured in Raleigh and Hamilton's *The Marriages of Mayfair*, when the villain Jim Callender attempts to flee from justice. On a stage of 80 feet by 80 feet, the production combined avalanche and equestrian business in an effort to elevate the sensation to new heights: an unsuccessful leap across the precipice on horseback (after a swift offstage swap of the actor for an acrobat) results in the villain's death, and, on more than one occasion – such was the risk to rider and animal – the horse was itself accidentally killed during the spectacle.

While sensation scenes continued to feature horses throughout the period, the population witnessed their gradual replacement by motor cars. Technology was transforming everyday life, and public unease about machines – trains, cars, and submarines, as well as hot air balloons (as in *The Ruling Passion* [1882] and *The Great Ruby* [1899]), zeppelins (as in Raleigh and Hamilton's *Sealed Orders* [1913]), and even the fire engine and humble omnibus (no longer horse-drawn, but first electric and later motor-powered) – offered a topical and abundant source for sensation scenes as well as the very means to create the spectacles, which used the same machinery that the public felt was invading their lives. One of the machines to constantly appear on the London stage, in ever-advancing form, was the boat, ship, yacht, steamer, and, eventually, the submarine. While some plays continued to feature the historical form of the Spanish galleon (*The Armada* and *The Best of Luck*), others looked to maintain utmost contemporaneity. Means of sea travel for passengers and for naval personnel, ships were vulnerable to a range of hazards and dangers; boiler explosions, storms, sandbanks, collisions, typhoons, even rocks led to fatalities on the *Anglo-Saxon* (1863), *London* (1866), HMS *Captain* (1870), RMS *Atlantic* and *Northfleet* (1873), HMS *Juno* (1880), *Kapunda* (1887), *Utopia* (1891), and the HMS *Victoria* (1893). In 1860, Tom Taylor's *The Overland Route* focused on the homebound journey of the Simoon Steamer, which runs aground on rocks, leaving her passengers shipwrecked on Mazzaffa Reef. The 'visible terrors consequent on the ship's foundering' left *The Times* in no doubt of the 'air of thorough reality' that the scene presented.[36] In 1907, *The Sins of Society* was influenced by two maritime disasters: the HMS *Birkenhead* in 1845 and the *Princess Alice* disaster (1878), the latter occurring when, during the return leg of a 'moonlight' pleasure cruise from London Bridge to Gravesend, the SS *Princess Alice* collided with the SS *Bywell Castle*, split in two, and, within four minutes, had sunk beneath the Thames. Newspaper coverage was extensive, and in the days and weeks after the event, the bodies of those onboard continued to rise to the top of the Thames. Rather than out at sea or in a region of the empire, this disaster had struck the city; and when the HMS *Beachy Head*, in *The Sins of Society*, sank on stage, it must have evoked a powerful sensation – born of memory – and a realism all too close to contemporary reality.

Ships also provided a dramatic setting for action, as in *A Chain of Events* (1852), *The Scuttled Ship* (1877), *Harbour Lights* (1885), and *A Million of Money* (1890); with passenger steamers out at sea in *Sealed Orders* (1913), submarines in *A Fight for Millions* (1904), and sunken yachts in *The Price of Peace* (1899) and *The White Heather* – the latter of which realistically depicted an underwater battle by the use of an aquarium with real fish and magic lanterns:

> The diver slowly descends. The boat above him is raised into the flies, giving the effect of remaining static, producing a 'panning down' effect for the audience. Finally, the attendant boat disappears. The diver reaches the sea bed and the stage presents a complete underwater scene.[37]

While an underwater battle was an uncommon sight for the audience, motorized vehicles were an increasingly everyday sight. In particular, the motor car, as symbolic of modernity, represented a threat to the status quo, a threat to horse culture, and a threat to life – for both passengers and pedestrians. Like the train, the motor car was a product of an increasingly industrialized world. Unlike sensation scenes inspired by the forces of nature, spectacles featuring an engine-powered vehicle (either train or car) put machine and man at the core of the scene, and a character's relationship with the vehicle was often the cause of disaster.

Why was it, as *The Graphic* wondered, 'that people will not only pay money to see an imitation on the stage of realistic objects of which they can see the originals every day for nothing, but will behold the imitation with feelings of excitement that are altogether wanting in the presence of the bona fide article'?[38] The reasons were twofold: first, audiences were startled by the feat of imitation itself (what Richard Altick terms the 'shock of actuality'); and second, they paid to see the 'situation', brushes with death between man and machine – something they could read about daily but were thrilled to 'see' happen in the theatre.[39] Part of their excitement was the result of this blurred boundary; audiences accepted the realism of the imitation and were aware of its illusion, but they were also aware of the potential for machinery to fail in real life.

In the 1890s motor cars were becoming an increasing presence on British roads and so too were reports of car-related accidents in the press. International motor-car races, especially in Europe, were reported alongside questions of 'Was it worth it?' when drivers and pedestrians were killed by collisions, engine explosions, and 'dangerous driving'. In part as a PR bid, the newly founded Motor Car Club proposed a race from London to Brighton in 1896 to 'give the public a practical demonstration of the capabilities and characteristics of the new vehicle and under normal circumstances of road traffic'.[40] The race set a new record (under four hours, at a maximum speed of 30 miles per hour) and established a growing trend for races around the UK. By 1901, motor-car races were listed as the 'Talk of London' (Figure 9.3), with 'motor-car fever fast spreading in this country'; yet the same article reported multiple deaths because of the 'reckless juggernaut'.[41] Clearly the public's relationship to the motor car was a problematic one – simultaneously regarded as symbol of the modern world and an overpowering, uncontrollable force ready to crush those in its path.

In September 1901, *The Great Millionaire* drew directly from current events: earlier in the year, a British car 'came to grief' at Sedan during a race from Paris to Berlin; in the play, a motor-car race ends in tragedy when Isaac Grant attempts to throttle Digby Grant, plunging them both off the moonlit road and down a precipice, resulting in the villain's death (Figure 9.4).

As with the horse race in *The Derby Winner* (1894), the two motor cars raced downstage towards the audience, filling 'the theatre with the smell of petroleum' and leaving the audience in 'no doubt about the reality of the motor cars' – which had cost over £700.[42] The sensation scene was

THE GREAT AUTOMOBILE RACE FROM PARIS TO BERLIN: MR. EDGE'S BRITISH-MADE CAR GOT ON ALL RIGHT
NEAR THE START (BUT CAME TO GRIEF, ALAS! AT SEDAN).

Figure 9.3 A 'juggernaut' out of control, veering off road during the Paris to Berlin race. 'The Talk of London', *The Penny Illustrated Paper and Illustrated Times,* 6 July 1901, Issue: 2093

judged unconvincing, however, mainly because the scene played against a cinematograph projecting a moving landscape.[43]

Eight years later a motor car would again feature on the stage at Drury Lane, but this time in direct competition with a train, and, interestingly, in a sensation scene which positioned the car as the saviour of the horse – rescuing a colt known as 'the Whip' from its imminent destruction by the express train (though the motor car also crashes in the play). Raleigh and Hamilton's *The Whip* (1909) subtly examines the race of technologies and the increasing speed at which the contemporary world was revolutionizing daily lives. As with George Spencer's *Rail, River, and Road* (1868),

Figure 9.4 A sensational plunge over the precipice. (Postcard for *The Great Millionaire*, author's own collection)

*The Whip* brought together multiple components of previous sensation scenes, incorporating nature, machine, and horse, and featuring as the main spectacle 'the agent and icon of modernisation': the railway.[44]

The 'railway rescue drama' was a consistent sensation scene throughout the second half of the nineteenth century and into the twentieth, then translating its popularity to early silent film. While some dramas featured the train station (another symbol of modernity, where people of all classes mix) as a backdrop to action, as in *The Flood Tide*, or the railway carriage for 'incidents' on a train, as in *The Great World of London* (1898), most often characters were rescued from the path of an oncoming train – as in *Under the Gaslight, The Scamps of London* (1843), *The Odds* (1870), and *After Dark*. In *The Whip*, a horse rather than a human is saved from death on the tracks. Such scenes 'surpassed those of ordinary experience ... but the events portrayed nevertheless correlated, even if only loosely, with certain qualities of corporeality, peril and vulnerability associated with working class life'.[45]

Between the 1860s and 1900s railways accidents were regular occurrences, and while some incidents were the result of human error (an intoxicated or distracted driver or signalman) they were most often the result of mechanical failure: fractured wheels, boiler explosions, speed, signal error, faulty tracks, and even bridge collapse (Figure 9.5).

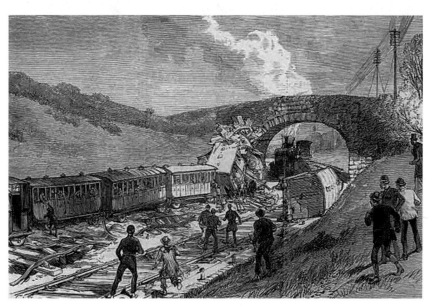

Figure 9.5 A typical illustration of a train collision – Wennington, near Lancaster, 1880. 'The Two Recent Fatal Railway Disasters', *Illustrated London News*, 21 August 1880, p. 184

In December 1866, the first underground accident took place on the London metropolitan line, killing three people, and less than two years later Boucicault's 'new drama of London life' *After Dark* saw Old Tom rescue Chumley from the oncoming train (also on the metropolitan line).

In 1880 alone there were thirteen severe railway accidents, one of which involved the death of a young child who was riding the engine of a mineral train when it derailed outside of Skinningrove, Cleveland. This scenario was utilized to escalate the drama of *Pluck*'s (1882) sensation scene when, after the first train crash at Hazlebury junction, the hero, Jack, rescues Ellen from the wreckage (Figure 9.6):

> ELLEN: My child, my child is in the carriage.
> GUARD: Here's the down train coming, and it must smash into us. Stand aside, everyone, for your lives!
> ELLEN (SCREAMS): My child – my child! For God's sake, save my child!
> *(During all this, people are being carried out of carriages)*
> GUARD: Too late, it is certain death!
> *(Business. Increasing noise of train approaching and blowing whistle. The train enters and dashes into the other one as Jack rushed from the carriage, and throws the child into Ellen's arms).*
> *(Second crash) Grand Tableaux!* (3:1)

In this instance, as with all sensation scenes, melodrama offered the audience a far happier ending than real life – using stagecraft to deliver the thrills and feelings of a temporal and physical proximity to actual catastrophes and disasters without the peril. During this 'reign of terror', 'no atrocity was too shocking, no calamity too appalling for representation', allowing sensation dramas to create a 'paroxysm of sensation' which 'disorganised [an audience's] condition histrionically'.[46] Rather than merely 'noxious trash ... filled with villains, suffering virtue and machinery', sensation scenes functioned, as David Mayer argues, 'as an essential social and cultural instrument' addressing – directly or indirectly – 'matters of daily concern', matters that kept 'a piece running so long'.[47]

Figure 9.6 Collision at Hazlebury Junction – an illustration of the sensation scene from *Pluck*. 'Pluck', *The Illustrated Sporting and Dramatic News*, 2 September 1882

## Notes

1. 'The Sensation Scene', *Fun* (9 May 1863): 73.
2. 'From Fun', *Manchester Times* (23 February 1867)
3. Aristotle, *Poetics*, trans. S. H. Butcher (New York: Hill & Wang, 1961), 64.
4. Augustus Harris, 'Spectacle', *Magazine of Art* (1899): 199.

5. *Ibid.*
6. *Ibid.*
7. Michael Booth, *Victorian Spectacular Theatre 1850–1910* (London: Routledge & Kegan Paul, 1981), 6.
8. Bernard Beckerman, 'Spectacle in Theatre', *Theatre Survey*, 25 (1984): 1–13.
9. Baz Kershaw, 'Curiosity or Contempt: On Spectacle, the Human and Activism', *Theatre Journal*, 55 (2003): 592.
10. 'A Cup of Tea with Mr Cecil Raleigh', *The Sketch* (13 September 1899): 322.
11. 'Green Room Gossip', *Daily Mail* (25 July 1900): 6.
12. 'Sensation Drama at the Theatre', *Hull Packet* (23 November 1877), n.p.
13. Amy Hughes, *Spectacles of Reform: Theatre and Activism in Nineteenth Century America* (Ann Arbor: University of Michigan, 2014), 15.
14. 'Lyceum Theatre', *The Times* (12 March 1882), 10.
15. *Ibid.*
16. 'Queen's Theatre', *The Caledonian Mercury* (28 June 1861)
17. *Ibid.*
18. Lynn M. Voskuil, 'Feeling Public: Sensation Theater, Commodity Culture and the Victorian Public Sphere', *Victorian Studies*, 44 (2002): 245.
19. 'To the Editor of The Times: Sensation Dramas', *The Times* (14 March 1882): 10.
20. *Ibid.*
21. 'Melodrama Ancient and Modern', *The Era* (20 July 1895), n.p.; 'Dramatic Improbabilities', *The Era* (30 October 1880)
22. 'Sensation Scenes', *The Era* (5 September 1885)
23. 'The Lyceum', *The Era* (22 December 1883)
24. Joslin McKinney, 'Sceneography, Spectacle and the Body of the Spectator', *Performance Research* (2013): 74.
25. 'Pleasure at Drury Lane', *Sunday Times* (4 September 1887): 5.
26. *Ibid.*
27. 'Reopening of Drury Lane Theatre', *Daily News* (5 September 1887)
28. *Tatler* review, quoted in Brian Dobbs, *Drury Lane Theatre: Three Centuries of the Theatre Royal* (London: Cassell, 1972), 171.
29. A bioscope show at the Palace Theatre, organized by Alfred Butt, displayed pictures of 'buildings still burning and survivors wearily picking their way through the ruins'. *Sunday Times* (10 January 1909): 7.
30. 'The Hope', *Sunday Times* (17 September 1911): 4.
31. *Ibid.*
32. Poster for the English adaptation of *Under the Gaslight*, in Michael Booth, *Hiss the Villain* (London: Eyre & Spottiswoode, 1964), 273.
33. 'Advertisements and Notices', *The Era* (12 April 1874)
34. 'Hearts are Trumps', *The Era* (23 September 1899)
35. 'Things Theatrical', *The Sporting Times* (23 September 1899): 2.
36. 'Haymarket Theatre', *The Times* (24 February 1860): 6.
37. Dennis Castle, *Sensation Smith of Drury Lane* (London: Charles Skilton Ltd, 1984), 104.
38. 'Theatres', *The Graphic* (18 November 1882)
39. Richard D. Altick, *Deadly Encounters: Two Victorian Sensations* (Philadelphia: University of Pennsylvania Press, 2000), 145.
40. 'Motor Car Race', *Financial Times* (8 October 1896): 4.

41. 'Talk of London', *The Penny Illustrated Paper and Illustrated Times* (6 July 1901): 1.

42. 'Drury Lane Theatre', *The Times* (20 September 1901): 4.

43. *Ibid.*

44. Nicholas Daly, *Literature, Technology and Modernity: 1860–2000* (Cambridge: Cambridge University Press, 2004), 216.

45. Ben Singer, *Melodrama and Modernity: Early Sensational Cinema and Its Contexts* (New York: Columbia University Press, 2001), 53.

46. 'The Beautiful in Dramatic Art', *The Era* (22 June 1879)

47. 'The Age of Sensational Things', *Glasgow Herald* (10 January 1865); David Mayer, 'Encountering Melodrama', in *The Cambridge Companion to Victorian and Edwardian Theatre*, ed. Kerry Powell (Cambridge: Cambridge University Press, 2004), 145.

# III
# Melodrama and Nineteenth-Century English Culture

# 10

KATHERINE NEWEY

# Melodrama and Gender

In this chapter, I am concerned with the performances of gender in melodrama, and the role of women in producing melodramatic texts. In melodrama of the nineteenth century, genre and gender intersected in a number of ways, and throughout the period melodrama developed as a vehicle for thinking about gender. Indeed, it could be argued that melodrama is, in all the media of its expression (drama, fiction, and latterly, film) *about* gender, and the contradictions of gender ideology. Melodrama placed the feeling individual at the centre of the drama to make powerful statements about human subjectivity and what it is to be human – and women and femininity were central to that melodramatic representation. This performance of emotion underpinned the politics of protest and reform of the period. The centring on women's actions and feelings is significant because in the first half of the nineteenth century, melodrama and the melodramatic were important ways of representing the strong emotional undercurrents, more generally, of a society under pressure of change.

Representations of the feminine have been a central focus of recuperative studies of nineteenth-century melodrama and the melodramatic on stage and in popular fiction, with particular interest in the transgressive woman of sensation fictions of the 1860s. The transgressive woman is to be found in a web of texts – novels, plays, paintings – clustered around the sensationalism of female desire which Lyn Pykett calls the 'improper feminine'.[1] The invention of the melodramatic heroine, as individuated feeling person, is one of the enduring legacies of melodrama's cultural work. This new kind of character – the active, feeling, suffering woman at the centre of the action – is an innovation of nineteenth-century melodrama which has been so thoroughly absorbed into popular culture that we no longer recognize her novelty, nor the revolutionary aspects of this character type. The genealogy of this melodramatic heroine starts with her position as suffering victim in the Gothic drama of the late eighteenth century. There are two later points of explosive development: the working class heroines of

149

the domestic melodrama of the 1830s and '40s, and the heroine-villains of sensation drama of the 1860s. While the creation of female characters who experience suffering and extreme feeling is not always an unalloyed good, melodrama gives female characters agency and voice, and a dominant physical presence on the stage throughout the century.

However, we cannot simply recover melodrama as a triumphantly feminist genre. Political expression in melodrama was uneven, oscillating between protest and conformity. Melodrama offered a critique of gender roles, but any subversive effect was ultimately contained. Heavy state regulation and censorship was maintained throughout the century, and this fed into the dramaturgical conventions of the genre, particularly in the restoration of class and gender hierarchy through the 'happy' ending of marriage – or the retributive deaths of transgressive female protagonists. The political force of stage melodrama was also undercut by critical condemnation of it as part of a declining and degraded popular culture, pandering only to the lowest audience desires for sensation, novelty, and cheap thrills. And yet, as Christine Gledhill comments about film melodrama, 'feminists found a genre distinguished by the large space it opened to female protagonists, the domestic sphere and socially mandated "feminine" concerns'.[2] For the rest of this chapter, I will explore that domestic feminine space that stage melodrama offers to look at the work of gender in the nineteenth century.

## Domestic Melodrama

The period from the late 1820s to the mid-1840s was a critical moment in the development of English melodrama, as a native English domestic melodrama developed from Romantic and Gothic drama. Stage melodrama of this period is often overlooked in studies of the sensational or transgressive female in melodramatic texts in various media. Yet the sensation writers of the late 1850s and '60s, such as Wilkie Collins, Mary Braddon, and Ellen Wood, all drew on the tropes, plots, characters, and registers of expression typical of early stage melodrama. An important ancestor in the genealogy of the 'improper feminine' is to be found in the domestic drama made popular in the minor (or 'illegitimate') theatres of London. Playwrights such as Douglas Jerrold, Edward Fitzball, John Baldwin Buckstone, William Thomas Moncrieff, John Thomas Haines, and George Dibdin Pitt all contributed to a set of melodramatic conventions which combined the story of a working woman in danger with scenes of contemporary life. This genre was so recognizable that by 1843, in the wake of Benjamin Webster's announcement of a £500 prize for the best new comedy, *Punch* could spoof Webster's competition:

Another Dramatic Prize. – The lessee of the [Victoria] theatre also offers a reward of one pound for the most absorbing domestic drama. It is indispensable that every piece sent in should contain a dream for the 'acknowledged heroine', and a suicide for the 'recognised tragedian'. All the pieces will be submitted to a committee of servant-girls, ill-used apprentices, and victims of oppression.[3]

Douglas Jerrold's domestic drama *Martha Willis the Servant Maid* (1831) is representative of melodramas which focused on young heroines and their battles with the wide world outside their homes and villages. First performed at the Pavilion Theatre, the coincidence of real-world theatre and fictional theatrical situation is also representative: the Pavilion served audiences living in the financial precarity of the day-labour and service industries of the growing working-class populations in London's East End, and relied upon its audience's sympathy and recognition of the stories told on the stage. For all that *Punch* was later to make such 'servant-girls' the butt of its satire, Jerrold's domestic dramas engage with his local audience's daily knowledge of the reality of the vulnerability of a young woman seeking her fortune in the big city, and offer central female characters as vehicles of sympathy as well as virtue. Martha is beautiful but innocent, and much loved by her familiars; importantly, she also creates social coherence and connection by her presence. As he delivers her to the busy London street, Scarlet the coachman articulates Martha's sympathetic power:

I tell you, Martha is a good girl, the darling of our village – all the folks there, love her like their own child. Why, I have had her weight in bank notes given to my care, and less fuss about it than the people made when they entrusted me with Martha Willis. (1:1)

Her spiritual power is almost occult. When her fiancé Walter is finally taken to Newgate prison, after resorting to crime to pay his gambling debts, he speaks his vision of Martha as a restorative icon of the purity of the country-side and the community of the village. In the midst of his dissipation, he declares:

Martha would sometimes rise in my thoughts, and still she'd come, mingled with objects bright and beautiful – the sunny fields, the green trees, the song of birds, my own home, and the throng of youthful friends, treading the honest path of humble life – (3:3)

In these melodramas, heroines play the role of carrier of hegemonic patriarchal values. Yet, as Frederick Burwick points out, female characters such as Martha are 'credible counterparts of the courageous women of the riots and the protests' beyond the theatres in the late 1820s and '30s.[4] Martha's attempt at saving her fiancé from the gallows puts her voice, her body, and the purity she represents centre stage to articulate a feminine version of honour in a plea to her dissolute lover:

> none who have the love of a woman suffer alone. 'Tis true, you may despise my prayers. *(kneels)* Thus kneeling at your feet, you may scorn my supplications, be blind to my tears – you may fly to death – but you will take me with you – you may perish, but one grave must hold us both. (3:3)

This speech – and many like it in the melodramas of these decades – encapsulates the paradox of the representation of femininity in melodrama. Martha speaks of self-sacrifice, but her defiance of evil, her emphatic physical and vocal presence – these elements of excess in performance – suggest a character with greater agency than her socially determined role allows.

In contrast, John Baldwin Buckstone's 'she-drama' *Agnes de Vere; or, the Wife's Revenge* (1834) offers a juicy story of female excess and emotion in which the female protagonist overtly breaks the bounds of orthodox femininity. In this play – one of the 'Adelphi screamers' Buckstone produced for the fashionable Adelphi Theatre in the 1830s – the possibilities of ambivalent or oppositional readings of melodrama are well illustrated. Agnes is forced into wrongdoing by the very strength of her commitment to a properly 'feminine' role as devoted wife and mother. In desperation at her husband's infidelity, she plans to trap him and his lover, the dancer Lydia, at a masked ball. Agnes goes to the ball disguised as Lydia, where she tells her husband of his wife's true devotion, while Alfred (thinking he is speaking to Lydia) falls on his knees and offers her all he possesses. Centre stage and alone after this declaration, Agnes soliloquizes on her fate, and finds a pistol to shoot herself. But she stops herself when she thinks of her child, and instead decides to seek revenge by shooting her husband and Lydia, although she does not kill them. Agnes then becomes delirious and escapes to her home, where she expresses her pain and suffering:

> Why did I follow him? Why did I go to the ball, seeking for misery that I too surely found, and which is now mine for ever? . . . 'twas in the hope to find that I had been deceived – in the mad hope to gain some knowledge that might have proved me to have been in error – but I was *not*; no, no! 'twas all truth – terrible, maddening truth. How did I escape? How came I home again? – I know not – I recollect nothing distinctly – cries of pursuit – the street filled with carriages – lights flashing to and fro, and no more. I found myself at home – at my drear, wretched home. I dread to think on what I might have done; – but I could not see him embrace her – I was frantic – mad – I knew not what I did – death was in my thoughts – its means were in my hand – as I think – as I reflect – I feel my mind changing. Am I mad? – Yes, yes; I am mad, miserably mad. – *(She falls in a chair on the L.H.)* (3:1)

Her madness continues when Alfred and Lydia enter, and Alfred treats his wife as a servant; when Alfred asks for chocolate, Agnes gives him a poisoned cup, and then, confessing all, dies of a broken heart.

This set speech for the star actress, Elizabeth Yates (playing Agnes), presents the language of female emotion in a physical as well as verbal representation. Her expression is codified and formalized into a set of gestures, vocal usages, and physical poses, which became visual icons of femininity under stress. Contemporary illustrations and acting manuals recommend extreme facial expressions, extended arm gestures, and heightened volume, enunciation, and tone of voice for these kinds of set speeches. Through impassioned set-piece speeches, female characters indicate realms of experience and emotion beyond the quotidian limits of the domestic sphere, and in this gesture towards broader experience, they provide a partial model for liberation. And this is the paradox of femininity represented in melodrama: for the female character – no matter how much she is finally restricted by the action of melodrama – the very taking of the stage as a physical, vocal, passionate, active, and self-activating human being is significant. She articulates the paradox within which she is caught: partial and still problematic, as heroines in melodrama must die for their transgressions; but liberating in the power and energy of expression that is afforded them.

## Masculinity

Studies of melodrama and the melodramatic which explore its transgression and representation of protest have generally focused on the feminine – we tend to think of gender as women's business. However, the heightened emotional temperature of melodrama also cuts across the pressure on normative representations of the bourgeois male subject. 'Manliness' in the period was stereotypically represented as emotionally reserved, respectable, brave, and honourable. In melodrama, heroes are brave, courageous, and honest, particularly in relation to the heroine's honour, but they are anything but reserved and emotionally repressed. While most of the emotional energy of melodrama was invested in the melodramatic heroine and narratives of virtue in peril, the melodramatic hero faced his own challenges.

The melodrama hero articulates – often at length – his emotional states and dilemmas, undercutting stereotypes of manly reservation and emotional stability. Of course, the strong-feeling hero is not unusual in the repertoire of drama in English, and constitutes a thread of connection between melodrama and earlier forms. The set-piece soliloquy articulating otherwise private thoughts and feelings is a convention of early modern tragedy for protagonists and antagonists alike, and such soliloquies arguably established a convention of theatrical representation of the individual subject of Renaissance humanism. In melodrama, this becomes an almost compulsive necessity to speak everything, but it is not the prince, king, or duke who is given the stage in this way: it is the father, the working man, the beggar, and the criminal – characters usually relegated to comic scenes or introduced as functions of the plot in tragedy.

One example of the early formation of the melodrama hero as counter-hegemonic man will stand here for the hundreds of melodramas in which this type appears. John Thomas Haines's *My Poll and My Partner Joe* (1835) follows the conventions of nautical melodrama to tell of the privations of working men; it plays with the popular British national character type of the sailor, and it channels concerns about social conditions and class relations. But even in this masculinist scenario, patriarchal power is fractured – and not always benign; it is just as often wielded to discipline other men, as it is used to control women. In the examination of the masculine heroic in nautical and domestic melodrama, the intersections of gender and class are dramatized in often spectacular ways.

Two men love the same woman, Mary Maybud ('my Poll' of the title): Harry Hallyard (played by the famous stage sailor Thomas Potter Cooke) and Joe Tiller, Harry's friend and partner in his wherry business (played by Robert Honner). However, this is not a plot about the competition of two men for one woman, but about the power of masculine friendship and love. Harry, Mary, and Joe all work on the Thames at Wapping. Mary and Harry are to be married, but the night before their wedding, Harry is press-ganged and disappears for four years. The next act is set on the ship and offers Cooke an opportunity to reprise the language and character (and hornpipe and songs) of the brave midshipman he made famous in Douglas Jerrold's *Black-Ey'd Susan* (1829). Haines also uses the events at sea to make a sharp political point about the evils of slavery, pointing to parallels between press-ganging and slavery in the international commerce in human bodies. Harry and his shipmates free the slaves from the very mercenaries who press-ganged Harry in the first place. Far away from Wapping, Harry is reunited with friends from home, who give him a four-year-old letter from Mary. He is overcome, but declares

> Oh, I arn't ashamed of these drops; when the heart's brim full of love and happiness, it must run over somewhere, and where and why shouldn't it at the eyes? – I don't think a man has less fire and courage in him for having a little of the water of affection. (2:3)

However, when Harry returns to Wapping, he finds disaster. Harry's letters had not reached home, and he was reported dead; his mother has died from grief at his loss, and to fulfil the last wish of Harry's dying mother, Mary has married Joe. When Harry hears this news, his response is like that of a melodrama heroine – physical collapse and hysteria:

> HARRY. (*nearly falling*) Oh, is – is this – (*he tries in vain to speak, at length bursts into a passion of tears, and throws himself upon the shoulders of Sculler*) (3:3)

Later, Harry finds his voice and, in near-soliloquy watching the sleeping Mary, articulates his passion:

> Oh! if she could conceive how I love her! even *her* changing heart would weep for me; but she can't – no, no! she knows nothing of the holy hopes and the sweet longings of a real love – ... My soul is pouring out of my eyes in adoration! (3:4)

Contrary to the notion of a controlled and silent manly man, the men in *My Poll and My Partner Joe* speak out their feelings in heightened language and action. *My Poll* is particularly interesting for its presentation of a strong homosocial masculine culture within the framework of melodrama. In order to bring about the required happy ending, Haines solves the problem of Mary's first marriage by killing off Joe. Joe dies, uncomplainingly and movingly. At the climax of the play, assured of Mary and Harry's forgiveness, Joe declares

> Then I'm happy. – I'm dying! Harry! Mary!
> (*he pulls their hands together, joins them and dies across them*) (3:4)

In this play, representative of so many hundreds, the tropes of melodramatic masculinity emerge. Central to the characterization of the hero – such as Harry Hallyard – is emotion. The raw and explicit statement of emotion makes these characters curiously vulnerable: there is little power derived from reserve or self-discipline. Manliness in *My Poll* is nurtured in the domestic sphere; work is seen as a problem when it separates men from their families. But these emotional domestic men are also working men, and the representation of manual labour and its precarity is part of the way melodrama participates in the grand narrative of politics in the nineteenth century. Economic instability – real enough in the 1820s and 1830s – produces a new kind of hero: the working man encountering the impersonal and oppressive forces of industrial capitalism, and protesting them. Like the presence of sensational femininity in melodrama, and the trope of the transgressive woman, this model of a hero has become so central to popular culture that we forget quite how revolutionary it was.

## Women Writing Melodrama

So far, I have been looking at the ways in which gender was constructed through melodramas written by men. Although women have been active in the professional theatre in Britain since the end of the seventeenth century, generally all but their work as performers has been overlooked. Looking for women's theatre work is a choice: we usually need to look for it deliberately. When we find it we have tended to focus on the exceptional women – prominent entrepreneurs and managers such as Madame Vestris, or the prize-winning playwrights such as Catherine Gore or Netta Syrett. Elaine Showalter warned in 1978 of the dangers of erasing the female writing tradition by a focus on an elite group of writers.[5] But what of the ordinary, the unexceptional woman playwright, who wrote melodramas because the market required them? What can a study of this kind of writer tell us about melodrama and gender?

To answer this question, I turn to Mrs Denvil, playwright for several theatres in the East End of London.[6] Victorian playwrights of any kind have always been considered non-canonical, and Mrs Denvil was a playwright working about as close to the bottom of the aesthetic hierarchy of nineteenth-century writing as it is possible to find. Theatre and literary records of Mrs Denvil are scarce – there are a few scripts, fewer reviews, and no memoirs or other documentary sources, such as letters or family papers. Her given name of Mary Ann is retrievable only from the 1851 census and does not appear in archival sources related to her professional work – her professional identity is as a married woman, 'Mrs Denvil'. Under this name, she was present and active in the theatre in the mid-nineteenth century; however, her presence is only recovered now by catching at fragments of records and mentions of her name. The very obscurity of her activity offers an important view of the intersection between representations of and by women in melodrama.

Although evidence surrounding the context of Mrs Denvil's plays is almost absent from the documentary record, she was a relatively prolific and successful playwright. She wrote several short melodramas for various minor theatres, adapted from topical and popular novels of the time, or from other melodramas. A manuscript of her adaptation of Harriet Beecher Stowe's novel *Dred* (1856) for the Britannia Theatre in Hoxton survives. The Britannia had a strong identity as a centre of culture in a multicultural community, with manager Sarah Lane, a local celebrity who employed local writers to custom create pieces for her audience. The manuscript for *Dred* (1856/7?) reveals a writer taking a serious approach to the piece, aiming for fidelity to the novel and its issues, as well as demonstrating an understanding of staging practicalities. It is clearly a working manuscript, with various alterations, additions, and crossings-out. No visual records of the production survive, but from the manuscript we can speculate about ways in which the script and the production were produced: at speed, to catch the topicality of the novel, and in close collaboration with the theatre manager and stage manager. This evidence points towards Mrs Denvil as a busy working professional; other fragments and traces of her life and work in the archival record seem to confirm this.

Mrs Denvil's plays survive in material form in the Frank Pettingell Collection, held by the University of Kent at Canterbury (UK). The story of the formation of this collection is a reminder of how the survival of much of the archival record of the nineteenth-century theatre was fragile and contingent, especially records relating to theatres in working-class neighbourhoods, in popular genres, and in women's working lives. The Pettingell Collection comprises over 4,000 items, including scripts, manuscripts, pantomime 'books of the play', and theatrical ephemera such as playbills. It was acquired by the University of Kent from the estate of the actor Frank Pettingell. Pettingell had in turn acquired the collection from the son of the Victorian actor, Arthur Williams, and it may well be Williams's neat handwriting on the cover of the printed script of *Susan Hopley*, identifying the author as 'Mrs Denvil', the date of its performance (16 September 1844) and listing the other theatres her melodrama played at – the Royal Albert Saloon, and the Victoria. According to custodians of the Pettingell Collection, many of the scripts were collected by Arthur Williams as part of his stock tools of the trade. The collection as a whole certainly bears the hallmarks of a working collection of a jobbing actor with rehearsal notes, blocking directions, moves, casting notes, cuts, pasted-in pages, and clippings throughout the collection.

There is evidence from the material traces of surviving scripts and theatrical ephemera that Mrs Denvil was by no means as obscure in her own time and community as she is now. Playbills for the Pavilion theatre suggest that Mrs Denvil was a featured artist when the theatre was managed by her husband. These playbills advertise her benefit night of 15 March 1841.[7] Benefit nights were a seasonal bonus, and an indicator of popularity. Mrs Denvil tops the bill as author in a benefit performance of her melodrama, *Ela, the Outcast*. What is fascinating in this bill is the snapshot of women's contribution to the theatrical economy. As well as Mrs Denvil, featured performers at the top of the bill for the night included Mrs Honner, a widely respected comic actress, perhaps best known for playing Oliver in the adaptation of *Oliver Twist* played at Sadler's Wells in 1838 (before the novel's serialization was complete), and Mrs Grattan. The aspirant tragedian, 'Mr [Henry] Denvil', is also at the top of the bill as both manager and actor, suggesting that Mrs Denvil's contribution to the family business as playwright was central to her husband's management policy. As lessee of the Pavilion, Mr Denvil was able to maximize the profit by staging a benefit night for his wife, effectively doubling the contribution she made to the family business: not only did Mrs Denvil write for the theatre, but the popularity of her plays enabled her husband to restage them for further profit. Mr Denvil did not have to bear the cost of a writer's fee or negotiate copyright either, as married women could only rarely own property in their own right before the Married Women's Property Acts (1870 and 1882). In the East End, the family was an important unit in the theatrical economy, but while women's work in the family business of the theatre was key, the family could also obscure the presence of working women within it. It is only through a deliberate search of the archival record for women's work that their every-day economic contribution is made visible.

The play featured for Mrs Denvil's benefit, *Ela, the Outcast*, seems to be lost; it does not appear in major catalogues or lists of plays of the period. Its existence is recorded only by these playbills, and gestured towards in the frontispiece of the novel *Ela, the Outcast* from which Mrs Denvil adapted the play. The novel was by prolific author James Rymer, published in parts in 1841, by the publisher of many penny bloods, Thomas Peckett Prest (also an author of many penny bloods). Mrs Denvil adapted *Ela* for the Pavilion Theatre, together with *Emily Fitzormond; or, The Deserted One* (1841-2), another penny blood published by Prest. According to the Preface of the novel version of *Emily Fitzormond*, this was an ongoing collaboration between Mrs Denvil and Prest, who advertised that this novel 'as well as most of the former works of the author has been dramatized most skilfully by Mrs. Denvil'. The novel and play are an example of the circulation of plots across different media, in a remediative system of exchange and adaptation of both ideas and their representation. This was a circulatory process, and never only in one direction: the popular press drew as much from the theatre as the theatre exploited cheap fiction.

In 1841, *Punch* comments (rather less approvingly) on Mrs Denvil's industry and reputation as an adapter of trends. *Punch* uses the occasion of Lord Mayor of Dublin Daniel O'Connell's visit to London to invent a series of satirical invitations from London theatre managers plying their wares to O'Donnell. Each invitation parodies the style of the theatre, from the obse-quious invitation on behalf of William Macready's 'classic management' at Drury Lane, offering O'Connell the role of 'heroic functionary' in *Richard III* and a liberal allowance for hair-powder, to the offer from Henry Denvil at the Pavilion:

If you mean to come on the stage, come to me. I know what suits the public. If you can't come yourself, send your cocked hat, and Mrs Denvil shall dramatise it.[8]

This is cultural capital – of a sort. Mrs Denvil's reputation as a skilled adapter of *anything* is parodied here, and the managerial partnership of the Denvils was prominent enough to be included in *Punch*'s knowing and urbane parody. The snippet also illustrates the overlapping circles of London's various cultural industries and the position of theatre within them. In 1841, *Punch* was in its early, Bohemian stage, run by men such as Douglas Jerrold and Mark Lemon, who moved easily between the theatre, fiction, and journalism, belying contemporary pressures to control and hierarchize cultural production.

We can speculate about the style and impact of *Ela, the Outcast* by readings of similar plays which have survived, piecing together the evidence of Mrs Denvil's approach to melodrama from these fragments of information. *Ada the Betrayed*, and *Susan Hopley; or the Servant Girl's Dream* (first performed at the Queen's Theatre) were published by the Purkess's Pictorial Penny Press, which was, as the name suggests, also a publisher of prose fiction penny bloods. The play scripts are fragile pamphlets made in the same pattern as the penny bloods, comprising eight pages, and including a graphic front cover illustration. This front page also includes the original cast list. The text is crowded into two columns of small and clumsily printed type. They resemble the serial publication of plays in pamphlet form practiced since the late eighteenth century by Cumberland, Dicks, Lacy, and French, but are noticeably more flimsy and crudely produced. Considered as material objects, the play scripts were published as cheap souvenirs of popular performances, and for readers of penny bloods who wanted the 'tie-in' product of stage adaptation. They may have had a further life as scripts for amateur performers, following the practice of Thomas Hailes Lacy (and his successor, Samuel French) of aiming at the growing market of amateur performers. Yet, they were published, and in a time and place where play scripts of popular 'illegitimate' performance were not regarded as literature. There is evidence of the speed and improvisation of writers and managers in local popular theatres; the note attached by Mr Denvil to the cover of his wife's manuscript of *The Poisoner and His Victim; or, Revenge Crime and Retribution* (n.d.), submitted to the Lord Chamberlain's Examiner of Plays for licensing indicates the pressures of speed under which a theatre like the Pavilion worked. Denvil requested that, 'this piece being required for Monday Night, an early reading of the drama will be esteemed – as the interest of the Establishment depends on Novelty'.[9]

Mrs Denvil worked in a theatrical economy in the first half of the nineteenth century which was part familial and part commercial. A factor of the commercial power of her writing was its sensationalized treatment of domestic women in situations at once removed from, but also recognizable to, her audience. This is the point of intersection between Mrs Denvil's work as a woman, and the plays she writes about working women. *Susan Hopley; or, The Servant Girl's Dream* is an example of the fast and improvisatory style of adaptation in which Mrs Denvil specialized. The script condenses the long novel *Susan Hopley, Or, the Adventures of a Maid-Servant* (1841), by Catherine Crowe, probably via an initial adaptation into a penny blood. In the eight pages of closely packed text, Mrs Denvil's script focuses on the highly fraught events – murder, dream visions, revenge – of the novel, rather than the longer story of Susan's detective work to prove the truth of her dream about the disappearance of her brother, which comprises the longer narrative of Crowe's novel. Susan dreams of her brother Andrew's death, murdered while trying to save his master, Wentworth. The next day, when the murder of Wentworth is discovered, but there is no sign of Andrew, he is blamed for Wentworth's death. Like Martha Willis in Jerrold's domestic drama discussed above, Susan sets out to seek justice for her brother, sacrificing her reputation to clear his name. Typically for a melodramatic heroine, she articulates her commitment to the truth, at the expense of her own comfort:

> I may not live to see it – I may starve for want of food, to support my sinking frame, or without a home to shelter me from the cold, perish in the street before the time comes; still the day will come, when the memory of Andrew will be cleared from the foul stain of murder. (2:1)

Denvil's script places female action and agency at the centre of the drama. The melodrama conceptualizes the world from Susan's affective perspective, giving weight and importance to the feelings which motivate Susan's actions. In the bareness and speed of Denvil's adaptations, feeling becomes a way of perceiving, organizing, and understanding the world: an epistemological position, in other words. This focus on affect and the feeling individual is compliant with the increasingly hegemonic and conservative ideology of bourgeois femininity. Yet, the combination of class and gender in the character of Susan Hopley has explosive, radical possibilities: Susan's feelings *count*, and they concentrate attention on the agency and subjectivity of the traditionally feminine, domestic, obedient, and usually silent woman, if only for those moments on stage.

Mrs Denvil's history also places female activity and agency at the centre of theatre making: it appears that her skills as a writer were essential in supporting the family. Her husband was an actor and bankrupted manager, so the family needed her support and income to keep them afloat; in time, their daughters also contributed to the family income as child actors. In the end, this is a story of female agency, power, and matriarchy, on and off the stage. And in the theatre, Mrs Denvil was not so extraordinary as we might at first assume. Once we start looking for women theatre professionals, we see them everywhere, and we come to realize that they have always been there, as stage managers, writers, actors, costumers, dressers, chorus singers and dancers, and trainers of child performers. What is at stake in Mrs Denvil's career? She wrote to supply the family finances, that seems clear. But she could have chosen to work for her family in other ways. Writing is hard and unforgiving work: with the education which allowed her to adapt anything to order, she might have found employment in other areas of literate piecework to be done from the home, such as copying work or teaching. However, Mrs Denvil chose to create fictional worlds which celebrated the world of working people and the powerful feelings of working women. The worlds she created on stage were not random or incidental, no matter how formulaic her plots and dialogue may read now. Mrs Denvil wrote for her local community, and while her plays might well have been regarded by middle-class critics as inconsequential curiosities, she was publicly valued by that community. Her work in telling stories across media was a kind of resistance to the constraints of elite and polite culture. And if this was achieved through the pleasurable sensations of the 'horrid' and heightened emotional response in her audience, it was still important cultural work. The presence of the feeling woman on stage, reinforced by a performance practice which emphasized the significance of female experience through heightened voice, gesture, and movement, worked to create the sign of woman in which performance energy is concentrated and focused to a high degree. It is here that the transgressive potential of melodrama can be located, and here that the subversive politics of melodrama have most significance.

## Notes

1. Lyn Pykett, *The 'Improper' Feminine: The Women's Sensation Novel and New Woman Writing* (London and New York: Routledge, 1992).
2. Christine Gledhill (ed.), *Home Is Where the Heart Is: Studies in Melodrama and the Woman's Film* (London: British Film Institute, 1987), 10.
3. *Punch* (8 July 1843): 13.

4. Frederick Burwick, *British Drama of the Industrial Revolution* (Cambridge: Cambridge University Press, 2015), 115.
5. Elaine Showalter, *A Literature of Their Own* (London: Virago, 1978), 8.
6. Katherine Newey, *Women's Theatre Writing in Victorian Britain* (Basingstoke: Palgrave Macmillan, 2005), 86–9.
7. *East London Theatre Archive*, Web, www.elta-project.org/.
8. 'The O'Connell Papers', *Punch, or the London Charivari* (13 November 1841): 208.
9. Anon [Mary Ann Denvil], *The Poisoner and His Victim; or, Revenge Crime and Retribution*, Lord Chamberlain's Collection of Plays, British Library, Add Mss 42982, f. 722.

# 11

ROHAN MCWILLIAM

# Melodrama and Class

Consider the ending of two plays, first mounted in London during the year that witnessed the struggle over the Great Reform Bill as Britain threatened to disintegrate into tumult. The first is John Walker's *The Factory Lad*, nothing less than a Luddite melodrama, first performed in October 1832 at the Surrey Theatre in south London. Workers confront the factory owner Westwood, who has introduced steam into his factory and dispensed with their labour. In the final scene in a courtroom, the action freezes with a startling tableau as a labourer shoots Westwood. A woman faints into her husband's arms, others offer an 'attitude of surprise', and soldiers level their muskets at the assassin, who laughs hysterically (2:4). The second is Douglas Jerrold's *The Rent Day* (1832), performed at the beginning of the year at Drury Lane in London's West End. Stewards are seizing the property of a poor family in lieu of rent which they cannot afford to pay. They struggle over a chair, whose back is pulled off. Money bags fall out together with a secret will left by a relative which leaves the family his fortune. They are saved from eviction and all are happy.

Both plays are products of the same historical moment. Both are statements about the perils of poverty. Both are about the humiliations of a society indifferent to basic needs. The effect is, however, completely different. *The Factory Lad* offers a bleak tableau of social conflict in a theatre frequented by workers, whilst *The Rent Day* delivers a happy ending: the despair of poverty is overcome through a mysterious inheritance. Jerrold's play strikes the modern viewer as ridiculously contrived, and yet it was far more typical of the genre we label 'domestic melodrama' and was frequently revived during the nineteenth century. *The Factory Lad*, with its stark portrait of class hostility, was barely performed. It is *The Rent Day*, for all its ludicrous plot developments, that gives us a better insight into the way social issues were translated onto the popular stage and social class was depicted.

How did the class system shape melodrama? This essay disentangles the complex forms of political communication characteristic of the Janus face of

163

melodrama, offering comfort to the radical and the conservative. What follows is an attempt to sketch out a new approach to this problem, arguing that melodrama was marked by the continuity of essentially eighteenth-century ideas of social structure which determined its worldview.

Of course, melodramas varied and there was no precise melodramatic view of the world, still less a melodramatic ideology. There were, however, certain codes and worldviews that became the small change of popular theatre. Theatrical genres were a contract between performer, playwright, manager, and audience. Their very predictability provided a satisfying experience. Nineteenth-century plays and performances were assemblages of conventions and symbols that became a shared language between stage and audience, one that was not even dependent upon the words in the text for it to be present as part of a moment in the theatre. This shared discourse included the acknowledgement of class, inequality, hierarchy, and power relations.

## Social Class and the Nineteenth-Century Stage

But what do we mean by 'class'? Today, there is much debate about the validity of class analysis amongst historians and sociologists.[1] Marxist arguments about class, which shaped the social sciences in the 1960s, are now in decline. Many note that the existence of social classes does not necessarily lead to class struggle. Some find class analysis reductive and insensitive to issues such as race, status, gender, region, and religion, which shape people's lives at least as much. There has been a shift away from talking about the 'working class' in the singular back to the Victorian usage, which was to talk about the 'working classes', acknowledging the huge range in income, work, and outlook amongst manual workers (the same is true of the 'middle class'). Class is difficult to measure and is arguably as much about a range of subjectivities as it is part of economic structure, one form of identity among many. It is, however, difficult to understand the ways in which nineteenth-century society was stratified without some reference to class.

The vocabulary of social class emerged in the later eighteenth century and became a way of talking about the economic inequalities of modern society.[2] Melodrama burst onto the stage at the same time, and thus it is reasonable to seek connections between the two. Theatre reflected the way in which class was becoming an organizing social principle.

In this chapter, class is understood as a system based on wealth, property, and occupation. It is the division between those who work by hand and by brain. It determines (though not completely) the life opportunities available to people born into different economic backgrounds. Whilst it is true that some individuals managed to rise from the working class into the ranks of the bourgeoisie, lack of education and capital prevented most proletarians from making the ascent. Common economic bonds created distinctive forms of politics, culture, and outlook in the different classes. The inequalities generated by class shaped how people saw the world, but not everyone within a class saw the world in the same way. There were divisions over issues such as religion and respectability. Class disunity was as much a feature of working-class life as class-based solidarity. The British working class rarely threatened to become the revolutionary force that Marx and Engels predicted.[3]

Class became an important part of the moral chiaroscuro of melodrama. But the links between class, fantasy, and culture have never been clear-cut; for example, popular taste in fiction in the early nineteenth century veered towards the Gothic and domestic romance, rather than elaborate political critique. It is difficult to see these forms of fiction in clear, class terms. Working-class people found many ways to endow their lives with meaning, and forms of storytelling and fantasy (including melodrama and fairy tales) included elements that were trans-class. The ideals of respectability that drove working-class life may strike some as an example of bourgeois hegemony, but the evidence suggests that ideals of self-help, Christian moralism, and hard work could come from below as well. They were not simply imposed on workers.

Class was one reason why scholars became fascinated by the popular stage. Given its popularity, melodrama appeared to give us a point of entry to the popular mind in the nineteenth century. The rapport that actors and dramatists needed to have with their audiences gave melodrama a communal feel. Audiences could see people like themselves on stage (as opposed to the classical repertoire, which held that only the elite possessed lives of sufficient interest to be the subject of drama). The populism of melodrama also explains in part why historians and theatre practitioners in the 1980s began to recover its political potential and meaning (a process I label elsewhere as the 'melodramatic turn').[4] When modern audiences thrill to the musical *Les Miserables*, they recognize how nineteenth-century theatre can still say something about poverty and the injuries of class division.

Some of the scholarly literature on melodrama betrays a broadly Marxist approach, emerging as it did out of attempts to understand popular culture as a potential site of resistance to market capitalism. Martha Vicinus argued, 'Melodrama always sides with the powerless'.[5] It resisted the dehumanizing logic of the market place.[6]

Walter Scott worried about the way that the stage turned plebeians into heroes whilst presenting the elite as villainous. Dramatists, in his view, were perpetuating a form of 'intellectual Jacobinism' that subverted 'the natural order of things'.[7] The theatre censor George Colman complained in 1824 that plays tended to 'preach up the doctrine that government is Tyranny, that revolt is Virtue, and that rebels are Righteous'.[8] Indeed, there were affinities between melodrama and the language of radicalism. Melodrama had its roots in the French Revolution, as well as in the transgressive qualities of the Gothic novel. Thomas Holcroft, who introduced melodrama to Britain with A Tale of Mystery (1802), was a political radical. Melodrama (as we will see) echoed the arguments of radicals, blaming social problems on the corruption of the aristocracy.

But here we hit a problem. Most melodramas, far from being subversive or sites of class conflict, tended to reaffirm traditional hierarchy. They did not attack the social system as such, but blamed problems on the failings of bad individuals (a trait they shared with Dickens and much other popular fiction). Order resumed once the villain was dispatched at the end of the play. As we saw with the ending of The Rent Day, the solution to poverty was often dealt with not through rebellion but through the coming of a lucky windfall. Melodrama may have hymned the dignity of labour, but its route out of poverty comes through the discovery of unearned wealth. Many of the major issues in popular politics (such as the Chartist movement's promotion of universal manhood suffrage) barely found a space on the stage, though issues around empire, race, militarism, and the legal system were depicted.

Theatres proved poor vehicles for radical messages about class, in part because plays were policed by the Lord Chamberlain (who forbade overt political messages in plays under his jurisdiction), or were subject to self-censorship by anxious managements. Melodrama may have appealed to the working class, but it was not a form that came from it – though the class position of many actors and playwrights was ambiguous; they cultivated a bohemian air which resisted class definition. Theatres were commercial enterprises whose purpose was to entertain and generate profit, not places to stir class hostility. Antagonizing those who believed in a hierarchical society was imprudent or, sometimes, just bad business.

Critics keep asking the question: was melodrama radical or conservative? One answer is that the form was never the sole preserve of one social class, but a form of negotiation between different groups. Henry Irving's long-running success at the Lyceum in The Bells (1871) was just one example of the way melodrama appealed to all. Melodrama reminded diverse audiences of the values that they shared. By its very nature, it was a force for consensus that resisted too much focusing on class distinction. This rendered it politically ambiguous, or at least ostensibly apolitical.

And yet it is possible to find melodramas that contained coded political messages. Darryl Wadsworth has shown that stage adaptations of Dickens's

*Bleak House* (1852–3) varied according to whether they were performed in the West or East End of London. The death of Jo was depicted as an example of the plight of the poor in the East End; the West End version presented it in a much more conservative way, which lacked a clear class dimension.[9] The contrast between *The Factory Lad* and *The Rent Day* with which we commenced would also be an example of the way similar issues were treated in different ways depending on the venue. Theatres (at least in the early nineteenth century) could also be sites of political conflict. When the management at Covent Garden increased the cost of seats in 1809, the Old Price Riots ensued. Performances were disrupted with the waving of slogans and banners. This was essentially a class issue, as rioters wanted the return of a just price that working people could afford. Theatre (like society at large) seemed organized solely for the convenience of the aristocracy, giving the dispute a political dimension. Performances became impossible until the management offered cheaper tickets.[10]

## Melodrama's Political Imaginary

Melodrama was the product of a society where the languages of class were abundant and where popular culture reflected the class system. But what kind of interpretation of class shaped melodrama? By and large, what we find on the stage is not what Karl Marx was writing about: a capitalist society whose contradictions generated class struggle, as the proletariat was exploited and the bourgeoisie kept all the profits. Instead, the social portrait on stage can be understood as the continuation of eighteenth-century ideas about society, which viewed it as a seamless web in which the different ranks and orders knew their place and enjoyed complementary roles.[11] Melodrama was coloured by many of the assumptions of Hanoverian Britain, where status was as important as class – significantly, melodrama looked back not just to the Gothic but to eighteenth-century plays such as *The Beggar's Opera* (1728). This, it should be said, was a view of society promoted by the elite, and one that became increasingly obsolete in the nineteenth century. It did, however, still enjoy some popular assent because the 'good society' envisaged in many plays was one based on a chain of connections and mutual obligations: an organic community.

Class identity took time to develop. Melodrama's heyday was in the early to mid-nineteenth century, when attitudes to social relations were in flux and languages of class co-existed with older forms of economic identity, such as the view of society based on ranks and orders. The modern language of class (based on a three-class model of aristocracy, middle class, and working class) and a working-class identity based on trade unionism only started to really predominate when mass production went into the ascendant during the 1870s. Radicals had previously employed more ambiguous terms such as 'the people' when they described who they were supporting, though some Chartist leaders did speak unapologetically in class terms.[12]

For that reason, economic divisions between classes were acknowledged on stage, though they were often described as the difference between 'the rich' and 'the poor' (rather than through the starker language of class). Melodrama preferred to stress the ties that bind. Conflict in the plays emerged when these relationships were violated (for example, by rapacious landlords). Melodrama's stock in trade were the connections that ran across society and offered to link the classes. Thus the stage emphasized national identity, Christian morality, and the possibility of romantic love between individuals from different classes. The exploitation of sailors could be acknowledged in plays like Douglas Jerrold's *The Mutiny at the Nore* (1830), but this was eclipsed by the portrait of the Jack Tar as gallant national servant. What we find on the nineteenth-century stage is not so much class analysis in a radical form as a generous and slightly incoherent populism that celebrated the lives of the common people (though it also featured working-class people who were less than virtuous).

At the same time, it contained a view of the world in which the aristocracy is very much in control. In some respects, this is a testimony to its accuracy. Nineteenth-century historians now emphasize the continuing importance of the elite at all levels of society. The aristocracy, the gentry or, further down, the squirearchy remained (in some respects at least) the leaders of society up to the 1880s. As David Cannadine puts it, up to the 1870s, 'it was the country house not the counting house that was still emphatically in charge'.[13] The wealth of the middle classes expanded but patricians set the tone of the governing classes: even in 1900, the prime minister was the Marquis of Salisbury, a hereditary aristocrat.

The portrait of the aristocracy was bifurcated. Evil aristocrats abounded on the stage. However, the solution to the problem of the bad aristocrat was usually the good aristocrat, a male figure who was aware of his paternal obligations. In *The Rent Day,* the steward Crumbs demands rent to pay off the gambling debts of Grantley, the squire. Grantley, in fact, turns out to be a model landlord who returns in disguise to expose the way that his steward oppresses the poor. His failure has been that of an absentee landlord cut off from his tenants.

Between the rich and the poor is a set of accomplices of the elite, such as Crumbs. These include stewards, bailiffs, and lawyers. They are essentially parasites on the common people doing the bidding of the rich. This is a view of society in which the middle class barely exists. Such a view began to change from the mid-century onwards, reflecting the greater visibility of the middle class in the corridors of power, in local government and as drivers of the economy. There were plays that featured middle-class swindlers, bankers, and speculators, such as Tom Taylor's *Still Waters Run Deep* (1855). Another essentially middle-class figure was the miser; for example, Old Miers (an unsubtle anagram of 'miser') in Edward Fitzball's *The Negro of Wapping* (1838). The ubiquity of the figure of the miser in melodrama – Walter Hatherleigh in George Dibdin Pitt's *Simon Lee* (1839) is an another example – embodies the person possessed of money who fails to use it well. Pitt's Simon Lee says 'a miser is a rogue to his country, for he hoards up the vitality of commerce and thereby checks it' (1:2).

The peculiarity of melodrama is that it combined two things that should be antithetical: populism and deference. If populism locates virtue in ordinary experience, then it should be opposed to the values of deference and paternalism, in which plebeians bow to the wisdom and care of patricians. The stage was a matrix in which the two coexisted. Melodrama reflected the disappointment of a society which was becoming more atomized. On the stage, it is often the failure of the elite to remember its paternalist responsibilities that causes disorder. Melodrama thus dovetails with both radicalism and romantic Toryism. Many radicals, in trying to protect traditional rights, were in one sense conservatives. There was a strong strand of romantic paternalism that coloured the image of the social order on stage. For that reason, the one position that does not appear to be validated by melodrama is laissez-faire liberalism, arguably the dominant ideology of the nineteenth century (and one associated with the middle classes). Theatre, for this reason, could be appropriated by audiences as an oppositional space; its political imaginary included the space to conceive of different forms of social relationship.

Another constituent of the melodramatic frame of mind was patriotism. British melodrama emerged during the Napoleonic Wars and their aftermath, which appeared to vindicate the nation's virtue. Yet patriotism was not necessarily conservative; it was also part of the language of radicalism from the eighteenth century up to the 1870s. Radicals insisted that love of country included concern for the condition of the common people. In this view, it was the selfish elite that lacked patriotism; freeborn Englishmen had a duty to oppose it. Patriotism was both an integral part of political argument and a way of building social consensus – or at least expressing a desire that different parts of society might work together for the benefit of all. The cultural work of melodrama was to create utopian moments in which consensus could be achieved.

Nautical melodrama shows the relationship between class and patriotism by presenting positive portraits of working-class lives. The patriotism of honest Jack Tars had seen off Napoleon. They represented the values of the freeborn Englishman, a motif that animated popular politics for much of the nineteenth century.[14] The Jack Tar was a hero celebrated on stage but also in popular prints and Staffordshire figurines, an icon of British endeavour. There were links between what was on the stage and what people put on their mantelpieces. The figure also resonated with the soldiers and sailors who could often be found in the audience. The sailor was clearly working class, but his presentation cannot be reduced to class; he stood for a different set of values. In plays like Buckstone's *Luke the Labourer*, he seemed to speak a different language from landlubbers with his frequent nautical references ('strike my topmast', 'snatch my bowlines') and allusions (2:1). Douglas Jerrold's *Black Ey'd Susan* (1829) featured the sailor William, who is strong, heroic, plain-spoken, and adept at the hornpipe. The Jack Tar in popular culture was also a figure who spent his life being far from home. The image of the sailor's return, a frequent motif in many plays, was a familiar experience in many coastal communities and in the East End of London with its docks. It resonated with a society that was increasingly mobile as people moved around the country and around the world. *Black Ey'd Susan* commenced at the Surrey but later played at Drury Lane, where its patriotism proved a hit with an audience derived from across the classes. Jerrold's William was the expression of an age in which the possibility of universal manhood suffrage was entering the political agenda. Melodramas rarely backed democratic politics, but their structure of feeling told a different story. Virtue lay with people who did not have the vote.

If we argue that melodrama offered a form of heightened reality or a series of translations that rendered everyday experience in a mediated form, it does not follow that melodrama was an exercise in what Marxists call 'false consciousness'. This would suggest that melodrama was a means by which the dominant class lulled the working-class audience into accepting its subordinate role. Such a view fails to take seriously the complexity of cultural forms. We know that melodrama throughout its history was always open to parody and burlesque. Audiences did not simply buy into the worldview of the stage, but could greet its stories with applause or disdain. They were aware of being manipulated by stage conventions, but still lapped up the sensational stories. Melodrama could be appropriated by audiences in different ways. We need to think of audiences both as internally differentiated and as having some agency. They could see political messages even if there was nothing necessarily political in the text. The pictorial tableau, for example, offered opportunities that could not be policed. As we saw with the end of *The Factory Lad*, the stage could offer visual statements of class without words.

What, then, is the political imaginary that we discover on the melodramatic stage? It is one founded upon the Victorian belief in the importance of character. Virtue, fairness, altruism, and regard for others are the sources of order. The opposite is degeneracy: the total implosion of moral character. Virtue is defined in terms of honesty and chastity. The melodramatic imagination did not admit of complexity. It saw the world in the stark terms of binary oppositions: right and wrong, rich and poor, the mansion and the cottage, virtuous and 'fallen', free and unfree labour, human and supernatural. Then there are the stark oppositions: tradition versus modernity, the rightful heir versus the scheming relative, the freeborn Englishman versus the foreign tyrant, face-to-face relations versus the cold alienation of the market economy, justice versus injustice, family ties versus individualism, town versus country. Melodramas adopted the classic Victorian solution to the problems of modern society: philanthropy. Sam, the eponymous villain in Fitzball's *The Negro of Wapping*, blames his descent into crime on the local miser denying him a helping hand. Lack of charity is sign of deficient character.

## Visions of the Social Order

In *Time and Tide*, first performed at the Surrey Theatre in 1867, a character exclaims, 'Oh, London, as ye lie there before me, I could breathe a curse on your splendid streets – a curse on your squalid ways! You've turned a happy country lad into a miserable heart-broken man' (Prologue). Melodrama was, by and large, an urban form (though it often portrayed the countryside). It gave expression to the advent of great cities which were shaped by industrialization but, even more fundamentally, by the rise in population from the mid-eighteenth century onwards. It was in cities that class differentials became stark. The stage abounded with images of familiar urban landmarks and took upon itself the task of explaining what city life was all about.[15] For that reason it was implicitly about class. Urban life was registered as a place of anonymity and peril. It corrupted the simplicities of rural life, where the classes are part of a seamless web. As one rustic in *Luke the Labourer* (1826) says, 'most things that are larn'd in Lunnon [London] had better never to be know'd at all' (1:1). Class relationships in the play are those of the labourers and the squirearchy.

Melodrama spoke up for an organic society in which all are linked through mutual bonds. Above all, melodrama expressed the shift away from a world based upon custom and tradition in the face of the rise of the market and possessive individualism.[16] Hence it constructed an imagined, organic rural society which contrasted with the corruptions of city life. One bond that has

become endangered is the familial link through the generations. In melodrama, children search for lost parents and vice versa. A working-class
woman in Dibdin Pitt's *The Beggar's Petition* (1841) runs off with a wealthy
young man and, over the years, becomes indifferent to the plight of her
poverty-stricken parents, though they are reconciled at the end. The play
suggests that bonds of home and family are too important to be sundered
(although it also, during the course of the action, shows how these are
fragile).

The figure of the aristocratic seducer was a way of expressing class differences. Melodrama's stock in trade was the evil aristocrat who was indifferent
to the plight of the poor and had designs on a lower-class woman. Such
figures possessed a deadly glamour on stage. In *Luke the Labourer,*
Wakefield, the lord of the manor, is bent on the seduction of a farmer's
daughter, Clara. It played at the Adelphi, the leading 'minor' playhouse on
the Strand in London, which enjoyed a cross-class audience. All social groups
enjoyed the figure of the aristocratic seducer. It can be connected to popular
radicalism, which blamed the evils of society on an exploitative aristocracy
that dominated the political system and rigged the market in its favour. Yet
melodrama can also be linked to romantic Toryism, which complained of a
class that had forgotten its obligations to the poor – there are thus connections that can be made between melodrama and a novel like Disraeli's *Sybil*
(1845). Melodrama was built on the ambiguities of populism. Its tales,
gestures, and attitudes spoke of class, but drew back from talk of class
struggle. Warmth and sympathy were seen as more important.

At one level, melodrama reflected the point of intersection between
Romanticism and popular culture. It embodied the view that authentic
feeling and virtue was not to be found in the artificial civilization of the
elite but amongst ordinary folk. Certainly, the stage abounded with comic
rustics and yokels, not overly endowed with intelligence, but the stage did not
disdain workers' lives. Snobbery was never a virtue. In George Dibdin Pitt's
*Simon Lee*, the rich miser Hatherleigh turns his daughter out of his home for
daring to marry a poor farmer against whom he bears a grudge. The latter is
forced to become a poacher, whilst Hatherleigh allows his grandchildren to
live in a hovel. On the other hand, workers who get above themselves are
either the object of ridicule or villains. Humphrey Bacon, the former butler to
the squire who becomes his clerk in Dibdin Pitt's *The Beggar's Petition,* is
ridiculous because of the way he puts on airs.

Class was thus woven into melodrama in complex ways. The social
investigator Henry Mayhew found that east London dustmen liked going
to plays with 'plenty of murdering scenes in them'.[17] The fascination with
violence on stage represented an assertive popular culture unwilling to

submit to middle-class norms of respectability and good taste.[18] The Coburg Theatre in South London was so identified with depictions of violence that it became known as the 'Blood Tub'. It spoke to the kind of working-class culture that was not too concerned with respectability. There was a strong link between melodrama and the popular press, which featured lip-smacking accounts of horrible murders. When James Thurtell was put on trial for the murder of William Weare in 1823, both the Surrey and the Coburg theatres in South London offered melodramas inspired by the case.[19] One way of understanding working-class life is through the idea of the criminal under-world – a common theme in the early Victorian period, exploited by plays like W. T. Moncrieff's *The Scamps of London* (1843). These were plays that borrowed heavily from French examples. The figure of the French detective Vidocq and the novels of Eugene Sue captured the imagination of early Victorian popular culture, generating melodramas in which the city was viewed as a labyrinth that had to be penetrated and its puzzle solved. The law was frequently shown as unjust and biased against the poor (in Walker's *The Factory Lad*, the judge is called 'Justice Bias'). Denizens of the under-world were distinguished by their use of slang (rather like Jack Tars), render-ing a view of the working class as different through accent and vocabulary: part of a fascination, dating back to the eighteenth century, with an alter-native society based on the dangerous classes who live close to the respectable and law abiding. Crime was an integral part of the presentation of class.

In a preface to Buckstone's *Luke the Labourer*, we are told that 'the vices of the lower orders of society, for the most part, have their origin in drunkenness, which is the parent of sickness, poverty, and crime, and not only debases and destroys its victims, but renders him incapable of performing the duties of his station'.[20] The idea that each class has a 'proper station' suggests the idea of class as part of a seamless web, but class was constantly refracted through the lens of character. Temperance and the fear of drunkenness was a great popular cause to which the stage responded. By this account, the failings of the working class were rooted in issues of character. The use of character in melodrama is complex. On the one hand, it is rooted in nature; people of weak or bad character submit to dark desires. On the other hand, plays also feature redemption, in which a bad person (for example, the villain's sidekick) can change sides or move towards righteousness. The drunkard who turns away from intemperance shows how the 'movingness' of melodramas (their emo-tional connection with the audience) is based on redemption.

Another negative stereotype of the working class was the trade unionist or worker trying to improve his or her situation through industrial action. In G. F. Taylor's *The Factory Strike*, which first played at the Royal Victoria Theatre (later the Old Vic) in 1836, a factory owner wishes to introduce new machinery. Set at the time of the Luddite disturbances, his workers are, however, stirred up by a villainous agitator not only to strike but to burn down the factory. The agitator also murders the factory owner. However, in the moral lexicon of the play, the factory owner is a benevolent paternalist who is only seeking to do his best for his labourers (the equivalent of a benevolent squire). His death leads to poverty for the workers. At the end, the hero – a hardworking labourer who did not want to strike – exclaims 'all my sorrows, all my misery, I owe to that which has raised itself up in the land like a giant, and is worship'd by the working classes, like a demigod, I mean a strike!' (3:6). The play recognizes the source of workers' anger but neutralizes their demands by suggesting workers can easily be led astray by hot-headed agitators out to cause trouble. This is a different approach to *The Factory Lad*.

There was a shift towards the end of the century. As Michael Booth notes, 'West End melodrama virtually ceased to have a social conscience as it became more middle-class'.[21] Whilst melodrama continued at the Princess's and the Adelphi, other West End theatres went over to comfortable middle-class comedies. Increasingly, West End theatre dealt with the problems of the middle or upper class, and pursued a mode of realism that matched developments within the novel. This in turn required the use of more upper-class actors. The class system shaped the acting profession.[22] Theatre became increasingly middle-class, whilst working people looked towards the music hall – and later the cinema – for entertainment.

In conclusion: the deployments of the class system on the popular stage are one reason why melodrama transcended the proscenium arch. Its language and scenarios spoke to popular concerns and shaped reality more generally. It became a good device to think with or, in the words of Peter Brooks, a 'sense making system'.[23] Melodrama reflected social relationships and constructed them at the same time. It is no surprise to find writers, journalists, politicians, and even ordinary people employing language and scenarios that they acquired from the stage – especially the longing for social justice and fair play. Melodrama provided a utopian dimension to popular social thought and shaped how class was understood.

## Notes

1. Geoff Eley and Keith Nield, *The Future of Class in History: What's Left of the Social?* (Ann Arbor: University of Michigan Press, 2007).
2. Asa Briggs, 'The Language of "Class" in Early Nineteenth Century England', in *Essays in Labour History*, eds. Asa Briggs and John Saville (London: Macmillan, 1960).

3. Alastair J. Reid, *Social Classes and Social Relations in Britain, 1850–1914*, new edition (Cambridge: Cambridge University Press, 1995 [1992]).

4. Rohan McWilliam, 'Melodrama and the Historians', *Radical History Review*, 78 (2000).

5. Martha Vicinus, '"Helpless and Unfriended": Nineteenth-Century Domestic Melodrama', in *When They Weren't Doing Shakespeare: Essays on Nineteenth-Century British and American Theatre*, eds. Judith Law Fisher and Stephen Watt (Athens: University of Georgia Press, 1989), 175.

6. Elaine Hadley, *Melodramatic Tactics: Theatricalized Dissent in the English Marketplace, 1800–1885* (Stanford: Stanford University Press, 1995), 5–6.

7. Frank Rahill, *The World of Melodrama* (University Park: Pennsylvania State University Press, 1967), 155–6.

8. Michael Hays and Anastasia Nikolopoulou (eds.), *Melodrama: The Cultural Emergence of a Genre* (Basingstoke: Macmillan, 1996), ix.

9. Darryl Wadsworth, '"A Low Born Labourer Like You": Audience and Working-Class Melodrama', in *Varieties of Victorianism: The Uses of a Past*, ed. Gary Day (London: Macmillan, 1998).

10. Marc Baer, *Theatre and Disorder in Late Georgian London* (Oxford: Clarendon Press, 1992); Hadley, *Melodramatic Tactics*, 34–76.

11. David Cannadine, *Class in Britain* (New Haven and London: Yale University Press, 1998), 19, 25–8.

12. Eric Hobsbawm, 'The Making of the Working Class, 1870-1914', in *Worlds of Labour: Further Studies in the History of Labour* (London: Weidenfeld and Nicolson, 1984), 194–213; Patrick Joyce, *Visions of the People: Industrial England and the Question of Class, c. 1848–1914* (Cambridge: Cambridge University Press, 1991).

13. David Cannadine, *The Decline and Fall of the British Aristocracy* (New Haven and London: Yale University Press, 1990), 18.

14. E. P. Thompson, *The Making of the English Working Class* (London: Gollancz, 1963), chapter 4.

15. Michael R. Booth, 'The Metropolis on Stage', in *The Victorian City: Images and Realities*, eds. Harold James Dyos and Michael Wolff, vol. 1 (London: Routledge, 1973).

16. E. P. Thompson, *Customs in Common* (London: Merlin, 1991), 16–96.

17. Henry Mayhew, *London Labour and the London Poor*, vol. 2, reprint (New York: Dover, 1968 [1851]), 176.

18. Rosalind Crone, *Violent Victorians: Popular Entertainment in Nineteenth-Century London* (Manchester: Manchester University Press, 2012), chapter 4.

19. Crone, *Violent Victorians*, 124.

20. D-G, 'Remarks', in J. B. Buckstone, *Luke the Labourer* (London: Cumberland, 1830), 6.

21. Michael R. Booth, *Theatre in the Victorian Age* (Cambridge: Cambridge University Press, 1991), 154.

22. Booth, *Theatre in the Victorian Age*, 131–2.

23. Peter Brooks, *The Melodramatic Imagination: Balzac, Henry James, Melodrama and the Mode of Excess* (New Haven: Yale University Press, 1976), xiii.

# 12

MARTY GOULD

# Melodrama and Empire

In nineteenth-century Britain, melodrama was an important participant in the affective consolidation of an imperial public, translating imperial conflicts and conquests into cultural productions that satisfied a popular taste for emotionally stirring drama and exotic theatrical spectacle. Melodrama was a powerful – and popular – vehicle for transmitting the jingoistic ideologies, as well as the images of the national character, that formed the bedrock of popular imperialism. Of all the period's theatrical genres and modes, it is melodrama – a genre with wide popular appeal – that was the most particularly suited to representing the moral scope and physical scale of empire across a wide social spectrum. As that empire expanded and evolved, so too did melodrama's engagement with it, the generalized fantasy Orientalism of early melodrama giving way, by century's end, to more aggressively jingoistic plays with settings, characters, and plots borrowed directly from real-world events.

It was in large part through spectacle that empire communicated its victories and its values, forming and informing a metropolitan citizenry. Noting that 'it is thoroughly understood that the plays at Drury Lane are things rather to be looked at than listened to', theatre critic Dutton Cook's review of *Youth* at Drury Lane in 1881 reveals the importance of spectacle and scene painting in the success of imperialist melodramas: 'the embarkation of the troops at Portsmouth and the battle fought at Hawk's Point by innumerable well-drilled supernumeraries, these were excellent displays of stage art, and roused the audience to special enthusiasm'.[1] Similar reviews circulated in response to Augustus Harris's *The World* (1882), with one critic calling its scenery 'the *raison-d'etre* of the piece'.[2] Such reviews reveal the important role that visual effects played in the appeal of imperialist melodrama: even when a play seemed too wedded to convention or its plot was deemed improbable, striking visual effect alone could rouse the audience to patriotic fervour.

As Edward Ziter has argued, from its beginnings, melodrama provided a 'pictorial vocabulary that organized and interpreted the regions east of

Europe for a metropolitan citizenry curious about the complex, trans-global conglomeration of places, peoples, and cultures that made up the British Empire'.[3] In the early nineteenth century, the 'exotic East' offered fertile material for spectacular theatrical fantasies: strange animals, richly costumed characters, and unfamiliar landscapes made India and Eastern Asia a rich territory for theatrical exploitation. The staging of the exotic also encouraged an active desire that demanded further visual consumption, commercial import, and territorial acquisition of this imagined East. Thus feeding the cultural engines of imperial expansion, the theatre provoked the public's acquisitive interest in the world beyond Britain, not only providing a vicarious encounter with it, but also promising its conquest and domination.

India, the so-called jewel in Britain's imperial crown, was a popular setting for melodrama throughout the century. India's architecture lent itself to rich pictorial illustration, while its religious leaders and hereditary monarchs made for theatrically effective villains. While earlier plays set in India – *The Cataract of the Ganges* (1823), for example – focused on Britain's protection of indigenous women through the reform of cultural practices such as sati, in the wake of the Sepoy Rebellion of 1857, an event the Victorians knew as the 'Indian Mutiny', plays with Indian settings such as *Jessie Brown* (1858) struck a more stridently martial tone, with a focus on Britons in peril.[4] Africa was less frequently invoked on the nineteenth-century stage, though its historical association with slavery intensified dramas such as Harris and Rowe's *Freedom* (1883) and Harris and Pettitt's *Human Nature* (1885), which cast imperialist invasion as humanitarian liberation.[5] Australia, which evolved from prison outpost to settler colony over the course of the nineteenth century, was a setting well suited to melodrama's plots of crime, punishment, villainy, and retribution. In Edward Stirling's dramatization of *Margaret Catchpole* (1854), or the 1888 drama *The Binbian Mine*, for example, movement to and from Australia both expunges Britain's criminal element and enables an heroic character metamorphosis.

Whatever its setting, melodrama offered timely entertainment, very much engaged with the events of the day. For the Victorians, the imperial frontier was never farther than the closest stage. From galloping horses to live rifle and cannon fire, theatres went to great lengths to provide audiences a 'realistic' encounter with empire. Printed advertisements testified to the great efforts theatres made to create realistic stage pictures, which, as Heidi Holder has noted, generally meant 'that the geography depicted on stage was identical to that depicted in newspapers and journals'.[6] Playbills listed battle scenes in bold print that mimicked the newspaper headline, a typography that suggested a documentary impulse behind these entertainments. This pretension to a sort of pictorial realism was reinforced by mid-to-late Victorian staging practices and melodrama's readiness to engage with current events, as described in an anticipatory advertisement of Augustus Harris and Paul Merritt's *Youth* (1881):

> The new play will be ultra-sensational, and full of startling effects. It will deal with our late military troubles in South Africa. We are to see the departure of the troops from England, the leave-taking of the soldiers, and the clambering up of the huge sides of the transports, after the familiar pictures by O'Neil. There will be scenes representing the trenches and the hand-to-hand fight at Rorke's Drift.[7]

Built around incidents from the recently concluded Anglo-Zulu War (1879), the play promises to replay the troops' departure for service in a conflict already concluded, making the melodrama something of a memorial, the suspenseful uncertainty of its unfolding drama in tension with the reassuring closure promised by recent real-world events. The play's realization of Henry Nelson O'Neil's *Eastward, Ho!* (1858), a famous – and familiar – painting of troops departing for service in India at the time of the Rebellion is yet another, and a further, backward glance. On its premiere, the scenes in South Africa were shifted to Asia, so that the play could engage with the Second Anglo-Afghan War (1878–80). Revived in 1883, *Youth* was reworked again so that its scenes depicted events from the more recent Anglo-Egyptian War (1882).[8] Though its essential plot and characters remained the same, the play's settings could be shifted to engage more recent events abroad.

Although it was often highly timely and topical, melodrama frequently overlaid outrageously exaggerated military spectacles and wholly invented characters and conflicts with gestures of verisimilitude. Even when it was engaging with current events, melodrama, a theatrical form that tended to be more ideological than informational in its broader aims and cultural function, was not always wedded to factual accuracy. Harris and Pettitt's *Human Nature* (1885), for example, reimagined the fall of Khartoum as a British triumph, transforming the Empire's recent loss into a moment Drury Lane's audience could celebrate.[9]

Melodrama's conventional framing translated an expansive and complicated political concept into the more familiar theatrical idioms that allowed audiences of all classes to understand their nation's imperial project and to make sense of themselves as citizens of an empire. This citizenship was not limited to metropolitan audiences, as melodramas performed across the Empire played an important role in reinforcing colonial connections to 'Greater Britain'. Not only did enthusiasm for these entertainments persist across the nineteenth century, but the links forged between melodrama and empire on the nineteenth-century stage persisted into the film era, with twentieth-century colonialist cinema employing the representational strategies that authorized Western Europe's continuing cultural and political domination of the colonized world.[10]

## Origins and Development of Imperialist Melodrama

Generally considered by theatre historians to be a late-century development, imperialist melodrama is a form with deep historical roots in earlier melodramatic subgenres, including Eastern Gothic melodramas, melodramas about the slave trade, and nautical melodramas. Slave traders and overseers made effective melodramatic villains in the early nineteenth century, and the global sites of slavery – the west coast of Africa, the American plantation – were spectacularly effective locations for emotionally charged dramas that engaged the public and political controversies of the day. Melodrama's conventions reinforced the prevailing structures of power that sustained slavery. In its march towards restorative closure, the form itself works against the possibility of revolution: there was little – if any – room for emancipation in melodrama's commitment to normative hierarchical structures of order.[11] This generic resistance to revolution would remain a defining feature of the form as it expressed increasing interest in matters pertaining to empire. On the melodramatic stage, armed revolts – whether of slaves or the indigenous inhabitants of overseas colonies – are generally contained, quelled before the curtain descends on the drama. If liberty triumphs in melodrama, as the Indian Mutiny and Boer War plays later in the century demonstrate, it does so through heroic self-sacrifice rather than through violent social upheaval.

Liberty remained an important theme as the slavery melodramas of the early nineteenth century yielded the stage to more identifiably colonialist and imperialist melodramas. Appearing a year after France abolished slavery across its empire, Edward Stirling's *The White Slave; or, the Flag of Freedom* (1849) employs a French colonial setting that tempers its engagement with slavery in the United States, masking its critical involvement in a current political controversy as a dramatization of a matter of more distant, historical interest. In this play, British bodies are protected by Britain's national banner, 'under whose protecting folds the rich, the poor, the white man, and the slave, find equal shelter and support!' (1:1). This equation of the empire's flag with individual liberty redefines, perhaps oxymoronically, the nature and function of imperialism.

In plays such as *The White Slave* (1836), *Rattlin the Reefer* (1836), and *The Cabin Boy* (1846), we can see how slavery melodrama intersected with the nautical melodrama that was especially popular in the 1820s and 1830s.[12] Nautical melodrama established patterns by which Britain's battles abroad, from the Crimean conflict of the 1850s to the Boer War of the 1890s, would be translated into theatrical entertainment. Patriotic to their core, nautical dramas celebrated British naval superiority in a period of expanding British overseas mercantile activity. Satisfying public demand for images of British heroism, the sailor hero of plays such as J. T. Haines's *My Poll and My Partner Joe* (1836) promoted the capitalist energies that fuelled imperial expansion and embodied the military strength that secured the empire's vital trade routes.[13] This naval hero would evolve over the course of the century as melodrama negotiated changing public perceptions of empire.[14]

While slavery melodramas and nautical melodramas engaged with racial issues and global military conflicts in Britain's early empire, it was the Eastern Orientalist melodrama that served as the most direct antecedent to the stridently imperialist melodramas of the later nineteenth century. William Barrymore's *El Hyder; or, the Chief of the Ghaut Mountains* (1818) is an example of such dramas. Capturing the exotic visual delights on offer in this play, the cover of the published Lacy's edition labels *El Hyder* 'a grand eastern melodramatic spectacle'. The play's scenery, this edition notes, was 'taken from William Daniell's *Views in India*', a popular collection of picturesque sketches of India, published as a series of volumes between 1795 and 1808. Adding dramatic action to Daniell's illustrations, *El Hyder* satisfied public desire for visual consumption of India by capitalizing on images that were already enjoying wide public circulation.

On one side of the play's military conflict is Hamet, usurper of the throne of Hindustan, who has captured Delhi and taken as prisoners Princess Zada and her son the prince, who is the lawful heir to the throne. Standing against Hamet is El Hyder, the play's titular hero, who commands an army of warriors determined to overthrow the usurper and restore the rightful heir. The play leaves little doubt as to Hamet's status as villain. He is, in every way, the stereotypical Oriental despot: he arrives on stage atop an elephant, heralded by a grand procession of soldiers, harem wives, and slaves; he steals the throne from its rightful heir; he forces the captive princess to choose between being his consort or his slave.[15] With his elephant, armies, harem wives, and slaves, Hamet is surrounded by the stuff of Eastern fantasy; this exotic pageant is both an optical feast for the audience and an unmistakable marker of Hamet's immorality, self-indulgence, and authoritarianism.

To counter this despotic figure of Oriental fantasy, the play mobilizes a figure from history, Hyder Ali. Although the historical Hyder Ali had resisted British expansion in India, Barrymore's play imagines that he *invites* the aid of the British, who assist him in the restoration of the kingdom's lawful ruler. Barrymore's play looks to the past as a way of providing a political – and a moral – framework for more recent events, shifting its historical materials to create a drama that advances a view of Britain's empire-builders, not as conquerors, but as adjunct operatives in an indigenous struggle for justice: in the immediate wake of a fresh British conquest in India, the play characterizes colonial expansion as the commitment to a larger moral duty. Invoking – and altering – a figure from the Anglo-Mysore Wars at the conclusion of the Anglo-Maratha Wars, some thirty years later, the play collapsed both into a single, recurring ideological conflict.

In keeping with this re-characterization of imperial conquest as benevolent intervention, the dramatic focus of Barrymore's play is on internal, indigenous Indian politics; its British characters are relatively minor, providing occasional commentary and comic relief. For most of the play they remain on the sidelines, shadowy figures who watch the main drama as it unfolds. The British characters belong to the play's comic subplot, yet in the end they join Hyder and his men and become instrumental to the military triumph that brings the drama to a close. Though the audience is left with a final vision of British troops triumphant, the larger dramatic trajectory of the play recasts this as a chiefly moral, rather than merely military, victory: the vanquishing of tyranny by the forces of freedom.

Precursors to the imperialist melodramas that would develop through the latter decades of the century, early melodramas such as *El Hyder* imagined an exotic East woven from Romantic fantasies of Oriental luxury, despotic kings, and supernatural forces. In these early Eastern melodramas, Oriental despotism was defeated by the British, often, as in the case of *El Hyder* and *The Cataract of the Ganges*, while working alongside indigenous forces that had taken up arms against a repressive local regime. Within such dramas, British characters tended to play supporting roles, with the larger drama dominated by indigenous conflict and illustrated by grand Eastern spectacle. As the empire expanded and the level of public knowledge about empire grew, these somewhat abstracted early Orientalist fantasies gave way to more factually informed melodramas with geographically particular settings that somewhat more accurately resembled areas in which Britain operated either militarily or commercially.[16]

Evolving over the course of the nineteenth century, imperialist melodrama became ever more spectacular in its effects, patriotic in its sentiments, and jingoistic in its tone. With its enormous stage and capacious auditorium, Drury Lane easily accommodated imperialist melodramas designed on the grandest of scales: distant cities and foreign landscapes were imaginatively recreated by the theatre's scenic artists; large casts of actors paraded on the stage as horses galloped across it; battle sequences filled the cavernous theatre with the sounds of cannon and rifle fire. Drury Lane became, by the close of the nineteenth century, the acknowledged home of imperialist melodrama.[17]

In melodramas such as *The Heroine of Glencoe* (1899), the final close of the curtain is often preceded by scenes of soldiers arriving in Britain or parading through the city's streets to the strains of 'Rule Britannia' and 'God Save the Queen'. A review of an 1899 production of Harris and Pettitt's *Human Nature* testifies to the patriotic spirit that such large-scale melodramatic spectacle could arouse. The reviewer emphasizes that Harris and Pettitt's play, originally produced some fifteen years earlier, had assumed a new relevance given the nation's current embroilment in the Boer War:

> Scene II, 'The Fall of Khartoum', – is one of the most realistic stage pictures in melodrama, which is saying a lot – and Scene IV, 'The return of the soldiers in Trafalgar Square', when the spacious stage of the Grand Theatre has something like 120 persons on at once. This, including as it does three military bands, is guaranteed to rouse the loyalty and patriotism of any audience at the present time to an almost inordinate degree. On Monday the whole house rose to the strains of 'Rule Britannia', and heartily joined in with the National Anthem.[18]

In such boisterous scenes, the play's real-life audience joins the stage crowd in cheering for the soldiers' victorious return, transforming theatregoers into a celebratory public. Moreover, as in the case of *Human Nature*, when they were performed in the midst of an unresolved, active conflict, such scenes anticipated – perhaps even promised – the eventual celebration of a final British victory, offering the certain closure of dramatic scripting amidst the uncertainty of war.

In Arthur Shirley's *The Absent-Minded Beggar* (1900) we can see how music and spectacle combined to transform an audience into a patriotic public. *The Absent-Minded Beggar* shared its title with Arthur Sullivan's musical setting of Rudyard Kipling's popular poem (originally published in the *Daily Mail* in October 1899), an example of the stage operating in concert with other cultural forms and institutions (in this case the press and the music hall) to promote popular imperialist sentiment.[19] In the play, Gilbert Hay, a young Scot, imagines the Union Jack as the material embodiment of the jingoism celebrated in popular song: 'A flag is a regimental anthem. It is "The Old Folks at Home," – "The Girl I Left Behind Me," and "Rule Britannia" all done up in one silk wrapper. ... [It is] two or three yards of embroidered stuff that spells "God Save the Queen" all over the wide, wide world' (1:1). These were songs long associated with Britain's wars abroad, sung by audiences in music halls, by dockside crowds waving farewell to departing troops, and by soldiers on fields of battle from the Crimea to India and South Africa.[20] Uniting sight and sound, Hay's speech ingeniously interweaves the flag with what we might call the soundtrack of popular imperialism, amplifying the impact of music – a generic feature of melodrama – by fusing it with the flag, a visual emblem of empire. In plays such as *The Absent-Minded Beggar* and Merritt and Pettitt's *British Born* (1873), the Union Jack was more than a mere prop: it was a powerful emblem that made virtue patriotic and patriotism a virtue.

At century's end, Drury Lane's lavish imperialist spectacles increasingly reflected public anxieties about the possibilities of the loss of Britain's global supremacy to emerging rivals such as France, Germany, and the United States, all of which were eager to extend their own imperial shadows, aided by economies and militaries strong enough to mount serious challenge to a British hegemony that had been largely unopposed for most of the century. The intra-European conflicts of late-century imperialist melodramas represent not only an increasing anxiety about continental rivals but also concerns about the morally corrupting influence of foreign cultures and the effects of foreign contact on the British character.[21] In addition, colonial rebellions and hard-fought wars against powerful groups such as the Afghans, Boers, and Zulus cast doubt about the future growth and stability of the Empire. All of these anxieties are evident in the increasingly jingoistic content of melodramas (and the popular music hall songs many of them featured) from the 1870s onward.[22]

*The Absent-Minded Beggar* demonstrates these late-century cultural politics at play. Denouncing the British and their banner, Boer – and villain – Karl van Buren literally tramples the Union Jack as the curtain rises on the play's first act. Though his mother is English and his father German, Karl recognizes no allegiance to either of these Old World nations, declaring instead that he is an Afrikander [sic], and he vows to take up arms against the English in his country's fight for freedom. Guided by the dream of an English-free future for the Transvaal, Karl's genocidal fantasy involves the massacre of the wives and children of British settlers. Karl's villainy knows no bounds. He lays plans to eradicate the English, to replace Kruger as President of the South Africa Republic, and to enslave the native population. Identifying with the Boer cause yet born of an English mother, Van Buren suffers from displaced nationalist loyalties, a cultural dislocation that manifests in his moral failings.

Karl's allegiance to the Boer cause puts him at odds with the sentiments of Gilbert Hay, a young Scotsman, who believes that the Uitlanders – British settlers living in the Transvaal – deserve freedom from the despotic yoke of Boer rule. The political future of the Transvaal is not the only thing that the two men wrangle over, for Karl has eyes for Kathleen, Gilbert's young bride: this romantic rivalry echoes and underscores the conflict over the future of the Transvaal. Following a family financial disaster, in the third act Gilbert takes his wife and child to South Africa, where he hopes to escape the poverty that plagued them in England. In South Africa, surveying the carnage of the battlefield that surrounds them, Kathleen and Gilbert cast their thoughts to the slain soldiers' loved ones back in England, to the wives and children who await news of the husband and father who will never return home. Here, Shirley's play is grimly honest about the price to be paid for securing Britain's imperial frontier, but it quickly turns the notion of national sacrifice on its head, shifting the real burden onto its own audience. Gilbert appeals to both the 'big hearted men with fat purses [and the] big handed toilers, with as scantily filled pockets' who will alike give what they can 'to help the widows and orphans who have fallen in our country's cause' (3:1). His words are clearly directed at the play's audience, which is implicated – rich and poor alike – in the care of the widows and orphans created by this conflict. Voicing the play's opposition to the sort of narrow, separatist, colonial nationalism espoused by Karl, Gilbert's appeal embraces all classes – the men with fat purses as well as the hard-toiling working men: all are alike encouraged to recognize their common member- ship in, and duty to, an imperial family.

## Domesticating the Empire

Often representationally reductive, melodrama helped to domesticate the empire, fitting the foreign into the familiar through the use of archetypical characters, domestic situations, and conventional themes. Charles Reade's *It Is Never Too Late to Mend* (1865), an oft-revived melodrama that enjoyed wide popularity in the second half of the nineteenth century, is an example of how melodramatic conventions intersected with, informed, and were inflected by empire in the middle of the nineteenth century. Reade's drama gives a colonial twist to a somewhat familiar romance plot, following the movement of its hero from England to Australia and back again. This trajectory firmly reasserts the colony's place in service to metropolitan domestic success. Emigration to Australia is but a temporary dislocation that endows the hero, George Fielding, with the economic and masculine development that will render him suitable for marriage. As a field of oppor- tunity unavailable within Britain itself, the empire is called into service as a necessary adjunct to the nation, a space where villainy can be evaded, reputations restored, and fortunes made. This imperial frontier is a place where young British men can become heroes: melodrama's generic domestic imperative establishes a very specific and necessary relationship between Britain and its empire.

Shaped by generic conventions, melodrama's representation of empire effectively interwove heroism with patriotism, and virtue with national identity. Operating within a plot that unfolded in India or Africa, a melodramatic hero became, almost inevitably, a hero of empire. Hailing from the humbler ranks of the citizenry, a soldier or settler, and boasting an appearance that advertised virtue, physical strength, and bodily health, the ideal hero of imperialist melodrama was the very embodiment of middle-class British masculinity, and he represented the moral strength of the empire, his willingness to sacrifice himself for his beloved reflecting and reinforcing the higher ideal of self-sacrifice for the love and honour of his country.[23]

Shifted to a colonial context, melodrama's conventional romance plot assumed fresh political meaning. On the one hand, in plays such as *It Is Never Too Late to Mend,* the romantic union between the hero and heroine that closes melodrama suggests imperial territorial and cultural engagements as extensions of the normative domestic romance. On the other hand, the villain's abduction of the heroine, often coupled with threats of sexual violation, bestowed upon global events a sense of immediate domestic danger. In *Jessie Brown,* for example, a melodrama about the outbreak of the Indian Mutiny, a humble bungalow housing a Scottish soldier's widow and her children serves as the locus of the rebels' attack. By thus relocating the site of 'home' beyond the British Isles, the play shifts the imperial frontier to a more alarmingly familiar, domestic space. This domestic setting implies that it is not only India but also Britain that is facing danger, imparting a more urgent imperative to the army's victory over the rebels. In plays such as *Jessie Brown* and *Comrades in Khaki* (1899), where military threats emanating from the imperial margins are dramatically refigured as sexual assaults on British women, the heroine represents metropolitan culture at risk, the threatened assault on her body suggesting the violation of domestic borders.[24] Saving the heroine is, in these cases, not merely a melodramatic convention but a national, cultural imperative.

Melodrama's colonial settings invest the villain's sexual rapaciousness with fresh political signification, manifesting the dangers of contact with the imperial frontier as the threat of sexualized violence against British women. A sign of his Orientalization, the white, Western villain plots against feminine emblems of Western virtue, suggesting associations with the slave trade or harem and thus dramatizing the dangers of exposure to the unrestrained sexuality of the East. Even when the melodrama ends with the expulsion of the villain, to the extent that his violent, carnal impulses arise from, or are enabled by, exposure to the colonial environment, such plots suggests that empire is a source of danger, not only to British bodies and values, but to the British nation itself. In such villains we can detect the disruptive current that flows beneath melodrama's drive towards closure: alongside the salvation of the heroine, the triumph of the hero, and the restoration of the imperial order, the larger arc of the drama has revealed unwholesome and dangerous impulses emanating from colonial space. The audience itself is constituted against these threats, so that while individual audience members may have felt personal sympathy or class-based affiliations with a play's villain, every element in the melodrama militates against such perverse allegiance.[25]

By reconfiguring an expansive, ambiguous, and complex political and ideological structure to fit within legible generic categories, melodrama simplified the complex web of economic relationships, political imperatives, and cultural conflicts that formed the British Empire. When they weren't shunted to the periphery, difficult questions about the ethics of imperial conquest and administration, or the limits of nationalist sentiment and patriotic expression, or the intersection of ethnicity with citizenship and justice, were translated by melodrama's binary coding to fit into a simplified moral framework.

## Criticism, Questions, Challenges

The colonial setting of many Victorian melodramas serves as a crucible in which characters' moral qualities are revealed, tested, and refined. *The Heroine of Glencoe*, a melodrama about the Boer War, links masculinity, honor, and Britishness. Its hero, Paul Verdom, is ethnically Boer and thought by his British lover's father to be a coward, but under the pressures of war, his manhood is proven: Paul's Boer sympathies are purged, and his ethnic allegiances are broken, replaced by a British sense of self-sacrificial honor that redeems his character. A similar ethical 'conversion' of the ethnic Other is at the heart of *Vermuh Kareeda* (1857), whose title character, of mixed heritage, comes, through the course of the play, to denounce the Indian rebellion as immoral and irrational. Another example of the ethical alignment promoted by imperialist melodrama can be found in Boucicault's *Jessie Brown*. Torn between conflicting duties, Reverend Blount, a clergyman in India at the outbreak of the Mutiny, says that he feels rising within him 'an emotion that is evil, very evil – a sinful desire to smash the heads of these wretches, who butcher women and infants' (1:1). In this speech, the Reverend voices what was probably a prevailing sentiment among members of the play's audience who were likewise roused to

186

a vengeful fever having read accounts of the rebels' 'atrocities' in the newspapers. As the rebels approach, Blount, a reluctant soldier, pendulates between the call to pray for his enemies and the desire to wreak vengeance upon them, declaring himself a man of peace while physically arming himself in readiness to fight.

Boucicault's play portrays Britain's response to the Mutiny as a righteous defence against unjustifiable aggression, and it portrays the British defenders' use of deadly force as the fulfilment of their highest moral duties. In the second act, however, the play allows Nana Sahib, the rebel leader, to argue for the legitimacy of the rebellion: 'Did Allah send the Briton here to make us slaves, to clutch us beneath his lion's paw, and to devour the land? Inshallah! The voiceless word of Allah has swept over the people, and it says, "Sufferers, arise, ye shall be free!"' This potentially provocative defence of colonial rebellion as the divinely ordained resistance to an oppressive imperial order that deprives indigenous inhabitants of their rights and freedoms is immediately dismissed by Randal's even grander consideration of the divine will: 'Freedom was never won by murder, for heaven never yet armed the hand of an assassin' (2:1). Ignoring the rebels' criticism of the colonial order, the British soldier rejects the legitimacy of armed rebellion against established imperial order.

Like *Jessie Brown, Nana Sahib: A Story of Aymere* (1863) allows the colonized to voice challenges to the ethical and political legitimacy of empire. This play, also set during the Indian Mutiny, opens on a holy man addressing a group of Indian rebels. His speech deploys a rhetoric of liberty that portrays the British as tyrants and invaders whose presence in India is not only repressive but unholy. However, the play's romance plot finally and firmly silences a potentially sympathetic understanding of the Indian Mutiny as a nation's struggle for independence from a repressive foreign invader. As in *Jessie Brown*, the historical figure of Nana Sahib is portrayed as having romantic designs on a British woman. When she rejects him, Nana sentences her to death. As she awaits her execution, her lover, Danvers, comes to her rescue, and confronts the rebel leader:

NANA. Your threats are in vain. Your doom is fix'd. Invader of our land, you've trampled under foot our freedom. Now feel the Indian's retribution.

DANVERS. Stay, this is the first time my foot has trod this soil. I am ignorant of the cause of this revolt. I came not here to war with you or yours. I came to seek my bride, and nothing but death shall tear her from my arms. (3:3)

Nana's talk about just rebellion in the pursuit of freedom from a foreign occupying force is silenced by the Englishman's insistence that he has not come to oppress but to liberate. Roused by the triumph of romance, the play's audience is distracted from the proclamations of the revolution's legitimacy, seeing the liberation of imperilled British womanhood as more urgent than the political liberties claimed by the play's titular rebel.

As the examples of *Jessie Brown* and *Nana Sahib* show, the Indian Mutiny was a rich source for melodrama because the prevailing popular characterization of the event lent itself to melodrama's moral binarism. The Mutiny was popularly perceived as an attack on order and innocence; it was portrayed in fiction and on stage as a battle between Christian and heathen, honesty and treachery, heroism and villainy. Focusing on images of victims and villains, melodrama obscured the long and complicated history of British rule in India, marginalizing suggestions of British wrongdoing and reinforcing the overriding sense that this was more than a rebellion: it was an assault on higher British values.[26] At the end of the Mutiny melodramas, the British flag waves and the band trumpets the strains of Britannia's rule, yet the historical rebellion remains in the memory, given fresh imagery by the larger drama, which reminds audiences of British rule under threat, of British bodies violated, and of a British empire nearly lost. Behind the spectacle of British triumph remains the spectre of British tragedy. Moreover, the return of the hero and heroine to England at the close of the Mutiny melodramas, though admittedly a conventional ending, nevertheless structurally reinforces the message that domestic tranquillity is not to be found in India, that love, happiness, and security cannot be found on the imperial frontier, which can never be completely domesticated, never fully Anglicized, never truly be 'home'. The imperial adventure plot injects fresh urgency into melodrama's domestic imperative: the stage may look outwards at the empire, but its closing gaze returns again and again to Britain, reinforcing its audience's domestic identities and commitments.

While the larger trajectory of most melodramas justifies and celebrates an imperialist ideology that authorizes brute force, oppression, and economic exploitation, quite often the empire's darker underbelly peeks through this fabric. These critiques are, it is true, generally sidelined by the jingoistic triumphalism of the closing scenes, but the questions that they ultimately elide have been raised on stage and, subtle and partial as these critical articulations may be, they are evidence of melodrama's capacity to at least entertain counter discourses that subtly challenge the 'imperialist melodrama's' celebration of the imperial project.

Melodrama's critical glance was often trained not on the periphery but on metropolitan culture, invoking the colonies as places where opportunities denied at home were possible. For example, when young Frank Malden, the hero of George Day's *The Diamond Rush* (1895), is not only denied permission to marry his sweetheart Nelly but is also disinherited, his only option is to go to work in the South African diamond fields, 'Where toil has its reward' (1:1). This critical perspective on metropolitan culture is shared by *It Is Never Too Late to Mend*, where the hero's desire to remain in (and later, to return to) England exists in tension with the play's unflinching criticism of England's flaws, including limited economic opportunities and injustices of the penal system.[27]

And so, despite the fact that the melodramatic expression of the ideologies that motivated and sustained the imperial project was generally structured to promote the affective consolidation of an imperial public, melodrama was not univocally and unequivocally pro-imperialist. To be sure, nineteenth-century melodrama celebrated the triumph not only of the British flag but of the larger values it represents. And yet, even with this general trajectory and operating within the genre's conventions, many melodramas managed to voice criticism of the nation or to express opposition to the objectives – and methods – of Britain's overseas mercantile and military activities. Scenes of British military victory offered thrilling moments for audience celebration of the nation's strength and courage, yet they brought with them the reminder that the cost of empire is measured in British lives. While the action of these plays unfolded among foreign landscapes, the intricacies of character and the trajectories of plot often directed a quietly critical eye on Britain itself. The mere existence of British-born villains within a play undermined an otherwise clearly racialized binary of right and wrong, locating the potential for wrongdoing within the British character. If the imperial frontier, in many plays, forms a field of opportunity for honest but impoverished Britons – the space in which British masculinity is proven and perfected – the need for such figures to go abroad in search of opportunity underscores the nation's failure to fully address the conditions that fostered such domestic economic hardship. And while the melodramatic hero might find victory and fortune abroad, it is to England that he returns, and this movement homeward entails a turning away from further imperial adventure, a subtle suggestion that contact with the colonial frontier is best kept to a minimum even, perhaps, best confined to the stage.

# Notes

1. Dutton Cook, *Nights at the Play: A View of the English Stage* (London: Chatto and Windus, 1883), 466–7.
2. Augustus Harris, review of *The World* at the Grand Theatre, Glasgow, *Quiz* (13 Jan. 1882): 10; Martin Meisel, *Realizations: Narrative, Pictorial, and Theatrical Arts in Nineteenth-Century England* (Princeton: Princeton University Press, 1983), 198.
3. Edward Ziter, *The Orient on the Victorian Stage* (Cambridge: Cambridge University Press, 2003), 3.
4. Heidi Holder, 'Melodrama, Realism and Empire', in *Acts of Supremacy: The British Empire and the Stage, 1790–1930*, eds. J. S Bratton, Richard Allen Cave, Breandan Gregory, Heidi Holder, and Michael Pickering (Manchester: Manchester University Press, 1991), 130–1.
5. Ziter, *The Orient*, 180.
6. *Ibid.*, 182.
7. D. A., 'The Stage', *Bell's Life in London and Sporting Chronicle* (9 July 1881): 4.
8. Michael Booth, 'Soldiers of the Queen, Drury Lane Imperialism', in *Melodrama: The Cultural Emergence of a Genre*, eds. Michael Hays and Anastasia Nikolopoulou (New York: St. Martin's, 1996), 9; Jim Davis, 'The Empire Right or Wrong: Boer War Melodrama on the Australian Stage, 1899-1901', in *Melodrama*, eds. Hays and Nikolopoulou, 27.
9. Ziter, *The Orient*, 1.
10. Femi Okiremuete Shaka, 'The Politics of Cultural Conversion in Colonialist African Cinema', *Cineaction*, 37 (1995): 58–63.
11. Dana Van Kooy and Jeffrey Cox, 'Melodramatic Slaves', *Modern Drama*, 55 (2012): 461–3.
12. Kristie Allen, 'On Duties: Pirates, Jack Tars, the Anti-Slave Trade, and Nautical Melodrama in the Making of the British Nation-State', *Nineteenth-Century Studies*, 25 (2011): 2–4, 10–1, 22–3.
13. Matthew Kaiser, *The World in Play: Portraits of a Victorian Concept* (Stanford: Stanford University Press, 2012), 54, 61, 73; Jacky Bratton, 'Theatre of War: The Crimea on the London Stage, 1854–5', in *Performance and Politics in Popular Drama*, eds. David Bradby, Louis James, and Bernard Sarratt (Cambridge: Cambridge University Press, 1980), 119–37.
14. J. S. Bratton, 'British Heroism and the Structure of Melodrama', in Bratton et al., *Acts of Supremacy*, 42–59.
15. David Worrall, *Harlequin Empire: Race, Ethnicity and the Drama of the Popular Enlightenment* (New York: Routledge, 2015), n.p. (e-book).
16. Holder, 'Melodrama, Realism and Empire', 133.
17. Booth, 'Soldiers of the Queen', 5.
18. 'Before the Footlights', *The Birmingham Pictorial and Dart*, 1.207 (8 Dec. 1899): 13.
19. Jonathan Schneer, *London 1900: The Imperial Metropolis* (New Haven: Yale University Press, 1999), 95–6.
20. Jeffrey Richards, *Imperialism and Music* (Manchester: Manchester University Press, 1997), 337–40.

21. MacKenzie, *Orientalism*, 187; Holder, 'Melodrama, Realism and Empire', 141–4.
22. Penny Summerfield, 'Patriotism and Empire: Music Hall Entertainment, 1870-1914', in *Imperialism and Popular Culture*, ed. John MacKenzie (Manchester: Manchester University Press, 1986), 27–9.
23. David Haldane Lawrence, 'Masculine Appearances: Male Physicality on the Late-Victorian Stage', *Critical Survey*, 20 (2008): 50–3; Graham Dawson, *Soldier Heroes: British Adventure, Empire, and the Imagining of Masculinities* (New York: Routledge, 1994), 1–11.
24. Fred Radford, 'Domestic Drama and Drama of Empire: Intertextuality and the Subaltern Woman in Late Victorian Theatre', *Nineteenth-Century Contexts*, 20 (1997): 2–8.
25. MacKenzie, *Orientalism*, 180; Ian Henderson, 'Jacky-Kalingaloonga: Aboriginality, Audience Reception, and Charles Reade's *It Is Never too Late to Mend*', *Theatre Research International*, 29 (2004): 95–110.
26. Gautam Chakravarty, *The Indian Mutiny and the British Imagination* (Cambridge: Cambridge University Press, 2005), 38, 112.
27. Michael Hays, 'Representing Empire: Class, Culture, and the Popular Theatre in the Nineteenth Century', in *Imperialism and Theatre: Essays on World Theatre, Drama and Performance*, ed. J. Ellen Gainor (New York: Routledge, 1995), 136–44.

# 13

SARAH MEER

# Melodrama and Race

The heyday of melodrama coincided with the ascent of racial theory. Older explanations of human difference referred to climate and geography, or drew on the Old Testament – the descendants of Cain, or Noah's wayward son Ham, were supposed to have been black. But by the mid-nineteenth century, a number of medical writers were asserting that differences amongst humans were fixed, biological, and consequential. The Edinburgh anatomist Robert Knox claimed in 1850 to be articulating 'a new sense' for the term 'race'. He linked 'physical distinctions' between people to 'moral differences', and indeed to destiny: the 'Saxon' race to which he belonged was 'about to be the dominant race on earth'.[1] The 'races' Knox named were 'Gipsey', 'Coptic', 'Jew', 'Phoenician', 'Celtic', 'Slovenian', 'Sarnatian', and 'Darker Races'. Other writers' classification schemes were different, but equally hierarchical. *Types of Mankind* (1854), and *Indigenous Races of the Earth* (1857), published in the United States by Josiah Nott and George Gliddon, divided humanity into fifty-four races, which they represented in an 'Ethnographic Tableau', a fold-out table of facial portraits.[2] They declared that this inventory of physiognomic features 'establishes . . . the existence of *superior* and *inferior* races'.[3] Such writing was conscripted in Europe to justify imperialist projects, and in the United States to argue for slavery and the slaughter of Native Americans.[4] Science has long repudiated such claims, although their legacy is still with us.[5]

These modes of thinking made their way into melodrama too, but they interacted with stage traditions in specific and often unique ways. The nineteenth-century stage had its own taxonomic systems. Until 1843, there was the division between patent theatres, licensed to show 'legitimate' drama, and the rest – but there were other distinctions too. In general, West End theatres attracted wealthier audiences than those in the east of London or south of the Thames. Specific conventions distinguished dramatic genres – comedy, tragedy, farce, and pantomime, as well as melodrama. Within a company, each actor specialized in a certain kind of role – juvenile, low

or light comedy, heavy man, leading lady – and status and pay were cali-
brated accordingly.[6] Performances were shaped by the customary structure
and tone for the genre, the theatre, and the company; all of these factors
could condition 'race' in performance. In melodrama, 'race' was shaped as
much by theatrical traditions as by the new theories; racial ideas were
expressed within the formal constraints of the genre, with an eye to supplying
a particular range of roles – often, even, specific parts for individual actors.

Nevertheless, the theatre had a long-standing interest in 'types'. A variety
of characters, often comic, typified regional or national characteristics in
nineteenth-century drama. Stage Irishmen and Scotsmen, Yankees and
Backwoodsmen sported distinctive accents, dress and manners, marking
type as language and culture. And types could approximate to what Knox
called races, too. So, for example, Charles Mathews' virtuosic solo piece
*A Trip to America* (1824) included a large cast of American characters,
including a 'Yankee' called Jonathan Doubikin, and a 'runaway Negro'
called Agamemnon.[7]

Nineteenth-century British society was also stratified by class and other
social divisions. These were recognized on stage, but also subverted, and
sometimes fantastically reimagined. *Caste* (1867), Tom Robertson's society
comedy, chides the theatre for its romantic illusions about class – Captain
Hawtree warns his friend the Honourable George D'Alroy against marrying
a lowly ballet girl: 'all those marriages of people with common people are all
very well in novels and in plays on the stage ... but in real life with real
relations, and real mothers, and so forth, it's absolute bosh' (1:1). Then the
play reinforces those very illusions: by its end, George is happily settled with
his Esther, and his own mother has overcome her snobbery.

*Caste*'s title alludes to social divisions in India, whose 'caste system' had
become a byword in Britain for an extreme and rigid framework of distinctions. In 1860, an article in the *Cornhill Magazine* made an overt comparison
between Indian 'caste' and the actors' pecking order: 'A theatre is like
a Hindoo household, and all the men and women before you are divided
from each other by the law of caste.'[8] Nicholas Dirks has argued that the
British 'refigur[ed]' caste to support the Empire, while mythologizing it as an
'unchanged survival of ancient India'.[9] In Britain, the fixation on caste overseas coincided ironically with the proliferation of racial theory at home.

Robertson's play dramatizes marriage across class lines; racial theorists were
similarly preoccupied with marriage (or at least reproduction) between 'races'.
The children of such unions challenged their claims of incompatibility and
irreconcilable difference. Many race-writers used terms from animal breeding
to describe such children ('mulatto', for example: originally a young mule, or
offspring of a horse and a donkey). Robert Knox asserted that intermarriage

could not produce a stable strain or 'breed', and that this demonstrated 'race': the child of European and African parents could not 'hold his ground as a mulatto: back the breed will go to one or another of the pure breeds, white or black'.[10] Josiah Nott argued that 'mulattoes' were shorter-lived than their parents, and 'bad breeders' whose children generally died young. Where he had to admit that this was not the case, he supposed that the white parents had inherited 'blood' from French or Italian ancestors, 'and other *dark*-skinned races' (in other words, some whites were less white than others, and hence their mixed-race children were better 'breeders').[11] In Robertson's play, Captain Hawtree argues like one of these racial theorists, using the language of animal species to insist on impermeable class barriers:

> Caste! – the inexorable law of caste! The social law, so becoming and so good, that commands like to mate with like, and forbids a giraffe to fall in love with a squirrel. (1:1)

Hawtree's example is so improbable that it makes D'Alroy's case: by contrast with a giraffe–squirrel romance, his feeling for Esther is unremarkable.

As *Caste* suggests, socially unequal relationships were a venerable tradition on the stage, where characters of different origins fell in love without creating, in Knox's words, a 'monstrosity of nature'.[12] The most famous of these dramas, of course, was Shakespeare's *Othello* (1604). Although the hero's marriage to Desdemona inspires some crude comment among the soldiery, including puns on his dark skin, Othello's difference is arguably not the prime cause of the tragedy. Until at least the end of the eighteenth century, both play and protagonist tended to be conceived as 'grand [and] majestic', with Othello himself often distinguished more by his military prowess than by what writers like Knox meant by race.[13] During that period Othello usually wore the uniform of a British army officer – the staging minimized, rather than emphasized his otherness.[14] Virginia Mason Vaughan argues that for the first half of the nineteenth century, productions focused on Othello as 'adoring husband' and 'noble victim'; indeed, '[t]he Moor was now, in many respects, the protagonist in a domestic melodrama'.[15]

In theatrical culture, traditional representations persist in the repertoire alongside newer trends, and this has implications for acting and staging, and also for reception. Nineteenth-century melodramas shared audiences with *Othello*: they may have influenced each other. For example, Dion Boucicault's racial melodrama *The Octoroon* (1859) opened at the New Adelphi in the Strand on 18 November 1861; a month earlier, on 23 October, Charles Fechter played Othello at the Princess's Theatre in Oxford Street; John Ryder took on the role in the same theatre on 3 March the following year. Almost as significant was *Oroonoko* (1695), Thomas Southerne's dramatization of the novel by Aphra Behn. One of the most popular tragedies of the eighteenth century, and regularly revived, it has a rebel slave hero, and in the play his wife is white. Actors whose Othellos were acclaimed also often played Oroonoko, in an anti-slavery play which inspired a sentimental identification with its hero and heroine.[16] Again, this was a far cry from the racial theorists (Knox jeered at abolitionism, arguing that 'the dark races have been the slaves of their fairer brethren ... since the earliest times'; he predicted that 'the Saxon race will never ... be at peace' with 'black races').[17] Kwame Anthony Appiah has suggested that literature (and implicitly the novel) played a special role in encoding ideas of race in the eighteenth and nineteenth centuries.[18] Evidently some stage traditions resisted them.

Another distinguishing feature of theatrical 'race' was of course performance itself, the construction of theatrical illusion. Most Othellos and Oroonokos in the nineteenth century were played by white actors in black make-up, usually a mixture containing burnt cork. Their audiences suspended disbelief about performers' appearances just as they did about other aspects of staging: the success of the illusion depended on the skill of the production. Furthermore, some kinds of performance played entirely self-consciously with the spectacle of what Knox would call racial difference. Early in the 1830s, a comic-burlesque brand of performance emerged, called at first Ethiopian Delineation, and later blackface minstrelsy; by the 1850s, 'Negro Minstrels' were a popular phenomenon in Britain. They purported to be African Americans, but were in reality white performers blacked up. Minstrels sang sentimental and comic songs, often burlesques of contemporary hits, and they delivered puns, jokes, skits, and mock lectures, in supposedly black accents.[19] These were degrading caricatures, even if they testify to an oblique fascination with African American music, dance, and humour. Many minstrel jokes made ironic or metatheatrical reference to the 'blackness' of the characters, particularly allusions to household polishes, such as Day and Martin's boot blacking. Minstrelsy thus purported to represent racial difference, but also emphasized its own pretence and performance. Intensely popular in the 1850s, minstrel shows not only included parodies of melodramas, but also influenced other kinds of black characters on stage. Certainly, minstrelsy influenced the reception of black characters in other genres.

Yet although 'blacking up' was involved in most portrayal of black people, a few black actors did take on roles like Othello and Oroonoko. The most famous black performer in nineteenth-century London was the New Yorker Ira Aldridge, whose career in Britain stretched roughly from 1824 to 1865.[20]

Advertising Aldridge's first performance as Othello in London in 1833, Covent Garden Theatre stressed his exoticism, billing him as 'the African Roscius', and as 'a native of the wilds of Senegal'.[21] (Roscius was a famous actor in ancient Rome; the Senegal claim was pure fiction.) Aldridge's Othello, at a patent theatre, attracted uncommon attention, and from a number of theatre journals outright hostility, even before they had seen him play. The *Figaro in London* jeered at Aldridge's presumption in terms that aligned his colour with class: his daring to appear was an 'act of insolence', that 'dishonoured' the stage; the paper undertook to 'force him to find, in the capacity of footman or street-sweeper, that level for which his colour appears to have rendered him peculiarly qualified'.[22] Servants and crossing-sweepers were occupations particularly associated with black people in London, and a number of reviews made this connection. *Bell's Life in London* also implied that Aldridge had disturbed the social associations of his colour, connecting him with a black boxer called 'Young Molineux', and a black 'pantiler' (that is someone who creeps about on roofs).[23] *The Athenaeum* claimed that Aldridge had been a servant to the comedian Henry Wallack, and objected to the 'lady-like girl ... Miss Ellen Tree ... being pawed about by Mr. Henry Wallack's black servant'.[24] Once again, Aldridge's Othello was described as breaching boundaries of class, which seemed inextricable from colour. *The Age*, although praising 'a very clever piece of acting', and asserting that 'we see no just reason why one of the human race, with only the difference of *complexion*, should be debarred the opportunity of displaying on the London boards', could not resist a minstrel-type joke:

> The trial will prove the act, as Day and Martin, and other vendors of Japan [black lacquer], state in their advertisements.[25]

A few newspapers, however, gave Aldridge respectful consideration. The *Standard's* review indicates that Aldridge's Othello, like others in the period, was drawing inspiration from melodrama. It pronounced his acting 'essentially melo-dramatic', and described his 'impressive' death scene:

> after having stabbed himself, he staggered towards the lifeless body of *Desdemona*, reeled, and fell fearlessly with his back to the audience. The effect was immense, and the house rang with continued acclamations.[26]

Despite some critics' hostility, viewers evidently appreciated Aldridge's melodramatic Othello.

Twenty years later, another black actor, Joseph Jenkins, was also billed as 'The African Roscius', when he took Othello onto the rather less exalted boards of the Eagle Saloon in Hoxton. Jenkins's performance was also scrutinized in class terms. The African American writer William Wells Brown was in the audience: he later interviewed Jenkins, who, he discovered, was also a part-time crossing-sweeper. The son of a farmer, Jenkins had been born in East Africa, 'between Darfour and Abyssinia'.[27] On the bills, however, the Eagle Saloon had romantically designated Jenkins as 'Selim, an African prince'. Wells Brown's account suggests that for some audience members the emotion Othello elicited became oddly interwoven with the Eagle's promotional biography of its star:

> He soon showed that he possessed great dramatic power and skill; and his description to the senate of how he won the affections of the gentle Desdemona stamped him at once as an actor of merit. 'What a pity', said a lady near me to a gentleman that was by her side, 'that a prince of the royal blood of Africa should have to go upon the stage for a living! It is indeed a shame!'[28]

Jenkins's thespian success, which in this scene conveyed Othello's nobility and attractiveness, clearly engaged this audience member's sympathies. Her comment suggests that she also blurred Othello with the story the Eagle was selling about Jenkins. Her conviction that the actor was really a prince inverted the colour/class associations made by Aldridge's opponents. Moreover, in reading his acting as social decline, she invested his biography with a misfortune fit for melodrama.

Like *Othello* and *Oroonoko*, some early nineteenth-century melodramas seem untroubled by romance across what Knox would see as racial borders. One of the century's most-revived pieces combined sympathy and exoticism, in a spectacular fantasy of benign British intervention in India. William Thomas Moncrieff's *The Cataract of the Ganges! or, the Rajah's Daughter* (1823) was notable for the eponymous cataract scenery, for its equestrian displays, and for its large cast of Indian characters, in a plot of power-struggles between Indian states. The British characters consist only of an English officer 'attached to the Rajah … of Guzerat' and his servant Jack Robinson.[29] The higher status roles, in both class and stage terms, are Indian (the rajah, the emperor, the villain, the juvenile lead, and leading lady). The British characters are relatively marginal. The English Mordaunt is a subordinate officer; Robinson is a servant (probably a role for the light comedian). Robinson's romance with a woman called Ubra is a small sub-plot. He has qualms about his attachment, not from a reluctance to marry an Indian, but because he is comically obsessed with Robinson Crusoe, whose fictional life he tries to imitate. By that light, he feels that his ideal companion should resemble Man Friday. As Robinson struggles with his attraction to

Ubra, he focuses on physiognomical features, in the manner of racial theorists:

> You're my idol, you jade, you are … Oh, you are too interesting! What a pity it is you an't black, and that you hav'n't got thick lips, and wooly hair, and a humpty dumpty nose. (2:3)

The comedy here partly derives from Jack's insistence on a fictional ideal at the expense of real feeling. The joke also depends on 'racial' assumptions – that the attributes Jack wishes for are not conventionally desirable. However, in this early melodrama, the romance between English and Indian characters is not treated as remarkable in itself. Moreover, it is clearly intended to be touching, as well as funny.

By contrast, the central dilemma of Dion Boucicault's play *The Octoroon* is one of love versus difference. Both in Britain and the United States, *The Octoroon* appeared at a critical moment. In New York it was first performed four days after John Brown's execution for instigating an anti-slavery rebellion; in London, it opened in November 1861, amidst trans-Atlantic tensions over the British stance on the American Civil War. As the issue of American slavery plunged the United States into bloodshed, and threatened to involve the United Kingdom too, Boucicault's drama explicitly dramatized the preoccupations of racial theorists who justified slavery, like Knox and Nott.

'Octoroon' is itself a name that purports to quantify ancestry in racial terms. It signifies a heritage that is one-eighth black – that is, it means having one black great-grandparent (and implicitly seven white ones). The heroine, Zoe, looks white but is legally black, and she therefore cannot marry white George Peyton, who has fallen for her. Peyton initially does not know about Zoe's ancestry; when he does, he refuses to accept it as a barrier. Thus, Boucicault zeroes in on the issue that so exercised Josiah Nott. The very existence of women like Zoe challenged the race-theorists' insistence that some partnerships were biologically aberrant; third-generation descendants of such a union make a mockery of terms like 'bad breeders'. The scene in which Zoe enlightens George echoes the common metonymic use of 'blood' for parentage (Nott uses it, and so does the lady who admires Joseph Jenkins), but Zoe takes it further, implying that each drop represents a specific line of descent. She also alludes to the Old Testament explanations of human variation:

> ZOE. That – that is the ineffacable [sic] curse of Cain. Of the blood that feeds my heart, one drop in eight is black – bright red as the rest may be, that one drop poisons all the blood. Those seven bright drops give me love like yours, hope like yours – ambition like yours – life hung with

passions like dew-drops on the morning flowers; but the one black
drop gives me despair, for I'm an unclean thing – forbidden by the
laws – I'm an Octoroon!                                             (2:1)

Just as Zoe's speech holds ancient and modern ideas of 'race' in tandem,
Boucicault offers two perspectives on her situation: Zoe's is that '[t]here is
a gulf between us, as wide as your love – as deep as my despair' (2:1).
George's response is staunch indifference: 'Zoe, I love you none the less;
this knowledge brings no revolt to my heart, and I can overcome the
obstacle' (2:1). The play also equivocates about whether race is a merely
social or legal construct – 'forbidden by the laws' – or whether there are,
as the racial theorists would have it, physical differences that are inexor-
able. As Zoe leads George to her fateful revelation, Boucicault lets her
begin an explanation based on family background, but she pulls back, her
hesitation probably implying the circumstances in which her mother conceived a child. But in delicately sidestepping the issues of illegitimacy,
shame, and possibly rape, Zoe submits that she wears her 'race' on her
body like secret insignia:

ZOE. And what shall I say? I – my mother was – no, no – not her! Why should
    I refer the blame to her? George, do you see that hand you hold: look at
    these fingers, do you see the nails are of a bluish tinge?
GEORGE. Yes, near the quick there is a faint blue mark.
ZOE. Look in my eyes; is not the same color in the white?
GEORGE. It is their beauty.                                       (2:1)

George's compliment incidentally reveals something about the play. Just
as the supposed signs of 'race' are themselves what make Zoe attractive
to her lover, so the exploration of a racial dilemma, or racial liminality,
is what recommends the drama to audiences. That is precisely the
promise made by the racial term in the title. And there was something
provocative about declaiming that 'race' was a matter of ineradicable
signs, when on the stage it was entirely a function of theatrical illusion.
Apart from Zoe, five slaves are named in the dramatis personae, plus an
unspecified number of slave children; their black make-up would have
been designed to contrast with Zoe's apparent 'whiteness'. Zoe herself
was played in both productions by Boucicault's wife, Agnes Robertson.
A well-loved star in her own right, Robertson came from Edinburgh; she
was particularly renowned for playing Scottish and Irish girls. To the
extent that the audience found themselves immersed in Zoe's plight,
they forgot that they were watching Robertson. In believing in those
blue marks on her skin, they were enjoying Agnes Robertson's artistry

as an actress, and her ability to make them trust for a moment that the Octoroon's 'race' was real. The theatrical artifice was compounded by Boucicault himself, playing Wahnotee, 'an Indian chief of the Lepan tribe', and by the minstrel-type antics of the children.[30]

The inherent instability of theatrical representation was mirrored by inconstancy in the play's form. In New York, and in its first London performances, Zoe is threatened with enslavement to the play's villain, and takes poison, declaring only in her dying moment: 'George, you may, without a blush, confess your love for the Octoroon' (5:4). In December 1861, Boucicault changed the ending (in response, he claimed, to British disapproval of Zoe's suicide), allowing the lovers to 'seek refuge in some happy country where the "sacrament of love" may take place without impediment'.[31] It may have been true, as Boucicault suggested, that British audiences more readily accepted a happy ending for Zoe than American ones did, but his contention that her death challenged slavery is still surprising. In the 1860s, anti-slavery sentiments were less controversial in London than in New York; Britain had abolished slavery in its colonies in 1833, while the issue was tearing the United States apart. Moreover, it is the 'happy' ending that consigns 'race' to local convention, maintaining that 'race' is a construct. The 'happy' play is anti-racist, while the suicidal version deems the 'Octoroon' inherently tragic. It is more likely that Boucicault's rewriting, and his explanations in *The Times*, were a canny mode of advertising, and a way of extending his play's run into December, when an annual cattle show at Baker Street brought in new punters from the countryside. The *Times* observed sceptically that it was 'worthy of notice that the preservation of the Octoroon's life coincides with the commencement of the Cattle Show'.[32] Boucicault altered the structure again for an 1868 revival, and the Dicks Standard Plays and Lacy's Acting Editions show further variations, an adaptability that belies Boucicault's attribution of the first change to the prejudice of his audience.[33]

Whereas the theatrical context itself ironized *The Octoroon*'s naturalization of race, Mark Lemon and Tom Taylor's *Slave Life* (1852) consciously represented race as a performance. *Slave Life* was a dramatization of Harriet Beecher Stowe's anti-slavery novel *Uncle Tom's Cabin* (1852). Then emerging as an international bestseller, Stowe's novel would inspire over the next three years at least twenty different productions in London. Lemon and Taylor wrote *Slave Life* for the Adelphi Theatre, then managed by J. B. Buckstone and Céline Céleste [Madame Céleste]; their play featured particularly good roles for women, including – for Céleste – Cassy, the enslaved concubine of the villain Legree. As Jane Moody has observed, Céleste, who was herself French, was particularly successful in parts that required her to play exiled or outcast figures – especially national, or what

Knox would call 'racial', types. One of her best-loved roles was in Buckstone's *Green Bushes* (1845), as 'Miami', a Mississippi girl of French and Native American parentage.[34] This was probably why the *Standard* observed that Cassy was a part 'which it was obvious she would present with due earnestness and vehemence'; the *Examiner* judged that Céleste played it with 'quiet intensity'.[35] Other parts also seem to be well-designed for specific actors. Mary Anne Keeley was the slave girl Topsy: Keeley excelled in uniting comic ability with pathos, often in children's roles. The most famous example at the Adelphi was her Smike, in an adaptation of Charles Dickens's novel *Nicholas Nickleby* (1838–9).[36] In *Slave Life*, Topsy, like Smike, journeys from the droll to the poignant. She begins as a scamp, with the catchphrase 'I'se so wicked'; but eventually she demonstrates loyalty and affection, and braves savage dogs to help her friends escape. The play is particularly interesting in the position it gives George Harris, a clever man enslaved to a brute, who is tortured by his inability to protect his wife and child. As he does in the original novel, George voices the anti-slavery argument. Showing his wife Eliza his invention for cleaning cotton, he declares,

> I have proved I have a mind. That man, not heaven degrades us; that human laws war with the laws of nature. All men are equal in the eyes of heaven.　(1:3)

George then demonstrates this equality dramatically. In the course of escaping from slavery, and rescuing his wife and child from Legree, George, who is in Knox's terms 'mulatto', pretends to be a slave-owner. In passing for white, George performs race, permitting the Adelphi's actor, Alfred Wigan, to play 'black' playing 'white'. George and Topsy are in a tavern filled with slave hunters when George warns his friend:

> Only remember, Topsy, I am no longer George Harris, the mulatto slave, but Henry Butler, of Louisiana, the master of slaves, as insolent, as purse-proud, as ignorant and overbearing as themselves.　(2:3)

In this planter persona, George insults the black waiter who brings him a drink, with a minstrel-like joke about his colour: 'Thank you my lump of snow' (2:4). In the play, such race-jokes are the mark of inhumanity – Legree calls Topsy 'Snowball' – so George's imitation satirizes the slave-owners' colour-fixation (3:2). One planter thinks he recognizes George's voice, but then assumes that he is mistaken because George seems so cultured: he vacillates, repeatedly misled by George's impersonation. Finally, George visits Legree's plantation, now '*assuming a broad southern drawl*', and imitating a rough slave dealer – in the words of the *Examiner*'s reviewer, 'a long-headed cautious Southern trader'.[37] Legree offers to sell George his own son, and George affects a cynical indifference, feigning reluctance to take on the costs of a child's upbringing: 'Ah! but then there's the trouble o' raisin' (3:2). The *Standard* applauded Wigan's skill in this scene as portraying 'the quintessence of American nonchalance, and cool, whimsical cunning'.[38] George's whiteface act is reinforced by the indeterminate appearance of his wife and child; one character guesses that they are runaway slaves, but then hesitates: 'Yet she and [the] boy are white' (2:3). It is also supported by the fact that Topsy is *en travesti*: she has donned boys' clothing to help him. When George jokes, of his planter disguise, 'I've risen in the world, Topsy', she counters, 'So have I, mass'r; look at dem (*points to her trousers*). All de way to de superior sex' (2:3). The play is notably attentive to women's subordination, as well as to racial hierarchies; here they are provocatively counter-posed.

The Adelphi production of *Slave Life* exemplifies the way that theatrical conditions could shape and complicate contemporary notions of race on their way to becoming dramatic representations. It offered a perfectly fitted role for its manager Céleste, as for other members of the company, and it made dramatic capital of the fact that white actors would play mixed-race parts. Like all London's versions of *Uncle Tom's Cabin*, it also borrowed from minstrelsy (as did the novel itself). Apart from Cassy, George, and his wife, the slaves speak with 'black' accents, they sing numbers popular in the minstrel tradition ('I wish I was in Ole Varginny', 'Nelly Bly', 'Sich a gettin' up stairs') and they make jokes about each other's colour. In other words, the play alludes to another theatrical genre whose *raison d'être* is a grotesque impersonation of 'race', a knowingly stagey cross-reference. This metatheatricality reminds the audience that this is performance, a point that George's impersonations make much more overtly. *Slave Life* demonstrates that the melodramatic stage could ironize and complicate racial thinking, even if it also reproduced it.

In this respect, melodrama has an equally complicated and ironic modern heir. The contemporary playwright Branden Jacobs-Jenkins has returned to the genre in his burlesque of Boucicault's play, *An Octoroon* (2014). Jacobs-Jenkins imports substantial extracts of Boucicault's dialogue into his own work, in what his opening scene suggests is a substitute for therapy, a story offered in exploration of what it means to be 'a "black playwright"'.[39] Branden Jacobs-Jenkins is himself a character in the play: in the prologue he slowly dons whiteface and a wig before engaging in a verbal battle with Dion Boucicault, including a magnificent duel consisting entirely of variations on 'Fuck You'.[40] The drama is a rich and indigestible mix of confrontation, subversion, and almost-tender homage. It also offers a twenty-first-century update on nineteenth-century racial classification. The dramatis personae specifies the race of the actors who should play each character, 'with actor ethnicities listed in order of preference'. The list blends nineteenth-century categories with modern American ones, now offensive descriptors mingled with currently neutral or at least conventional terms.

> ZOE —played by an octoroon actress, a white actress, a quadroon actress, a biracial actress, a multi-racial actress, or an actress of color who can pass as an octoroon.
>
> DORA —played by a white actress or an actress who can pass as white.
>
> MINNIE —played by an African-American actress, a black actress, or an actress of color.[41]

The stipulations make modern and historical identities interchangeable, or at least substitutable; they also challenge such terms' stability of signification. In the prologue, the Assistant is described as '*an Indian actor – whatever that means to you*'; the character list suggests that might include '*a Native American actor, a mixed-race actor, a South Asian actor, or an actor who can pass as Native American*'.[42] The text is simultaneously prescriptive and permissive, stipulating 'racial' identities like quadroon which are now obsolete, or suggesting that a modern identity might 'pass as' a nineteenth-century one ('an actress of color who can pass as an octoroon'). The play both resists a nineteenth-century dramatic heritage and returns to it. Like George's impersonations in *Slave Life*, Jacobs-Jenkins's invocation of 'passing', an idea whose meaning entirely depends on a rigidly 'racial' understanding of society, reminds us that performing identity also happens outside the theatre. In a sense, acting is a professional 'passing' – just as racial identities are performed and imagined in real life – and the consequences can be significant and far-reaching in both cases. Passing reveals the flimsiness of the boundaries invented by race theorists. Just occasionally, nineteenth-century melodrama did this too.

## Notes

1. Robert Knox, *The Races of Men: A Fragment* (Philadelphia: Lea and Blanchard, 1850), 9, 13, 14, 15.
2. Josiah Clark Nott and George Robins Gliddon, *Types of Mankind*, ed. Robert Bernasconi (Bristol: Thoemmes Press, 2002 [1854]); *Indigenous Races of the Earth* (Bristol: Thoemmes Press, 2002 [1857]), 618.
3. Nott and Gliddon, *Indigenous Races of the Earth*, 637.
4. George W. Stocking Jr., *Victorian Anthropology* (New York: The Free Press, 1991 [1987]); Reginald Horsman, *Race and Manifest Destiny: The Origins of American Racial Anglo-Saxonism* (Cambridge: Harvard University Press, 1981), 3–6.

5. George M. Fredrickson, *Racism: A Short History* (Princeton: Princeton University Press, 2002).

6. [John Hollingshead], 'Behind the Curtain', *The Cornhill Magazine*, 2 (1860): 748, 744; Jerome K. Jerome, *On the Stage – And Off: The Brief Career of a Would-be Actor* (Stroud: Alan Sutton, 1991 [1884]), 31, 27.

7. See Tracy Davis, 'Acting Black, 1824, Charles Mathews' *Trip to America*', *Theatre Journal*, 63 (2011), 167.

8. Hollingshead, 'Behind the Curtain', 748.

9. Nicholas B. Dirks, *Castes of Mind: Colonialism and the Making of Modern India* (Princeton: Princeton University Press, 2001), especially 5, 12, 16.

10. Knox, *The Races of Men*, 161.

11. Nott and Gliddon, *Types of Mankind*, 373, 374.

12. Knox, *The Races of Men*, 66.

13. Julie Hankey, *Othello*, ser. *Shakespeare in Production*, eds. J. S. Bratton and Julie Hankey (Cambridge: Cambridge University Press, 2005 [1987]), 12; Virginia Mason Vaughan, *Othello: A Contextual History* (Cambridge: Cambridge University Press, 1994), 7.

14. Vaughan, *Othello*, 135.

15. *Ibid.*

16. Virginia Mason Vaughan, *Performing Blackness on English Stages, 1500–1800* (Cambridge: Cambridge University Press, 2005), 17, 149–50, 157.

17. Vaughan, *Performing Blackness*, 17; Knox, *The Races of Men*, 150, 161.

18. Kwame Anthony Appiah, 'Race', in *Critical Terms for Literary Study*, eds. Frank Lentricchia and Thomas McLaughlin (Chicago: University of Chicago Press, 1995 [1990]), 284–9.

19. On British minstrelsy and Ethiopian delineation, see Michael Pickering, *Blackface Minstrelsy in Britain* (Aldershot: Ashgate, 2008); Sarah Meer, *Uncle Tom Mania: Slavery, Minstrelsy & Transatlantic Culture in the 1850s* (Athens: University of Georgia Press, 2005); 'Competing Representations: Douglass, the Ethiopian Serenaders and Ethnic Exhibition in London', in *Liberating Sojourn: Frederick Douglass and Transatlantic Reform*, eds. Martin Crawford and Alan Rice (Athens: University of Georgia Press, 1999), 141–65; and W. T. Lhamon, *Jump Jim Crow: Lost Plays, Lyrics, and Street Prose of the First Atlantic Popular Culture* (Cambridge: Harvard University Press, 2003).

20. Herbert Marshall and Mildred Stock, *Ira Aldridge, the Negro Tragedian* (Washington, DC: Howard University Press, 1993 [1958]); Hazel Waters, *Racism on the Victorian Stage: Representation of Slavery and the Black Character* (Cambridge: Cambridge University Press, 2007), 58–88.

21. 'The Theatres', *The Satirist* (7 April 1833): 534.

22. 'Theatricals', *Figaro in London* (6 April 1933): 56.

23. 'The New Black and M'Keevor', *Bell's Life in London* (21 April 1833): 3.

24. 'Covent Garden', *Athenaeum* (13 April 1833): 236.

25. 'Theatricals', *The Age* (14 April 1833): 118.

26. 'Covent-Garden Theatre', *The Standard* (11 April 1833): 1.

27. William Wells Brown, *The American Fugitive in Europe*, rpt. in *The Travels of William Wells Brown*, ed. Paul Jefferson (New York: Markus Weiner, 1991 [1854]), 206.

28. Brown, *The American Fugitive in Europe*, 204.

29. William Thomas Moncrieff, *The Cataract of the Ganges! or, the Rajah's Daughter* (London: Simpkin & Marshall, 1823), ii.
30. 'Characters in the Play', Dion Boucicault, *The Octoroon; or, Life in Louisiana*, ed. Sarika Bose (Peterborough, Ontario: Broadview, 2014 [1859]), 21.
31. 'Adelphi Theatre', *The Times* (12 December 1861): 12.
32. *Ibid.*
33. 'Princess's Theatre', *The Times* (12 February 1868): 6; Sarika Bose, 'Note on the Text', in Boucicault, *The Octoroon*, 19–20.
34. Jane Moody, 'Céleste, Céline'. *Oxford Dictionary of National Biography*.
35. 'Adelphi Theatre', *The Standard* (30 November 1852): 1; 'Theatrical Examiner', *The Examiner*, 4 (December 1852): 773.
36. Joseph Knight, 'Keeley, Mary Anne', *Oxford Dictionary of National Biography*.
37. 'Theatrical Examiner', *The Examiner*: 773.
38. 'Adelphi Theatre', *The Standard*: 1.
39. Branden Jacobs-Jenkins, *An Octoroon* (London: Nick Hern Books, 2017), 10.
40. *Ibid.*, 17.
41. *Ibid.*, 8.
42. *Ibid.*, 17, 8.

# Extensions of Melodrama

# 14

CAROLYN WILLIAMS

# Melodrama and the Realist Novel

Let me begin by offering a definition of realism. Realism – in whatever genre or medium it occurs – is the representation of the world (understood as 'the world as it is', the world free of representation and independent of shaping human perception or desire) along with the clear indication that the representation itself is an artifice or construction, a mediated and therefore not a direct rendering of reality. In other words, realism, as the suffix '-ism' should inform us, decidedly does *not* depend on the naive assumption that representation could ever be unmediated or transparent. The nineteenth-century realists were never naïve in that way.

## Genre Matters

Melodrama and the realist novel practice their realisms in different ways, of course, developing them in close relation to one another across the nineteenth century. Both are devoted to representing the ordinary and the everyday; both aim to show characters in relation to social collectives or to a social whole. Melodramas based on recently published (or even not-yet-completely published) novels were common, driving authors to distraction and catalyzing the struggle for authors' rights – while the struggle for dramatic copyright also raged on. The case of Charles Dickens is illustrative. On the other hand, realist novels frequently make use of melodramatic characters, plots, and techniques, because signalling a turn away from melodrama was one crucial way to assert their realism; and here the case of George Eliot is most instructive.

Unfortunately, this novelistic strategy of including and yet signalling a turn away from melodrama – an example of the novel's formal logic as a genre – has too often led to the misapprehension that melodrama was not itself realistic; but it was. Accordingly, this essay will focus neither on the many melodramatic stage renderings of nineteenth-century novels nor on novelistic uses of melodrama – which have been much studied elsewhere – but will instead explore common ground between these two titanic bourgeois genres, before settling into a discussion of melodramatic realism in its own right.

Realism is always relative, and representations that are taken to be realistic are merely more realistic than other styles of representation. As George Levine put it, 'realism is a mode that depends heavily on reaction against what the writer takes to have been misrepresentation'.[1] Thus the realist novel positions itself relative to prior genres and modes, claiming to be more realistic than they were, internalizing or parodying them, including them ironically within its more comprehensive form. So, too, melodrama positions itself in relation to forms of representation that had come before. As the 'Remarks' to J. B. Buckstone's *Luke the Labourer* (1828) claim, 'The public have no relish for magnificent woe ... in blank verse'.[2] Written in prose and treating the toils of ordinary characters, melodrama was ostentatiously more realistic than its dramatic precursors.

In several respects, the relativity of realism is descendental – a term that should suggest not only its attention downward in the social hierarchy, its commitment to representing the common, the seemingly insignificant, and the low, but also its refusal of transcendental frameworks of understanding. Melodrama, in Peter Brooks's now-famous formulation, 'becomes the principal mode for uncovering, demonstrating and making operative the essential moral universe in a post-sacred era'; it develops in 'an anxious new world where the Sacred is no longer viable, yet rediscovery of the ethical imperatives that traditionally depended on it is vital'.[3]

Allegory and romance have been most frequently invoked in order to illustrate the 'misrepresentations' against which novelistic realism asserts itself early on. Think of *The Pilgrim's Progress* (1678) and one realistic response to it, *Oliver Twist, or The Parish Boy's Progress* (1837–9). (We should pause, too, to notice that the novel's subtitle, which acknowledges its debt to Bunyan and Hogarth, also imitates the form of a melodramatic playbill.) Or think of *Don Quixote* (1605, 1615) as a foundational moment in the history of the novel as a genre, since the Don's delusions, fostered by reading romances, must be demystified if he is to live in the real world. In studies of nineteenth-century realism, however, melodrama will provide a better genre for comparison.

*Jane Eyre* (1847), for example, whose coincidences are not fully rationalized (but are attributed to 'Mother Nature' and 'God the Father'), raises questions about realism's differences from romance. *Tess of the D'Urbervilles* (1891–2), on the other hand, raises questions not only about realism's relation to tragedy but also to tragedy's replacement, melodrama. *Tess*'s narrator laments – though also rationally explains – the novel's coincidences, while dismissing, with bitterly ironic quotation marks, the notion that '"Justice" was done' in the end. But though the novel aggressively fails to provide a characteristically melodramatic happy ending – one mark of its realism – Tess is surely reminiscent of the suffering but virtuous melodramatic heroine, while Alec D'Urberville is surely reminiscent of the melodramatic villain. As in melodrama, we are meant to recognize her abiding virtue; the novel's subtitle is *A True Woman Faithfully Represented*. When the narrator claims that the 'President of the Immortals had ended his sport with Tess', that narrator suggests tragedy as a reference, only to remind us at the same time how far from tragedy we are, since the central character is so low in the social scale as to be unnoticed in the general scheme of things – another mark of the novel's realism.

For Dickens, Eliot, and Hardy, for all the writers of sensation fiction, and for most other English novelists as well, melodrama provides the most salient reference point against which to create or test a realist vision.

## Probability and Improbability

In the history of the English novel, when the claim to historicity (the claim that the narrated events actually happened) gives way to the claim of probability, the crucial conditions for the development of realism have been prepared. The emerging novel no longer purports to tell a story that really happened, but instead offers an imitation or model of what *could* realistically have happened (as opposed to the fantasy, wishful thinking, or supernatural intervention that characterizes such genres as romance or fairy tale).[4] Within this context, the conventional happy ending of melodrama has often seemed improbable: too sudden and too dependent on coincidence. However, since these happy endings blatantly display their social importance – the reconstitution of families, restitution of lost relations, rescue or escape from the injustices of the law – we should try to understand rather than dismiss them; and in this respect, their very improbability is the crucial key. The melodramatic plot, building inexorably toward a tragic outcome, clearly might *not* have ended happily.

The sudden melodramatic resolution both acknowledges the artifice of the plot and bespeaks the sense of social crisis in which a happy ending seems all but impossible to imagine. What might be considered 'probable' was changing in terrifying ways. We should, in other words, appreciate the sense of fearful instability that raises this urgent question: to what nearly unbelievable lengths must a plot go in order to imagine a happy ending? Within this context, the happy ending is startling, satisfying, and quite a relief. Melodrama responds directly to the post-Enlightenment and especially post-Revolutionary breakdown of an older order and the social chaos that ensued. Not only a 'post-sacred era', the period was also an era of great social instability. In 'Refugee Theater', Matthew Buckley vividly describes this sense of crisis, when 'the very bases of social structure' seemed to have been 'undermined', 'fracturing kinship systems, rendering obsolete the performative rituals of civil society, and engendering, finally, a widespread loss of belief in the efficacy of language itself'.[5] Now lacking absolute authority, the emerging civic order demanded faith in the just execution of human law, which was quite easily seen to be frighteningly fallible and frequently unjust.

Thus perhaps we can see the sociopolitical significance of a plot structure that threatens the existential perils of tragedy, only to swerve away from them at the very end – giving its audiences ways to think about their new world, while also offering relief from it. David Mayer aptly calls melodrama 'a metaphor through which to approach disturbing subjects temporarily', for it 'tames those subjects, offering relief as the problem . . . becomes emotionally intelligible'.[6] From this perspective, melodramatic happy endings retrospectively highlight the relative realism of melodramatic middles.

Melodrama was excoriated in its early days, as well, for its focus on common people. According to Walter Scott, melodrama committed the 'affectation of attributing noble and virtuous sentiments to the persons least qualified by habit or education to entertain them; and of describing the higher and better educated classes as uniformly deficient in those feelings'. Thus, from Scott's point of view, the melodramatic critique of the high and the elevation of the low was not only a political fault, 'the ground-work of a sort of intellectual Jacobinism', but was therefore also a fault against probability.[7] In our own day, by contrast, the happy endings of melodrama are often accused of being conservative, insofar as they restore social order while seeming to gloss over the problematic nature of the status quo. However, at the very least we should notice that Scott, himself a famous conservative, thought that the genre was radical – since it envisioned an inversion of the social hierarchy. Thus we might well disagree with Michael Booth when he writes that melodrama represents 'a dream world, inhabited by dream people and dream justice'.[8] Instead, we might agree with Daniel Gerould, who argues that 'the graphic depiction of social misery is itself incendiary', even when that misery is alleviated in the end.[9]

## Type and Individual

The characters of melodrama are typified. Especially early on in the history of the genre, they are relatively static, do not develop, and represent one primary motive, set of feelings, or social function. Later on they become more mixed and complex.[10] For example, Michael Booth discusses seven stock types in English melodrama: the hero, the heroine, the villain, the old man and woman, and the comic man and woman. But within these main types, he acknowledges, others may figure, too – such as the villain's accomplice, who often has second thoughts, turns against the villain, and swings the plot toward its resolution.[11] These main character types cluster in thematically significant ways, allowing the plot to represent historical change in compressed form. For example: an absent father is often replaced by an evil or ineffectual uncle, as in Thomas Holcroft's *A Tale of Mystery* (1802). The fact that the head of the family is an oblivious surrogate for an absent father allows one and the same plot to suggest both destructive sibling rivalry in the older generation and also damage to the younger generation through the absence of the fatherly, authoritative guidance they might need. Selina, the heroine, seems to be an orphan – perhaps illegitimate – and the plot clusters around this problem as well. How is the family organized? For that matter, who, even, is part of the family?

Another form of organization is even more significant, for English melodrama is known for alternating between scenes of high and low life, tragic and comic action. Dickens famously defends this convention in Chapter 17 of *Oliver Twist*, using his now-famous metaphor of 'streaky bacon' to claim that these alternations are in fact realistic, very much like 'the transitions in real life'. Jacky Bratton further explains, through her formulation of the 'contending discourses' of melodrama, that the lower, comic characters represent a point of view from which the attitudes of the high characters can be ironized or criticized.[12] For example, the servant Beckey Butterfly in Edward Fitzball's *The Inchcape Bell; or, The Dumb Sailor Boy* (1828) keeps two lovers on the string, unlike her mistress, who pines for her one lover with a high, uncompromising fidelity. Beckey explains that her hedge against heartbreak is realistic and practical, given her lower social position: 'as for heart-breaking, we servants have to pay for breakages, and that always makes me very careful' (1:2). Thus the easy-going, often outspoken characters in the low plot represent good common sense, an anti-authoritarian energy, and a looser attachment to high virtue. Their speech is peppered with comic malapropisms, making their low class position unmistakably audible.

In short, the character types of melodrama function in their own genre-specific ways and should be better understood. For one thing, each of the types that Booth identifies must be further differentiated. The term 'heroine', for example, merely names a plot function, and of course it is indeed crucially important that the woman occupies the central place in so much melodrama. But all heroines are not alike; the heroine of any given play might represent 'the erring daughter' (as in W. T. Moncrieff's *The Lear of Private Life; or,*

*Father and Daughter* [1820]) or 'the helpless wife' (as in Douglas Jerrold's *Black Ey'd Susan; or, All in the Downs* [1829]), or 'the ill-treated servant' (as in George Dibdin Pitt's *Susan Hopley; or, The Vicissitudes of a Servant Girl* [1845]). The character may still be seen as a type, but should be seen as a much more particularized type, the suffering woman under duress within very specific social circumstances. This differentiation within the type is one way melodrama explores the problems, issues, and double binds of femininity. (Of course the male types are also differentially represented, and through them we can see melodrama's analysis of masculinity, as well.)

Above all, melodrama represents these types in a systematic relation to one another, figures of 'gender' often representing 'class' and 'nation' in a complex intersection. In other words, to understand the melodramatic types, we must imagine them together, within the ensemble. Functions relative to a plot structure, they are also functions within the stock company, an economic structure of ensemble playing in which actors and actresses would specialize in certain roles. Together the melodramatic ensemble of types represents a schematic model of social relations, expressed through the figure of the family. This is melodrama's way of gesturing toward social totality, the genre's systematic abstraction of social roles, with the family as the nodal point of and synecdoche for the social whole. The rise of melodrama corresponds roughly with the historical development of domestic fiction, and grasping this historical parallel can lead us back to the realist novel. The ostentatiously 'representative' character system of melodrama is certainly different from, but no more dubious than the character systems of the realist novel.

The long-standing critical discourse about the relative weight of individual and type in the constitution of novelistic character can be instructive for an understanding of melodrama as well. In his description of formal realism, Ian Watt emphasizes the representational turn away from the type, by which he chiefly means the allegorical type, referring to an earlier historical moment than the one we are considering now.[13] Michael McKeon focuses on exemplarity as crucial to the early development of realism. In the interplay of precept and example (that is, the interplay of an idea being illustrated and the illustrative instance of it), the realistic reference is to the type or 'species', which is then illustrated through an individual character, who is understood to be a fictional example of the type.[14] Thus exemplarity in characterization leads us back again to probability; for the 'fictional' part (the individual) must be developed against the background of its species or type in a realistically plausible way, and it is this group abstraction – the species or type – that refers to the real world outside the text. Catherine Gallagher continues this line of argument for nineteenth-century realism, pointing out that 'the type is the presumed referent while individuals are presumed to be fictional'. She emphasizes the fact that novelists assume this reciprocal relation between type and individual: 'types are induced from persons in the world and ... characters are deduced from types'.[15] Here, then, is another angle from which we can learn to value the melodramatic types, for they, too, express a general realism beyond the fiction of particular characters.

Thus, while the characters of melodrama are typified, the main characters of realist fiction are individualized. But, crucially, individualized realist characters are always grounded in the type – whether the organizing principle of the type is construed in any given case as social class, gender, race, nation, ethnicity, or indeed any other generalized social category. So, for example, when Jo the crossing-sweeper dies in *Bleak House* (1852–3), the narrator reminds us of the many others of his poverty-stricken class who are 'dying thus around us, every day' (Chapter 47). Or, for example, in *Middlemarch* (1871–2), the story of Dorothea Brooke is positioned by the novel's 'Prelude' against the 'epic life' of Saint Theresa. Of the 'many Theresas' born in a later, secularized age, 'who found for themselves no epic life' because there was 'no coherent social faith and order' to support their ambitions, Dorothea is understood to be only '*a* Saint Theresa', one individual among many who invisibly aspire ('Prelude', italics mine).[16]

These relations of generalization and particularization – both in the novel and in melodrama – are neither allegorical nor idealizing, but sociological. An 'individual' can *only* be apprehended as it is embedded within specific social conditions and groups.[17] Comparing melodrama and the realist novel thus reveals a process of generalization through which the categories of modern social analysis – class, gender, nation and state, race, ethnicity, sexuality – are themselves being developed and understood as ways of describing modern social organization.

This historical dimension of the novel's analytical force has long been understood, but melodrama participates in these cultural formations as well.

## Melodramatic Realism

An art form grounded in live public presentation – involving bodies, speech, music, and a vast array of visual sensations – will necessarily display a different kind of realism from one grounded in (mostly) private and silent reading. But it is important to understand that melodrama was understood to some extent to be realistic almost from its beginnings. In the early decades, an interest in Gothic spectres soon gave way to an interest in civil or domestic disorganization and distress, whereas the spectacularly fictive imaginings of exotic other lands soon gave way to the thrilling reenactments of recent military conflicts and family difficulties at home. The present, not the past, becomes the focus of melodrama as early as the 1820s and '30s, at which point domestic melodrama has firmly established the focus of the genre in the ordinary, everyday world. By this time, too, melodrama has adopted its penchant for representing contemporary crimes and disasters; it becomes almost journalistic in its bid to reenact well-known, contemporary events.

Melodrama depends on various forms of recognition, using conventions that lend a sense of the real to the experience of its spectators. For example, the convention of physiognomic legibility – which holds that facial features and expressions accurately convey psychological states, including motivations and intentions – assured spectators that they could readily recognize the types. Thus the villain could be hissed upon his first appearance. Never mind that this convention was not always upheld; to be sure, melodrama often conveys scepticism about any easy deduction from appearances, sometimes parodying or violating the convention altogether. Nevertheless, it was a melodramatic convention still; and, as in the history of any genre, revision of its conventions – even to the point of overturning them – is to be expected. Dickens, one of the most melodramatic of the nineteenth-century novelists, practices a version of this physiognomic aesthetic – and its sonic equivalent – giving his characters individualized physical attributes and speech tics, while Eliot's realism constantly subjects this convention to critique. A well-known, humorous, and brief example appears in Chapter 1 of *Adam Bede* (1859): 'If Gyp had had a tail he would doubtless have wagged it, but being destitute of that vehicle for his emotions, he was like many other worthy personages, destined to appear more phlegmatic than nature had made him.' True, Gyp is a dog, but the point explicitly refers to human 'personages' as well. Expression often goes awry; appearances do not necessarily reveal psychological interiority.

Sound, too, fosters audience recognition in melodrama. For one thing, the characters repeatedly announce their feelings and intentions. And in their famous 'asides' they tell the audience directly what they feel and what they plan to do. Despite the artificiality of declamation as a style of speech, the fact that it was uttered in prose (not verse) tips it toward the realism of ordinary, everyday life. Characters who could not speak at all for one reason or another – often because they had been traumatized or wounded in the past – 'spoke' in pantomime, using gestures that were understood by the virtuous characters in the play. (Thus, silence was an important element in the soundscape of melodrama.) Speech in melodrama also supported the realism of social class distinctions. The romantic heroine and hero spoke perfect English – unless the hero was a Tar, in which case his speech was divided between densely nautical jargon and the sentimental, manly eloquence he employed when speaking of his wife, his home, or his nation; but other roles often employed 'low' or colloquial speech, regional dialect, professional jargon, or slang. Through dramatic speech, in other words, spectators could recognize the socially typed characters by hearing as well as seeing.

Meanwhile, melodramatic music guides the audience's affective response at every turn. Whether original music played by a full orchestra (for lavish productions) or snatches of readymade music available in collections (like crib sheets) and played by only a few instruments, melodramatic music was thematic – insofar as it set and guided the mood of a scene. There were *agitatos* ('agits' for short) or *furiosos* ('hurries') for chase scenes or scenes of combat, *andantes* ('slows' or 'pathetics') for sentimental scenes, *tremolos* or *mysteriosos* ('mysts') for scenes of suspense, or for eerie, uncanny phenomena like visions, dreams, or ghosts.

Melodramatic music alternately rises and falls, starts and stops, dividing the dramatic action into passages. The music could be ostentatiously interruptive, suddenly demanding attention – as in melodrama's famous crashing chords – while sometimes a song might be included, set like a cameo within the ongoing dramatic action. But often the music fades into the background while continuing to play softly, operating on its auditors unconsciously, much as film music, its direct inheritor, would later do. Spectators of melodrama and, later, of film learn this convention; they become accustomed to the music guiding their responses subliminally. When we are most aware of it, however, melodramatic music stands out as something no written text could ever convey. Thus, it may at first seem unrealistic. But the music provides one powerful condition for affective absorption or immersion, lending spectators the feeling of 'being there', enfolded within the dramatically represented world. The sense of sympathy engendered in realist fiction has been well understood as an affective form of engagement, a route to epistemological and aesthetic awareness. Thus we should be able to see that if 'a knowledge won by way of the emotions' could describe George Eliot's realism, it could also – in a different way – describe the effects of melodramatic music.[18]

However, the visual – and, in particular, the pictorial – realism of melodrama is even more easily grasped. Tableaux punctuate the melodrama with moments of visual stasis, moments when acting bodies freeze to form a still picture (and in fact the tableau was often called 'Picture' in the playtexts of the period). Thus the narrative form of melodrama depends on intermittent pictorialization, a form that Martin Meisel has also found in illustrated novels and narrative painting throughout the nineteenth century.[19] Representing the crucial 'situations' or 'points' of the plot in visual terms, the tableaux create suspense, as if the narrative line were actually suspended on a series of these pictorial points. But the tableau's sudden stillness and silence might be even more important than its intermittence and seriality – for its sudden representational difference from the dramatic action creates a sense of shock, interrupting spectators' absorption and calling on them to pause, to shift their orientation toward the representation, and to interpret the picture. Thus the dramatic action starts and stops, punctuated by still pictures; Meisel has called this narrative form 'serial discontinuity'.[20] This same dynamic – movement interrupted by stasis – may also be seen on the micro-level in the melodramatic acting style, a 'pointed' style in which acting bodies perform broad sweeping gestures that come to a 'point' in brief poses or 'attitudes' that then dissolve or flow into the next gestural sequence.

Furthermore, the stage itself becomes more and more like a framed picture over the course of the nineteenth century, as the proscenium arch gradually becomes an inviolate boundary, separating the place of representation from the place of spectatorship. Though Madame Vestris had introduced the box set as early as the 1830s, this pictorialism reached its apogee in 1880, when Squire and Marie Bancroft at the Prince of Wales's Theatre extended the gilt proscenium arch across the bottom of the stage as well, forming a four-sided frame that explicitly called attention to the nineteenth century's pictorial dramaturgy. The strictly planar orientation of the play behind an imaginary 'fourth wall' emphasizes the artifice of the representation: in other words, what looks 'real' is tacitly acknowledged to be a staged picture.

Tableaux took many different forms. Domestic tableaux were usually sentimental, meant to produce an affective response, to be sure, but were used also to suggest – through the positioning of bodies in the composition – plot complications that might yet unfold. A more blatant form of suspense could be activated through the tableau of recognition, when two characters suddenly 'start back' from one another, then freeze briefly, staring intently at each other. This stage picture of suddenly immobilized astonishment alerts spectators to a relationship in the past that will eventually be revealed. And while the two characters stand still for a moment, forming a tableau for the audience, each one also appears as a tableau for the other.

In the tableau 'realization', acting bodies on stage would compose themselves as a well-known work of art. Early on, realizations were usually based on paintings – such as in Douglas Jerrold's *The Rent Day* (1832), when the curtain opens to disclose a tableau performance of David Wilkie's *The Rent Day* (1807). Later on, spectacular realizations could imitate scenes from contemporary life, their initial stillness giving way to movement, the stage picture coming to life. For example, *The Lights o' London* (1881) by George Robert Sims features a scene of the 'Boro' Market in Southwark on a Saturday night, complete with minutely realized costermongers' barrows, a greengrocer's shop, a cobbler's shop, a public house, and much more (5:1). But the imitation of painting continued in this play as well, with the realization (4:2) of Luke Fildes's well known painting of a Victorian workhouse, *Applicants for Admission to a Casual Ward* (1874). When the stage tableau imitates a painting, it explicitly acknowledges the artifice of its own representation, based as it is on a prior work and another genre of realistic representation.

When George Eliot's narrator acknowledges a debt to a previous realistic genre, her realism adopts a similar strategy. In Chapter 17 of *Adam Bede*, 'In Which the Story Pauses a Little', the narrator extols 'Dutch painting' for its depiction of non-idealized characters shown in 'homely' domestic routines. The narrator acknowledges the constructed nature of the realism, claiming that the narrative provides not things as they are, but 'a faithful account of men and things as they have mirrored themselves in my mind'. Thus Eliot's realism explicitly announces itself as a reconstruction, both of past experience and of a prior art form. Her use of 'Dutch painting' as a metaphor for her own practice should interest us for two other reasons as well: one, because an invocation of the pictorial makes the story 'pause a little', one primary aesthetic effect of the tableau in melodrama; and two, because the melodramatic tableau, like Eliot's manifesto, is based on genre painting, mediated through the dramaturgy of Diderot.[21]

Realist fiction has generally been thought to have the advantage when it comes to representing interiority. But melodrama has its own ways of accomplishing this feat. From the earliest days of melodrama, the mise-en-scène, along with the music, could expressively represent a mood – as in the wild, rocky, mountainous defiles and storms in Act 2, scene 3 of *A Tale of Mystery* (1802). Somewhat paradoxically, these conventions have contributed to the reputation of melodrama as relentlessly 'external', when what is at stake is the transfer of affect to an audience, affect that matches the look of the stage picture. Like physiognomic legibility, this technique in the mise-en-scène depends on recognition, evoking feeling from what spectators see (and hear). Melodrama mobilizes spectators to feel what they see, and see what they feel. But melodrama develops other powerful conventions for representing psychological interiority in audiovisual form.

For example, the melodramatic tableau develops techniques for representing internal states. This aspect of melodrama relates to the earliest Gothic attempts to represent ghosts and spectres, which present the epistemological problem of rendering the invisible in visible terms – the same representational problem posed by psychological phenomena, whether dreams, fears, projections, or memories. As Gothic becomes increasingly psychologized, an evolving conventional relation between forestage and backstage allows for the 'vision scene', in which present external reality would be represented in the forestage with interior psychological reality (whether present or past) represented in the backstage. *The Corsican Brothers* (1852), an adaptation by Boucicault of the novella by Alexandre Dumas *père* (1844), and *The Bells* (1871), an adaptation by Leopold Lewis of Erckmann-Chatrian's *Le Juif polonais* (1867), provide the best examples.

In *The Corsican Brothers*, the two brothers – one who has remained in Corsica while the other goes to Paris – share a romantic form of extrasensory communion, whereby one brother feels stricken whenever the other is in danger. In the concluding tableau of Act 1, the brother in Corsica feels a pang, and the backstage opens to reveal the other brother in Paris, dying after being wounded in a duel. The entirety of Act 2 then shows what has precipitated that duel in Paris, whose results we have already seen. At the moment of the Parisian brother's death (2:4), the backstage opens to reveal the other brother at home in Corsica, precisely as we saw him at the end of Act 1 in the forestage. Thus the two acts fit together like puzzle pieces, with each concluding forestage tableau showing what is happening there and then, in that act, while the backstage opens to reveal what is happening at the exact same moment elsewhere. The structural relation of these two double tableaux has been credited with developing the stage representation of simultaneity in time.[22] Admittedly, *The Corsican Brothers* still relies on non-realistic, supernatural elements, but my point here is simply that psychological interiority is projected visually in the backstage as extrasensory vision.

The backstage tableau is similarly deployed as a place of interiority in *The Bells*, whose visions are fully psychologized; that is to say, they refer to no supernatural powers, but only to ordinary psychological states of memory and guilt. Mathias robbed and murdered a Polish Jew fifteen years before the play opens, and his wealthy burgomaster's life has been founded on that secret crime. But he is haunted by the sound of the bells on the murdered Jew's sleigh. Melodramatic music reproduces the sound of those bells with increasing urgency, and thus the audience is forced to participate in Mathias's feeling of obsessive, inescapable memory. At the end of Act 1, Mathias watches from the forestage as his guilty secret is externalized in a shocking backstage tableau that represents his past crime in the act of being committed; he sees himself on the verge of reenacting that crime. Jointly through the music and the tableau, then, his hidden secret is visually projected and 'realized' outside himself.

In order to make something visible that is by its very definition invisible – whether ghosts and spectres or secrets and memories – melodrama must wrestle with its own audiovisual mandate, using its very 'externality' to overcome and surpass the limits of its form.

### Revising the History of Realism on the Nineteenth-Century Stage

The very old argument that stage realism lagged far behind novelistic realism could – and should – be revised; and our understanding of nineteenth-century stage realism should be modified, too, with melodramatic forms of realism in mind. This would be one important way to show that theatre history can take melodrama seriously. While the scope of this essay cannot do justice to this much larger project, in conclusion we might point the way. This essay has considered several different conceptual banners under which to think about realism: genre differences; sociological thinking; domestic focus; affective or sympathetic spectatorship; and pictorial representation or spectacle. Let me now dwell again on the last, for the spectacular has too often been thought to rule out realism.

We might take the 1860s as an exemplary moment, when two movements diverged from one another and yet worked together toward greater theatrical realism; their relation is dialectical. One movement may be illustrated by T. W. Robertson's understated 'cup and saucer' realism, for his typical setting, the middle-class drawing room, could be no place to stage melodramatic excess. While engaging in ostentatiously trivial stage business, Robertson's characters spoke in an understated style; a great deal was left unsaid, and not everything said was significant. This style seemed the very opposite of melodramatic grandiosity.

However, the other movement grows from within melodrama itself. Sensation melodramas of the 1860s were at one and the same time over the top and hyper-realistic in their staging of extreme situations. They were also tightly engaged with the sensation fiction popular at this time. Dion Boucicault's 'sensation scenes' – burning tenement buildings, exploding steamships, rapidly approaching trains (in *The Poor of New York* [1857], *The Octoroon* [1859], and *After Dark* [1868] respectively) – were realistically depicted, arousing and engaging the eyes, ears, minds, and bodies of their spectators, encouraging them to feel immersed in the dramatic representation. However, these elaborate displays only intensified and made explicit what melodrama had always done. Sensation melodrama names and discloses the shock and astonishment inherent in modern, everyday life. It tells us that the understated, quiet interior does not exhaust the limits of realism, for the shocking external events of the modern world are realistic, too. In this view, spectacle and sensation are not the opposite of realism, but are primary expressions of it.

# Notes

1. George Levine, 'Introduction: George Eliot and the Art of Realism', in *The Cambridge Companion to George Eliot*, ed. George Levine (Cambridge: Cambridge University Press, 2001), 7. See also his *The Realistic Imagination: English Fiction from Frankenstein to Lady Chatterley* (Chicago: University of Chicago Press, 1981).

2. D-G [George Daniel], 'Remarks' to *Luke the Labourer; or, The Lost Son* (London: Cumberland's Minor Theatre, vol. 2 no. 3, 1830), 5.

3. Peter Brooks, *The Melodramatic Imagination: Balzac, Henry James, Melodrama, and the Mode of Excess*, second edition (New Haven: Yale University Press, 1995 [1976]), 15, 19.

4. Michael McKeon, *The Origins of the English Novel* (Baltimore: Johns Hopkins University Press, 1987), especially 53–55, 120; Douglas Lane Patey, *Probability and Literary Form: Philosophic Theory and Literary Practice in the Augustan Age* (Cambridge: Cambridge University Press, 1984); Robert Newsom, *A Likely Story: Probability and Play in Fiction* (New Brunswick: Rutgers University Press, 1988).

5. Matthew Buckley, 'Refugee Theater: Melodrama and Modernity's Loss', *Theatre Journal*, 61 (2009): 179.

6. David Mayer, 'Encountering Melodrama', in *The Cambridge Companion to Victorian and Edwardian Theatre*, ed. Kerry Powell (Cambridge: Cambridge University Press, 2004), 151.

7. Walter Scott, 'Essay on the Drama', in *The Miscellaneous Prose Works of Sir Walter Scott, Bart, Vol. 6: Essays on Chivalry, Romance, and the Drama* (Edinburgh: Robert Cadell, 1834), 386.

8. Michael Booth, *English Melodrama* (London: Herbert Jenkins, 1965), 14.

9. Daniel Gerould, 'Melodrama and Revolution', in *Melodrama: Stage, Picture, Screen*, eds. Jacky Bratton, Jim Cook, and Christine Gledhill (London: British Film Institute, 1994), 185, 188.

10. Mayer, 'Encountering Melodrama', 150, 158–60.

11. Booth, *English Melodrama*, 15–36.

12. Jacky Bratton, 'The Contending Discourses in Melodrama', in *Melodrama*, eds. Bratton, Cook, and Gledhill, 38–49.

13. Ian Watt, *The Rise of the Novel* (Berkeley: University of California Press, 1964), 11–34.

14. Michael McKeon, 'Prose Fiction: Great Britain', in *The Cambridge History of Literary Criticism*, vol. 4, eds. H. B. Nisbet and Claude Rawson (Cambridge: Cambridge University Press, 1997), 250–4.

15. Catherine Gallagher, 'George Eliot: Immanent Victorian', *Representations*, 90 (2005): 62.

16. Gallagher makes this point, *ibid*.

17. On this point, see *Aspects of Sociology*, Frankfurt School for Social Research, trans. John Viertel, with a preface by Max Horkheimer and Theodor W. Adorno (Boston: Beacon Press, 1972), 37–53.

18. Nicholas Dames, 'Realism and Theories of the Novel' in *The Oxford History of the Novel in English: The Nineteenth-Century Novel, 1820–1880*, eds. John Kucich and Jenny Bourne Taylor (Oxford: Oxford University Press, 2012),

305. See also Rae Greiner, *Sympathetic Realism in Nineteenth-Century British Fiction* (Baltimore: Johns Hopkins University Press, 2012).

19. Martin Meisel, *Realizations: Narrative, Pictorial, and Theatrical Arts in Nineteenth-Century England* (Princeton: Princeton University Press, 1983).

20. Meisel, *Realizations*, 38.

21. Dames, 'Realism and Theories of the Novel', 300; Carolyn Williams, 'Moving Pictures: George Eliot and Melodrama', *Compassion: The Culture and Politics of an Emotion*, ed. Lauren Berlant (New York and London: Routledge, 2004), 105–44.

22. Martin Meisel makes this point in '"Scattered Chiaroscuro": Melodrama as a Matter of Seeing', in *Melodrama*, eds. Bratton, Cook, and Gledhill, 65–81.

# 15

## DAVID MAYER

# Melodrama in Early Film

The same reasons that made melodrama the principal theatrical genre to enhance serious themes throughout the nineteenth century led to its unquestioned absorption into early film. Audience perceptions, real and imagined, of a rapidly changing, unstable, threatening, and increasingly secular world, where explanations for suffering, poverty, imperial expansion, urbanization, and social upheaval were not immediately apparent, continued into the new medium. It was still far easier and far more theatrically effective to blame villainy, human malevolence, greed, lust, or jealousy than to identify and analyze – let alone dramatize – their root causes. Melodrama's basic structure – villain-driven depredations on innocents and the eventual exposure and discomfit of the villain, with the concomitant restoration of stability and harmony – worked as well in motion pictures as it had on the stage. Furthermore, scenes of physical and large-scale action, the 'sensation scenes' of the late Victorian theatre – battles, fires, catastrophes, horse-racing, civil unrest, and episodes involving numerous actors – could be more effective on the screen than on a confining stage. On one level it was so simple a transference as to make explanations almost unnecessary, but on quite another level there were complications, and an uneven narrative of adaptation and acceptance.

That uneven narrative of transference is the substance of this chapter. I will offer an account of the chronology and processes through which melodramas became the staple (and, often, the preferred fare) of cinema audiences. The chapter will outline the changing technologies that enabled melodramas briefer than ten minutes in duration to be recast in versions exceeding two hours. It will locate the more immediate source for film melodrama, not in full-scale stage melodramas but in vaudeville's and the music hall's far briefer playlet or dramatic sketch. The chapter will note which melodramatic genres transferred more readily to film than others. It will explore film parodies of stage melodrama, as filmmakers and film audiences increasingly sensed the greater popularity of motion pictures over live drama. It will deal with the problems faced by actors, filmmakers, and audiences who, deprived of the spoken dialogue of theatrical melodrama until about 1928 and the arrival of sound motion pictures, adjusted to technology-imposed silence (except that 'silent' films, augmented with musical accompaniment and occasional sound effects, were never wholly silent). Intertitles, translated into in the language of exhibitors and audiences, freed films from the explicitness of the specific languages of their makers and conferred the advantage of almost-universal intelligibility. I insist that early filmmaking was rarely entirely separate from theatrical practice and that filmmakers repeatedly used theatrical strategies and theatrical praxis in individual films. Beneath all runs my conviction that it is possible, when viewing those early film melodramas which survive, to glimpse elements – but only elements – of the Victorian and Edwardian stage: narratives, scenery and stage machinery, acting, recognizable performers, and other supposedly lost remnants of the earlier live theatre captured, preserved, and performed on celluloid. Finally, throughout this chapter, I will highlight those film melodramas which survive and are accessible to modern scholars and – less frequently – to modern audiences. These are listed in two appendices: those available on DVDs and in libraries, and those viewable on the internet at YouTube.

Melodramas are not a part of the earliest history of the movies. Those earliest years, from 1895 through 1900, are a period of experimentation and a time of developing competing cameras and projectors, film stock of different gauges, faster and more sensitive emulsions (the light-sensitive surface coatings which capture and retain images on film); quarrels over devices and patents; questioning whether there were really audiences for film, or whether film was little more than a fugitive novelty; and doubts about audience attention span, as movies gradually and irregularly appeared in vaudeville houses and music halls. A visual novelty, the film program following live variety acts offered a series of mixed brief films in which there was little narrative content apart from the occasional one-shot anecdote: a passing train, a festive or celebratory procession, a journey by train or ship or automobile, a celebrity appearance.

It was precisely this placement of film on the American, Dutch, French, and British variety bill that accounts for narrative film and, by extension, the earliest film melodramas and comedies. From about 1900, individual films, most shorter than two minutes, were spliced together on a single reel to provide a program of film viewing approximately a half-hour in duration. Immediately before the films was the last *live* act, the dramatic sketch. The sketch had come into existence following the British Theatres Act of 1843, which not only clarified the distinction between the 'legitimate' (i.e., dramatic) playhouses licensed by the crown, and the 'minor' playhouses licensed by local magistrates, but also created the condition for the music halls, by definitively separating drinking and smoking from dramatic productions. While the Theatres Act focused on the exclusive right of playhouses to offer spoken drama but forbade the sale and consumption of alcohol in their auditoria, the music halls, immediate successors to the public houses, were denied the right to perform spoken drama, but were permitted to sell alcohol on the premises and allowed both smoking and drinking in their auditoria.

By the 1880s, British music halls had found a way around the severity of this law through the dramatic sketch: a brief narrative playlet, limited to no more than six actors, accompanied by music, with dialogue limited to occasional sentences or the dramatized action made intelligible by a narrator who, standing to one side of the stage, explicated the situation or sang an explanatory narrative that described the performers' actions and their emotional states. By agreements negotiated between theatre and music hall managements and acknowledged by a Parliamentary commission, sketches were limited to eighteen minutes. Dramatic sketch companies passed easily across the Atlantic to America and into Europe. Because narratives were sung or given to audiences in the form of program notes, the pantomime performances of the actors – with only scant dialogue – were always intelligible to their audiences.

We see the effect of this ruling in John 'Jew' Lawson's internationally successful melodramatic sketch *Humanity* (1896), billed on 'the halls' and in trade papers of America and Britain as '*Humanity* in 18 Minutes'. Lawson, an acrobat and comedian, had travelled from Manchester to America in 1883, taking the role of a comic Jew in a melodrama entitled *Humanity; or, Passages in the Life of Grace Darling* (1882). Subsequently acquiring full rights to this largely unsuccessful drama, Lawson cut away the first three acts and refashioned it into a vaudeville sketch, incorporating an 1860s London crime in which two disputants fought with pistols, knives, and fists, setting fire to the apartment in which the quarrel began, and crashing down the blazing stairs to their deaths. Lawson, now taking the character of a wealthy Jew and identifying his adversary as the seducer of his gentile wife (both of whom justified their adultery with the reiterated statement, 'Remember, he's only a Jew'), confronted and fought with his adversary, the pair smashing the contents of the apartment, and, locked together, tumbling down the fiery staircase. At the bottom, Lawson arose from the wreckage to sing 'Only a Jew'.[1]

Meanwhile, from the mid-1870s theatres, both their auditoria and stages previously brightly illuminated by gas, responded to the introduction of electric stage lighting by reducing illumination or wholly darkening their auditoria. Now both theatre and music hall audiences sat in the dark gazing onto a lighted stage at a melodramatic narrative. Thus, when they were shown in variety houses, films were visible because they were viewed from darkened auditoria. It would have been impossible otherwise.

The next step – as filmmakers became more adroit, as music hall audiences were seen to be accepting of motion pictures, as copies of film were more readily available from the by-now-numerous studios in New York, Fort Lee (New Jersey), London, Brighton, and Paris, and as the dramatic sketch (or the alternative narrative ballet) was perceived as an expensive and unnecessary luxury – was to replace the dramatic sketch with a filmed sketch. Since motion picture studios sold their films to exhibitors, pricing them by the linear foot, it was far cheaper to buy the film-print than to support the stage company. For a time, Lawson held onto his sketch and continued to tour it along with other sketches he had devised. Other actors similarly retained their properties until age, physical disability, or other reasons prompted their surrender to the filmmakers. Lawson delayed filming *Humanity* until 1912 (by which time the permitted duration of the sketch had stretched to thirty minutes), removing the adulterous relationship and adding a few further characters. Meanwhile, by 1903, film studios were supplying music halls with sketches and, crucially for the holiday season, French *féeries*, brief 'fairy' dramas produced by Gaumont and Pathé that were deliberately structured to resemble the traditional English Christmas pantomime. Despite the longer performance time allowed to them, live narrative sketches were slowly driven from the variety houses of Europe and America, to be replaced by cheaper and more popular motion pictures – cheaper both to make and to sell as multiple prints.

It is hard to date exactly when the first melodramatic film narratives appeared. In 1901, the American Mutoscope and Biograph Company (hereafter Biograph) filmed the temperance melodrama *Ten Nights in a Barroom*. Because American audiences were widely familiar with Timothy Shay Arthur's 1854 novel and William W. Pratt's 1858 stage adaptation, separate episodes of the narrative were sold to exhibitors as discrete parcels, and it was left up to the discretion of the nickelodeon and variety theatre proprietors how much of the complete plot would be acquired and shown. It wasn't until 1903 that the entire film was assembled and released as a complete entity.

Concurrently in Britain, *Tally Ho!* (1901) was filmed, based on a live thirty-minute comedy-melodramatic sketch, devised by W. H. Risque and staged by Frank Parker, that had been performed twice daily at the London Hippodrome from June to December 1901. The film was not intended for general commercial viewing but commissioned as a promotional piece for the

Moss Empires (a variety theatre chain), and was exhibited in other Moss theatres as an inducement to patronize Edwin Moss's flagship variety house. Shot on the Hippodrome's stage and circular arena, capable of being rapidly converted into a water tank and reliant on trained animals and numerous 'Hengler's Plunging Horses', the drama enacted a vicious squire's refusal to marry his daughter to the man of her choice, and the younger man's sub-sequent ruse to elope with the girl during a local stag hunt. The hunt is diverted by a stag, which lures the squire and entire hunt of some dozens of male and female riders into the village pond. Unfortunately, this film, some six minutes in duration and in all likelihood the earliest film to be shot indoors in a theatre, has vanished. Six minutes of film in 1901 is substantial. Films in the period between 1900 and 1909 eventually reached a length of about twenty minutes, although most ran for fewer than fifteen minutes.

Also in this decade many of the theatrical melodramatic genres appeared on film, more than a few shaped by conventions of the touring combination company.[2] Audiences who had experienced stage melodramas soon found filmed westerns, temperance melodramas, 'sporting' (i.e., boxing and horse-racing) and detective plays, 'togaplays' and other dramas set in the ancient world, abducted child dramas, dramas which combined the perils of urban life with domestic strife, and, in many of these varieties, dramas which questioned the role of women and which spoke to nascent female emancipa-tion. Melodramatists who had made modest livings in the theatre began to realize that motion pictures offered further opportunities, and deserted the stage to turn screenwriter. These relocated writers included Frank Boggs, Wallace McCutcheon (father and son), Scott Marble, J. Searle Dawley, Alicia Ramsay, Rudolph de Cordova, and, crucially, D. W. Griffith.

Early in this decade two melodramas stand out, both shot by Edwin S. Porter for the Edison Company and both reflecting the structure of the American melodramatic combination company. In *The Great Train Robbery* (1903), loosely based on Scott Marble's 1897 stage melodrama bearing the same title, as well as an assortment of unnamed western dramas, the robbery of an American baggage and passenger train is interrupted by a dance performed by cowboys and cowgirls before the drama of pursuit, shootout, and capture is effected. Porter's *Uncle Tom's Cabin* (1903), filmed later that same year, approaches twenty minutes in length and uses two companies, one consisting of the actors, white and blacked-up, who perform a narrative loosely based on Harriet Beecher Stowe's novel and the Aiken playtext, and a second company of black actor-dancers who perform in three dance scenes extraneous to the plot, and serve as set-dressing in scenes carried forward by the white performers. This film is one in which we may view the actual stage sets used by an unidentified 'Tom' company, caught by

Porter as they toured New Jersey, and, as Eliza and her baby cross the frozen Ohio River, glimpse stage machinery in operation. Despite its unusual length, *Uncle Tom's Cabin* stopped short of scenes which fully developed Stowe's narrative. Rather, audiences, probably to some degree familiar with stage versions, witnessed abridgements of the narrative, each scene's contents explicated by intertitles – some of the first to be employed – which stated the subject matter of the scenes. Intertitles containing dialogue lay some years in the future.

This approach to adapting stage melodramas foreshadows the manner in which popular narratives, not protected by copyright legislation until 1911 and constrained in duration to less than twenty minutes, would be scavenged for key episodes or presented in a sequence of brief dramatic episodes. One of the better known early film sequences to survive, *Rescued from an Eagle's Nest*, depicts a baby carried off by a predatory eagle, and the child's rescue from the eagle's mountain eyrie by her woodsman father (played by D. W. Griffith), an episode lifted in its entirety in 1907–8 by Edwin Porter from the second act of Con Murphy's Irish-American melodrama, *The Ivy Leaf* (1884). Concurrently, Sidney Olcott, filming Klaw and Erlanger's six-act *Ben Hur* for the Kalem Company in 1907, reduced William Young's adaptation to seven brief 'tableaux'. Similarly, Siegmund Lubin's 1907–8 adaptation of Henry Herman and Henry Arthur Jones's *The Silver King* (1880) retains the original four-act structure and, in brief action scenes, offers the play's key actions unexplicated by intertitles. Physical movement, gesture, and audiences' prior knowledge of the stage version evidently sufficed.

Earlier, in 1902, Porter had filmed *The Life of an American Fireman*, a six-minute film that dramatized an American fire company alerted by an alarm, newly patented suspended harnesses dropping onto waiting fire horses, and the company engines and firefighters racing to a smoke-filled house where they extinguish the blaze, rescuing a mother and child. The film lacked a villain to obstruct the firemen, but was melodramatic in its use of action scenes. Porter's film conspicuously draws on Joseph Arthur's stage drama *The Still Alarm* (1887). It is probable that Porter was further influenced by a second stage melodrama, Scott Marble's *The Patrol* (1891), which retained elements of Arthur's plot but exchanged the firemen's horse-drawn engines for police paddy wagons racing to apprehend criminals. The enduring popularity of the stage *Still Alarm* (with touring productions and revivals in America, Britain, and France) assured that three further silent films with this title, each adding fierce conflagration episodes to Joseph Arthur's plot, followed in 1911, 1918, and 1926.

Modern spectators viewing these early, pre-1909 films will be conscious of how much of the action was filmed outdoors. External filming at first was a necessity. Limitations in existing lenses, slow and sometimes unpredictable emulsions, and the slow development of indoor lighting meant that exteriors and action sequences were easier to film than interior domestic scenes, although the problem of interior settings was sometimes solved by constructing sets in the open air, often on rooftops where fluttering canvas flats and drops betray passing breezes.

Outdoor filming was necessary not merely for reasons of available light, but also to make space for animal action, for the few attempts to adapt Georgian and Victorian equestrian melodramas to the screen. In 1910, Frank Boggs successfully adapted Henry Milner's *Mazeppa; or, The Wild Horse of Tartary* (1831), with the California landscape standing in for the Carpathian Mountains, but his film no longer survives. However, an eccentric adaptation of this most popular hippodrama appears in *The Cheyenne's Bride* (1911), a film by James 'Young Deer' Thomson, who claimed to be Native American, and, frequently costumed as a Plains brave, took the leading role in numerous films he wrote and directed for Pathé Frères – usually performing opposite his co-star wife, a genuine Winnebago, self-styled 'Princess Red-Wing'. *The Cheyenne's Bride* enacts the rivalry between Sioux and Cheyenne warriors as they compete for the favour of the Sioux chieftain's daughter. The chief has his daughter, whose preference is for the Cheyenne, bound à la *Mazeppa* to the back of a horse, the horse turned loose and sent galloping across California scrubland and forest with the rivals in pursuit, until the favoured suitor finally overtakes and rescues his bride. Bizarre as this sequence is, it is our only filmed vision of the great Astley spectacle, *Mazeppa; or, The Wild Horse of Tartary*, dramatized from Lord Byron's poem by Henry Milner and Andrew Ducrow and staged at Astley's Amphitheatre in 1831.

Filming indoors brought further problems. Simple electric bulbs were inadequate, and stage lanterns had yet to be invented. The London Hippodrome's *Tally Ho!* had been filmed using unfiltered and unshaded arc lamps, hitherto only occasionally used for street lighting, with the result that cast and crew experienced temporary blindness and were obliged to rest in darkened rooms. By 1906, banks of tubular lamps provided an overall lighting wash, but key or atmospheric lighting effects were slower to arrive.

The visibility of actors necessarily raises the question of melodramatic acting styles, and whether motion pictures in any way curtailed the various gestural alphabets and vocabularies that were so characteristic of stage melodrama. As far as one can observe in early film melodramas, actors who migrated from the stage to film brought with them practiced, sometimes large, gestures of the Delsarte school – an approach to emotional and gestural acting brought to America from France in the 1880s by François Delsarte –

and the various British acting academies, but were generally subtle in their use and careful not to over-gesticulate. French actors, already influenced by the Naturalistic stage, seem somewhat more nuanced in their performances – but not always – while those actors who entered the profession directly through the film studios and who had witnessed, but not practiced, stage acting were the least subtle, until they gradually learned their craft. Film parodies of stage melodrama, increasingly common from 1909, make a point of depicting actors whose gestures are inappropriately large and empty of meaning, and who needlessly repeat the same gesture mechanically. Such parodies taunt the stage as an anachronistic relic harbouring actors whose performance styles are ludicrously obsolete, whilst implying (but not overtly stating) the superiority of motion pictures. Overall, however, there was no consistency in melodramatic acting, even as the silent era was coming to a close. Because there was a continual flow in both directions of actors crossing the Atlantic, no gestural language, European or American, predominated and became standard. Even as the camera moved closer to the actor with the use of the medium shot, the 'American shot' (actors filmed from the waist up), or even the close-up, individual actors' gestural performances varied from scene to scene and film to film. In film melodramas as late as 1922, it is not unusual to find an actor, who has otherwise played with restraint, responding to a crisis with gestures that are large and which, even in the context of that moment, appear excessive; but those large gestures can also seem deeply moving and entirely appropriate.

A further legacy of stage melodrama affected gestures, their timing, and their fluency: the use of music both as the actors filmed their scenes and in the venues where films were exhibited. Reminiscences of silent era actors and photographs of film studios testify to the presence of pianos and the occasional small string orchestra to accompany filming, which had the desired effects of setting the emotional tones of the scene being filmed and supporting the actors' gestures, enabling them to sustain or elaborate an attitude or extend an outstretched limb. When films were exhibited, pianos (in the lesser venues) and orchestras (in the more upmarket cinemas) played throughout the screening. Music publishers hired composers to compose piano 'melos' and issued albums of all-purpose tunes sold to nickelodeon pianists. When the films were exhibited, the extent to which music was appropriate to the drama and was synchronized with the moment enacted depended upon the circumstances and venue. Many film melodramas were accompanied by a house pianist who improvised and used stock melodies. Other house musicians used all-purpose music supplied by publishers and – occasionally – by the studio. A few orchestras – those located in first-run houses – played music again provided by the studio or commissioned and closely supervised by the director: Joseph Karl Briel's score for Griffith's *The Birth of a Nation* (1915) was closely synchronized to every moment of this three-hour film.

In 1908 Griffith began his motion picture career, first as a scenarist writing scripts for Biograph and as an actor appearing in several Biograph films, but, later that same year, as a director of his own narratives. And while Griffith is far from the only writer-director representative of that period, his film melodramas, both original and derived from earlier dramas and novels, are among the best preserved and the most accessible. Griffith's *The Adventures of Dollie* (1908), his debut film as a director, exploits a prevailing fear that Romany immigrants, entering America from Eastern Europe, steal children to extract ransom. *The Adventures of Dollie* enacts in twelve minutes the anguish of a family when their small daughter Dollie is kidnapped by gypsies. Hidden in a barrel stowed at the rear of the gypsy caravan as the gypsies flee with their prize, the child (still in the barrel) falls into a river, tumbles over a waterfall and is carried along on the current until fished out by a boy who helps to restore Dollie to her distraught parents. Griffith's film follows an earlier British film melodrama, Cecil Hepworth's seven-minute *Rescued by Rover* (1905) in which the faithful family dog leads the father to a gypsy lair where his kidnapped daughter is held captive.

By 1911, Griffith had graduated to more elaborate original melodramas. His sixteen-minute *The Lonedale Operator* (1911) enacts the peril and resourcefulness of a female telegraph operator when her railway express office is attacked by tramps intending to steal a satchel holding a mining company's payroll. Telegraphing for assistance and keeping her attackers at bay with a monkey wrench held as if it were a pistol, she is saved by her sweetheart, a locomotive engineer, who races his engine to her timely rescue.

Meanwhile, however, Griffith had turned to the theatrical repertoire for many of his Biograph films. Among these is *A Drunkard's Reformation* (1908), based on the late Charles Warner's performance in Charles Reade's *Drink* (1879), a British adaptation of Emile Zola's *l'Assommoir* (1877). Griffith's attempt at a temperance melodrama for American audiences enables direct comparison with its immediate contemporary, the French-made *l'Assommoir* (1908), directed by Albert Capellani for Pathé Films. Griffith worked from Biograph's Manhattan studio and the Players' Club, where he had gone to recruit actors for his films. When Warner committed suicide in February of 1908, Griffith, who had observed Warner onstage on the vaudeville circuit when Warner was touring a cut-down version of *Drink* as a dramatic sketch, quickly devised a framing plot in which a family, threatened by the father's alcohol addiction, is rescued when he accompanies his small daughter to the theatre, where he witnesses Warner's performance. Coaching a Biograph actor in Warner's mannerisms, Griffith devised a replica *Drink* that recalled Warner's harrowing performance of the lead character's death, brought on when the villainess Virginie, whose advances Coupeau has ignored, deliberately poisons his frail body by placing before him a bottle of cognac and rejoices as he consumes it, rapidly producing delirium tremens sufficient in their horror to drive the errant spectator-father to permanent sobriety.

Concurrently, Capellani, drawing on his own theatrical background and his association with Andre Antoine and his naturalistic Théâtre Antoine, recruited a cast of experienced stage actors from the Paris theatres and, using exterior and interior settings as environments appropriate to his working class Parisians, dramatized Zola's entire narrative, including Gervaise's seduction and abandonment, the scandalous washhouse fight between female rivals, Coupeau's fall from a scaffold deliberately weakened by the 'adventuress' (villainess) Virginie, Coupeau's subsequent lapse into alcoholism, and his horrid death tormented by visions of attacking reptiles and demons. Like Griffith, Capellani staged a temperance melodrama, one which demonstrates that pictorial realism and somewhat less gestural acting were yet another facet of melodrama.

A further approach to European melodrama emerged in 1910 with the Danish actress Asta Nielsen performing the lead role in *Afgruden* (*The Abyss*). Directed by Urban Gad, it enacts the mesmeric decline of a modest piano teacher who, engaged and seemingly settled, is abruptly, unexpectedly, overcome by lust for a travelling showman, abandoning respectability and comfort as she is drawn into the life of an itinerant cabaret performer. She sings and dances for pennies, desperate to keep a tenuous hold on her fickle lover. As her life plummets into an abyss of degradation, she is confronted with a rival and – again suddenly – erupts into a violently jealous, self-destructive virago, and stabbing her lover in her fury. An initial impulse might be to view Nielsen's piano teacher as a stock role in late-nineteenth-century 'bad girl melodrama', not the 'adventuress' or the seductress, but the '[good] girl who loses her character'. Such roles required the transgressive heroine to suffer before rehabilitating herself in the drama's final act, at last regaining self-possession and respect. Melodrama, after all, encourages us to view characters in moral terms and to search for moral coherence and eventual stability as the narrative moves toward its conclusions. But with *The Abyss* those expectations mutate. In contrast to expectations conditioned by melodrama and popular fiction, we don't witness the woman's rehabilitation or the return of her moral compass. Rather, her journey is in one direction only. If she isn't a melodramatic heroine, neither is she the drama's villain, but is instead a pathetic victim of her own passions. Her character corresponds to the male hero-villain of late Victorian melodramas,

such roles as Mathias, as played by Henry Irving in Leopold Davis Lewis's
*The Bells* (1871) – as well as Irving's numerous other fractured and morally
divided characters for the Lyceum stage.

Although the Biograph Studios (with Griffith) and the Edison, Kalem,
and Lubin Companies' films are the better known to historians from this
early period of filmmaking, it was the Thanhouser Film Corporation that
best illustrates the transition from live performance to filmed melodrama.
At the close of the nineteenth century Edwin Thanhouser, a former actor,
managed profitable stock theatres in Wisconsin and Chicago where he
staged numerous stage productions. After he married the actress
Gertrude Homan in 1900, the couple together observed the advent of
motion pictures and, in 1909, moved their family to New Rochelle, New
York, where they established a film studio in a former roller-skating rink:
Edwin managing the business, Gertrude choosing scripts, casting, and
editing films. Their films were drawn from classic novels, Dickens especially, and the stage – Shakespeare, Ibsen, comedy, and melodrama – but a
substantial number of the films produced by the company between 1910
and 1917 were original melodramas, many of them mysteries, detective
thrillers, and domestic dramas. Most of the over 1,000 Thanhouser films
have been lost, but 225 have been recovered and preserved, and sixty-three
are available both on the internet and as DVD box sets (which readers are
urged to view).[3] I cite but two here, both dating from 1912 and taken
directly from stage plays: *Dr. Jekyll and Mr. Hyde*, based on the 1888
stage adaptation by Thomas Russell Sullivan and Richard Mansfield and
starring Mansfield in the double role of Jekyll/Hyde, and *Under Two
Flags*, adapted for the stage in 1901 by Paul M. Potter from Ouida's
1867 novel. Following the theatrical version, Thanhouser's *Dr. Jekyll
and Mr. Hyde* bestows upon Jekyll a fiancée, Thanhouser's leading actress
Florence La Badie, who is baffled and then repelled by his chemical
transformation. However, unlike in the stage play, the role of Jekyll was
performed by the former stage actor James Cruze, while the part of Hyde
was performed by Harry Benham, transformations between the two identities effected by optical dissolves and careful editing. A less compact
narrative – 'Five Acts and Nine Tableaux' – *Under Two Flags* begins
with the hero Bertie Cecil escaping from England to shield and divert
attention from his brother, who has stolen from regimental funds.
Joining a French cavalry unit in Arabia, he is befriended by a young
woman, 'Cigarette', who falls in love with him but then, to save his life,
sacrifices herself before a firing squad when Cecil's fiancée appears.

Of Thanhouser's original melodramas, *The Evidence of the Film* (1913) is
their most self-referential, as its plot depicts the studio in operation: a

messenger boy accused of stealing the bonds he was to deliver is rescued by his sister, a Thanhouser film editor, who finds among the studio's film out-takes evidence of her brother assaulted by the villain and the bonds stolen from him. Further Thanhouser original melodramas include *An Elusive Diamond* (1914), a detective drama, *The Pasha's Daughter* (1911), a narrative of an American erroneously jailed in Turkey for plotting against the government who is rescued by a pasha's daughter, and *In the Hands of the Enemy* (1915), a spy thriller reflecting war in Europe and anticipating American involvement. The search for more of these revealing Thanhouser films continues.

The years 1912–13 mark a watershed in motion pictures and, consequently, a change in the nature of filmed melodrama. Music halls, formerly the principal venues for exhibiting and watching film, were increasingly replaced by purpose-built cinemas that attracted middle-class audiences, a newer, more affluent clientele. Filmmakers recognized those newer patrons' preferences for longer dramatic films with artistic content. The habit of cinema-going was stimulated by their ability to make and – significantly – market films of greater length, with running times in excess of an hour and with some exceeding two or three hours. As early as 1908, French cinema had become accustomed to the *film d' art* movement, with such dramatized reenactments as *L'Assassinat du duc de Guise* (1908). In 1912, Adolph Zukor, forming a partnership with Daniel, Gustave, and Charles Frohman to create the Famous Players Studio ('Famous Players in Famous Plays'), engaged Sarah Bernhardt and Lou Telegen to produce *Les Amours de la reine Elizabeth* (1912) in Paris. Famous Players' first studio production had Edwin Porter directing an overweight James O'Neill in his famous melodramatic stage vehicle, *The Count of Monte Cristo* (1913).

More significant, because it established some of the conditions for Biblical melodrama, was D. W. Griffith's *Judith of Bethulia* (1913). Begun by Griffith in 1912 but held back until 1913 by Biograph executives angered at its seemingly excessive cost, the film enacts the siege of the walled city of Bethulia by the Assyrian general Holofernes. To save the city, the recently widowed Judith comes into the enemy camp, beguiles Holofernes, gets him drunk, and – briefly but painfully hesitating because she has sensed his sexual aura – decapitates him, returning to Bethulia with his severed head, an act that demoralizes the Assyrians and leads to their defeat but also leaves Judith, hailed as a heroine, again bereft.

*Judith* is not the earliest melodrama set in the ancient world. As early as 1901 Ferdinand Zecca had filmed *Quo Vadis?*, now lost. Henryk Sienkiewicz's novel, set in the reign of Nero and dramatizing the emperor's persecution of Christians and their converts, was again filmed by Enrico

Guazzoni in 1912, and once more by Georg Jacoby and Gabriellino D'Annunzio in 1924.[4] Wilson Barrett's enduring stage drama, successful on both sides of the Atlantic and in the colonies, *The Sign of the Cross* (1895) – another melodramatic togaplay in which pagan Rome and imperial Romans were challenged by upstart Christianity and proselytizing Christian maidens – was directed by Frederick Thompson (1914 – only partly complete). Decadent, orgiastic pagan Rome was depicted in Louis Feuillade's *Heliogabale* (1911), many of the scenes realizing the paintings of Laurence Alma-Tadema. Lew Wallace's novel *Ben Hur* (1880) was twice filmed, briefly by Sidney Olcott in 1907 and again, impressively, by Fred Niblo in 1925. The destruction of Pompeii in AD 79, the subject not only of Bulwer-Lytton's 1834 novel *The Last Days of Pompeii* but also English and American stage and pyrodramatic versions, came to the screen as *Gli Ultimi Giorni di Pompei* (1913), directed by Mario Caserini and Eleuterio Rodolfi. However, the dominating film melodrama of the ancient world is *Cabiria* (1914). Directed by Giovanni Pastrone and split into five full-length episodes, it enacts the defeat of Roman armies by Hannibal, the abduction from Sicily to Carthage of the girl Cabiria, her enslavement and eventual rescue by a strongman Maciste, and – by the fourth episode – the defeat of the Carthaginians by the Roman general Scipio Africanus.

From this point, there is a veritable explosion of feature-length film melodramas, continuing into and beyond the coming of sound. Those cited here are among the more available. One of the forms this explosion takes is the sudden burgeoning of serials intended to be viewed in weekly or monthly tranches. Although few individual episodes were longer than fifteen minutes, the total length of these pocket melodramas more than exceeded the typical feature film. What further distinguishes film serials is that many featured a physically active, adventurous, danger-seeking and danger-surviving female as their lead character, a woman who could pursue and apprehend robbers, wrestle villains to the ground, ride dangerous vehicles and stand on top of speeding trains, ascend rock faces, buildings, or iron-work bridges, leap into lakes and rivers, endure hostile climates, and solve complex criminal cases all in the name of restoring justice. The titles of the competing serials readily identify their heroine: *Adventures of Kathlyn* (1912), *The Perils of Pauline* (1914), *The Active Life of Dolly of the Dailies* (1914), and *Les Vampires* (1915) (featuring the heroine-villainess Irma Vep, an anagram of vampire). The most enduring of these was *The Hazards of Helen*, the Kalem Company's adventure series that played out over 119 twelve-minute episodes (totalling nearly twenty-four hours of film) released over a span of slightly more than three years between 1914 and 1917.

Students of melodrama will be aware of the large-scale productions through the 1890s and up to about 1918, most notably Drury Lane's 'autumn dramas' (all of which were melodramas). In 1889, and annually thereafter, Charles and Daniel Frohman began importing these dramas to New York, where the scale of production and the vivid sensation scenes continued to draw audiences and lead to tours along the East Coast. Broadway producers Lee, Jacob, and Sam Shubert, acquiring motion picture rights, formed Paragon Pictures and engaged the French émigré director Maurice Tourneur to direct those autumn dramas that continued in popularity. Paragon produced *Sporting Life* (1917 and 1925), *The Whip* (1917), *The White Heather* (1919), and – later – *The Two Orphans* (1933), Tourneur's version of Eugene Corman's and Adolphe D'Ennery's 1874 *Le Deux Orphelines*, challenging Griffith's *Orphans of the Storm* (1922). Of these, only *The Whip* survives and, together with a filmed parody of the stage play, offers insight into both the stage drama and the measures taken when adapting it for the screen.

The stage version of *The Whip* (1909), a drama by Henry Hamilton and Cecil Raleigh, enacts a somewhat typical British 'sporting drama' narrative: an ancestral home and dukedom are at risk unless a racehorse can recoup a lost fortune by winning a crucial national derby, so that the cash-strapped duke might marry a horse-loving heiress. But problems intervene. The horse's owner is threatened by a villain who woos the heiress, attempts to blackmail the duke, manages to strand the railroad boxcar in which the horse is travelling to the racecourse in the path of a crushing locomotive, and, when all else fails, contrives to have the horse's jockey arrested just as the race is to begin. Tourneur, apparently under instruction to Americanize both characters and setting, crafts characters in the mold of southern gentry and translates the action to Virginia country estates, to the Armory horse show and the Eden Musée waxworks in Manhattan, and to the running of the rich Travers Stakes at Saratoga. And although the pursuit by fast car to intercept the boxcar carrying the nearly doomed horse and the resulting rail smash are vivid and exciting, Tourneur's *coup de théâtre* lay in replacing the arrested jockey (who in the stage version is wrested from the police by an angry mob, and thrust upon his mount to compete and win) with the heroine, disguising her gender in racing silks, who rides to victory. In this decision, Tourneur borrows from two earlier dramas, Charles T. Dazey's *In Old Kentucky* (1893) and Edison's film, *The Trainer's Daughter; or, The Race for Love* (1907), both of which feature their heroine in disguise, compelled by circumstances to substitute for the abducted jockey, and riding the winning horse.

But Tourneur's *The Whip* is not the final word on this stage melodrama. A remarkably close version, in some respects more faithful to the live drama, replacing the somewhat preposterous narrative scenes with absurdly comic travesties, is the parody *Pimple's The Whip* (1916).[5] 'Pimple' and Pimple films were the invention of two brothers, Fred and Joe Evans, originally members of a family music hall act. Fred played Pimple in clown whiteface, wearing a frightwig and turned-up putty nose; Joe played villains. With the decline of the dramatic sketch, the brothers followed other family members into movie-making with Folly Films, producing comic sketches that soon turned into slapstick, punning parodies of well-known stage plays, sketches, and successful films. In their version of *The Whip*, based not on the movie but the still-popular Drury Lane autumn drama, Fred's Pimple takes the leading role as the man who is dependent on his racehorse – a pantomime horse: two men in a horse costume complete with broomstick tail – to recoup his fortune. He is opposed by his brother, playing Lord Elpus, who seeks to injure The Whip so that he cannot compete. Cleverly parodying the attempt to sabotage the horsebox carrying *The Whip*, Lord Elpus, climbing aboard an evidently rickety cardboard train, disconnects a visibly cardboard horse-box which glides to a swerving stop. The Whip is belatedly rescued, by Pimple arriving on a bicycle, who remonstrates with stagehands before being knocked over as the locomotive finally arrives. The climactic Derby, formerly managed onstage with real horses on moving treadmills galloping in front of a painted moving diorama, is here run with a melee of pantomime horses, running through suburban streets lined with bemused gaping onlookers, tumbling in heaps, carrying their full-size jockeys to the finish line, a backcloth painted to recall William Powell Frith's 1858 painting *The Derby Day*.

But Pimple is not the first to parody melodrama. The very best of these, *Why Girls Leave Home*, has an uncertain provenance.[6] Twice filmed by Edison in America in 1909 and 1912 for the British market, the film originally dramatized the concern of a local vicar distressed because a supposedly unwholesome melodrama, modelled on the Melville Family's 'Bad Woman' plays, was to appear at the town's Opera House. The vicar's daughter and his secretary defy his wishes and attend the drama. All that survives of the longer film is the Opera House drama, loosely based on G. H. Macdermott's *Driven from Home* (1871), with the imagery and costumes taken from *Stageland* (1889), Jerome K. Jerome's slender satiric book ridiculing the conventions and characters depicted in English melodramas.[7] The melodrama the pair views takes to task the clichés of bad melodrama – exaggerated gestural acting, sentimental plotting with a deserted mother (presumably unmarried) roaming the streets with her child, a malicious villain, clumsy, unnatural staging (the child, abducted by a full seven of the villain's henchmen from her mother's lap, passes unnoticed from hand to hand), and refractory or misplaced stage machinery – 'snow' that is dumped from its cradle on only a segment of the stage, flying apparatus that jams, leaving a would-be suicide dangling from her harness above the Thames, and visible stagehands casting handfuls of rice to simulate splashes – and does so with the confidence of filmmakers who believe that the public's acceptance of motion pictures now outweighs that of theatrical melodrama.

Despite these parodies, however, melodrama's day was far from over. Melodramatic films of the mid-to-late-teens and twenties are characterized by the restaging of classic, long-popular dramas, some of these melodramas featuring known artists recreating their original stage roles. Producers and audiences in the years 1916 and 1917 were particularly receptive to those melodramas reconfigured for the screen. In addition to Maurice Tourneur's *The Whip*, we can view the late Victorian stage through re-cast film versions of three plays: Henry Irving's 1877 Lyceum adaptation of Charles Reade's *The Lyons Mail* (1854) (also performed as *The Courier of Lyons*); the actor William Gillette's stage adaptation of Arthur Conan Doyle's short stories, *Sherlock Holmes* (1899); and Joseph Arthur's *Blue Jeans* (1890).

Two years after his father Henry's death in 1905, H. B. 'Harry' Irving had formed his own theatre company to tour, successfully, 'replica' productions of Lyceum favourites, performing the double roles of the benign, harmless Joseph Lesurques and the murderer Dubosc in *The Lyons Mail*. In 1916, under the direction of Fred Paul, he committed these roles to film. Sadly, only the first reels of this film survive, but they offer enough evidence about how the Irvings, father and son, approached their roles. *The Lyons Mail* (1916) enacts the consequences possible when two men, one an innocent husband and father, the other a vicious, hardened criminal, so closely resemble one another that the innocent man can be misidentified by confused witnesses as the robber of the Lyons mail coach and the murderer of its driver. Such errors send the innocent Lesurques to the guillotine; Dubosc remains unaccused and free. The elder Irving had specialized in roles where a man's outer identity hid deep inner guilt. A student of criminology, Harry Irving relished playing both roles.

Only recently rediscovered and restored, William H. Gillette's *Sherlock Holmes* (1916) recreates the original stage drama with fidelity to plot – in which an austere and sometimes aloof Holmes and the heroine fall in love (after her victimization at the hands of villainy has been resolved) – and to characterization, allowing modern audiences to witness a major late-Victorian actor at his exquisitely detailed work. Gillette staged his drama in five interior scenes, giving the piece urgency and intense compression. Arthur Berthelet, the film's director, only partly resisted the temptation to 'open the film out' to needless 'London' (actually Chicago) exteriors, and thus lost the compression and urgency of the stage piece. The restoration of this film is a compromise; the 1918 French serial format has been retained, breaking the original film into episodes, each episode introduced by exposition (translated to English) that often gives the plot away.

John Collins's *Blue Jeans* (1917) was made without its original stars but, instead, with an exceptional film actress, Viola Dana, in the leading role.[8] Collins, formerly a director for the Edison company, and an emerging independent director until his death in the Spanish influenza epidemic of 1918, remounted Joseph Arthur's 1890 melodrama set in 'the blue jeans district' of rural Indiana, preserving Arthur's plot and key incidents, including the famous sawmill scene in which the hero Perry Bascom, knocked unconscious and dragged onto the table of a buzz saw, is rescued by the heroine who, wielding a chair, bashes her way out of a locked office and drags her husband from the whirring blade. Collins inflects his narrative, originally evenly balanced between the distinct plights of hero and heroine, to favour his actress-wife Viola Dana, who plays June, a woman struggling against malicious accusations to prove her marriage and child legitimate. She is eventually vindicated, of course, and emerges as a figure of moral integrity – but also as a female character able to rise to strong physical action.

Two more adaptations from the live stage all but complete the roster of important – and available – silent film melodramas. These are again notable for casting in their leading roles the actors who made their names in the stage versions: Augustus Thomas's *The Copperhead* (1919) starring Lionel Barrymore, and *The Only Way* (1899) with John Martin Harvey. *The Copperhead* (1920) immediately followed its Broadway run, enacting the circumstances visited upon an Illinois family loyal to the Union, when, at the behest of President Lincoln, the husband and father agrees to go undercover in the guise of a Southern sympathizer (a 'copperhead') to report on and frustrate the rebels' activities.[9] Rejected by his wife, who blames but never understands, desolate at the death of their son, further isolated by his wife's eventual death, and shunned by the community, he drifts into old age until events bring his silent sacrifice to light. Eloquently performed by Barrymore and Doris Rankin, who sequentially plays his wife and granddaughter, it is as much a domestic melodrama as a Civil War play.

*The Only Way*, Frederick Longbridge and Freeman Wills's stage adaptation of Charles Dickens's *A Tale of Two Cities* (1859), was successfully toured for twenty-seven years before Harvey was willing to submit his money-spinner to Herbert Wilcox's direction.[10] That decision, in part, was an error, as Wilcox's film version of *The Only Way* (1926) unwisely restored some of the characters and episodes that the dramatists had excised in the interest of a clearer narrative. However, Harvey's depiction of Sidney

Carton, especially in the tribunal episodes where Charles Darnay faces the wrath of the Paris mob, enables the spectacle of a major Victorian/Edwardian actor in full gestural flow – as well as the expressive restraint of these gestures, as he holds a battered felt hat that he shuffles between his hands.

The reader will notice that, apart from *Judith of Bethulia*, the full-length melodramatic films of D.W. Griffith haven't been cited. This choice is deliberate. Griffith's mature melodramas clearly clamour to be recognized, for Griffith, in my view, is the dominating movie-maker of the silent era, and his films are among the more accessible – on DVD, video, the internet, and at public screenings – for those wishing to study melodrama on early film.[11] However, four films – the more significant of his later films – are briefly described here: *The Birth of a Nation* (1915), *Intolerance* (1916), *Way Down East* (1920), and *Orphans of the Storm* (1922).

*The Birth of a Nation* has received the most attention of the Griffith melodramas because of its vicious racist content, which culminates in the rescue of the white heroine from the clutches of South Carolina's threatening black governor by the timely arrival of Ku Klux Klan horsemen, led by her Southern lover. The film was initially publicized by the title of the play on which it was partly based, Thomas Dixon's *The Clansman* (1905). However, the success of the film lies in the fact that *The Birth of a Nation* is not one melodrama but two antithetical dramas, skilfully annealed with a dramatization of President Lincoln's assassination. Griffith has prefaced the plot of *The Clansman* with the characters, strategies, and structure of the typical 'Northern' Civil War melodrama, in which Northern and Southern couples fall in love in the antebellum period, then separate along ideological lines as war breaks out. This approach generates expectations of how fractured relationships will heal and how the great national dilemma of racial antagonism will be resolved. The subsequent *Clansman* narrative confounds those expectations.

Two fused narrative strands in *The Birth of a Nation* might appear unambitious when compared to the four discrete narratives in Griffith's lengthy *Intolerance*. The basic premise is that three of these strands, 'The Judean Story' (Jesus's crucifixion at the hands of an intolerant clergy), 'The French Story' (the St Valentines massacre of Paris's Huguenots by an intolerant Catholic monarch), and 'The Babylonian Story' (the fall of the Babylonian Empire, brought about by the treachery of an ambitious priest) are major cultural tragedies occasioned by prejudice, and religious and moral intolerance. There is no single villain in any of these; rather, biased, intolerant society is the villain of the piece. These plots interweave and play against 'The Modern Story', a melodrama in which a young worker is wrongly accused of murder and sentenced to execution; he and his wife have their baby taken from them by obsessively puritanical social do-gooders; and the wife's ultimately successful rescue journey is accomplished by speeding car with a pardon that exonerates her husband and restores their child. By contrast to the other 'stories', the modern episode is banal, its episodes sometimes heavy-handed and clichéd, but it is also suspenseful, fast-paced, and melodramatically optimistic in its depiction of intolerance overcome by desperate acts of justice.

Both *Way Down East* and *Orphans of the Storm* are adapted from notably successful, long-lived stage melodramas, the former from Lottie Blair Parker and Joseph Grismer's 1897–8 play of the same title, the latter from *Les Deux Orphelines* (1874) by the French dramatists Adolphe d'Ennery and Eugène Cormon, itself adapted for the American stage by A. M. Palmer and Jackson N. Hart. Both melodramas, successful in Britain and America, continued to be performed by professional and amateur companies for some decades, even after Griffith's films had been released and applauded. In both instances, Griffith explored multiple versions of the plays that had been attempted as the drama evolved, expanding the original narratives to include richly detailed back stories for his characters, adding weight to the villains' perfidy and casual brutality, and ending both films (as he had *The Birth of a Nation* and 'The Modern Story' in *Intolerance*) with harrowing rescues from deadly peril. In *Way Down East* the heroine, stunningly performed by Lillian Gish, is rescued, unconscious, from an ice-floe sweeping toward a waterfall. In *Orphans of the Storm* one of the two heroines, again Lillian Gish, is saved from the Terror's guillotine by breathless mounted rescuers.

A final word. This account must remain provisional because many more stage melodramas were translated into films that have – at least for the present – disappeared. Some, or many, may be lost forever, but other films are hidden in archives and in the vaults of private collectors, and they may yet surface. I believe in that possibility, and will continue to search for these films; and for moments in film that illuminate Victorian stage melodrama.

# Appendix 1
## Melodramas Available on DVD

Edwin S. Porter's *The Life of an American Fireman* (1902) and *The Great Train Robbery* (1903); the sequence *Rescued from an Eagle's Nest*; and J. Searle Dawley and Edwin S. Porter's *The Trainer's Daughter; or, The Race for Love* (1907) can be found on the DVD set *Edison: The Invention of the Movies, 1891–1918* (Kino Video/ MoMA, 2005). D. W. Griffith's *The Adventures of Dollie* (1908) and *Judith of Bethulia* (1913) can be found on *Griffith Masterworks: Biograph Shorts* (Kino Lorber, 1992). Albert Capellani's *l'Assommoir* (1908) is included on the *Coffret Albert Capellani* DVD set (Pathé, 2011). Urban Gad's *Afgrunden* (1910) can be found on *Danish Silent Classics: Asta Nielsen* (Danish Film Institute, 2005). Fred Niblo's *Ben-Hur: A Tale of the Christ* (1925) is available in a four-disc collector's edition (Warner Home Video, 2006), as well as in other formats. Maurice Tourneur's *The Whip* (1917) is best viewed on the DVD *Maurice Tourneur's The Whip* (Grapevine Video, 2014). Arthur Berthelet's *Sherlock Holmes*, starring William Gillette, can be found on the dual-format DVD and Blu-ray set *William Gillette: Sherlock Holmes* (Flicker Alley, 2015). In addition, D. W. Griffith's *The Birth of a Nation* (1915), *Intolerance* (1916), *Way Down East* (1920), and *Orphans of the Storm* (1922) are all available on DVD; consistently the best versions, with better musical scoring, are those in Kino's *Griffith Masterworks* series. Available as a viewing print through the Library of Congress: Siegmund Lubin's *The Silver King* (1907–8); D. W. Griffith's *A Drunkard's Reformation* (1908); Edwin S. Porter's *The Count of Monte Cristo* (1913); Frederick Thompson's *The Sign of the Cross* (1914); Fred Paul's *The Lyons Mail* (1916) (truncated); and Maurice Tourneur's *The Whip* (1917).

# Appendix 2
## Melodramas Available on YouTube

Edwin S. Porter's *The Great Train Robbery* (1903) and *Uncle Tom's Cabin* (1903); the sequence *Rescued from an Eagle's Nest*; Sidney Olcott's *Ben Hur* (1907); André Calmettes and Charles Le Bargy's *L'Assassinat du duc de Guise* (1908); D. W. Griffith's *The Adventures of Dollie* (1908), *A Drunkard's Reformation* (1908), *The Lonedale Operator* (1911), *The Birth of a Nation* (1915), *Intolerance* (1916), *Way Down East* (1920), and *Orphans of the Storm* (1922); Urban Gad's *Afgrunden* (1910) (poor quality version); James Thomson's *The Cheyenne's Bride* (1911); Louis Feuillade's *Heliogabale* (1911); Mario Caserini and Eleuterio Rodolfi's *Gli Ultimi Giorni di Pompei* (1913); Giovanni Pastrone's *Cabiria* (1914) (first film); several episodes of the film serial *The Perils of Pauline* (1914); the complete series of the film serial *Les Vampires* (1915); and several non-consecutive episodes of *The Hazards of Helen* (1914–17), are all viewable on Youtube.

## Notes

1. H. Chance Newton, *Crime and the Drama; or Dark Deeds Dramatised* (London: Stanley Paul & Co, Ltd., 1927), 94–5. Why Lawson's villain was depicted as an anti-Semite is not clear, though the sketch's date suggests the influence of the Alfred Dreyfus affair, which began in 1894.

2. Combination companies took their name from the bringing together in a single drama, usually a melodrama or comedy, of two discrete groups of players: those who performed the dramatic plot and a second group of variety specialist performers. In films requiring visual acts, these specialists tended to be acrobats and dancers.

3. Twenty-six Thanhouser films are available in four commercially available box sets (twelve total DVDs) as *The Thanhouser Collection* (Marengo, 2003): vols. 1–3 [1910–1916]; vols. 4–6 [1910–1917]; vols. 7–9 [1910–1917]; and vols. 10–12 [1910–1916]. But all have also been made available on YouTube.

4. Both versions survive: the 1912 film by Guazzioni is held by the British Film Institute, and the 1924–5 version by D'Annunzio and Jacoby is held by the Netherlands Film Archive.

5. Viewing print held by the British Film Institute. Also available through The BFI Online, but one must be a subscriber to view.

6. The original print from the Will Day Collection is held by CNC Archives Français du Film, but the BFI also holds a viewing copy.

7. Jerome K. Jerome, *Stage-Land: Curious Habits and Customs of its Inhabitants* (London: Chatto & Windus, 1889).

8. As of 2017, a viewing print is held by the George Eastman Museum, and a digital cinema package (DCP) is available on loan. However, a full restoration is in progress. Meanwhile the sawmill scene and June's reconciliation with her grandparents are viewable on YouTube.

9. The George Eastman Museum holds the viewing print. Bootleg DVDs also circulate.

10. The British Film Institute holds two slightly different versions, one made for British audiences (still on nitrate film stock) and a second – viewable – print made for the American market.

11. But these films, many adapted from earlier stage dramas, have already been the subject of longer, more thorough analysis in the twelve volumes of *The Griffith Project*, ed. Paolo Cherchi-Usai (London: British Film Institute, 1997–2008) and in David Mayer, *Stagestruck Filmmaker: D.W. Griffith and the American Theatre* (Iowa City: University of Iowa Press, 2009).

# 16

JANE M. GAINES

# Moving Picture Melodrama

We can no longer speak of 'film' melodrama, although motion picture *film* was what audiences watched in theatres between 1915 and 2015. What is referenced in the term 'film' is a century of motion photography, of scenes shot on light-sensitive film stock, printed, and theatrically projected onto large screens to produce the illusion of movement. Today, moving image drama is less and less giganticized on wide screens, and more and more miniaturized on handheld devices. Still, even tiny moving image dramas, digitally shot, edited, and streamed, emulate cinematic conventions and replicate the photorealistic look of motion picture film. These videos keep alive the aesthetic of the cinema century: the frame, the cut, and the use of deep space before the camera. More importantly, these digital emulators share with their film predecessors the double meaning of 'moving'. That is, they use onscreen 'movement' in its capacity to affectively 'move' audiences.[1] What we still see today then, in more venues and formats, from the home to the theatre, are 'moving pictures'. Contemporary viewers, like their predecessors, may be awestruck, horrified, or moved to tears, depending upon the genre. They may even be 'moved' to see new points of view, an acknowledgement of the rhetorical power of melodrama. And if melodrama is a rhetoric, its power to move aligns us with or against social forces in our time.

Access to popular moving image melodrama is today easier than ever before. Indeed, moving pictures have usurped the place of written literature as well as theatrical drama in the English-speaking world. But this usurpation *should not* be cause for despair over the incursion of illiterate barbarians or the victory of hyperbole over nuance. The academic elevation of melodrama, a once-despised mode, involves recognizing it everywhere – in televised serial family drama and masculine action genres – the western, the thriller, and the gangster film. That is, melodrama is now understood not as a single genre but as a cross-generic mode.[2] This critical vogue also entails seeing melodrama as structuring elite culture – not only because key dramatic devices have been perfected in moving image form, but also, as film melodrama theorists now assert, because from the nineteenth-century stage to the present, melodrama has been the cultural dominant. Finally, if the dominance of melodrama has been secured by moving pictures, it is surely time to forgo the hierarchy of linguistic over audio and visual signifiers, and to accord respect to the carriers of the magnified 'melos' that so enhance the drama. Using the term 'melos', Greek for 'music', both signals the analogy between music and cinematic effects and harkens back to the definition of the kind of drama in which musical accompaniment serves as emotional heightener.

It is time as well to revive theatre's gift to the moving picture, to see that contribution in the expressivity of the gestural continuum, the resonance of the voice, the eloquence of the staged scene, and the ingenuity of the narrative *situation*.[3] Such a revival refuses the superiority of the word over the wordlessness of pre-sound bodily performance.[4] At last, literary studies must defer to other worlds of signs. These other signs, carriers of meaning that make direct appeals to sense perception, are not routed through the word but arrive via musical tonality, color, scale, shape, and all means of visual patterning, from pantomime to cutting to special effects. The challenge that moving picture melodrama poses to the sustained study of its literary antecedents is thus twofold: first, to see and to read, not a deferential hierarchy, but a shared structure in the narrative *situation*. Second, to see, starting in the silent film era, the triumph of *wordless mimesis* over words on a printed page.

Literary studies is further called upon to view moving picture melodrama as germane to understanding the ideological successes of nineteenth-century 'sentimental fiction'. This critical reversal entails a detour through film genre theory and the evolution of characteristic devices. Why is this? It is because *every* cinematic technique is also a melodramatic device: the tracking or travelling shot, slow and fast motion, the zoom in and the cut to the close-up, as well as the freeze frame, descendant of the *tableau*. Consider here one of the most basic adaptations of nineteenth century stage melodrama to the motion picture – the scene and shot juxtaposition that Tom Gunning calls the 'contrast edit'. Here, melodrama's 'moral dualism' is technologically enhanced, sharpened. Two characters or situations are put in opposition, sometimes by means of *parallel editing* – the patterned alternation of two or more scenes separated in space.[5] Or, in a dramatic alternative to the 'contrast edit', the split screen might be used to depict two simultaneously occurring scenes by dividing the frame down the middle.

Such techniques were deployed on either side of the ideological spectrum. Some one-reel dramas passed judgment on the capitalist rich, others were critical of labour. Exemplifying the latter, Alice Guy Blaché's *The Strike* (1912) melodramatizes the labour-capital opposition with the use of a split screen. A double image shows the factory workers voting to strike on one side and a fire breaking out in the home of the labour organizer on the other, implying a causal connection between the strikers and the fire. But the owner speeds his car to the worker's home and rescues his family, and, as a consequence, the strikers back down: a race against time resolves the labour dispute in favour of the owner. Blaché's anti-labour drama is thus in stark political contrast to D. W. Griffith's more progressive screen adaptation of Frank Norris's 'A Deal in Wheat'.[6] A *Corner in Wheat* (1909) uses the contrast edit to juxtapose the poor buying bread with wealthy wheat speculators partying extravagantly (Figures 16.1 and 16.2). The ending condemns the greedy capitalist by having him fall backwards into his own wheat bin, where he drowns.

Sergei Eisenstein noted the commonalities between Griffith's dualistic worldview and that of English author Charles Dickens. The Soviet Socialist filmmaker took the American capitalist director to task for the patterned 'alternations' he used to contrast scenes of the rich and the poor, the metaphor for which, that famous 'slab of streaky bacon', is found in the pages of *Oliver Twist*.[7] Eisenstein thought that Griffith's narratives 'resolved' class differences too easily, rather than sharpening them. Furthering Eisenstein's political analysis, film melodrama theory since the 1970s has urged us to consider the raw social material that melodrama stages. In effect, this move credits melodrama for taking up seemingly irresolvable problems – class conflict, inequality, domestic abuse, labour strife, and racial discrimination.

## The Raw Material of Contradiction

Feminist melodrama theory, picking up where Eisenstein left off, and thinking of the cultural conflicts stemming from gender and race difference, has proposed that melodrama finds its material in *contradiction* – that is, as inconsistencies manifest as cruel social injustice, the fallout from which is suffering. In the 1970s feminist analysis, the contradiction stems from the maintenance of capitalist patriarchy, which engenders situations at odds with official morality. Again and again, love dispels hate, but love of country justifies war; 'money does not buy happiness', although it often does; and persons cannot be property, but they are nonetheless bought and sold. Melodrama's most replayed dramatic situations stem from such consequential social predicaments, from such early film adaptations as *Uncle Tom's Cabin* (Edwin S. Porter, 1903; Figure 16.3) to *Imitation of Life* (Douglas Sirk, 1959), to the more recent *Twelve Years a Slave* (Steve McQueen, 2014). In these examples, the sharpest contradiction is that between biology and family, and the failures of familial love are enacted as flight, renunciation, fratricide, and abandonment. In a racist society, the biological cannot be made to line up with the familial, and that impossibility forms the basis of

Figures 16.1 and 16.2 Frame enlargements. *A Corner in Wheat* (D.W. Griffith, Biograph, 1909) Courtesy: Museum of Modern Art.

dramatic tension in *Imitation of Life*. Although Annie is the biological mother of light-skinned Sarah Jane, Annie cannot *be* a mother to a daughter who looks white. Sarah Jane is led to reject association with her mother, only to later express demonstrative remorse at her mother's funeral. The social orders of marriage and family, property and personhood, biology and family

248

Figures 16.1 and 16.2 (cont.)

are at odds with one another, the fruits of which are the illegitimate child and unwed mother, the unmarried daughter, the unfaithful wife, or the disinherited son. Here is melodrama's typology of fraught and torn characters. In this way, film melodrama theory has taught us to be skeptical of all happy outcomes. Of the American family melodrama it is often said that so much remains unresolved that there can only be 'false happy endings'.[8]

Figure 16.3 Frame enlargement. *Uncle Tom's Cabin* (Edwin S. Porter, Thomas A. Edison Co., 1903). Courtesy: Museum of Modern Art.

Considering 1950s Technicolor family melodramas, Laura Mulvey observes that 'the strength of the melodrama form lies in the amount of dust the story raises along the road, a cloud of over-determined irreconcilables which put up resistance to being neatly settled in the last five minutes'.[9] Thus one critical approach to analyzing warring positions is to ask what narrative enigmas are left unresolved or are resolved unsatisfactorily.

One explanation for unsatisfactory resolutions, as well as 'tacked-on' endings, lies with the impossible standard of 'the good' that so many melodramas uphold – the measure of which is the idealized 'home'. Critics derive this yardstick from Peter Brooks's observation that one way to distinguish melodrama from tragedy is that the former often begins with, and must return to, a 'space of innocence'.[10] Here the home is that imaginary space of beginning and belonging, of security and stability, the measure of value and the seat of tradition, the locus of all that is thought to be 'good and true'. There is no better primer for studying this space than US silent shorts of the 1910s. Yet in titles like *The Unseen Enemy* (D. W. Griffith, 1912) or *Suspense* (Lois Weber and Phillips Smalley, 1913), the cozy family space is under attack. In these instances, threats to that space establish the antithesis of 'the good' that seeks *recognition* – the new evil that lurks 'unseen' – whose deadly animosity must be recognized in order for the community to survive.[11] Whether shark attacks in *Jaws* (Steven Spielberg, 1978), or terrorist bombs exploded in Boston in *Patriots Day* (Peter Berg, 2016), recognition is requisite to making home communities safe again. However, 'home' may be totally imaginary and unrealizable within the drama. In the television serial 'The Wire', as Linda Williams analyzes it, even tough urban melodramas must imagine a 'good home' community as what the characters most need: what Baltimore hopes the city yet 'could be' but may 'never have been', given the elusiveness of justice for its black citizens.[12] It is, then, never so simple as good versus evil.

## The 'Melos' Given to the Drama

While studies of high culture venerate uniqueness, studies of mass culture value borrowing and repetition. Motion picture film genre study focuses on the use and reuse of narrative and iconographic conventions as well as character types. Such study is interested in how the novel *East Lynne* (1861), dismissed by English literary critics as 'sensation fiction', was re-melodramatized in multiple stage and motion picture film adaptations. Here screen adaptation also means transposition into a fuller range of signs – signs carrying an extra charge of expressivity. What the 'melos' gives to the drama via cinematic signifiers is often exemplified by the close-up on the trembling hand, or the sweeping crane shot from the vantage of the chandelier. Perhaps these examples explain why such cinematic conventions have been critically lumped together as mere embellishment or aesthetic 'excess', that is, 'in excess of' the norm of classical realism, a point to which we will return.

This is not to deny the camera's enlargement of signs or dynamic movement through space, the basic ways and means of moving picture drama. But more importantly, moving image melodrama is also a structured sensibility whose signal achievement is its accessibility. The best answer to the charge of 'overblown' is to say that in melodrama *nothing is left unclear*. Similarly, English 'sensation fiction' ensures that nothing is left ambiguous – so ordered are its antinomies – the most basic of which has historically been the 'powerful' set against the 'powerless'. Here is melodrama's signature inversion – the reversal that elevates the powerless over the powerful by virtue of their moral superiority. Or as Christine Gledhill describes the workings of moving picture melodrama, the material it takes up is 'thrust' into poles, but always to pedagogical ends. The use of 'heightened contrasts and polar oppositions', she says, functions to make events morally comprehensible.[13] Such structures make sense of the world, engaging viewers and readers in the narrative struggle to separate the villainous from the victimized, to bring about that recognition of the innocent whose true worth, while evident to us, remains unrecognized by other characters.[14] Viewers must be aligned one way or another, their feelings recruited against or on behalf of historical ideologies as well as characters, remembering the function of melodrama as a rhetoric. One might add, however, that sympathy for victims can be used to any ideological end, the most notorious example of which in the history of cinema is the white supremacy argument orchestrated by means of every shot and cut in *The Birth of a Nation* (D. W. Griffith, 1915).

Feeling, then, is not randomly evoked but belongs to an ideologically ordered system. Here, however, Peter Brooks's emphasis on the morally 'legible' may be too literary a term, since it implies a writing that is made clearly readable or easily grasped.[15] Above and beyond the word, whether spoken or read, moving picture melodramatic effect relies on a wide range of unlike signifiers, each governed by different codes and conventions – the summary pose of the *tableau*, the framed composition, the blue-tinted night sky, the insert cut away within the scene – a new mixed repertoire at the disposal of the earliest crossovers from the Victorian stage. Viewers *do* register visual valuations quickly, and ease of iconic recognizability does play a part. Yet since there may be a distance between what makers encode and what viewers intuit or infer, no audio or visual signifier ever has a guaranteed effect on audiences.

At the same time, it is clear that the 'photoplay', as the moving picture was called in the 1910s, *was* easier to grasp than the theatrical play or the novel, its realizations significantly enlarged for maximum effect. Additionally, in the one-reel shorts and (after 1915) full-length features of American film, a system was developing for the most economic use of every device: doubling, recurring, and paralleling. In such formal patterning we again see the challenge that mass culture melodrama poses to high literary tradition in its refusal of obscurity or illegibility. For it wants only to strike the heart, directly and forcefully. Since popular melodrama strives for immediate impact, to fault the mode for failing to complicate is to miss the affective-aesthetic achievements of the moving picture, best exemplified by the cross-cut sequence.

## The Cross-Cut Sequence: From *Way Down East* (1920) to *Interstellar* (2014)

As Linda Williams says of the melodramatic narrative structure – in which suffering is inflicted and a rescue required in order to right a wrong – at its most heart-wrenching, 'pathos requires action'. And in this we see how pathos followed by action is such a powerful vehicle for clarifying the moral scheme of things.[16] Two moving pictures a century apart – *Way Down East* (D. W. Griffith, 1920) and *Interstellar* (Christopher Nolan, 2014) – testify to the resilience of the cross-cut sequence, the editing technique that so spectacularly displays the narrative requirement that suffering be met by action. Nearly a century apart but united by the image of the home endangered, the one looks back to the Victorian home menaced by the sexual predator while the other looks forward to the ecological threat to our planetary 'home on earth'.

A solid bridge between nineteenth-century English and American melodrama is the domestic narrative in which the vulnerable woman falls prey to seduction. Melodrama, specializing in extremity, narrativizes our worst fears – unwanted pregnancy, desertion, public denunciation – all the better to declaim the injustice of condemning virtuous victims. *Way Down East*, a classic example, is Griffith's adaptation of the Lottie Blair Parker play, a confluence of the popular 'Annie Laurie' and the thousands of 'Uncle Tom's Cabin' theatrical performances[17]: before unwed mother Anna Moore (Lillian Gish) was thrust out into the snowstorm, mulatto Eliza had crossed the icy river from slave to free state, and a child bride was thrown into the cold lake by her aristocratic husband in Dion Boucicault's The *Colleen Bawn* (1860). *Way Down East* uses the baby born out of wedlock as a melodramatic prop to establish naïve innocence, for Anna tries to breathe life into the cold hands of the dead baby she continues to rock.

*Way Down East*, wildly successful and world-renowned, was remade in China as *Orphan of the Storm* (Zhang Huimin, 1929). In Russia, the ice floe cross-cut sequence was deployed in the service of the revolutionary USSR at the end of *Mother* (V. I. Pudovkin, 1926). Here again is parallel editing, but more noticeably it also overrides or reverses the usual one-way narrative cause and effect. That override is achieved in *Way Down East* with the technical 'cut back', repeatedly, to rescuer David (Richard Barthelmess), effecting the suspense-producing delay in narrative outcome.[18] While David searches for her, Anna is carried downriver on an ice chunk towards the treacherous drop (Figure 16.4). Her 'nick of time' rescue at the edge of the falls is reinforced by the boldest but most maligned of devices – what theatre critic Eric Bentley once called 'outrageous coincidence'.[19] Denigrated as the most preposterous of melodrama's store of tricks by the measure of cultural probability, the narrative coincidence marks the moment in which an intervening force either fails by a hair or succeeds by a second. Rather than assailing the coincidence, then, we might better applaud it, not only for the

Figure 16.4  Location still. *Way Down East* (D. W. Griffith, 1920). Courtesy: Museum of
Modern Art.

miraculous turn of events it effects but also for the rhetorical power it wields
on behalf of 'the good'.

Here we should also credit the parallel back and forth that by convention
leads the viewer to expect a narrative agent to intervene by coincidence in the
course of events – even when the intervention we are prepared to expect never
happens – as in the case of *Interstellar*. Our anticipation of an intervening
'rescue' is set up by a cross-cut parallelism over planetary time and space,
incorporating the most improbable 'cut back' in the history of moving
pictures. Former astronaut Cooper (Matthew McConaughey) is battling
the imbalanced villain Mann (Matt Damon) on a desolate planet seven
light years away from Earth. The film cuts from there to Earth and
Cooper's astrophysicist daughter Murph (Jessica Chastain), driving to save
her brother and his family from cornfields on fire. Then it cuts back to
Cooper, the agent who we expect will save Earth, struggling to retrieve his
life-support device. Alternating between the two spaces, the film aims to
make the viewer feel that the two are causally linked, that Cooper can
intervene to save Earth despite a seven-year time difference and diverting
wormholes in space.

With so very much at stake – the fate of planet Earth – one might well ask if
there is some risk in the recourse to a convention whose achievement entails
the abandonment of so-called reality. But such judgment against

254

melodrama's overstatement is again critically mistaken, especially when we consider how the mode specializes in the aggrandisement of threats to human existence. Discussing the science fiction disaster film subgenre, Despina Kakoudaki argues that we look to moving picture melodrama for its attempt to express the deepest concerns of the historical moment. If the nation is obliterated in the 1990s disaster film typified by *Independence Day* (Roland Emmerich, 1996), she says, this is because 'destroying what looked like home is necessary in order to reaffirm what home really means'.[20] If home is the 'one place on earth' to which you can always return, then consider what happens if there is no longer a habitable Earth to call home. If we understand that *Interstellar* melodramatizes a new threat to home on earth – catastrophic climate change that is burning up an overheated planet – then we can see the film's overblown devices as straining to stand for the enormity of that threat. The spectacularity of the onscreen destruction is proportionate to its existential significance – whether what is represented is the collapse of social order, the erosion of community, or the annihilation of the human species.

## How Many Realisms?

Behind the criticism of moving picture melodrama as overblown is always some notion of realism. Failing the test of probability, such drama may be faulted for abandoning realism, and be derogatorily called 'unrealistic'. Paradoxically, however, the moving picture has also been charged with the opposite – not for being unrealistic but for delivering a realism that is too mimetic. Operative here is an older opposition between low representational 'realism' and high Modernism. Much like nineteenth-century literary realism, motion photographic realism, in contrast with Modernism, is considered too tied to the world, too accessible and too easy. Even today, an old bias against moving pictures as 'easy' underwrites high-culture value judgments found in film reviewing as well as academic writing. Here is where we may better understand why moving picture melodrama is thought to exceed or violate the standard of representational realism. Indeed, melodrama has always been associated with aesthetic excess, although this formulation, too, is now ripe for reexamination, given the move to define melodrama not as an aberration but as an entertainment norm.

Most importantly, however, since moving picture melodrama theory holds that there are ways in which melodrama needs some realism, we want to know which of the many realisms this means. Perhaps it helps to acknowledge that melodrama is associated with both the preposterously incredible *and* the sociologically credible that goes by the name of 'realism'.

Further, since one period's realism is another period's unrealistic, some historical comparison is required. As Rick Altman has argued, in the technological history of motion pictures, the rule of thumb is that every innovation is greeted as an advance in realism, the supplanting technology seen as realistic relative to the technology it succeeds.[21] This principle even applies to the idea advanced by the first theatre historians that silent motion picture film melodrama achieved in realism what the theatrical stage could not. An earlier version of the transition held that, for instance, Eliza's escape across the treacherous ice floe in all of the *Uncle Tom's Cabin* stage plays could leap from the constraints of the stage to the new realism in staging that the photoplay delivered. But such an abrupt leap is not in the interests of seeing historical continuity in melodrama as mode. We might better acknowledge the theatre's use of lifelike painted scenery and mechanical props that Ben Singer calls the striving towards 'spectacular diegetic realism', a phenomenon of nineteenth-century theatrical melodrama.[22] In retrospect, this spectacular realism shares with nineteenth-century literary realism an aspiration to precise and credible depiction that in its staging, however, strived to be not credible but amazing. But in the end, the theatre's spectacular realism was succeeded by photorealism, an image of lifelikeness that photoplays of the 1910s so effortlessly achieved with the motion picture film camera turned on the world.

In a century of moving picture criticism, other realisms have held sway. No longer contrasted with the less-than-real realism of the theatrical stage, the Hollywood motion picture, evolving from 1917 to 1960, as one major account has it, perfected yet another realism in its continuity system of editing.[23] In the continuity style, scenes were pieced seamlessly together and cuts covered, all the better to create the impression of uninterrupted reality. So it is that 'realism', along with 'harmony', 'proportion', 'self-effacement', and 'narrative story-telling' is understood as one of the defining features of the 'classical' mainstream film.[24] Recently, however, the dominance of classical realism has come into question with the rise in melodrama scholarship, and a strong case is now being made that melodrama is the 'dominant form'.[25] Some, however, may argue that there is no mutual exclusivity since classical realism is a style and melodrama is a mode. A century of popular American cinema may be illustrative of melodrama *as well as* classicism, both ways of interpreting the same canonical titles such as *Stella Dallas* (King Vidor, 1937) and *Now, Voyager* (Irving Rapper, 1942). Some confusion around the term 'realism' lingers as a consequence of the conflation of classical Hollywood with the 'Classic Realist Text', associated in the 1970s with the 'ideology of realism', a critique of the way the motion picture delivered a *version* of reality as if it were reality itself.[26] This question remains pressing because it is also a matter of what to call the form that the US, beginning in 1917, exported to the world. Was it classical continuity style or melodrama?

Melodrama theory has also been interested in cultural realism, those realities of conventionality ruled by assumptions about who wins, who gets blamed, and who will pay in the long run. This is the historically specific realism without which melodrama would not resonate with its audience.[27] What is meant here may be best grasped by what Steve Neale calls *cultural verisimilitude* – read 'familiarity' – met in popular motion pictures by conventional rules of *generic verisimilitude*.[28] It would be deference to cultural verisimilitude that explains why popular melodrama depends upon what is taken to be true in the wider society: as today, for instance, the idea that gender transgression will not go unpunished, or that abuse of power *will* go unchecked. Such cultural truisms, however, may contrast with the innocence that viewers are drawn to recognize and to which bigoted characters are stubbornly blind, as in *Philadelphia* (Jonathan Demme, 1993), which took a sympathetic approach to the question of discrimination against people with AIDS.

Clearly, then, melodrama as a popular genre does not necessarily allow cultural truisms aligned with reactionary positions to stand. Thus it could be said that at the same time that melodrama relies on a conventional realism, better grasped as cultural verisimilitude, it also pushes the limits of what is thought to be real and true, even undermining the social realism that is the basis of the problems it dramatizes. In this, melodrama could arguably be a critical anti-realism, reaching beyond what is recognized and familiar. One might consider in this regard the new super-expressivity of video and audio: the Dolby Atmos sound system enlargement of theatrical space to produce envelopment, as in *The Revenant* (Alejandro González Iñárritu, 2016), or the computer-generated imagery (CGI) special effects simulation of gigantic waves in *The Perfect Storm* (Wolfgang Petersen, 2000). These technologies are heir to the mechanized ice floe in *Uncle Tom's Cabin* that produced the spectacular realism of an earlier stage melodrama. Here, in addition, is where melodrama abandons the constraints of realism as credibility and verifiability, advancing the improbable in its reach for another kind of truth, one unavailable to us if we insist on reality checks. Overabundant expressivity, then, might best be understood as a sign of the very difficulty of signifying the immeasurable, the inarticulable, and the incomprehensible towards which melodrama gestures.

## Progressive or Reactionary

Common sense may encourage viewers and readers to think that melodrama, dedicated as it is to traditional values, must be reactionary by definition. Over the last two centuries, however, two traditions have supplied the theoretical justification for seeing melodrama as potentially progressive: nineteenth-century women's sentimental fiction, and 1930s German experimental theatre, where Bertolt Brecht's notion of self-reflexivity was developed. A unique application of Brecht appeared at the confluence of 1970s film theory and feminism in the British analysis of the 1950s Technicolor melodramas of Douglas Sirk. Theorists fastened on the connection between German émigré Sirk and his earlier work with Brecht in devising a theory of aesthetic subversion at the level of the motion picture *mise-en-scène*. While Brecht's anti-identificatory and anti-illusionist devices were designed for a political theatre, critics found them exemplified as well in the Universal Pictures family melodramas that Sirk later directed in Hollywood. Melodrama theory then borrowed the auteur director Sirk to justify the emphasis on the interior décor as itself a running commentary on the shallowness of the American middle-class family. Although *Imitation of Life* and *All That Heaven Allows* (1955), might not be easily seen on first viewing as self-reflexive works, the idea that the *mise-en-scène* can comment ironically on the narrative action, ultimately undercutting it, has become critically attached to such examples of the family melodrama genre. Here the excess attributed to melodrama functions as a critique of the characters' vapid lifestyle. Thus analyzed as ironic in their excessiveness, Sirk's Hollywood pictures were credited with a progressive point of view. As Christine Gledhill further explains, although Sirk as auteur director may have originally justified the development of stylistic 'subversion', in the 'slippage' between auteur and genre, subversive stylistics came to be attributed to film melodrama as a mode.[29]

Second, from women's 'sentimental fiction' comes the idea that melodrama is political protest, a tradition revived retrospectively and extended from *Uncle Tom's Cabin* to the novels of Olive Higgins Prouty: *Now, Voyager* and *Stella Dallas*.[30] Here, the home is a holdout from violent conflict, and motherhood itself is transgressive, its values the antithesis of those of cutthroat capitalism. The mother, however, is placed in the contradictory position of upholding patriarchal order while standing in opposition to it. As E. Ann Kaplan has argued: 'To make Motherhood a universal value is transgressive – while patriarchy may have invented the Ideal Mother as balance for excessive male drives ... [it] never intended male attributes of desire, ambition (on which capitalism depends) to be undermined.'[31] If patriarchy is seen as the source of the Maternal Mother how could she turn against the Father and the Law? In her transgression she may fall outside patriarchal norms and risk condemnation, but melodrama may find a way to take her side. How other than by always having it both ways? The narrative must demonstrate that a woman who has committed adultery can still remain emotionally faithful to her husband and a good mother in spite of her lapse. Lady Isabel in *East Lynne*, for example, reenacts the contradictoriness of this message to women: you cannot be expected to be true, but you will be; it is in your character to be weak, but you will be morally strong. You must forgive, but you can never be forgiven. All of the bromides of Victorian England are espoused and dramatized, but shown to be insufficient to deal with errant wives and tyrant fathers, the loss of fortune and property, the demise of the aristocratic family, and the erosion of social class distinction. Feminist analysis finds as well in the *East Lynne* narrative the double message to women: do be sensitive but don't be emotional; be helpless but withstand suffering. Here is insight into the historic infantalization of women to whom the double message is that it is your fault but not your fault, because how could you know any better? You must defer but transcend, accept your subjugation but refuse it. Do take authority in the home and over the realm of emotions, but never *be* the authority.

Other objections to a benevolent Victorian view of the home arise because for many women the home has historically been, not the safest, but rather the most dangerous place on earth – no haven but rather the place of maximum vulnerability. Consider the versions of the husband as his wife's murderer exemplified by *Gaslight* (George Cukor, 1944) or *Suspicion* (Alfred Hitchcock, 1941). Everyone knows as well that 'they' are in our homes, confirmed by the horror genre adaptations of Bram Stoker's *Dracula*, from *Nosferatu* (F. W. Murnau, 1921) to *Interview with the Vampire* (Neil Jordan, 1994) to the *Twilight Saga* films (2008–12). Conventionally, sexual predators rise from their coffins or break out of prison, lurk in the suburbs, and find the last space of innocence – the girl in the bedroom. Generic verisimilitude requires that the scourge always rise from the dead and can never be killed. But in the slasher film *Halloween* (John Carpenter, 1978) Jamie Lee Curtis as the babysitter doesn't know this convention, and she fends off the monster who finds her hiding in the closet of the upstairs bedroom. The androgynous Curtis is the victorious 'final girl' whom Carol Clover identifies in the slasher subgenre.[32] The final girl is followed by Jody Foster's astronaut in *Contact* (Robert Zemeckis, 1997), precursor of the female astronauts in *Gravity* (Alfonso Cuarón, 2013) and *Interstellar*. Crossing genres, from horror's slasher subgenre to science fiction, we find the female as species survivor. The point is that although melodrama, as the 1930s and 1940s 'woman's film', has been faulted for women's capitulation to marriage in the end, the mode has undergone and will continue to undergo cyclical updating as it crosses popular genres.

The question as to whether female characters are empowered or disempowered in popular melodrama, however, is best referred to the larger politics of mass culture that seeks to explain the appeal of moving picture entertainment relative to the degree of hope held out to the widest audience. Here is where melodrama's reactionary reputation comes back into play, its nostalgia read as an espousal of traditional values. The tendency to look back to innocent beginnings may certainly be interpreted as the conservatism of the mode. Often, the hoped-for 'yet to be' is none other than the past all over again. In this analysis, melodrama tells us that the lost 'good' from which we have strayed *must* be located in the past. While the future may hold the 'better', this future 'better' can only be imagined relative to 'the good' of social tradition and established values. So in the yearning for a future that will be as it was in the past, we find the paradoxical wish for the new to be like the old. Still, there is yet another vantage on this problem, one useful in assessing the relative progressiveness of moving pictures with female characters – the standpoint of the 'double movement' of the popular. Simply put, in order to appeal to its audiences, melodrama would have to offer something to counter its reactionary tendencies.[33] Moving pictures structured as melodrama are then always looking two ways at once, this two-way view a wish for *both* the future and the past. Because if the future holds the better, that promise cannot be abstract, but must mean that things could or would be *even better* than they have been before – that the future, on which all hopes are pinned, would have to be different.

## Notes

1. Linda Williams, *Playing the Race Card: Melodramas of Black and White from Uncle Tom to O. J. Simpson* (Berkeley: University of California Press, 2001), 13.
2. Christine Gledhill, 'Rethinking Genre', in *Reinventing Film Studies*, eds. Christine Gledhill and Linda Williams (London: Arnold, 2000), 227.
3. Kristin Thompson, 'Narrative Structure in Early Classical Cinema', in *Celebrating 1895: The Centenary of Cinema*, ed. John Fullerton (London: John Libbey, 1998), 230, finds the term 'situation' – a staple term of nineteenth-century dramaturgy – in screenwriting manuals from the 1910s.
4. Jane M. Gaines, 'Wordlessness, To Be Continued . . . ', in *Researching Women in Silent Cinema: New Findings and Perspectives*, eds. Monica Dall'Asta and Victoria Duckett (Bologna: University of Bologna, 2013), 288–302.
5. Tom Gunning, *D. W. Griffith and the Origins of American Narrative Film* (Urbana and Chicago: University of Illinois Press, 1991), 77, 134–45.
6. Frank Norris, 'A Deal in Wheat', in *The Pit: A Story of Chicago* (New York: Modern Library, 1934).
7. Sergei Eisenstein, 'Dickens, Griffith, and the Film Today', in *Film Form*, ed. and trans. Jay Leyda (New York: Harcourt Brace Jovanovich, 1977).

8. John Mercer and Martin Shingler, *Melodrama: Genre, Style, Sensibility*. (Wallflower: New York and London), 60.
9. Laura Mulvey, 'Notes on Sirk and Melodrama', in *Home Is Where The Heart Is*, ed. Gledhill, 76.
10. Williams, *Playing the Race Card*, 28; Peter Brooks, *The Melodramatic Imagination: Balzac, Henry James, Melodrama, and the Mode of Excess*, new edition (New Haven: Yale University Press, 1995 [1976]), 29.
11. Linda Williams, 'Mega-Melodrama! Vertical and Horizontal Suspensions of the "Classical"', *Modern Drama*, 55 (2012): 524.
12. *Ibid.*, 536.
13. Gledhill, 'Rethinking Genre', 234.
14. Brooks, *The Melodramatic Imagination*, 26–8.
15. Brooks, *The Melodramatic Imagination*, 42–3.
16. Williams, *Playing the Race Card*, 25.
17. David Mayer, *Stagestruck Filmmaker: D. W. Griffith and the American Theatre* (Iowa City: University of Iowa Press, 2009), 195–6.
18. Eisenstein, *Film Form*, 200.
19. Eric Bentley, *The Life of the Drama* (New York: Atheneum, 1964), 201.
20. Despina Kakoudaki, 'Spectacles of History: Race Relations, Melodrama, and Science Fiction/Disaster Film', *Camera Obscura*, 17 (2002): 113.
21. Rick Altman, *Silent Film Sound* (New York: Columbia University Press, 2004), 18.
22. Ben Singer, *Melodrama and Modernity: Early Sensational Cinema and Its Contexts* (New York: Columbia University Press, 2001), 50.
23. David Bordwell, 'Part One: The Classical Hollywood Style 1917-60', in *The Classical Hollywood Cinema: Film Style and Mode of Production to 1960*, eds. David Bordwell, Janet Staiger, and Kristin Thompson (New York: Columbia University Press, 1985), 3–4.
24. Christopher Williams, 'After the Classic, the Classical and Ideology: The Differences of Realism', in *Reinventing Film Studies*, eds. Gledhill and Williams, 213.
25. Williams, *Playing the Race Card*, 21–3.
26. Williams, 'After the Classic, the Classical and Ideology', 207.
27. Gledhill, 'The Melodramatic Field: An Investigation', in *Home Is Where The Heart Is*, ed. Gledhill, 31.
28. Steven Neale, 'Questions of Genre', in *Film and Theory: An Anthology*, eds. Toby Miller and Robert Stam (Oxford: Blackwell, 2000), 158–9.
29. Gledhill, 'The Melodramatic Field', 7.
30. Lauren Berlant, *The Female Complaint: The Unfinished Business of Sentimentality in American Culture* (Durham: Duke University Press, 2008), Chapter 1.
31. E. Ann Kaplan, 'Mothering, Feminism and Representation: The Maternal Melodrama and the Woman's Film 1910-40', in *Home Is Where The Heart Is*, ed. Gledhill, 120.
32. Carol J. Clover, *Men, Women, and Chainsaws: Gender in the Modern Horror Film* (Princeton: Princeton University Press, 1992).
33. Jane M. Gaines, 'Dream/Factory', in *Reinventing Film Studies*, eds. Gledhill and Williams, 106–10.

# 17

## SHARON ARONOFSKY WELTMAN

# Melodrama and the Modern Musical

It should be no surprise that melodrama, the most popular theatrical genre of the nineteenth century, would carry forward into the twentieth and beyond. Media scholars point out that popular films such as *Star Wars* (1977) and television soap operas use stage melodrama's signature elements.[1] These include sensational plots, exciting special effects, escapist entertainment, a recognizable vocabulary of sweeping physical gestures, identifiably good and evil characters, heroes rewarded and villains punished, and musical underscoring to manipulate a strong emotional reaction from the audience. These features also appear frequently in musicals, along with a few others inherited from melodrama, such as closing scenes with emphatic tableaux, alternating comedy and drama, and oscillating between speech and musical numbers throughout the show. But the modern musical's many-threaded debt to melodrama is a tangled one. Like so much of twentieth-century Modernism's rejection of the Victorians, the twentieth-century musical also has tried to assert its modernity by setting itself apart from its ancestor, dismissing Victorian melodrama as simplistic, overwrought, overacted, and overly sentimental.

The ambiguity of the relationship between melodrama and the musical is especially pronounced in the two musicals that vie for designation as the first modern musical, *Oklahoma!* (1943) and *Show Boat* (1927). Of the two, *Oklahoma!*, composed by Richard Rodgers with book and lyrics by Oscar Hammerstein, is more often credited as the first to integrate songs and dances fully into a serious plot.[2] Many other scholars give that honour to *Show Boat*, composed by Jerome Kern, with book and lyrics also by Hammerstein.[3] Some push the point of origin all the way back to *The Black Crook* (1866).[4] All three creation stories (which I will tell in a moment) involve Victorian melodrama in multiple ways in birthing the new entertainment we now call simply 'the musical'.

*Oliver!* (1960) and *Sweeney Todd* (1979) exemplify both the modern musical's debt to melodrama and its effort to distance itself from that debt.

These musicals not only employ many conventions drawn from theatrical melodrama but also derive from Victorian novels, *Oliver Twist* (1837–9) and *The String of Pearls* (1846–7), which had *already* been influenced by, and had contributed to, Victorian stage melodrama. These novels were initially written, as Elaine Hadley puts it, in the 'melodramatic mode', meaning that they 'include graphic depictions of gruesome incidents, scenes of physical danger and inflicted torture, plots premised on criminal behaviour, affected verbalizations of overwrought emotion, an aura of atmospheric menace, and narratives of familial and social crisis'.[5] Upon their initial publication (or even before the serial publication was complete), both were immediately adapted to the Victorian melodrama stage, setting up complex lines of inheritance, demonstrating the intertwined set of relationships among each novel, melodrama, film, and musical. Tracing these lines reveals the degree to which the modern musical, for all its innovations, is fundamentally a reshaping of Victorian melodrama.

### Reviewing the Situation: A Brief History of Melodrama in the Broadway Musical

In 1866, a ballet company arrived in New York from Paris to perform the *féerie* extravaganza *La Biche au Bois* (*The Doe of the Forest*) (1845), a Romantic confection of woodland sprites like those we still enjoy in such ballets as *La Sylphide* (1832). But at the last moment, their theatre, the Academy of Music, burned down. Meanwhile, the melodrama *The Black Crook* (1866) by Charles M. Barras, also involving a plot about fairies in the forest, was set to open in New York at Niblo's Garden. *The Black Crook* incorporated the Parisian ballet troupe, interleaving their dances between scenes of dialogue and song. The outcome was a groundbreaking five-and-a-half-hour spectacular,[6] racking up an unheard of 474 performances.[7] It was New York's first show to run more than a year,[8] at a time when a play running only a few weeks was considered a success.[9]

Even before incorporating the *féerie* extravaganza, *The Black Crook* had already included songs and musical underscoring that served to heighten emotion, as would any melodrama; these are constitutive elements in defining theatrical melodrama (or melody-drama, as the genre was earlier called). Also in concert with melodrama conventions, and before the *féerie*'s involvement, *The Black Crook* ended some scenes with arresting tableaux, and it alternated comic and dramatic episodes; as we have noted, these basic features of melodrama are familiar characteristics of the modern musical, as well. It was *The Black Crook*'s blending with *La Biche au Bois*'s thematically connected and beautifully executed dances by professional dancers, the redoubling of spectacular scenery, costuming, and stage effects, plus the addition of other eye candy that made what had been a fairly conventional melodrama into a recognizable antecedent of the modern musical. But perhaps its crowning achievement was its long theatrical run of over a year, which in time became the attainable goal of modern musicals and eventually a requirement for their financial viability.

In 1867, Mark Twain reviewed this 'Grand Spectacular Drama', explaining its triumph:

> the scenic effects – the waterfalls, cascades, fountains, oceans, fairies, devils, hells, heavens, angels – are gorgeous beyond anything ever witnessed in America, perhaps, and these things attract the women and the girls. Then the endless ballets and splendid tableaux, with seventy beauties arrayed in dazzling half costumes, and displaying all possible compromises between nakedness and decency, capture the men and boys.[10]

Twain reiterates how the ballet dancers' sex appeal made up a large part of the show's notoriety and success: 'Beautiful bare legged girls ... [are] dressed with a meagerness that would make a parasol blush ... with more tights in view than anything else. They change their clothes every fifteen minutes for four hours, and their dresses become more beautiful and more rascally all the time.'[11] Such attractions became staples of the Broadway musical, including the plethora of dazzling women in revealing costumes, so prominent from the 1890s to the 1930s in popular revues such as the *Zeigfield Follies*. Yet what Twain's gendered commentary elides is that if audience delight was generated solely by gorgeous scenic effects and dancers' skimpy attire, then the ballet alone would be sufficient entertainment. But only the combination of fabulous visual elements with the song, dialogue, and sensational spectacle of melodrama pulled in the record crowds.

The successful mash-up of melodrama and ballet makes a good story – so good that a 1954 Broadway musical, *The Girl in Pink Tights*, is based on it – but it leaves out a lot. Revues, minstrel shows, variety shows, and European operettas became and remained popular during the nineteenth century and through the early twentieth; all importantly influenced the musical as we now know it. Perhaps the most important influence is W. S. Gilbert and Arthur Sullivan's. But their invention of the English comic opera is also predicated on the precursor genres of melodramas and extravaganza,[12] compounding melodrama's impact. This manifold pedigree is particularly clear in *Show Boat*. Its duets are squarely in the tradition of European operetta, and its comedy draws from American minstrelsy. From melodrama, it derives plot elements, character types, spectacular sets, and more. Yet at the same time,

*Show Boat* also uses melodrama to cast off its Victorian origins and to proclaim – in its difference – its own middle-class, middlebrow modernity. We see this modulated use of melodrama in character, plot, and set. Gaylord Ravenal and Steve Baker are deeply flawed – one a gambler and the other a hot-tempered actor – even when they behave admirably. Although they suit a melodramatic world of strong emotion rather than psychological nuance, they are neither heroes nor villains. Instead, their roles are to fit poorly into a culture in which people of different races are forbidden to marry, and in which men who are less successful breadwinners than their wives are made to feel inadequate and unmanly. This change is an extension of the shift within Victorian melodrama by the 1860s, away from earlier clear-cut characterizations and toward 'temperance' and other sub-genres portraying male protagonists who would be good if they could, but who suffer in the effort. Unlike most melodrama, no happy ending awaits the male romantic leads in *Show Boat*, part of its modification of melodrama to suit the middlebrow audiences who have been raised on the realistic late-nineteenth-century plays of George Bernard Shaw, August Strindberg, and Henrik Ibsen. The only outright villain in *Show Boat* is Pete, a minor character who derives directly from melodrama; his actions trigger the main storyline, a further indication of this play's melodramatic structure since, as David Mayer points out, 'melodrama is villain-driven'.[13] Attracted to Julie – the secretly mixed-race star of the show boat's stock company, who is illegally married to its leading man, Steve, who is white – Pete divulges her racial status in revenge for her refusal of his advances. Plus, for an extra dollop of evil, he blackmails her. His sudden revelation forces Julie and Steve to leave their jobs and causes their fortunes' tragic decline.

The climactic shock of recognizing racial or class difference connects this plot closely to many Victorian stage melodramas, such as Dion Boucicault's *The Octoroon* (1859). Likewise, a colossal riverboat recreated on stage comes straight from Victorian melodrama, which glories in crafting believable trains, bridges, and burning houses to astonish audiences. Examples are Augustin Daly's *Under the Gaslight* (1867), which introduced the much-copied spectacle of a train barrelling down on a victim tied to the tracks; Elizabeth Polack's *The Echo of Westminster Bridge* (1835), with its hyper-realistic set depicting the bridge to enthusiastic response[14]; and Mrs Henry Young's *Jessy Ashton; or, The Adventures of a Barmaid* (1862), in which the heroine must leap from a burning building. *The Octoroon*, for its part, featured a riverboat engulfed in flames. Making the link between melodrama and the modern musical, Matthew Sweet calls the melodrama's sensation scene the 'Victorian equivalent of today's "helicopter moment"', invoking the chief spectacle of *Miss Saigon* (1989), in which the male lead

265

spectacularly evacuates from the roof of the American embassy in Vietnam,[15] itself based (via opera and film) on David Belasco's melodrama, *Madame Butterfly* (1900), and its source text.

Moreover, *Show Boat* incorporates melodrama openly in its use of a play within a play: the Cotton Blossom, as the show boat is named, mounts productions of melodramas to entertain their local-yokel patrons in port after port. The remarkably faithful 1936 film version directed by James Whale (widely regarded as one of the best stage-to-film adaptations of all time) shows the Cotton Blossom's clientele hissing at the stage villains, just as they laugh obstreperously at a blackface minstrel show. There is some historical accuracy to this: for example, audiences in Victorian London's working-class neighbourhoods could rambunctiously express their approval by throwing onto the stage practical but hefty gifts such as rounds of beef, umbrellas, sausages, and trousers in lieu of flowers.[16]

The function of the film's meta-theatrical scenes (besides their own entertainment value for the movie-goers) is twofold. First, they establish for the sophisticated musical theatre and cinema audiences of the early twentieth century how much modern musical stagecraft has improved since 1887, when Act I of *Show Boat* is set. For example, we see the showboat's clunky, amateurish attempts at special effects (such as a rising moon managed by a handheld lantern that projects a shaky circle onto a scrim from backstage). However, sophisticated scenic effects were de rigueur in Victorian melodramas mounted in opulent venues that catered to mixed-class audiences, such as the Bowery in New York and the Britannia and the Surrey in London, so that the scene serves in part to create a narrative of difference between melodrama and the modern musical that audiences read to their own current advantage. The scenes also allow the twentieth-century audiences to congratulate themselves on how much more dignified they are (seated without hissing or knee-slapping in their own plush theatre seats on solid ground) than their gullible and demonstrative parents or grandparents might have been while devouring melodramas before the century's turn. In other words, in 1927 or 1936, *Show Boat*'s most explicit purpose in representing Victorian melodrama is to distinguish itself from it, pushing against its own melodramatic heritage. Yet there would be no Cotton Blossom without melodrama, and there would be no *Show Boat* either.

Seventeen years later Hammerstein partnered with Richard Rodgers to create *Oklahoma!*, widely regarded (despite numerous exceptions) as the first integrated musical. In an integrated musical, the songs and dances are woven fully into the plot, propelling the story; moreover, this plot might well involve serious drama with heart-wrenching developments, sad endings, and social critique. This is in contrast to the majority of musical theatre in the decades just before *Oklahoma!*, when the genre of musical comedy reigned. In musical comedy, the songs and dances largely interrupt the light-hearted plot, providing interludes of pure entertainment.[17] These musical numbers are often so unnecessary to the forward propulsion of the narrative that a love song could be plucked out of one show and dropped into another at the appropriate moment with no damage to the storytelling. As in nineteenth-century extravaganzas, they sometimes recycled non-original music with new words. After *Oklahoma!*, musical theatre would never be the same. *Show Boat*, also largely integrated, did not have the same immediate sway, despite its success.[18]

Both *Show Boat* and *Oklahoma!* deal thoughtfully with grave issues (racial persecution, community unrest, murder), reacting against the frivolity of musical comedies. But the old genre of melodrama already depicted slavery, alcoholism, tenants exploited by landlords, sailors forcefully impressed into service, and injustice of all kinds; examples are George Aiken's *Uncle Tom's Cabin* (1853), Tom Taylor's *The Bottle* (1847), and Douglas Jerrold's *The Rent Day* (1832) and *Black-Ey'd Susan* (1829). The modern integrated musical's innovation in introducing meaningful topics into musical theatre is in a sense a recuperation and reworking of Victorian melodrama for modern audiences who, on the one hand, often crave narrative coherence and weighty subjects rather than the illogical fluff provided by musical comedies, but who, on the other hand, still love beautifully executed songs, dances, and spectacles as a part of their evening out.

*Oklahoma!*, set just before statehood when Oklahoma was a divided community needing to pull together to succeed, is manifestly melodramatic in its clearly distinguishable hero (the cowboy, Curly), heroine (the ingénue, Laurey), and menacing villain (the farmhand, Jud Fry). Moreover, Jud is punished by death after having earlier posed a coercive sexual threat to Laurey – all familiar melodramatic tropes. *Oklahoma*'s exciting death scene involving a secret knife was heralded as an innovation, moving the genre of the frolicsome musical comedy toward that of an earnest musical play; in musical comedy, characters are not likely to die on stage. Yet the villain's onstage death is in large part a device propagated directly from melodrama, where it is fairly commonplace, as in the first stage version of *Sweeney Todd* (1847).

Long before *Oklahoma!*, *Show Boat*, or even *The Black Crook*, melodramas at times integrated music meaningfully into the plot and signified important narrative information musically. Until the Theatre Regulation Act of 1843, only three London theatres (Drury Lane, Covent Garden, and, in the summer, the Haymarket) had an exclusive patent on purely spoken drama. Other theatres were permitted to mount only less prestigious musical entertainments. Musical underscoring and a minimum of five songs meant that melodramas were classified as musical rather than spoken drama, despite their dependence on dialogue. Some melodramas interpolated songs that were simply popular ditties of the day, interrupting a seamless dramatic experience. But sometimes songs helped to propel the story. For example, Jacky Bratton points out that W. T. Moncrieff wrote the song 'The Watchman' to build to the dramatic climax of his 1830 play *The Heart of London; or, The Sharper's Progress*, first performed on 15 February at the Adelphi.[19] Likewise, Tracy Davis explains the integrative underscoring for Dion Bouciault's *The Relief at Lucknow* (1858):

> Jessie interjects Scottish tunes as multigenerational conditioning, teaching the child Charlie about his traditional culture, holding the regiment true to its Highland roots, and (Ophelia-like) demonstrating how privation has unhinged her. Thus, song is naturalized while it also serves as shorthand for characters' emotional states. The final sequence utilizes folk song, popular song, military slogan, and nationalistic anthem into a fully-motivated (diegetic) coup de théâtre wholly justified by civil and military tradition to stir a metropolitan audience.[20]

A rich musical soundscape is among the constitutive elements of melodrama, long employed with shrewdly expressive effect. *Show Boat* and *Oklahoma!*, the two Broadway shows most identified with inaugurating the modern integrated musical, are thoroughly grounded in melodrama, including in their use of music to further the plot. In other words, even the highly touted innovation that defines the modern musical as a sophisticated mode of dramatic narrative was at its core a melodramatic technique.

## Food, Glorious Food! Or, Well-Cured Bacon and Meat Pies

After *Oklahoma!*, integrated musicals became the norm in New York; this style of storytelling through song and dance became synonymous with the Broadway musical. In London, however, musical comedies (with some integrative elements) reigned supreme among British playmakers throughout the 1940s and 1950s – think of the fun of Noel Coward or Ivor Novello – until Lionel Bart adapted Charles Dickens's novel *Oliver Twist* to the musical stage. The young pop songwriter Lionel Bart was paying attention to the wild popularity and aesthetic value of imported Broadway musicals such as *Oklahoma!* and *South Pacific* (1949); the blockbusters *My Fair Lady* (1956) and *West Side Story* (1957) both premiered in London in 1958. *Oliver!* opened at the West End's New Theatre on 30 June 1960. An immediate hit, it was the longest running musical in London until

Andrew Lloyd Webber's huge success with *Jesus Christ Superstar* (1972). In fact, Webber credits Bart as 'the father of the modern British musical',[21] and *Oliver!* as 'one of the greatest musicals of all time'.[22] Bart wanted to write a 'British musical to rival the Americans'.[23]

*Oliver!*'s melodramatic ancestry can be traced not only through American innovations in developing the integrated musical but also to Victorian melodrama directly. *The Tatler* described *Oliver!*'s 1960 premier as 'a roaring transpontine melodrama'[24]; 'transpontine' here is a reference to the sensational theatrical fare offered in London neighbourhoods on the south side of the Thames river (in other words, across the bridge), which were in the Victorian period home to a large working-class community who liked their drama filled with blood, crime, and excitement. At the Surrey, for example, nineteenth-century audiences of sailors and dockworkers were particularly attached to nautical melodrama.[25] By calling a show opening in 1960 in London's pricey West End 'a roaring transpontine melodrama', the reviewer not only defines it generically as a melodrama but also places it geographically, socioeconomically, and temporally as a particular kind of old-fashioned entertainment that would have appealed to working-class audiences of a bygone age, still accessible in living memory. In that living memory, for example, would be E. T. Cook's widely read 1902 travelogue *The Highways and By-ways of London*, with reprints as late as the 1920s: 'Even the dramatic tastes of the people "over the water" are now supposed to be primitive; and "transpontine" is the adjective applied to melodrama that is too crude for the superior taste of northern London.'[26] Like *Oklahoma!* but also like melodrama (transpontine or otherwise), *Oliver!* is both comic and serious; as in *Oklahoma!*, in *Oliver!* a murder occurs onstage, when Bill Sikes kills Nancy (although the most gruesome aspects occur out of sight of the audience). While in part its melodramatic elements derive indirectly through earlier integrated musicals such as *Oklahoma!*, the musical *Oliver!* also inherits melodrama directly through a complex genealogy of prior stage and film dramatizations of the novel *Oliver Twist*.

In general, Dickens's novels appeared on stage immediately upon publication; in fact, because Dickens published his novels serially, they were often performed before he had written – let alone printed – the concluding episodes. There were no copyright protections addressing theatrical adaptation for authors of novels. The final instalment of *Oliver Twist* appeared in *Bentley's Miscellany* in April 1839; George Almar's *Oliver Twist: A Serio-Comic Burletta* premiered at the Surrey Theatre (one of those transpontine playhouses) in the autumn of 1838. In witnessing a performance, Dickens was so embarrassed that he lay down in the corner of his box during the first scene and did not rise again until the final curtain fell.[27] The same year,

C. Z. Barnett's melodrama *Oliver Twist, or, The parish boy's progress* (1838) hit the stage; there were probably at least three others produced before the novel's concluding instalment appeared. Indeed, Philip Bolton notes that *Oliver Twist* was Dickens's most adapted novel in the nineteenth century, with at least 200 versions performed in England or America by 1900, quickly followed by more theatrical adaptations – and soon, cinematic versions – of the various stage plays.[28]

One example is the 1909 *Oliver Twist* directed by J. Stuart Blackton and starring Edith Storey as Oliver, maintaining the nineteenth-century stage melodrama convention in which an actress plays the orphan boy, and indicating the tremendous fluidity between the melodrama stage and early film.[29] Likewise, Ivy Millais played Oliver in the 1912 Hepworth film, directed by Thomas Bentley. Marie Doro had portrayed Oliver on Broadway in the 1912 revival of J. Comyns Carr's melodrama *Oliver Twist* (1905) at the New Amsterdam Theater; in 1916, Jesse Lasky produced a Paramount film directed by James Young based on it, casting Doro in a reprise of her role of Oliver. As Bolton explains, 'actresses would step back and forth between the two media. Playwrights became screenwriters. Plays became films'.[30] But soon actresses performing boys largely disappeared from film. In the 1922 silent *Oliver Twist* directed by Frank Lloyd, Jackie Coogan played Oliver. With the innovation of synchronized sound, silent films that had been based on stage plays were in turn remade into talkies, the first sound *Oliver Twist* being the 1933 movie directed by William J. Cowan, with Dickie Moore playing Oliver. But most important in this lineage of films leading to *Oliver!* is David Lean's acclaimed but controversial *Oliver Twist* (1948), starring Alec Guinness as Fagin. When we reflect that the musical was then itself remade into Carol Reed's Oscar-winning film *Oliver!* (1968), the connections between stage and screen are even more obvious: John Romano points out that the director 'Reed stole shot for shot Lean's version for the narrative portions of the musical. The story boards are the same.'[31]

In addition to the melodrama legacy inherent in all modern musicals and in the line of melodrama stage and screen adaptations haunting the show, the melodramatic identity of *Oliver!* is also triply overdetermined. Its source, *Oliver Twist*, is itself a melodramatic text at its very foundation. Elaine Hadley has written on the melodrama of *Oliver Twist*, arguing that Dickens 'adopted the melodramatic mode in order to resist the alienating and classifying effects of The Poor Law Amendment Act of 1834'; she explains that the novel's 'melodramatic techniques ... create a familial and communal identity for Oliver'.[32] Sally Ledger points out that Dickens's use of the aesthetics of melodrama serves the aesthetics of class protest in *Oliver Twist*.[33] Dickens himself famously compares *Oliver Twist* to a melodrama and defines its aesthetic architecture as melodramatic. He explains that he has consciously chosen to structure his novel melodramatically, alternating scenes of comedy and tragedy like slabs of streaky bacon, as found in stage melodrama:

> It is the custom on the stage: in all good, murderous melodramas: to present the tragic and comic scenes, in as regular alternation, as the layers of red and white in a side of streaky, well-cured bacon. The hero sinks upon his straw bed, weighed down by fetters and misfortunes; and, in the next scene, his faithful but unconscious squire regales the audience with a comic song. We behold, with throbbing bosoms, the heroine in the grasp of a proud and ruthless baron: her virtue and her life alike in danger; drawing forth her dagger to preserve the one at the cost of the other; and, just as our expectations are wrought up to the highest pitch, a whistle is heard: and we are straightway transported to the great hall of the castle: where a grey-headed seneschal sings a funny chorus with a funnier body of vassals.[34]

Dickens claims that such interleaving of humour and heartbreak is genuinely a kind of realism: 'Such changes appear absurd; but they are not so unnatural as they would seem at first sight. The transitions in real life from well-spread boards to death-beds, and from mourning weeds to holiday garments, are not a whit less startling; only, there, we are busy actors instead of passive lookers-on.'[35] In other words, in addition to its other melodramatic endowments, the melodrama in *Oliver!* is acquired directly from the very construction of *Oliver Twist*, bequeathed by the novelist himself. Dickens even reminds us that melodramas included singing choruses, making the novel even riper for musicalization. Dickens's theory of realistic fiction as melodramatic complicates the effort of both the modern musical and the late nineteenth-century realist drama it partly emulates to reject melodrama as by definition unrealistic.

For all the melodrama that *Oliver!* inherits directly from *Oliver Twist*, or indirectly from previous theatrical and cinematic adaptations, or from the genre of the integrated musical, there is one major area in which Bart's adaptation importantly departs from all three kinds of antecedents: the character of Fagin. Though based in part on the historical Ikey Solomon, a notorious fence of stolen goods convicted in 1830, the character of Fagin, as Juliet John observes, 'obviously borrows heavily from the stereotype of the stage Jew and the reader's response to Fagin relies on his or her recognition of, and openness to, well-worn theatrical, literary (and racist) conventions'.[36] With his fiery red hair and devilish appearance (first encountered in the novel with smoke surrounding him and a toasting fork in hand), Fagin shares many characteristics with the 'stage Jew', a stock character going back at least to Renaissance drama. William Shakespeare's Shylock from *The Merchant of Venice* (1605) and Christopher Marlowe's Barabus from *The Jew of Malta* (1592) are Fagin's ancestors, usually portrayed in red-headed wigs, presenting a 'hooked nose, shuffling gait, and long gabardine coat and broad-brimmed hat',[37] just as George Cruikshank's originally illustrated Fagin in Dickens's novel. Even the real-life Ikey Solomon as inspiration for Fagin is mediated directly through the stage stereotype: Edgar Rosenberg points to the 'stage Jew' character originally named Barney Fence in William Thomas Moncrieff's melodrama *Van Dieman's Land* (1830); a clear precursor for Dickens's Fagin, Moncrieff renamed his own Barney, choosing the name Ikey Solomon for the character, to capitalize on the news story's popularity.[38]

Victorian stage adaptations of *Oliver Twist* would often realize on stage Cruikshank's repulsively large-nosed and servile illustrations of the novel's Fagin. *Realization* was a popular Victorian theatrical effect in which the actors would freeze in a tableau to create an exact replica of a familiar visual image audiences already knew. So popular and predictable was this phenomenon that illustrators created images to look like stage tableaux, making them easy to realize.[39] Cruikshank's influence remained powerful throughout the shift from stage to screen (and back again), so that more than a century after the novel's initial publication and appearance on stage, David Lean's *Oliver Twist* visually represents Fagin as a realization of Cruikshank, early stage adaptations, and previous film versions. This is most obvious in Alec Guinness's monstrous prosthetic nose, prompting charges of anti-Semitism and riots in Berlin. It could not be released in the United States until twelve minutes were cut, primarily of Guinness in profile.[40] Bart's inspiration to retell the story as a musical upon seeing the film when he was eighteen may have been a desire to recuperate it, to present it without the anti-Semitism.[41]

Bart's rewriting of Fagin as an endearing scamp – a nurturing, off-kilter parental figure rather than an inciter of murder and a corrupter of children – is not only a rejection of the character portrayed in David Lean's film and Dickens's novel but also a rejection of the stage Jew from which both derive. By concluding the stage version of *Oliver!* with Fagin going off unscathed into the sunrise as a kind of Wandering Jew, instead of cowering in his death row cell as in *Oliver Twist*, Bart invokes another traditional image with medieval roots, often thoroughly anti-Semitic but also often less damaging and perhaps more sympathetic than the typical stage Jew that became popular in Victorian melodrama. Leopold Lewis's *The Bells* (1871) and *The Wandering Jew* (1873), both adapted from earlier nineteenth-century sources, depict less villainous itinerant characters in what is arguably the tentative beginning of melodrama's amelioration of the stage Jew caricature, which Bart in turn draws upon for his reprobate but loveable Fagin.

Even more explicitly a modernized melodrama than *Oliver!* is *Sweeney Todd: The Demon Barber of Fleet Street*. In 1979, composer-lyricist Stephen Sondheim and book-writer Hugh Wheeler adapted Christopher Bond's 1973 play of the same name, which is itself based on a long series of stage, film, and even music hall ballad adaptations. Like *Oliver Twist*, which it imitates blatantly, the anonymously published novel *The String of Pearls* appeared serially; again like *Oliver Twist*, George Dibdin Pitt's dramatization (later renamed *Sweeney Todd*) appeared before the novel's concluding instalment appeared. Like all melodramas, it included incidental music and songs, such as a rousing chorus praising Mrs Lovett's meat pies, and others by favourite performers advertised on the playbill.[42] Like every previous version, Sondheim's musical relates the saga of Sweeney Todd, the barber who murders his customers and disposes of the bodies by dropping them into the cellar of the pastry shop next door to be made into Mrs Lovett's meat pies. The most obvious difference between the modern musical and the Victorian melodrama is in the character of Todd, who shifts from the mercenary brute of the novel and previous screen and stage versions (except for Bond's, of course) to a law-abiding family man who first seeks justice and then retribution against the cruel judge who raped his wife, stole his daughter, and transported him for life on a trumped up charge.[43] And of course all this character work is managed through Sondheim's complex music and brilliant lyrics.

Whereas Bart took the stage Jew Fagin and made him likable and funny, Sondheim, Wheeler, and Bond took the melodrama villain Todd and made him a sympathetically tragic anti-hero, giving him the psychological motivation that realism requires. Sondheim's appropriation of melodrama remakes the often despised working-class entertainment into something that critical and art elites can champion, as evidenced by the volumes of scholarship devoted to this musical, and frequent performances by grand opera companies. Notwithstanding the show's ample humour (some gently mocking Victorian melodrama), Sondheim defines melodrama 'simply as being high theater', 'larger than life – in emotion, in subject, and in complication of plot'; he sees little difference between melodrama and tragedy.[44] Explicitly returning the musical to its roots in melodrama, Sondheim lays bare the melodrama that is always inherent in the modern musical.

## Conclusion

How does our understanding of modern musicals change when seen as melodrama? How does our understanding of melodrama change when seen as incipiently the modern musical? From its inception, no matter which origin story one chooses, or whether *The Black Crook* or *Show Boat* or *Oklahoma!* is the genre's 'first', the musical owes its existence to melodrama. What is true of the whole form is true of specific examples. Long before their musical-dramatization in twentieth-century London or New York as *Oliver!* and *Sweeney Todd*, both the novels *Oliver Twist* and *The String of Pearls* were already bound up in melodrama, both in their own derivation and in their earlier progeny on stage and screen.

But do melodramas and musicals perform similar cultural work? Both genres have been criticized as valuing spectacle and sentiment over intellect, offering the escapist entertainment deplored by Bertolt Brecht instead of incitement to political action.[45] When the offspring exposes too much of its parentage, melodrama poses a threat to the musical's prestige, as can be seen in reviews of the 1985 London premiere of *Les Miserables* (1980) – 'a lurid Victorian melodrama', says Francis King in *The Daily Telegraph* – or the 2006 film adaptation of *Phantom of the Opera* (1976): 'impressively free of anything that does not smell of unpasteurized melodrama', says Anthony Lane in *The New Yorker*.[46] But Victorian stage melodrama is also under-stood to offer cultural critique along with its escapism, beginning in the French Revolution and the imported French *melo-drame*.[47] Although the modern musical remakes this working-class medium into a middle-class, middlebrow entertainment (evidenced by hefty ticket prices), it too offers social criticism along with entertainment, and all the twentieth-century musicals we have discussed demonstrate this. Moreover, the working-class origins of melodrama thoroughly underwrite *Oliver!* and *Sweeney Todd*. Both tell stories about the oppressed underclass; their often biting lyrics and the music that manipulates our emotions rework their sources to negotiate what has always been melodrama's tension between escapism and cultural critique.

## Notes

1. See Jeffrey Mason, 'The Face of Fear' in *Melodrama*, ed. James Redmond (Cambridge: Cambridge University Press, 1992).
2. Raymond Knapp, *The American Musical and the Formation of National Identity* (Princeton: Princeton University Press, 2005), 122–3.
3. Geoffrey Block, *Enchanted Evenings: The Broadway Musical From* Showboat *to Sondheim and Lloyd Webber*, second edition (Oxford: Oxford University Press, 2009), 19–39.
4. Cecil Smith and Glenn Litton, *Musical Comedy in America: from* The Black Crook *to* South Pacific, *from* The King & I *to* Sweeney Todd (New York: Routledge, 1987), 1.

5. Elaine Hadley, *Melodramatic Tactics: Theatricalized Dissent in the English Marketplace, 1800–1885* (Stanford: Stanford University Press, 1995), 78.
6. Katherine Preston, 'American Musical Theatre Before the Twentieth Century', in *The Cambridge Companion to the Musical*, second edition, eds. William A. Everett and Paul R. Laird (Cambridge: Cambridge University Press, 2008), 18.
7. Knapp, *The American Musical and the Formation of National Identity*, 23.
8. Gerald Bordman, *American Musical Comedy* (Oxford: Oxford University Press, 1982), 18.
9. Nathan Hurvitz, *A History of the American Musical Theatre: No Business Like It* (London and New York: Routledge, 2014), 37.
10. Mark Twain, 'Model Artists', reprinted from the San Francisco *Daily Alta*, 28 March 1867, in *The American Stage: Writing on Theater from Washington Irving to Tony Kushner*, ed. Laurence Senelick (New York: The Library of America, 2010), 79–80.
11. Twain, 'Model Artists', 80; see also *The Letters of Charles Dickens*, Vol. 12, ed. Graham Storey (Oxford: Clarendon- Oxford University Press, 2002), 81.
12. Carolyn Williams, *Gilbert and Sullivan: Gender, Genre, Parody* (New York: Columbia University Press, 2010), 75.
13. Mayer, 'Encountering Melodrama', in *The Cambridge Companion to Victorian and Edwardian Drama*, ed. Kerry Powell (Cambridge: Cambridge University Press, 2004), 150.
14. *Figaro in London*, 3–4.188 (11 July 1835): 118.
15. Matthew Sweet, *Inventing the Victorians: What We Think We Know About Them and Why We're Wrong* (St. Martin's Press, 2001), 5.
16. Jim Davis and Victor Emeljanow, *Reflecting the Audience: London Theatregoing, 1840–1880* (Iowa City: University of Iowa Press, 2001), 88.
17. Block, *Enchanted Evenings*, 147.
18. Todd Decker, *Show Boat: Performing Race in an American Musical* (Oxford: Oxford University Press, 2013), 4. Camille Forbes points out that *Show Boat* was also the first racially integrated book musical (one which tells a story) on Broadway, although revues such as *Ziegfeld Follies* casting black and white performers had already appeared by 1927, in *Introducing Bert Williams: Burnt Cork, Broadway, and the Story of America's First Black Star* (New York: Basic Books, 2008), 273.
19. Jacky Bratton, 'William Thomas Moncrieff', *Nineteenth Century Theatre and Film*, 42 (2015).
20. Tracy C. Davis, *Broadview Anthology of Nineteenth-Century Performance* (Peterborough: Broadview Press, 2011), 324.
21. Eric Pace, 'Lionel Bart, 68, Songwriter; Created the Musical "Oliver!"', *The New York Times* (5 April 1999), www.nytimes.com/1999/04/05/theater/lionel-bart-68-songwriter-created-the-musical-oliver.html, accessed 22 March 2009.
22. '*Oliver!* creator dies after cancer battle', BBC (3 April 1999), http://news.bbc.co.uk/2/hi/uk_news/311100.stm, accessed 12 March 2017.
23. David Roper, *Bart!: The Unauthorized Life and Times, Ins and Outs, Ups and Downs of Lionel Bart* (New York: Pavillion, 1994), 8.
24. Samantha Ellis, 'Lionel Bart's Oliver!, June 1960', *The Guardian* (18 June 2003), www.guardian.co.uk/stage/2003/jun/18/theatre.samanthaellis/print, accessed 26 March 2011.

25. Michael Booth, *English Melodrama* (London: Herbert Jenkins, 1965), 102.
26. Emily Cook, *Highways and By-Ways in London* (London and New York: Macmillan and Co, 1902), 128.
27. Phillip Cox, *Reading Adaptations: Novel and Verse Narratives on the Stage, 1790–1840* (Manchester: Manchester University Press, 2000), 121.
28. H. Philip Bolton, *Dickens Dramatized* (Boston: G. K. Hall and Company, 1987), 104–5.
29. Sharon Aronofsky Weltman, 'Investigating Early Film and the Nineteenth-Century Theatre', *Nineteenth Century Theatre and Film*, 42 (2015): 119–20.
30. Bolton, *Dickens Dramatized*, 106.
31. Gerhard Joseph, 'Dickens, Psychoanalysis, and Film: A Roundtable', in *Dickens on Screen*, ed. John Glavin (Cambridge: Cambridge University Press, 2003), 18.
32. Hadley, *Melodramatic Tactics*, 5.
33. Sally Ledger, *Dickens and the Popular Radical Imagination* (Cambridge: Cambridge University Press, 2007), 101.
34. Charles Dickens, *Oliver Twist*, ed. Fred Kaplan (New York: W. W. Norton, 1993 [1837–9]), 117–18.
35. Dickens, *Oliver Twist*, 118.
36. Juliet John, *Dickens's Villains: Melodrama, Character, Popular Culture* (Oxford: Oxford University Press, 2003), 129.
37. Harry Stone, 'Dickens and the Jews', *Victorian Studies*, 2 (1959): 233.
38. Edgar Rosenberg, *From Shylock to Svengali: Jewish Stereotypes in English Fiction* (Palo Alto: Stanford University Press, 1960), 134.
39. Martin Meisel, *Realizations: Narrative, Pictorial, and Theatrical Arts in Nineteenth-Century England* (Princeton: Princeton University Press, 1983), 247–65.
40. Joss Marsh, 'Dickens and Film', in *The Cambridge Companion to Charles Dickens*, ed. John Jordan (Cambridge: Cambridge University Press, 2001), 218–19.
41. Jack Gorman, *Knocking Down Ginger* (London: Caliban Books, 1995), 138.
42. Sharon Aronofsky Weltman (ed.), 'The Playbill', *Nineteenth Century Theatre and Film*, 38 (2011): 25–7.
43. Sharon Aronofsky Weltman, 'Boz versus Bos in *Sweeney Todd*: Dickens, Sondheim, and Victorianness', *Dickens Studies Annual*, 42 (2011): 55–63.
44. Stephen Sondheim, 'Larger than Life: Reflections on Melodrama and Sweeney Todd', in *Melodrama*, ed. Daniel Gerould (New York: New York Literary Forum, 1980), 3–14.
45. Millie Taylor, *Musical Theatre, Realism and Entertainment* (Aldershot: Ashgate, 2012), 89–90.
46. Francis King, 'Glum-Show', *Sunday Telegraph* (13 October 1985): 16; Anthony Lane, 'The Current Cinema: Unmasked', *The New Yorker* (3 January 2005), www.newyorker.come/magazine/2005/01/03/unmasked-3, accessed 26 March 2011.
47. Rohan McWilliam, 'Melodrama', in *A Companion to Sensation Fiction*, ed. Pamela K. Gilbert (Malden and Oxford: Wiley-Blackwell, 2011), 56.

# 18

## PETER BROOKS

# Psychoanalysis and Melodrama

### The Melodramatics of Psychic Enactment

Freud's mentor Josef Breuer provided the clue. Speaking of a woman's increasingly hysterical behavior, he remarked to Freud:

> 'These things are always *secrets d'alcôve!*' I asked him in astonishment what he meant, and he answered by explaining the word *alcôve* ('marriage-bed') to me, for he failed to realize how extraordinary the *matter* of his statement seemed to me.[1]

One could dwell on the game of hide and seek going on here: James Strachey's use of a French metonym (*'secrets d'alcôve'*) for the hidden places of sexual transactions, where Freud writes *'Geheimnisse des Alkovens'*; Breuer's (or Freud's?) decorous gloss of the word *alcôve* as marriage bed (*'des Ehebettes'*), as if that were the only place and kind of sex; and Freud's claim that Breuer has failed to understand the extraordinary importance of what he's just said – extraordinary, at least, in the understanding of his disciple, whereas Breuer, it seems, took fright at it: at least, fled Anna O., the patient at the origin of psychoanalysis, when she flung herself into his arms, leaving Freud to exploit the secret and build his career on it.

Like melodrama, psychoanalysis assumes that there is a certain hiddenness to the wellsprings of existence, but also that these can be, and must be, brought into the open, to overt enactment, in order for understanding to take the place of bafflement and for the process of cure to proceed. The melodramatic quality of the enactment is ensured by the repression that keeps it from discovery until analytic pressure brings it forth. Consider two examples of the emergence of the hidden in Freud's descriptions of his analytic work with patients. First, the very early case of Miss Lucy R., from *Studies on Hysteria* (1895):

> And now, under the pressure of my hand, the memory of a third and still earlier scene emerged, which was the really operative trauma and which had given the scene with the chief accountant its traumatic effectiveness.[2]

And then from his most famous case history, that of the 'Wolf Man' (*From the History of an Infantile Neurosis*, 1918), at the moment when analysis of the traumatic wolf dream leads to the discovery of the 'primal scene':

> But what picture can the nightly workings of his sexual desire have conjured up that could frighten him away so violently from the fulfillment for which he longed? ...
>
> What sprang into activity that night out the chaos of the dreamer's unconscious memory-traces was the picture of copulation between his parents, copulation in circumstances which were not entirely usual and which were especially favorable for observation.[3]

Discovery in Freud has a melodramatic cast because, as in stage melodrama, the behind is breaking forward, coming to occupy the front of the proscenium. Freud called dream *'ein anderer Schauplatz'*, another stage, an alternative theatre where enactments happen free of waking censorship. Stage melodrama, in my understanding of it, offers something very similar: a theatre in which repression can be lifted for the duration of the performance, where emotion can be spoken and acted out in its primal fullness. If that is the case, psychoanalysis does not merely appear melodramatic: psychoanalysis and melodrama share the same aesthetic and moral goals.

I argued in my book *The Melodramatic Imagination* that psychoanalysis can be read as a systematic realization of the melodramatic aesthetic, brought to bear on the structure and dynamics of mind.[4] Psychoanalysis is necessarily melodramatic in the way it conceives of psychic conflict, as a struggle of different forces that is fierce, unremitting, often disabling to the ego. The unconscious harbours melodramatic villains. The dynamics of repression and the dramatic return of the repressed mimic the plots of melodrama. Acting out is inevitably excessive: what needs to be dramatized and resolved is primal and essential, like the integers of good and evil embodied in melodramatic characters. The Manichaeism of melodramatic persons and the emotions they incarnate find their counterparts in the structure of ego, id, and superego, which itself constitutes a kind of dynamic matrix of the melodramatic enactment. One could read the whole of Freud's crucial essay of 1923, *The Ego and the Id*, as the schematics of psychic melodrama, because of the dramatically conflictual relations of those psychodynamic categories: where the ego is seen to be only an apparent master in its own house, like 'a man on horseback, who has to hold in check the superior strength of the horse', and is often obliged to let it go where it wants.[5] Freud's later formulations of the psychic process in the dualism of Eros and Thanatos, perpetually struggling to bring the organism into life and then back to primal quiescence, only make the melodrama of psychoanalysis the more grandiose.

Melodrama (as critics have recognized) often resembles the world of dreams, especially those we call nightmares.[6] Analysis of the dream was, of course, from the outset for Freud the 'royal way' to the processes of unconscious life. The enactments of dreams closely resemble the expressionist mute actions that so many melodramas stage, as in recognition of the genre's derivation from pantomime: these are gestures that clearly signify and point to meanings that can't be stated but must eventually be brought to articulation. The drama of articulation in melodrama – finding the words to say the moral universe – has its counterpart in psychoanalysis, the 'talking cure' which ought to lead to a full articulation of what has been repressed from conscious memory, manifested instead as uncontrolled acting-out or as bodily symptom. Like melodrama, psychoanalysis is a drama of recognition: of finding the place of the 'truth', of the narrative that explains (and therefore maybe cures), of making the individual and the universe legible.

The convergence of the matter and mode of melodrama and psychoanalysis can be seen with particular clarity in the problem that Freud addressed from the outset of his career: hysterical conversion, the way that desire writes its unconscious histories on the body as symptom. The hystericized body is one invested with meaning, a body that both conceals and reveals what it has to say, that must be brought into the realm of rational discourse. Learning to read the hysterical body is the task of psychoanalysis from *The Studies on Hysteria* onward. This may be true as well in melodrama, especially in its mute action, and becomes especially evident in silent cinema, which perforce borrows a repertory of gestures, postures, and actions from melodrama and pantomime.

An example can be found in the work of D. W. Griffith – object of study for a number of the theorists of film melodrama.[7] In *Orphans of the Storm*, his silent film of 1921, based on a masterful melodrama of 1874 by Adolphe Dennery, *Les Deux orphelines*, we are in the 'storm' of the French Revolution, as if Griffith had reached back to the moment at which melodrama originated, in that greatest of upheavals and stark conflicts. The muteness of silent cinema is thematized, as it were, when the two orphan sisters, Henriette and Louise (played by the Gish sisters, Lillian and Dorothy), are separated. As Henriette talks anxiously with the Countess (her mother: neither has yet recognized the call of the blood, though they are feeling it), Louise, who is blind, and has been enslaved by the evil La Frochard and made to beg in the streets of Paris, appears in a deep shot, at the end of the street, forcing herself to sing at La Frochard's command. Henriette's face begins to register a preconscious recognition. Then she begins to tremble, her body seized with the drama of a possible discovery that is not yet complete. She breaks from the Countess to rush onto the balcony. She leans toward her blind sister in gestures of yearning, hope, despair, desperately seeking reunion. You have the impression she might throw herself into the street. Meanwhile, Louise down below casts about for the source of the voice calling to her.

Bodies here are fully hysterical, if we understand by hysteria a bodily representation of that which cannot otherwise be said. Hysteria gives us the maximal conversion of psychic affect into somatic meaning: meaning enacted on the body. The emotional hyperbole of the scene cannot reach release and relief because the recognition is interrupted, censored, by the arrival of soldiers to arrest Henriette: the father of her aristocratic suitor, the Chevalier de Vaudrey, to get her out of the way has had recourse to a *lettre de cachet*, an Old Regime agency of censorship and repression by way of imprisonment in the Bastille. This will lead to another scene of an extra-ordinary hystericized body: Henriette is in a tumbrel on her way to the guillotine, and makes a last farewell to Louise, in the street (the scene is formally intertitled, 'The Farewell'). As she leans from the cart for a final kiss, and their lips meet and are held long together, Henriette's body appears to be in a nearly impossible posture, tilted from the cart, rigid, already almost inanimate, like a puppet or a mummy, an image of her imminent death. It is a striking image of victimization, and of the body wholly invested with meaning – the body ceasing to function in order to become the place on which messages of life and death are inscribed. Melodramatic and psychic representation converge seamlessly in this bodily writing. Embodied signs are symptoms, to be deciphered and read.

The semiotics of melodrama and psychoanalysis, then, are similar, possibly identical. Freud's understanding of that semiotics is stated, almost melodramatically, in the case history of *Dora*:

> He that has eyes to see and ears to hear may convince himself that no mortal can keep a secret. If his lips are silent, he chatters with his fingertips; betrayal oozes out of him at every pore. And thus the task of making conscious the most hidden recesses of the mind is one which it is quite possible to accomplish.[8]

One could take this as advice from a theatre director to his actors – how to play without words, so that the body itself conveys meanings. It is of course more nearly advice to the audience: how to read what the bodies are telling us. In the case of both theatre and psychoanalysis, the premise is the same: the world is replete with meaning, but you have to know how to find that meaning, bring it to light, make it overt. Freud at times called himself 'conquistador' because of his conquest of the domain of apparent non-meaning, showing that everything, even the apparently trivial gestures of everyday life, slips of the tongue, and all the other 'parapraxes' were in fact full of meaning, if only you knew how to find it. *The Psychopathology of Everyday Life* (1901) reads as a manual of everyday melodrama that looks forward to Hollywood 'domestic melodrama', showing how seemingly banal quotidian situations and gestures can be freighted with a potentially explosive drama. He that has eyes to see and ears to hear can find the drama of the everyday, and give it the swelling music of film.

## Irreducible Sadism

At nearly the same moment that Freud was postulating the source of the Wolf Man's trauma in the 'primal scene' of his parents' copulation – which was given its sexual and frightening charge of affect and meaning only later, in the wolf dream that retrospectively makes the primal scene pathogenic – Marcel Proust was creating his fictive persona's own primal scene in the '*drame du coucher*' of *Swann's Way (Du côté de chez Swann,* 1913), the drama of the mother's withheld kiss. Later in the same volume, Marcel will discover the chilling evil of sadism when, as a voyeur looking through the window, he witnesses the scene between Mlle Vinteuil and her woman lover, where sexual arousal depends on profanation of the image of Mlle Vinteuil's father (the composer), her lover spitting on her father's photograph. After recounting the scene, the narrator goes on to reflect on Mlle Vinteuil's sadism, on what happens to this otherwise 'scrupulous and tender soul' when it enters 'the inhuman world of pleasure'. It's not that evil appears pleasurable to her, but rather that pleasure appears evil, that pleasure cannot exist without its being evil. This leads to a reflection on the melodramatic theatricality of sadism as the starkest form of evil:

> To be sure, in Mlle Vinteuil's ways of doing things the appearance of evil was so complete that one would have trouble finding it realized to this degree of perfection except in a sadist; it's under the footlights of a Boulevard theatre rather than in the lamplight of a real country home that one can see a daughter make her friend spit on the portrait of a father who had lived only for her; and it is really only sadism that gives a foundation in real life to the aesthetics of melodrama.[9]

The excessive representations of melodrama might have no justification in reality were it not for the very real existence of sadism. That kind of evil force in the world tells you that melodrama is for real, that its enactments have a psychic underpinning.

Much later in the novel, Proust will clarify further the linkage of sadism and melodrama in positing a link of sadism to death and destruction – he is now in the midst of World War I, and the German bombardment of Paris. Freud, from the other side of the front in the Great War, would also discover that sadism, though a component of erotic life, ultimately derives from the death drive. Marcel witnesses though a peephole the Baron de Charlus being whipped by hired hands, which leads to a discussion, not of masochism (which Proust sees as derivative) but of sadism. For Charlus, the narrator tells us, pleasure didn't exist without 'a certain idea of cruelty of which I hadn't before now measured the full force'.[10] Then, explaining Charlus's disappointment and exasperation by the evidently simulated cruelty of his hired tormentors, we are told that even authentic thieves and assassins would not have satisfied him because they do not speak their crime, don't discourse of it. 'And there is moreover in the sadist – however good he may be, all the more the better he is – a thirst for evil [*une soif de mal*] that evildoers working toward other goals cannot satisfy.'[11] As I read this, it makes sadism an independent moral condition, so to speak: one that is not derivable from Eros, that rather stands closer to the death drive. In fact, nothing produced by Charlus's hired hands could ever satisfy him erotically. 'Nothing is more limited than pleasure and vice. One can truly say, in this sense, in changing the sense of the expression, that one turns always in the same vicious circle.'[12] The grim pun suggests the problem: 'vice' cannot satisfy the sadist because it really has nothing to do with his destructive urge.

Freud at the same time, during the Great War, was also discovering that sadism was not derivable from the erotic. It was rather a product of the death drive, which was forced on his attention by the coming of a war destructive of all that European civilization had attained. First in *Thoughts for the Time on War and Death* (1915), then in the major revision of his thought of *Beyond the Pleasure Principle* (1920), inflected by work with shell-shocked patients from the war whose dreams returned over and over to their traumatic experiences, in apparent contradiction of the wish-fulfilment theory of dreams, Freud came to the realization that the pleasure principle did not explain everything. Beyond that lay the death drive, more primitive, working to undo the life forces and return the organism to the primal quiescence that preceded and followed life.

Unlike the pleasure principle, the death drive is largely invisible. Its one clear manifestation is sadism. Sadism is the urge to destruction turned outward to wreak havoc on the world, the death drive turned from within the organism to be directed toward the destruction of others. Aggression and destructiveness are as constitutive of humans as love. War is regressive, it strips away the veneer of civilization, it lays bare primal emotions and drives in an unrepressed state. The death-dealing of the Great War leads to another stage of the Freudian melodrama. Now he is able to declare, in melodramatic paradox: 'The aim of all life is death.'[13] Freud's thought here glosses Proust's claim that sadism is the emotion that justifies the aesthetics of melodrama: it has that irreducible primacy that melodramatic enactment reveals.

## Freud Reads Balzac, Balzac Reads Freud

At the very end of his life – just before he asked his physician Max Schur to fulfil a long-held promise to inject him with a lethal dose of morphine when the pain of his cancer had become unbearable – Freud finished what was to be his final reading. 'Freud did not read at random', Schur tells us, 'but carefully selected books from his library.'[14] His choice now fell on a novel from 1831 by Honoré de Balzac, *La Peau de chagin* (*The Fatal Skin*, in the English version, by Atwood Townsend): Balzac's first fully achieved novel, which lays out the melodramatic premises of his work to come. When Freud had finished – the day before he called for the fatal injection – he remarked to Schur: 'This was the proper book for me to read; it deals with shrinking and starvation.' Balzac's novel is indeed about that, but shrinking and starvation are the result of desire and its fulfillment. The young hero of the novel, Raphaël de Valentin, on the verge of suicide from despair at his utter destitution and his failure to make his chosen woman love him, is given a magic wild ass's skin, a *chagrin*, by an old antiques dealer (who has reached the age of 102). The magic skin realizes any wish one makes on it. Yet with every realized wish it shrinks. The metaphor is overtly sexual, but this is largely generalized in the lesson given to Raphaël by the antiques dealer when he presents the skin: 'Man depletes himself by two instinctive acts that dry up the sources of his existence. Two verbs explain all the forms taken by these two causes of death: DESIRE and POWER. . . . *Desire* sets us afire and *Power* destroys us.' ['*Vouloir* nous brûle et *Pouvoir* nous détruit.'][15] So that the realization of desire, or Eros, always at the same time does the work of Thanatos, leading us more quickly to destruction. But there is an alternative, says the old man: 'but KNOWLEDGE leaves our frail organism in a perpetual state of calm'.

Freud's choice of this last novel to read before death seems too predetermined, *more freudiano,* to be a matter of chance, but I can offer no more information on how he came to select it, or it to select him. Note, though, that this flamboyant, melodramatic, parabolic tale already contains within itself the essential, world-determining struggle posited by the pre-Socratic Empedocles of Agrigentum, which Freud had come upon in a book by Wilhelm Capelle published in 1935. As Freud explains in one of his last essays, *Analysis Terminable and Interminable* (1937), Empedocles saw the world as the war of *philia* and *neixos,* love and strife, which Freud reconfigures as Eros and the death drive (later titled Thanatos by Wilhelm Stekel), thus reinscribing the argument of *Beyond the Pleasure Principle* under ancient authority. Those two grandiose drives or instincts, Eros and the death drive, by their conflict determine the course of life. In *The Fatal Skin*, once Raphaël discovers the power of the talisman given to him by the old antiques dealer (for whom Raphaël, in turn, wishes a passion for a dancer from the opera, contradicting the dealer's choice of knowledge and calm passivity – a wish that will, of course, be realized, to the old man's destruction), he plunges headlong into the world of desire and power, summoning up a drunken orgy peopled with beautiful women.

The morning after, he discovers that he has inherited an immense fortune from an unknown uncle in Calcutta. At once, he sets the magic skin against the outline he traced of it the night before – to measure the shrinkage that this realization of desire has caused: 'A horrible pallor etched all the muscles of the wilted face of this legatee, his features contracted, the relief of his face blanched, the cavities became dark, the mask was livid, his eyes became fixed. He saw DEATH.'[16] The discovery of the realization of desire, in all its fullness, is equally the discovery of death, as the inevitable outcome of desiring. If the death drive serves the pleasure principle, assuring the discharge of libido, in a deeper sense the pleasure principle is the servant of the death drive, assuring that the organism is led back to what Freud in *Beyond the Pleasure Principle* identifies as primal quiescence, the death that precedes and follows life. At the tail end of the orgy, all Raphaël can pronounce is: '*I desire nothing.*'[17]

To desire is ultimately to choose death. In his desperate attempt to prolong his existence, Raphaël tries to live will-lessly, all his needs taken care of by a servant who is never to ask what his master wants. He has made for himself a set of opera glasses that purposely distort the lines of the world, rendering everything seen through it ugly – in particular, transforming women from objects of desire into monsters. Yet it can't work. Life without desire is sterile. When Raphaël's old love from his student days, Pauline, reappears, he tosses away the talisman and devotes himself to a life of loving. But the death drive quickly does its silent work – the talisman reappears, now reduced to the size of a leaf, and Raphaël begins coughing his life away. He retreats to mountain spas, to no avail. At the last, Pauline reappears again, and he calls to her, overcome by desire. She now is holding the skin:

> Seeing her embellished by terror and love, he was no longer master of his thoughts: memories of scenes of caresses and of the delirious joys of his passion triumphed in his long sleeping soul, and blazed like a smoldering hearth.
> 'Pauline, come! Pauline!'

A terrible cry rose from the throat of the young woman, her eyes dilated, her eyebrows, moved by a pain never known, opened with horror, she read in Raphaël's eyes one of those furious desires, once her glory; but as this desire swelled, the Skin, contracting, tickled her palm.[18]

Raphaël, with an inarticulate cry that becomes a death rattle, dies on her breast. It is an appropriately melodramatic and Gothic ending to a highly coloured tale of what is at stake in desire, power, knowledge, and death.

The Fatal Skin is about 'shrinking and starvation', as Freud said to Schur; it's also about everything on the way to that finality. The Fatal Skin belongs to Balzac's 'philosophical tales', which claim to reveal the hidden reasons of social effects. It is one of those novels in which the plane of everyday reality keeps opening up to something fantastic, in the manner of Balzac's beloved Thousand and One Nights, but always a fantastic that he stipulates as of the real: a principle on which the real resides. The seemingly irrational in fact never is: it is reason itself on a deeper level of motivation and causation. The very principles that govern life are dug out, brought to the light of day in the novel. It offers a rich allegory of life choices in an economy of desire governed by the ultimate arbiter of death. In fact, all of Freud's late system of thought already resides in this first of Balzac's great novels. He realizes in analytic discourse what Balzac has already dramatized.

I would suggest also that the highly coloured, Gothic, melodramatic mode of Balzac's novel brings out, in a logic of anticipation and retroaction that Freud might have appreciated, the Gothic and melodramatic aspects of psychoanalysis itself. Psychoanalysis offers a melodramatization of psychic life, just as Balzac offers a highly charged psychodrama. Balzac and Freud – and it is this that makes the choice of Freud's final reading so interesting – stand in an unrealized relationship to one another, each bringing out, as it were, an essential aspect of the other. It's not that there are many indications of an influence of Balzac on Freud – though Freud clearly knew the novelist's major works. And Schopenhauer, cited in Beyond the Pleasure Principle, might have taught Freud various Balzacian lessons. It is rather that the two enterprises, the Balzacian and the Freudian, stand in a remarkable relation. They share a semiotic, by which all is at the same time hidden and knowable.

Balzac, in a letter, offered his own summary definition of The Fatal Skin: 'everything in it is myth and figure'.[19] Freud was not unaware that one could say the same about his work from Beyond the Pleasure Principle, where in the absence of biological explanations of the origins of sexuality he turns to Plato's myth of the androgyne, and onward. In his last major work, Moses and Monotheism (1939), Freud creates a new, different mythology, casting himself in the role of the lawgiver eventually disobeyed by his people, who rise up and murder him. Myths and figures everywhere. One can imagine that Balzac's novel appealed to Freud through its attention to the quotidian while simultaneously claiming, and demonstrating, that everyday life contains a mythic drama of meaning, that it is subject to analysis in terms of the basic forces governing human existence. Balzac's projected *Pathologie de la vie sociale,* like Freud's *Psychopathologie des Alltagslebens,* claims to lay out the principles for analyses of everyday social life. Yet the largest claims to understanding can't be entirely contained within a semiotic: they exceed it, to engage those mythic and figural forces beyond immediate apprehension but everywhere at work in the movement from life to death.

The very foundation of society, in Freud's thought, lies in the murder of the primal father, which from *Totem and Taboo* (1913) onwards comes to have ever-greater explanatory force in accounting for the role of guilt and law in the creation of human community. One could say that psychoanalysis comes to be a discourse where explanation has the same melodramatic quality as the phenomena to be explained. As Freud states in an astonishing sentence in one of his very last essays, 'Constructions in Analysis' (1937), where he has been discussing the 'ultra-clear' hallucinations of patients, which he thinks must contain a kernel of historical truth: 'The delusions of patients appear to me to be the equivalents of the constructions which we build up in the course of an analytic treatment – attempts at explanation and cure.'[20] That seems to plunge psychoanalysis back into the enactments of melodrama itself, hallucination met by hallucination.

## Desire, Aggression, Kultur

The linguistic turn of psychoanalysis post-Freud, in the work of Jacques Lacan, seems to me largely to confirm the close relations of psychoanalysis and melodrama. Lacan's reading of Freudian symbology raises the stakes of meaning (if that's possible), seeing in symptom, for instance, the structure of metaphor, and in desire the working of metonymy, as the two fundamental poles (referring here to Roman Jakobson) of language.[21] For instance, Lacan writes, 'And the enigma that desire presents to any "natural philosophy," its frenzy miming the gulf of the infinite, the intimate collusion in which it envelopes the pleasure of knowing and that of domination in pleasure, belongs to no other unhinging of instinct than its being caught up on the rails – stretching toward *the desire of something else* – of metonymy.'[22] And on metaphor: 'It is the truth of what this desire has been in his history that the patient cries out through his symptom, as Christ said that the stones themselves would have cried out if the children of Israel had not lent them their voice.' We seem to witness here an unexpected melodramatization of linguistics. Another instance that goes to the heart of Freud's thinking may be found in Lacan's translations/adaptations of Freud's famous dictum, '*Wo es war, soll Ich werden.*'[23] The phrase is usually given the optimistic translation: 'Where id was shall ego come to be.' Lacan proposes three darker versions. In 'The Freudian Thing' (*La chose freudienne*, 1955): 'Where it was, one could say, there where being occurred, we would have it understood, it is my duty that I come to be.' One senses the drama in the formulation of a coming into selfhood in the place marked out by id. In 'The Agency of the Letter' (*L'Instance de la letter*, 1957), he simplifies: 'There where it (id) was, I (ego) must come into being (or: arrive).' And then yet again, in 'Knowledge and Truth' (*La Science et la vérité*, 1965): 'There where it was, there as subject must I come to be.'[24]

Freud calls this coming of ego to the place of id *Kulturarbeit*, comparing it to Faust's draining of the Zuyder Zee (in Part 2 of Goethe's drama).[25] But that cultural work, as I hope my examples have suggested, is not so simple as the building of dykes and the creation of arable land. If the dykes may figure repression, holding at bay the raging force of the sea, we know that such a solution, such a construction, can only be provisional (as Mephistopheles in fact tells us), and that we will have to find ways to accommodate that which has been blocked from the civilized world. His late work, *Civilization and Its Discontents* (1930) – written as the rise of German National Socialism was beginning to shadow Europe – is all about the price we pay for trying to live in a world that tries to hold murderous forces at bay. The price paid by the 'instinctual renunciation' required by life in society turns out to be more than humanity can bear. If the creation of community is the work of Eros, the very renunciations that community requires will feed aggression and destruction. The result is the malaise of life within civilization, *Kultur*, and the nurturing of differences among communities that will unleash the murderous rages that pit nations one against the other, to the potential destruction of civilization itself. It is a melodramatic book – though not more so than the reality it was trying to explain. That may suggest, once again, why melodrama is a central expressive mode of the modern world, and why psychoanalysis, in its attempt to explain everything about the way humans behave, including their nightmarish, self-destructive behaviours, becomes itself part of melodramatic discourse.

## Notes

1. Freud, 'On the History of the Psychoanalytic Movement', in *Standard Edition of the Complete Psychological Works*, ed. James Strachey, vol. 14 (London: Hogarth Press, 1957), 13.

2. Freud, *Standard Edition*, vol. 2, 120.
3. Freud, *Standard Edition*, vol. 17, 36.
4. See Brooks, *The Melodramatic Imagination: Balzac, Henry James, Melodrama, and the Mode of Excess*, second edition (New Haven: Yale University Press, 1995 [1976]), 201–2.
5. Freud, *Standard Edition*, vol. 19, 25.
6. See in particular Eric Bentley, 'Melodrama', in *The Life of the Drama* (New York: Atheneum, 1964), 195–218.
7. See my 1995 preface to *The Melodramatic Imagination* (where I acknowledge some of the important critical and theoretical work on this topic), and Brooks, 'Melodrama, Body, Revolution', in *Melodrama: Stage, Picture, Screen*, eds. Jacky Bratton, Jim Cook, and Christine Gledhill (London: British Film Institute, 1994), 11–24.
8. Freud, *Standard Edition*, vol. 7, 77–8.
9. Marcel Proust, *A la recherche du temps perdu*, vol. 1 (Paris: Bibliothèque de la Pléiade, 1987), 163. Translations are my own.
10. Proust, *A la recherche du temps perdu*, vol. 4, 356.
11. *Ibid.*, 406.
12. *Ibid.*
13. Freud, *Standard Edition*, vol. 18, 38.
14. Max Schur, *Freud Living and Dying* (New York: International Universities Press, 1972), 572.
15. Balzac, *La Comédie humaine*, vol. 10 (Paris: Bibliothèque de la Pléiade, 1979), 85. Translations are my own. The best available English translation is *The Fatal Skin*, trans. Atwood Townsend (New York: Signet, 1963).
16. *Ibid.*, 209.
17. *Ibid.*, 210.
18. *Ibid.*, 291–2.
19. Balzac, letter to M. de Montalembert, 25 November 1831, cit. Maurice Allem in his introduction to *La Peau de chagrin* (Paris: Garnier, 1967), vi.
20. Freud, *Standard Edition*, vol. 23, 268.
21. See Roman Jakobson, 'Two Aspects of Language and Two Types of Aphasic Disturbance', in *On Language* (Cambridge: Harvard University Press, 1995), 115–33.
22. Jacques Lacan, 'L'Instance de la letter, ou la raison depuis Freud', in *Écrits* (Paris: Editions du Seuil, 1966), 751. My translation.
23. Freud, *Standard Edition*, vol. 22, 80.
24. Since translation of Lacan is always problematic, involving a considerable interpretation in the rendering, I give here the original French:

> *La chose freudienne:* 'Là où c'était, peut-on dire, là où s'était, voudrions-nous faire qu'on entendît, c'est mon devoir que je vienne à être.'
> *L'instance de la lettre:* 'Là où fut ça, il me faut advenir.'
> *La Science et la vérité:* 'là où c'était, là comme sujet dois-je advenir.'

25. See Freud, *Standard Edition*, vol. 22, 80.

# 19

JULIET JOHN

# Metamodern Melodrama and Contemporary Mass Culture

[M]odern art has typically felt itself to be constructed on, and over, the void, postulating meanings and symbolic systems which have no certain justification because they are backed by no theology and no universally accepted code. . . . There is a desperate effort to renew contact with the scattered ethical and psychic fragments of the Sacred through the representation of fallen reality, insisting that behind reality, hidden by it yet indicated within it, there is a realm where large moral forces are operative. . . . The melodramatic mode can be seen as an intensified, primary, and exemplary version of what the most ambitious art, since the beginnings of Romanticism, has been about.

Peter Brooks, *The Melodramatic Imagination* (1976)[1]

I like to spend my time with kind of feisty people that I also disagree with quite a lot. . . . just a bit of combativeness is a fun thing to be around.

Katie Hopkins ('Britain's Most Hated Woman'), in Series 15 of *Celebrity Big Brother*, Channel 5 (29 January 2015)

A senior academic once asked a doctoral student of my acquaintance how he could be both serious about post-structuralism and a committed football supporter. It was a joke that succeeded in drawing attention to the gap between the student's theoretical belief in a decentred, relative world and the emotional energy he invested in a game structured around a binary battle between two opposing sides, which asks supporters to believe simply in one side or the other. The comment led to soul-searching on the student's part about the consistency and sincerity of his philosophical beliefs, but this essay will argue that the apparently contradictory worldview he espoused is typical rather than exceptional in the age of global mass media, and integral to its workings.

Cultural theory has been heavily influenced in the postmodern era by the idea that an 'incredulity towards meta-narratives' shapes experience and that this scepticism has resulted in what Baudrillard calls a 'loss of the real' – or the replacement of trusted 'truths' or meta-narratives with conflicting and constructed fictions.² The prevailing intellectual assumption in the western academy is that experience is fractured, relative, and multiple and that postmodern consumers are aware of this. Melodrama offers, this essay will argue, an alternative conceptual frame for understanding global structures of feeling and communication. From its stage origins to its broader cultural manifestations, it has been central to popular culture and experience. Melodrama depends on moral polarity and clarity, conflict between good and evil which has its origin in myth and religion, externalized aesthetics which render depths visible, and the elevation of raw emotionalism above the 'mere rationalization' which tends to dominate 'our thin-lipped, thin-blooded culture', in the memorable words of Eric Bentley.³ Its dependence on an almost childlike belief in an essentialized moral universe appears opposed to the logic of postmodernism. This is perhaps one of the reasons why, while there has been a great deal of work on melodrama on screen and stage, its central importance to the workings of the broader contemporary media remains overlooked as an object of serious academic enquiry; this is despite overwhelming evidence of the persistently melodramatic tastes of the mass public and the melodramatic techniques used by media producers.

The relationship between the melodramatic worldview and the postmo-dern is dialectical rather than oppositional, however. The mutually consti-tutive relationship between absolute and relative ideologies has tended to evade even those theorists of 'post-postmodernism' who have sought to reinstate the importance of belief into prevailing intellectual narratives of scepticism or suspicion, but can share with postmodern theorists a binary logic predicated on the assumption that overarching concepts like truth or the real are either credible or they are not. A fine exception to this is Timotheus Vermeulen and Robin van den Akker's concept of metamodern-ism, a term they use to denote the emergence of a new sensibility in the 2000s which oscillates between postmodern (or 'sceptical') and modern (or 'uto-pic') ways of viewing the world, and thus allows for the coexistence of belief and disbelief.⁴ While I see the 'utopic' as pre-modern rather than modern, and would figure the relation between the modern and postmodern as exist-ing on a spectrum, rather than as the kind of opposition that the authors in many ways work to undermine, their identification of a 'metamodern' sen-sibility which incorporates modes of experience that are both whole and fragmented is incisive and enabling, especially for new ways of understand-ing the dynamics of mass media consumption.

My appropriation of the term 'metamodern', however, assumes a dual sensibility which operates as much through double consciousness as through oscillation; I associate the emergence of this sensibility, moreover, with the inception of melodrama, and its relationship with Romanticism, in the late eighteenth century. While Vermeulen and van den Akker claim to be the first academics to observe the re-emergence of a Romantic sensibility in post-millennial culture, they do not acknowledge or understand the history of the twinned relationship between Romanticism and melodrama, or the importance of melodrama to the dual sensibility they identify. It is melodrama, more than Romanticism, which offers, as Peter Brooks argues in the epigraph to this essay, a secular, 'primary' moral vision to a 'post-sacred' age; but it is in the relationship between the two modes that the dialectical metamodern consciousness is born. The familiar omission of melodrama from theoretical narratives has important consequences in terms of skewing the historical frame and rendering intellectually invisible the importance of melodrama to structures of feeling in a mass media age. Melodrama is the modern form of the 'utopic', rooted in the transcendence and belief system of myth, yet born in response to 'the void' of the modern world.

This is nowhere more apparent than in the most popular forms of mass culture: reality television, sport, and tabloid newspapers all offer the public 'a dream world inhabited by dream people and dream justice . . . [a]n idealization and simplification of reality', to quote Michael Booth's well-worn definition of melodrama.[5] My contention is that successful global media exports are all characterized by the techniques, as well as the emotional and ethical structures, of melodrama. As the melodramatic mode always finds its essentialized, primary moral and emotional vision in dialogue with forms of scepticism, it is central to the metamodern sensibility in ways that have gone largely unexplored. And to the extent that it posits a utopic vision that is conscious of the potential 'void' which creates a need for that vision, melodrama is itself metamodern. The metamodern media consumer is required to adopt not simply a Coleridgean 'suspension of disbelief', but a simultaneous suspension and adoption of both belief and disbelief. The most viewed Channel 5 series of the UK version of the global reality TV show *Celebrity Big Brother*, for example, was ostentatiously filtered through the dual lens of metamodern melodrama from the outset, the presenter Emma Willis taking on the role of a fairy-tale narrator and archly announcing, 'Our fairy tale is about to begin. . . . Will they live happily ever after? . . . Fat chance.' In the case of shows like the *Big Brother* franchise, as the concept has evolved and become increasingly fixated on celebrity, the focus has shifted away from relatively ordinary, un-self-conscious contestants whose moral fibre and social sensitivity the audience were asked to judge, to contestants whose business is celebrity, sensation, and manipulation of the relationship between belief and disbelief. To date, there have in fact been more series of *Celebrity Big Brother* than of the original *Big Brother*, though the 'stars' entering the Big Brother house are increasingly minor.

The key contestants in series fifteen of the show were Katie Hopkins, a celebrity often dubbed 'Britain's Most Hated Woman' who has become famous (or notorious) for straight-talking offensiveness on screen as well as in her tabloid column, and Perez Hilton, 'Hollywood's Hottest Celebrity Gossip', as he describes himself.[6] When tasked with writing lyrics for a charity single, their fellow contestants, soul singer Alexander O'Neal and former pop star Kavana, produced the lines: 'Does anybody really know just who I am? Does anybody really care how good I am? Does anybody really care it's all about me?' (12 January 2015). Their words sum up the series' consistent direction to viewers to question appearances. This invitation to cynicism is combined throughout with the encouragement to simple moral judgement. Katie Hopkins is announced as the 'wicked witch', who is well known for 'telling it as it is' (7 January 2015). Thus we have the moral paradox of someone who is seen as bad because she claims to be honest. The audience is encouraged to ask whether she is in fact faking nastiness to further her 'brand' and her newspaper column, and may in fact be both less nasty and less honest than she seems.

Hopkins and Hilton vie for the position of supreme villain in the tabloid coverage of the show, which colludes with the series' framing of itself as a camp fairy tale. At the same time, inside the house, both 'villains' paradoxically vie for the position of moral arbiter by defining themselves as truth tellers in a fabricated celebrity world. In claiming 'I always tell the truth' and espousing transparency, Hopkins claims the moral high ground which she otherwise affects to despise (7 January 2015). She tells viewers that her plan was to be 'consistent' and 'true to myself' (6 February 2015). Transparency is of course normally the hallmark of goodness in melodramatic aesthetics, because it is presumed that sincerity aids community. In claiming that she felt as if she had 'slayed the dragon' when Perez appeared to walk out, she purports to stick up for the vulnerable who do not have the courage to defend themselves against his acid tongue (6 February 2016). Hopkins's archrival from the world outside the house, glamour model and eventual series winner Katie Price, refuses to believe in her claims to honesty: 'You are playing a massive game', she tells her and it is 'all an act' (29 January 2015). Unlike Hopkins, Hilton uses the language of therapy and psychoanalysis to convey his own sincerity: 'I am a work in progress', he claims, 'So much of what I am doing is based out of fear' (8 January 2015; 12 January 2015).

Thus, metamodern melodrama does not abandon the idea of a moral code, but makes the very existence of moral content the dramatic and ethical battleground. Brooks positions psychoanalysis as the 'systematic realization of the melodramatic aesthetic, applied to the structure and dynamic of the mind'.[7] Psychoanalysis is in fact both like and unlike melodrama, in that it looks inward rather than outward for meaning, fetishizing the inner life, and yet the requirement to externalize inner confusion recognizes the health and social benefits of rendering the hidden visible. In a post-sacred era, in western culture at least, the inner life is often positioned as offering substance or depth in a world 'constructed on, and over, the void', to echo Brooks. The language of psychoanalysis is thus regularly invoked in the most popular media products – whether on chat shows like the Oprah Winfrey show, series like *Celebrity Big Brother*, or global talent show franchises like *The X-Factor*, the ability of the individual to communicate his/her emotional and psychological 'journey' to the public is positioned as offering an ethical content which seems as important in selling these shows as talent or celebrity.

In its original incarnation, melodrama was partly a reaction against the individualism of high Romanticism and the 'turn inwards' valorized in nineteenth-century culture.[8] Such is the flexibility of the melodramatic mode, however, that it has metamorphosed to survive, and, indeed, flourish in differing cultures and contexts. It has therefore proved itself to be a uniquely powerful vehicle of mass communication, neutral in itself and ideologically malleable. As such, in contemporary mass culture, melodrama often works to further and celebrate individualism, working in collusion with discourses of psychology and psychoanalysis, for example, which were anathema to its founding elevation of communal values over concern for self. For reality TV villains like Hopkins and Hilton, the idea that they are true to themselves or in touch with themselves is posited, by themselves at least, as a kind of good: the suggestion is that they at least have selves to be true to. To possess 'content' which one is prepared to exhibit, whether good or bad (in terms of an older moral framework), is presented as authentic and courageous in itself. Hopkins describes herself as 'a witch with a heart of stone', but presumes that the public vote for her because she is 'prepared to say what everyone is thinking' (7 January 2015). The implication (echoed by other contestants on this and other reality TV shows) is that honesty, even if it hurts others, is preferable to tact or sensitivity because it preserves the individual's integrity or relationship with his/her own self, even at the cost of relations with others. *Celebrity Big Brother* is more about 'psychological warfare' than 'Roman gladiators', in the words of contestant Ken Morley, evicted for political incorrectness (12 January 2015). In this version of melodrama, goodness is regularly associated with authenticity and individualism, even if the assertion of the self is enabled through battle and conflict which disturbs the collective.

Renée Sgroi voices a frequently held assumption that 'reality TV's use of melodrama produces "authentic" selves with which viewers can engage'.[9]

As reality TV has evolved, however, I would argue that its main driver is no longer primarily the production and consumption of authentic televisual selves, but the interrogation of the idea of the authentic self. This is not to say that viewers all watch reality TV shows in a state of disbelief, but that reality TV produces a double consciousness which tends toward belief and scepticism simultaneously. In the case of shows like *Keeping Up with the Kardashians*, for example, the narrative generated across multi-media platforms is driven, not by the local dramas of this self-made celebrity family, but by the questioning of the 'reality' of reality TV itself. The reality or otherwise of Kim Kardashian's bottom – memorably captured in her front page cover for *Paper* magazine, which aimed to 'break the internet' – symbolizes the invitation to question the concept of authenticity which drives reality TV and celebrity culture more widely.[10] While the theoretical narratives of Vermeulen, van den Akker, and other academic commentators emphasize the increasing role of belief in post-postmodern culture, I would argue that the public has been – and has been encouraged to be – more rather than less sceptical in recent years, partly in response to celebrity culture, yet without abandoning belief. Belief may be gaining more attention in cultural theory, but it has always been foundational in popular cultures across the globe. As so often, cultural narratives generated by the academy are skewed by taking slight notice of public perception.

Metamodern melodrama of all guises in the mass media age revolves around the theme of content versus surface, which is morally inflected. This seems a long way from the stage melodrama of the Romantic and Victorian period, which was predicated on an externalized aesthetic through which surfaces were instantly legible signifiers of moral depths. However, it is crucial to the success of reality TV that the idea of authenticity as a moral good is promoted, however consistently it is interrogated. As Beverley Skeggs and Helen Wood argue, 'it is the connection to the moral . . . that gives reality television some purchase on the social'.[11] At the same time, the ways in which the moral is defined are obviously socially and culturally conditioned. Thus, while series of *Big Brother* across the globe have witnessed sex between housemates (to the extent that viewers have almost come to expect it), explicit sexual acts (like masturbation with a wine bottle), nudity, regular verbal abuse, foul language, alcoholic excess, and aggression bordering on 'warfare' between housemates, in the UK, exclusion from the house has mainly been reserved for those whose politically incorrect language and behaviour violates the show's alignment of itself with an equality and diversity agenda. In 2016, Andrew Tate was evicted for racist tweets; in 2015, Jeremy Jackson was thrown out for exposing Chloe Goodman's breast and cautioned for common assault; and in the same series, Ken Morley was expelled for 'offensive and wholly unacceptable language' after twice using the word 'negro' and for repeatedly announcing his unashamed enjoyment of ogling the female bodies on view. Ken's refusal to see what was wrong with declarations of admiration for women's 'arses' prompted Perez Hilton to warn him, 'If I were you, when I'd leave this house, I'd be afraid for my safety', and Nadia Sawalha to say that she wanted to call the police to remove him (12 January 2015).

Morley is perhaps the most interesting of the evictees, as his offensive behaviour is clearly deliberate and designed to test the moral contradictions of the show, rather than born of ignorance or lack of discipline. While several series have featured a 'type' whose non-PC views are offensive, what differentiates Morley is his adoption of an intellectually formalized position on political correctness, and his deconstruction of the business imperatives underpinning the show's claims to a moral and pedagogic function. He is an anti-PC theorist who seeks to expose the hypocritical or selective moral code of a show which gains viewers partly by encouraging and selling the prospect of sex and bullying, and then affecting to disapprove of it. His sarcastic rant about 'boring boring political correctness, like a latter-day Victorianism' after Jeremy's eviction from the house, is designed to draw attention to what he regards as the intolerant disciplinary politics of a sham show which purports to promote tolerance and inclusivity (11 January 2015). At his departure, while Hopkins complains that people shouldn't get 'censored out of here' and Perez exclaims with melodramatic verve that he feels free of 'cancer' and 'evil', the show's narration milks the situation to announce that Morley's 'exit to left' has left behind 'a nice hot steaming pile of drama' (13 January 2015).

However antipathetic to the values of most viewers, Morley's right-wing critique of the equality and diversity agenda underlying the UK series draws attention to the fact that the central theme of political correctness is the closest it comes to having moral content or commitments, and that the authentic individualism it appears to celebrate is selective. UK *Big Brother* stakes its claim to morality on its protection and promotion of the rights of some marginal and disempowered groups and individuals, functioning in some ways pedagogically to promote its politics. The model of community it creates is a community of individuals which welcomes those who have shown particular courage in expressing their identities in a social environment in which they are subject to discrimination. Its fan base is hugely supportive of LGBT rights, voting Brian Dowling (who went on to become the first openly gay children's TV presenter) the winner of the UK's *Ultimate Big Brother* in 2010, and on several occasions crowning him the favourite *Big Brother* housemate ever. In 2004, Nadia Almada became the first transgender winner of the series; her trans status was kept hidden from her housemates but was relayed to the public, and she won with 74 per cent of the vote.[12] Long-time presenter of the series Davina McCall has confessed that Nadia was her favourite housemate of all time.[13]

Nadia 'single-handedly "saved" the Big Brother franchise', according to Barbara Ellen in the *Observer Magazine*, turning the show into 'a cultural barometer' because she had a 'real story to tell'.[14] The media response to her win, like the more recent coverage of the transitioning of Bruce Jenner into Caitlyn Jenner, was framed as a celebration of the ability of the individual to express or be their true self in public. Like coming-out narratives more broadly, trans narratives adopt and celebrate a melodramatic aesthetic which promotes synonymity between inner and outer selfhood in a social environment that allows for it. There is an essentialist dimension to the popular coverage of coming-out and transitioning stories which coexists interestingly with a seemingly opposed emphasis on what Judith Butler and queer theorists have celebrated as gender performativity. Thus, in Caitlyn Jenner's 2015 confessional interview on *20/20* with Diane Sawyer, the former Olympic gold decathlon champion once regarded as 'a symbol of masculinity as interwoven into American culture as the Marlboro Man' describes herself more than once as having 'the soul of a female'.[15] The essentialism evoked by Jenner is primarily religious (she introduces the concept of a female soul in the context of a semi-humourous opening anecdote about the process God went through in making her) but also psychological ('my brain is much more female than it is male'). Her neglected adult daughter Cassandra later comments, in the extended piece in *Vanity Fair* on Caitlyn Jenner's transition (with photos by Annie Liebowitz), that she feels like Jenner was a better parent when [s]he was 'moving towards his [sic] authentic self', also described by her as 'his true identity'.[16] The paradox of 'moving towards' or creating what you actually are is re-emphasized by a tearful Leibowitz, who claims that during the photo shoot, 'I felt like I saw the making of Caitlyn', and by the closing emphasis on Cassandra's reaction to hearing Caitlyn speak: 'she saw a vulnerability and authenticity she had never experienced before'.[17]

James Bennett argues rightly that celebrity culture tends to emphasize an 'entrepreneurial self'; however, this entrepreneurship or performativity often co-exists with an emphasis on essences which is foregrounded in the popular media but downplayed in academic discourse.[18] The extraordinary story of Caitlyn Jenner distils the contradictions of metamodern melodrama, not simply because her gender dysphoria led a person once dubbed 'the greatest athlete in the world' to undermine the moral integrity associated with the Olympic ideal by living a life of lies. Jenner was an object of fascination even before her transitioning, because her role as the emasculated, comic father figure in the long-running reality TV series, *Keeping Up with the Kardashians* had taken her so far away from her former Olympian image, into the nether regions of reality TV at its most commercial, and celebrity culture at its most decadent. At her transitioning, there were thus many who were sceptical that this was yet another story to boost publicity for the reality show or a spin-off. *Variety* magazine focused less on the question of authenticity than on the sophisticated media operation orchestrated by Jenner to allow for her decision to transition to be received, like an old-style melodrama, as a triumph of truth over dissembling. Both the Sawyer 20/20 interview special and the *Vanity Fair* cover were described by *Variety* as part of a 'masterful' media campaign strategized by Alan Nierob, 'a seasoned showbiz publicist and longtime exec at Rogers & Cowan' who had previously 'handled crisis PR for some of Hollywood's biggest names including Robert Downey Jr. and Mel Gibson'.[19] It is perhaps inevitable in the age of global media that even the most genuine and personal announcement by a major celebrity would need to be carefully thought through, even staged. One of the positive outcomes of Caitlyn Jenner's successful PR campaign was that she was awarded the Arthur Ashe Courage Award at ESPN's ESPY (Excellence in Sports Performance and Achievements) awards in July 2015. The award had previously been awarded to Muhammad Ali, Nelson Mandela, and Billie Jean King, and is made for contributions which transcend sport. After initially realizing fame as an American 'supercharged hero' who appeared to embody all the moral virtues claimed by the Olympics and 1970s America, and a subsequent long period of appearing to deconstruct her heroic image as athlete, Jenner reconstructed herself as Caitlyn Jenner, a very different kind of hero.[20] Jenner's life had not so much turned full circle as given the circle a twist.

It is Jenner's past as an iconic sporting hero which makes her unusual story extraordinary, destabilizing not just gender codes but media narratives and genres. While the media representation of celebrity culture shares with that of the transgender community a focal concern with the relationship between essence or reality and show or performativity, the popular presentation of the cultural value of sport focuses on its purist claims to uphold and further simple moral values at odds with the ethical relativism of postmodernity. Sports rhetoric embraces an undiluted version of the melodramatic mode in its celebration of heroism, its elevation of passion, its dependence on excess, its demands that athletes project themselves truthfully, its expulsion and demonization of those who do not follow collective rules, and lastly its persistent promotion of un-cynical spectatorship. Strikingly, this melodramatic frame persists even in the face of its obvious violation. Perhaps most notoriously, Lance Armstrong, once the all-American hero, is now pilloried as villain for betraying the dream he seemed to represent. The rise and fall of Oscar Pistorius inflects so many characteristics of melodrama through the global media lens that it could not have been scripted if it had not been real. The same could be said of the fall of the erstwhile American football hero, O. J. Simpson.

Whatever the reality of the multibillion dollar industry that is sport today, sport is one area which rejects the archness of reality TV and other areas of mass entertainment. Dependent on Olympian ideals and ancient heroic myths, sports broadcasting harnesses melodramatic techniques originally designed to communicate to diverse audiences in large theatres, in the service of the global communication of utopic dreams to diverse publics. It offers 'audiences the fulfilment and satisfaction found only in dreams ... an allegory of human experience dramatically ordered, [a world] as it should be rather than it is'.[21] Jenner's explanation to Buzz Bissinger, in *Vanity Fair*, of why she 'became determined in sports' echoes Booth's language: Bruce Jenner had pursued sport not only 'because he was gifted, but also because it helped to prove his masculinity, since, as he told me, "that's what everybody wants to believe"'.[22]

What is striking about Jenner's description of her desire to give herself and the public the fairy tale that she believed to be a product of the collective will is its similarity to Lance Armstrong's explanation of his own motivation for cheating so ruthlessly in the sport of cycling over so many years. One of the more credible parts of his confessional interview with Oprah Winfrey comes when he tries to explain the psychological state he was in during his career of lies – specifically the stories he told himself and came to believe.[23] Much has been written about Armstrong's individual psychology and life story, but much less about the interplay between his distinctive psyche and the cultural narratives which surround sport. 'This story was so perfect for so long', Armstrong says in the language of a literary critic:

> And I mean that ... as I try to take myself out of the situation, and I look at it. You overcome the disease, you win the Tour de France seven times, you have a happy marriage, you have children, I mean it's just the mythic, perfect story.

When Oprah asks if it was 'hard to live up to that picture', Armstrong describes himself, again in literary terms as 'a flawed character' (as opposed to a flawed person). His response to Oprah's pointed question, 'Didn't you help paint that [perfect] picture?' is fascinating in its analysis of the powerful interaction of spin and the will to believe in the making of media myths. While on the one hand conceding that the blame for painting a false picture was his, on the other, he explains that 'a lot of people' helped to create and sustain the story:

Behind that picture and behind that story was momentum. Whether it's fans or whether it's the media, it just gets going and I lost myself in all that.

It would be easy to write off what Armstrong says here as a form of moral evasion, but his explication of the dynamics of modern sporting myths is sophisticated and, in general terms, accurate. Modern sporting narratives are melodramas built on the structures and values of myth and circulated to the public via the mass media. What is interesting is that such stories of heroism, extraordinary feats, raw passion and the triumph of virtue over adversity, still have traction in an age of virtual reality where sophistication about appearances always verges on scepticism. Armstrong's will to win is often linked to the pursuit of money and a dominant ego, but another consistently dominant driver for most sportsmen and women, cheats or not, is the desire to inhabit an heroic role in the eyes of others, to take their place in 'the mythic, perfect story'. The drive to live the dream is propelled by the longing to believe in the dream and sustain it, for competitors, sports fans, and indeed cultures across space and time. One of the most succinct and incisive analyses of Armstrong's ability to succeed in perpetuating a lie for so long comes from Alastair Campbell, Tony Blair's spin doctor-in-chief and author of *Winners: And How They Succeed* (2015). 'The reason Armstrong was able to live his lie for so long was', Campbell argues, because 'so many people wanted it to be true. Partly it was the cancer survival story. But it was also the desire people have to celebrate specialness in sport'.[24]

By all accounts, Armstrong had a genuine belief in his own 'specialness' from his early days. His rise to become a 'cycling superman' was thus no doubt at some level the fulfilment of a narcissistic narrative that he had predetermined but it was also the product of a psyche steeped in melodramatic narratives about exceptionalism, excess, pushing boundaries, fighting all comers, and victory against the odds.[25] Armstrong's understanding of stories plays into his undoubted media and business skills, but his relationship to narrative is not always that of the detached cynic. He talks often of his ability to 'control the narrative' but less often about his tendency to live and control stories simultaneously, perhaps because the living is not always in his control. Those admirers of Armstrong who remain are swayed not just by his argument that doping was endemic in cycling but by the verve and excess with which he inhabited the lie: there is a reckless courage about this which positions Armstrong as extraordinary, even if this extraordinariness is that of a sociopath or anti-hero. The novelist and sportswriter Benjamin Markovits captures the strange lack of surprise that greeted the eventual and categorical exposure of Armstrong. Confessing to personal reasons for liking Armstrong, who had helped his brother-in-law get the same pioneering cancer treatment that had saved Armstrong himself, Markovits muses after some praise for this generosity:

> But if you'd asked me even while all this was going on if Armstrong had doped for his seven Tour wins, I think I would have answered: 'Probably'. One of the curious features of the recent series of revelations is that they haven't really changed the way people see him. ... Revelations are supposed to shock us into revaluations – in this case all that's happened is that we've had some of our almost-certainties confirmed.[26]

While it is doubtful that all fans would share Markovits' calm sense of resigned scepticism, there can be few who followed Armstrong's story and the media narratives attending it without to some degree adopting the kind of double consciousness that Markovits describes. Armstrong was always one of the most openly suspected sportsmen of all time, not least by his nemesis, the *Sunday Times* sportswriter David Walsh, who doggedly pursued the truth about him in the face of bullying and intimidation over many years. What is most interesting from a broader cultural perspective about Walsh's book detailing his obsessive pursuit of the cyclist, however, is not so much the detail or eventual exposure but the melodramatic worldview that the adversaries share. The subject of Walsh's *Seven Deadly Sins* is not just Armstrong but the role of romance and fairy tale in the sports business.[27] Like Armstrong, Walsh points to a collusion between the drug cheat 'hero', the media, and sometimes the fans in producing a fake fairy tale. His story is as much his own as Armstrong's, a story of a journalistic triumph of virtue over adversity, and of heroism over villainy. While he dismantles Armstrong's claims to extraordinariness, sources like Betsy Andreu and Emma O'Reilly are rendered unambiguously heroic.

This is not to undermine Walsh's moral claims – after all, Armstrong foisted a lie on the public while Walsh sought to expose it – but it is to demonstrate that both hunter and prey were enmeshed in a metamodern melodrama centred on the relationship between belief and disbelief. Armstrong and Walsh are well matched in their grasp of the unusual combination of commerce and myth which propels the sports industry, with Walsh reminding readers, for example, that the Tour de France was established in order to sell newspapers and that the media perpetuates its romance. The Tour was the product of 'the imagination of journalists' who are 'sentimental creatures', and 'the success of the Tour is built on emotion and memory'.[28] The paradox of sport in the modern era is that while it holds firm to a purist *raison d'être*, it is also a global form of mass entertainment, subject to the mechanisms of a media whose portability depends on money and image. Doping is of course sport's most publicized doppelgänger, shadowing its claims to moral purity so determinedly that the relationship between cheating and fair play threatens to become the drama which over-shadows all sporting dramas. But doping is perhaps as much effect as cause of the corruption in sport, the inevitable result of the business of selling stories of sporting glory which travel as widely as possible. It is the product of the increasingly melodramatic taste for spectacle and sensation which gained impetus in the need to be legible and audible to huge audiences in the large theatres and audiences of the nineteenth century, and has evolved in an increasingly capitalist context.

This essay has emphasized the role of melodrama as a form of belief expressed in the mass media and the symbiotic relationship of belief with forms of scepticism. 'It is as children and dreamers ... that we enjoy melodrama', as Eric Bentley argues; melodrama can thus offer us a conduit to innocence, an affective experience of 'monopathy' or emotional wholeness, to quote Robert Heilman.[29] Melodrama has, however, another function, and that is, paradoxically, to operate as a signifier of superficiality. A mode which uses surfaces transparently to signify depths can work to render an intensified experience of large moral forces, as captured in Brooks's wonderful description of melodrama as 'the expressionism of the moral imagination'.[30] But if there is a synonymity between surfaces and depths, logic also dictates that there may be no such thing as depths. This goes some way to explaining what Barbara Klinger calls 'the particular affinities between melodrama and a mass camp sensibility'.[31]

Melodrama developed in step with the mass market for culture, the staple fodder of large theatres catering to working-class audiences with little education who wanted the effect of their entertainment to be immediate and intense. The array of strategies it developed as a result, with their emphasis on surface, spectacle, emotion, and sensation, thus equipped it to survive and thrive in the mass media age of image and sound bites. Its projected moral purity is in many ways the product of 'post-sacred' realities and impurities. It is thus always potentially a dialectical mode, containing within itself that negotiation between content and surface which provides the international mass media with its central melodrama.

It is tempting to conclude that metamodern melodrama is the representative form of post-postmodernity, a mode which brings together belief and disbelief, authenticity and performativity, surface and depth. But the truth is that melodrama's internal and external entanglement with discourses of scepticism is nothing new; it has been part of melodrama's history since its inception. Although Peter Brooks has described melodrama as 'a central fact of the modern sensibility', even his own attempt to position melodrama centre stage at times unintentionally replicates the cultural subordination of melodrama to twinned modes like Romanticism and psychoanalysis familiar in dominant cultural histories and theories.[32] It thus remains marginal to cultural maps of modernity, rendering its status as a central 'fact' of the modern sensibility more dependent on popular experience than on the written cultural histories which tend to establish such 'facts'. The evolution of the global mass media and the changed cultural and economic dynamics which have allowed for them should make the centrality of melodrama to transnational ways of understanding and communicating too obvious for melodrama to remain at the margins of academic cultural histories and theories. Donald Trump's rise to the presidency, to end with an unavoidable recent example of a global mass media phenomenon, would have been less of a surprise if the cultural commentators who Trump likes to label the liberal elite had possessed a better understanding of melodrama's power as a populist tool of mass communication. Harnessing melodramatic techniques like exaggeration, sensation, and the play of moral absolutes to social media platforms like Twitter, Trump has managed to promote himself to many as authentic and straight-talking while at the same time running roughshod over truth in the pursuit of power. Experiencing and projecting himself as a theatrical character, he personifies the doubleness of metamodern melodrama. Moreover, he understands and exploits the dual sensibility which leads his supporters to accept his fictions as truths while at the same time knowing and accepting that they may not be. He understands, moreover, the media's appetite for entertainment in politics which can make the news – and make the news commercially successful.

Trump's strategies take us back to Thomas Holcroft, the founding father of British melodrama, whose stated aim was 'to fix the attention, rouse the passions, and hold the faculties in anxious and impatient suspense'.[33] Since Holcroft imported the genre from France to Britain in the Romantic period, melodrama has offered the post-sacred world across countries and continents the reassurance of a worldview 'postulating meanings'; but melodrama also contains within itself a dialectical sense of the void necessitating those postulations. It is this tension that has always been a 'central fact of the modern sensibility', though it has played out increasingly melodramatically in the modern mass media.

## Notes

1. Peter Brooks, *The Melodramatic Imagination: Balzac, Henry James, Melodrama, and the Mode of Excess*, second edition (New Haven: Yale University Press, 1995 [1976]), 21–2.

2. Jean-Francois Lyotard, *The Postmodern Condition: A Report on Knowledge* (1979); Jean Baudrillard, *Simulacra and Simulation* (1981). There has of course been highly influential work on the way in which collective belief is structured, by Benedict Anderson and Lauren Berlant among others, but the keynote of the dominant narratives of postmodernism has been scepticism.

3. Eric Bentley, *The Life of the Drama* (New York: Atheneum, 1964), 198.

4. Timotheus Vermeulen and Robin van den Akker, 'Notes on Metamodernism', *Journal of Aesthetics and Culture*, 2 (2010): 12.

5. Booth, *English Melodrama* (London: Herbert Jenkins, 1965), 14.

6. http://perezhilton.com, accessed 30 July 2016.

7. Brooks, *The Melodramatic Imagination*, 22.

8. See my *Dickens's Villains: Melodrama, Character, Popular Culture* (Oxford: Oxford University Press, 2001), 1–48.

9. 'Authentic Reality TV Selves: The Case for Melodrama', in *Television, Aesthetics and Reality*, ed. Anthony Barker (Cambridge: Cambridge Scholars Press, 2006), 225.

10. *Paper* (Winter 2014), http://papermagshop.com/collections/frontpage/products/phase-2-break-the-internet-double-issue-2014, accessed 30 July 2016.

11. *Reacting to Reality Television: Performance, Audience and Value* (London: Routledge, 2012), 26.

12. Barbara Ellen, 'The more people criticised, the stronger I became', *Observer Magazine, The Guardian* (22 August 2004), www.theguardian.com/theobserver/2004/aug/22/features.review17, accessed 30 July 2016.

13. Ann Gripper, 'Davina McCall says she won't be crying for end of Big Brother', *The Mirror* (1 June 2010), www.mirror.co.uk/tv/tv-news/davina-mccall-says-she-wont-be-crying-225566, accessed 30 July 2016.

14. *Ibid.*

15. Buzz Bissinger, 'Caitlyn Jenner: The Full Story', *Vanity Fair*, www.vanityfair.com/hollywood/2015/06/caitlyn-jenner-bruce-cover-annie-leibovitz, accessed 30 July 2016; '*Bruce Jenner: The Interview, ABC News*' 20/20 (24 April 2015), http://abcnews.go.com/2020/fullpage/bruce-jenner-the-interview-30471558, accessed 30 July 2016.

16. Buzz Bissinger, 'Caitlyn Jenner: The Full Story'.

17. *Ibid.*

18. James Bennett, *Television Personalities: Stardom and the Small Screen* (London: Routledge, 2011). Bennett taps into work influenced by Michel Foucault's idea of the 'entrepreneur of the self' in *The Birth of Biopolitics; Lectures at the Collège de France, 1978–79*, translated by Graham Burchell (New York: Palgrave Macmillan, 2008), 226.

19. Cynthia Littleton, 'The Secret Mastermind behind Caitlyn Jenner's Transformation' (5 June 2015), *Variety*, http://variety.com/2015/tv/news/bruce-jenner-caitlyn-jenner-transition-new-york-times-story-1201513335, accessed 30 July 2016.

20. Buzz Bissinger, 'Caitlyn Jenner: The Full Story'.

21. Booth, *English Melodrama*, 14.

22. Buzz Bissinger, 'Caitlyn Jenner: The Full Story'.

23. 'Lance Armstrong: The Worldwide Exclusive' (Parts 1 and 2), *Oprah's Next Chapter, Oprah Winfrey Network* (17 and 18 January 2013).

24. 'Lance Armstrong liked to play the long game, David Walsh has played even longer, and won' (20 January 2013), *Alastair's Blog*, www.alastaircampbell.org/blog/2013/01/20/lance-armstrong-liked-to-play-the-long-game-david-walsh-has-played-even-longer-and-won, accessed 30 July 2015.
25. Alex Gibney (Director), *The Armstrong Lie* (Sony, 2013).
26. Benjamin Markovits, 'In Defence of Lance Armstrong', *LRB Blog, London Review of Books* (21 January 2013), www.lrb.co.uk/blog/2013/01/21/benjamin-markovits/in-defence-of-lance-armstrong, accessed 30 July 2016.
27. David Walsh, *Seven Deadly Sins: My Pursuit of Lance Armstrong* (London: Simon & Schuster, 2012).
28. *Ibid.*, 46.
29. Bentley, *The Life of the Drama*, 204; Robert Heilman, *Tragedy and Melodrama: Versions of Experience* (Seattle: University of Washington Press, 1968), 243.
30. Brooks, *The Melodramatic Imagination*, 55.
31. Barbara Klinger, *Melodrama and Meaning: History, Culture and the Films of Douglas Sirk* (Bloomington: Indiana University Press, 1994), xix.
32. Brooks, *The Melodramatic Imagination*, 21; John, *Dickens's Villains*, 46–8.
33. Preface to *A Tale of Mystery* (13 November 1802, Covent Garden); quoted by Joseph Donohue, *Theatre in the Age of Kean* (Oxford: Blackwell, 1975), 106, from the playbill at the Henry E. Huntington library.

# GUIDE TO FURTHER READING

## Primary Sources: Selected Anthologies

Booth, Michael (ed.). *English Plays of the Nineteenth Century Volume 1: Drama 1800–1850 and Volume 2: Drama 1850–1900*. Oxford: Clarendon Press, 1969.

—— (ed.). *Hiss the Villain: Six English and American Melodramas*. London: Eyre and Spottiswoode, 1964.

—— (ed.). *The Lights O'London and Other Plays*. Oxford: Oxford University Press, 1995.

—— (ed.). *The Magistrate and Other Nineteenth-Century Plays*. Oxford: Oxford University Press, 1974.

Cox, Jeffrey (ed.). *Seven Gothic Dramas, 1789–1825*. Athens: Ohio University Press, 1992.

Davis, Tracy C. (ed.). *The Broadview Anthology of Nineteenth-Century British Performance*. Peterborough: Broadview Press, 2012.

Franceschina, John (ed.). *Sisters of Gore: Gothic Melodramas by British Women*. New York: Routledge, 2000.

Rowell, George (ed.). *Nineteenth Century Plays*. Oxford: Oxford University Press, 1972.

Smith, James L. (ed.). *Victorian Melodramas: Seven English, French and American Melodramas*. London: J. M. Dent, 1976.

Wischusen, Stephen (ed.). *The Hour of One: Six Gothic Melodramas*. London: Gordon Fraser Gallery, 1975.

*The Victorian Play Project*. http://victorian.nuigalway.ie/modx/.

## Secondary Sources

Andrin, Muriel, Anne Gailly, and Dominique Nasta (eds.). *Le mélodrame filmique revisité / Revisiting Film Melodrama*. Brussels: Peter Lang, 2014.

Archer, William. *Masks or Faces? A Study in the Psychology of Acting*. London: Longmans, 1888.

Astbury, Katherine. 'Music in Pixérécourt's Early Melodramas'. *Melodramatic Voices: Understanding Music Drama*. Ed. Sarah Hibberd. Farnham: Ashgate, 2011. 15–26.

Aston, Elaine, and Ian Clarke. 'The Dangerous Woman of Melvillean Melodrama'. *New Theatre Quarterly*, 12 (1996). 30–42.

Backscheider, Paula. *Spectacular Politics: Theatrical Power and Mass Culture in Early Modern England*. Baltimore: Johns Hopkins University Press, 1993.

Baer, Marc. *Theatre and Disorder in Late Georgian London*. Oxford: Clarendon Press, 1992.

Barker, Clive. 'The Audiences of the Britannia Theatre, Hoxton'. *Theatre Quarterly*, 9 (1979). 27–41.

Bartley, J. O. *Teague, Shenkin and Sawney: Being an Historical Study of the Earliest Irish, Welsh and Scottish Characters in English Plays*. Cork: Cork University Press, 1954.

Bentley, Eric. *The Life of the Drama*. New York: Atheneum, 1964.

Berlant, Lauren. *The Female Complaint: The Unfinished Business of Sentimentality in American Culture*. Durham: Duke University Press, 2008.

Block, Geoffrey. *Enchanted Evenings: The Broadway Musical From* Showboat *to* Sondheim and Lloyd Webber. Second edition. Oxford: Oxford University Press, 2009.

Boaden, James. *Memoirs of the Life of John Philip Kemble*. 2 vols. London: Longman, Hurst, Rees, Orme, Brown, and Green, 1825.

Booth, Michael. 'A Defence of Nineteenth-century English Drama'. *Educational Theatre Journal*, 26 (1974). 5–13.

*English Melodrama*. London: Herbert Jenkins, 1965.

'New Technology in the Victorian Theatre'. *Theatre Notebook*, 46 (1992). 122–36.

'Soldiers of the Queen, Drury Lane Imperialism'. *Melodrama: The Cultural Emergence of a Genre*. Eds. Michael Hays and Anastasia Nikolopoulou. New York: St. Martin's Press, 1996. 3–20.

*Theatre in the Victorian Age*. Cambridge: Cambridge University Press, 1991.

*Victorian Spectacular Theatre 1850–1910*. London: Routledge & Kegan Paul, 1981.

Bordwell, David. 'Happily Ever After, Part II'. *The Velvet Light Trap*, 19 (1982). 2–7.

Bradby, David, Louis James, and Bernard Sharratt (eds.). *Performance and Politics in Popular Drama: Aspects of Popular Entertainment in Theatre, Film and Television*. Cambridge: Cambridge University Press, 1980.

Bratton, Jacky. *The Making of the West End Stage: Marriage, Management and the Mapping of Gender in London, 1830–1870*. Cambridge: Cambridge University Press, 2011.

*New Readings in Theatre History*. Cambridge: Cambridge University Press, 2003.

'Romantic Melodrama'. *The Cambridge Companion to British Theatre, 1730–1830*. Ed. Jane Moody and Daniel O'Quinn. Cambridge: Cambridge University Press, 2007. 115–27.

Bratton, Jacky, Jim Cook, and Christine Gledhill (eds.). *Melodrama: Stage, Picture, Screen*. London: British Film Institute, 1994.

'The Contending Discourses of Melodrama'. *Melodrama: Stage, Picture, Screen*. Eds. Jacky Bratton, Jim Cook, and Christine Gledhill. London: British Film Institute, 1994. 11–24.

Bratton, J. S. 'British Heroism and the Structure of Melodrama'. *Acts of Supremacy: The British Empire and the Stage, 1790–1930*. Manchester: Manchester University Press, 1991. 18–61.

Bratton, J. S., Richard Allen Cave, Breandan Gregory, Heidi J. Holder, and Michael Pickering. *Acts of Supremacy: The British Empire and the Stage, 1790–1930*. Manchester: Manchester University Press, 1991.

Brewster, Benjamin, and Lea Jacobs. *Theatre to Cinema: Stage Pictorialism and the Early Feature Film*. Oxford: Oxford University Press, 1997.

Briggs, Asa. 'The Language of "Class" in Early Nineteenth Century England'. *Essays in Labour History*. Ed. Asa Briggs and John Saville. London: Macmillan, 1960. 43–73.

Brooks, Peter. *The Melodramatic Imagination: Balzac, Henry James, Melodrama, and the Mode of Excess*. Second edition. New Haven: Yale University Press, 1995 [1976].

Buckley, Matthew. 'The Formation of Melodrama'. *The Oxford Handbook to the Georgian Stage*. Eds. Julia Swindells and David Taylor. Oxford: Oxford University Press, 2014.

(ed.). *Modern Drama*, 55 (2012). Special issue on melodrama.

'Refugee Theatre: Melodrama and Modernity's Loss'. *Theatre Journal*, 61 (2009). 175–90.

'Sensations of Celebrity: Jack Sheppard and the Mass Audience'. *Victorian Studies*, 44 (2002). 423–63.

*Tragedy Walks the Streets: The French Revolution in the Making of Modern Drama*. Baltimore: Johns Hopkins University Press, 2006.

Burwick, Frederick. *British Drama of the Industrial Revolution*. Cambridge: Cambridge University Press, 2015.

*Illusion and the Drama: Critical Theory of the Enlightenment and the Romantic Era*. University Park: Pennsylvania State University Press, 2010.

*Romantic Drama: Acting and Reacting*. Cambridge: Cambridge University Press, 2009.

Cannadine, David. *Class in Britain*. New Haven and London: Yale University Press, 1998.

Clark, Anna. 'The Politics of Seduction in English Popular Culture, 1748–1848'. *The Progress of Romance: The Politics of Popular Fiction*. Ed. Jean Radford. London: Routledge and Kegan Paul, 1986.

Cockett, Stephen. 'Acting with Music: Henry Irving's Use of the Musical Score in His Production of The Bells'. *Europe, Empire and Spectacle in Nineteenth-Century British Music*. Eds. Rachel Cowgill and Julian Rushton. Aldershot: Ashgate Press, 2006. 235–48.

Cockrell, Dale. *Demons of Disorder: Early Blackface Minstrels and their World*. Cambridge: Cambridge University Press, 1997.

Cox, Jeffrey N. *Romanticism in the Shadow of War: Literary Culture in the Napoleonic War Years*. Cambridge: Cambridge University Press, 2014.

'The Ideological Tack of Nautical Melodrama'. *Melodrama: The Cultural Emergence of a Genre*. Eds. Michael Hays and Anastasia Nikolopoulou. New York: St. Martin's Press, 1996. 167–90.

Crone, Rosalind. *Violent Victorians: Popular Entertainment in Nineteenth-Century London*. Manchester: Manchester University Press, 2012.

Cross, Gilbert B. *Next Week – East Lynne: Domestic Drama in Performance, 1820–1874*. Lewisburg: Bucknell University Press, 1977.

Davis, Jim. *Comic Acting and Portraiture in Late-Georgian and Regency England.* Cambridge: Cambridge University Press, 2015.

'Melodrama On and Off the Stage'. *The Oxford Handbook of Victorian Literary Culture.* Ed. Juliet John. Oxford: Oxford University Press, 2014. 686–701.

'The Empire Right or Wrong: Boer War Melodrama on the Australian Stage, 1899-1901'. *Melodrama: The Cultural Emergence of a Genre.* Eds. Michael Hays and Anastasia Nikolopoulou. New York: St. Martin's Press, 1996. 21–37.

(ed.). *The Britannia Diaries 1863–75: Selections from the Diaries of Frederick C. Wilton.* London: Society for Theatre Research, 1992.

'The Gospel of Rags: Melodrama at the Britannia, 1863–74', *New Theatre Quarterly,* 7 (1991). 369–89.

'British Bravery or Tars Triumphant'. *New Theatre Quarterly,* 4 (1988). 122–43.

Davis, Jim, and Victor Emeljanow. *Reflecting the Audience: London Theatregoing, 1840–1880.* Iowa City: University of Iowa Press, 2001.

Davis, Tracy C. *Actresses as Working Women: Their Social Identity in Victorian Culture.* London and New York: Routledge, 1991.

(ed.). *The Broadview Anthology of Nineteenth-Century British Performance.* Peterborough: Broadview Press, 2012.

*The Economics of the British Stage, 1800–1914.* Cambridge: Cambridge University Press, 2000.

Davis, Tracy C., and Peter Holland (eds.). *The Performing Century: Nineteenth-Century Theatre's History.* New York: Palgrave Macmillan, 2007.

Davis, Tracy C., and Thomas Postlethwaite (eds.). *Theatricality.* Cambridge: Cambridge University Press, 2003.

Davis, Tracy C., and Ellen Donkin (eds.). *Women and Playwriting in Nineteenth-Century Britain.* Cambridge: Cambridge University Press, 1999.

Decker, Todd. *Show Boat: Performing Race in an American Musical.* Oxford: Oxford University Press, 2013.

DeLong, Kenneth. 'Arthur Sullivan's Incidental Music to Henry Irving's Production of *Macbeth* (1888)'. *Henry Irving: A Re-Evaluation of the Pre-eminent Victorian Actor-Manager.* Ed. Richard Foulkes. Burlington: Ashgate Publishing, 2008. 149–84.

Diamond, Michael. *Victorian Sensation: Or, the Spectacular, the Shocking and the Scandalous in Nineteenth-Century Britain.* London: Anthem Press, 2003.

Diderot, Denis. *The Paradox of Acting.* Trans. Walter Herries Pollock. London: Chatto and Windus, 1883.

Disher, Maurice Willson. *Blood and Thunder: Mid-Victorian Melodrama and Its Origins.* London: Muller, 1949.

Donohue, Joseph (ed.). *The Cambridge History of British Theatre, Volume 2: 1660 to 1895.* Cambridge: Cambridge University Press, 2004.

Duckett, Victoria. *Seeing Sarah Bernhardt: Performance and Silent Film.* Urbana: University of Illinois Press, 2015.

Eisenstein, Sergei. 'Dickens, Griffith, and the Film Today'. *Film Form.* New York: Harcourt, Brace, 1949.

Elsaesser, Thomas. 'Tales of Sound and Fury: Observations on the Family Melodrama'. *Home Is Where the Heart Is: Studies in Melodrama and the Woman's Film.* Ed. Christine Gledhill. London: British Film Institute, 1987. 43–69.

Guide to Further Reading

Eltis, Sos. *Acts of Desire: Women and Sex on Stage, 1800–1930*. Oxford: Oxford University Press, 2013.
Emeljanow, Victor. *Victorian Popular Dramatists*. Boston: Twayne Publishers, 1987.
Estill, Robin. 'The *Factory Lad*: Melodrama as Propaganda'. *Theatre Quarterly*, 1 (1971). 22–6.
Evans, Bertrand. *Gothic Drama from Walpole to Shelley*. Berkeley and Los Angeles: University of California Press, 1947.
Fisher, Judith L. 'The "Sensation Scene" in Charles Dickens and Dion Boucicault'. *Dramatic Dickens*. Ed. Carol Hanbery MacKay. New York: Palgrave Macmillan, 1989. 152–67.
Fitzball, Edward. *Thirty-Five Years of a Dramatic Author's Life*. London: Newby, 1839.
Fitzgerald, Percy. *The World Behind the Scenes*. London: Chatto and Windus, 1881.
Frank, Frederick. *The Origins of the Modern Study of Gothic Drama*. Lewiston: Edwin Mellen Press, 2006.
Frank, Marcie (ed.). *Criticism*, 35 (2013). Special issue on melodrama.
Gaines, Jane M. 'Even More Tears: The Historical Time Theory of Melodrama'. *Melodrama Unbound*. Eds. Christine Gledhill and Linda Williams. New York: Columbia University Press, 2018. 325–39.
    '*4 Months, 3 Weeks, and 2 Days*. Where is Marxism in Melodrama Theory?' *Le mélodrama filmique revisité / Revisiting Film Melodrama*. Eds. Muriel Andrin, Anne Gailly, and Dominique Nasta. Brussels: Peter Lang, 2014. 277–91.
Garcia, Gustave. *The Actor's Art*. Second edition. London: Simpkin, Marshall & Co., 1888.
Gardner, Vivien and Susan Rutherford (eds.) *The New Woman and Her Sisters: Feminism and Theatre, 1850–1914*. Ann Arbor: University of Michigan Press, 1992.
Garlington, Aubrey S. '"Gothic" Literature and Dramatic Music in England'. *Journal of the American Musicological Society*, 15 (1962). 48–64.
Gerould, Daniel (ed.). *Melodrama*. New York: New York Literary Forum, 1980.
    'Melodrama and Revolution'. *Melodrama: Stage, Picture, Screen*. Eds. Jacky Bratton, Jim Cook, and Christine Gledhill. London: British Film Institute, 1994. 185–98.
Gledhill, Christine (ed.). *Gender Meets Genre in Postwar Cinemas*. Urbana: University of Illinois Press, 2012.
    (ed.). *Home Is Where the Heart Is: Studies in Melodrama and the Woman's Film*. London: British Film Institute, 1987.
    'Rethinking Genre'. *Reinventing Film Studies*. Eds. Christine Gledhill and Linda Williams. London: Arnold, 2000. 219–43.
Gledhill, Christine and Linda Williams (eds.). *Melodrama Unbound*. New York: Columbia University Press, 2018.
Glenn, George D. 'Nautical "Docudrama" in the Age of the Kembles'. *When They Weren't Doing Shakespeare: Essays on Nineteenth-Century British and American Theatre*. Eds. Judith L. Fisher and Stephen Watt. Athens: University of Georgia Press, 1989. 137–51.
Goldberg, Jonathan. *Melodrama: An Aesthetics of Impossibility*. Durham: Duke University Press, 2016.

309

Gould, Marty. *Nineteenth-Century Theatre and the Imperial Encounter*. London: Routledge, 2011.

Graziano, John. 'Invisible Instruments: Theater Orchestras in New York, 1850–1900'. *American Orchestras in the Nineteenth Century*. Ed. John Spitzer. Chicago: University of Chicago Press, 2012. 109–29.

Hadley, Elaine. *Melodramatic Tactics: Theatricalized Dissent in the English Marketplace, 1800–1885*. Stanford: Stanford University Press, 1995.

Haggerty, Sheryllynne. *Merely for Money: Business Culture in the British Atlantic, 1750–1815*. Oxford: Oxford University Press, 2012.

Hambridge, Katherine and Jonathan Hicks (eds.). *The Melodramatic Moment, 1790–1820*. Chicago: University of Chicago Press, 2018.

Hays, Michael and Anastasia Nikolopoulou (eds.). *Melodrama: The Cultural Emergence of a Genre*. New York: St. Martin's Press, 1996.

Heilman, Robert. *Tragedy and Melodrama: Versions of Experience*. Seattle: University of Washington Press, 1968.

Hibberd, Sarah (ed.). *Melodramatic Voices: Understanding Music Drama*. Farnham: Ashgate, 2011.

Hibbert, H. G. *Fifty Years of a Londoner's Life*. London: Grant Richards, Ltd., 1916.

Holder, Heidi J. 'Melodrama, Realism and Empire on the British Stage'. *Acts of Supremacy: The British Empire and the Stage, 1790–1930*. Manchester: Manchester University Press, 1991. 129–49.

Hollingshead, John. *My Lifetime*. London: Sampson Low, 1895.

Hulme, David Russell. 'Orpheus with his Lute: Sources of Edward German's Music for the Victorian and Edwardian Drama'. *Brio*, 37 (2000). 36–47.

Hultgren, Neil. *Melodramatic Imperial Writing: From the Sepoy Rebellion to Cecil Rhodes*. Athens: Ohio University Press, 2014.

James, Louis. *Fiction for the Working Man, 1830–1850*. Oxford: Oxford University Press, 1963.

Jerome, Jerome K. *Stage-Land: Curious Habits and Customs of Its Inhabitants*. London: Chatto & Windus, 1889.

John, Juliet. *Dickens's Villains: Melodrama, Character, Popular Culture*. Oxford: Oxford University Press, 2001.

'Melodrama'. *Oxford Bibliographies: Victorian Literature*. 2 March 2011. www.oxfordbibliographies.com/view/document/obo-9780199799558/obo-9780199799558-0042.xml.

'Melodrama and Its Criticism: An Essay in Memory of Sally Ledger'. *19: Interdisciplinary Studies in the Long Nineteenth Century*, 8 (2009). http://doi.org/10.16995/ntn.496.

Johnson, Ray. 'Tricks, Traps and Transformations: Illusion in Victorian Spectacular Theatre'. *Early Popular Visual Culture*, 5 (2007). 151–65.

Jones, David. *Gothic Machine: Textualities, Pre-Cinematic Media and Film in Popular Visual Culture, 1670–1910*. Cardiff: University of Wales Press, 2011.

Knapp, Raymond. *The American Musical and the Formation of National Identity*. Princeton: Princeton University Press, 2005.

Leaver, Kristen. 'Victorian Melodrama and the Performance of Poverty'. *Victorian Literature and Culture*, 27 (1999). 443–56.

Ledger, Sally. *Dickens and the Popular Radical Imagination*. Cambridge: Cambridge University Press, 2007.

Lewes, George Henry. *On Actors and the Art of Acting*. London: Smith, Elder & Co., 1875.

Lhamon, W. T. *Jump Jim Crow: Lost Plays, Lyrics, and Street Prose of the First Atlantic Popular Culture*. Cambridge: Harvard University Press, 2003.

Loren, Scott and Jörg Metelmann (eds.). *Melodrama After the Tears: New Perspectives on the Politics of Victimhood*. Amsterdam: Amsterdam University Press, 2015.

MacKenzie, John. *Orientalism: History, Theory, and the Arts*. Manchester: Manchester University Press, 1995.

Marcus, Sharon. *The Drama of Celebrity*. Princeton: Princeton University Press, forthcoming.

'Salome!! Sarah Bernhardt, Oscar Wilde, and the Drama of Celebrity'. *PMLA*, 126 (2011). 999–1021.

Marks, Martin. *Music and the Silent Film*. Oxford: Oxford University Press, 1997.

Marsan, Jules. 'Le Mélodrama et Guilbert de Pixérécourt'. *Revue d'Histoire littéraire de la France*, 7e Année, no. 2 (1900). 196–220.

Mayer, David. 'Encountering Melodrama'. *The Cambridge Companion to Victorian and Edwardian Theatre*. Ed. Kerry Powell. Cambridge: Cambridge University Press, 2004. 145–63.

*Henry Irving and* The Bells. Manchester: Manchester University Press, 1980.

'Nineteenth Century Theatre Music'. *Theatre Notebook*, 30 (1976). 115–22.

(ed.). *Playing Out the Empire: Ben Hur and Other Toga Plays and Films, 1883–1908: A Critical Anthology*. Oxford: Clarendon Press, 1994.

*Stagestruck Filmmaker: D. W. Griffith and the American Theatre*. Iowa City: University of Iowa Press, 2009.

Mayer, David and Matthew Scott. *Four Bars of 'Agit': Incidental Music for Victorian and Edwardian Melodrama*. London: Samuel French, 1983.

Mayhew, Henry. *London Labour and the London Poor*. 4 vols. Reprint. New York: Dover, 1967.

McConachie, Bruce A. *Melodramatic Formations: American Theatre and Society, 1820–1870*. Iowa City: University of Iowa Press, 1992.

McWilliam, Rohan. 'Melodrama'. *A Companion to Sensation Fiction*. Ed. Pamela K. Gilbert. Chichester, West Sussex: Wiley-Blackwell, 2011. 54–66.

'Melodrama and the Historians'. *Radical History Review*, 78 (2000). 57–84.

Meer, Sarah. *Uncle Tom Mania: Slavery, Minstrelsy and Transatlantic Culture in the 1850s*. Athens: University of Georgia Press, 2005.

Meisel, Martin. *Realizations: Narrative, Pictorial, and Theatrical Arts in Nineteenth Century England*. Princeton: Princeton University Press, 1983.

'Scattered Chiaroscuro: Melodrama as a Way of Seeing'. *Melodrama: Stage, Picture, Screen*. Eds. Jacky Bratton, Jim Cook, and Christine Gledhill. London: British Film Institute, 1994. 65–81.

Mercer, John and Martin Shingler. *Melodrama: Genre, Style, Sensibility*. London: Wallflower, 2004.

Metayer, Léon. 'What the Heroine Taught, 1830–1870'. *Melodrama: The Cultural Emergence of a Genre*. Eds. Michael Hays and Anastasia Nikolopoulou. New York: St. Martin's Press, 1996. 235–44.

Moody, Jane, and Daniel O'Quinn (eds.). *The Cambridge Companion to British Theatre, 1730–1830*. Cambridge: Cambridge University Press, 2007.

*Illegitimate Theatre in London, 1770–1840*. Cambridge: Cambridge University Press, 2000.

Morosetti, Tiziana (ed.). *Staging the Other in Nineteenth-Century British Drama*. Bern: Peter Lang, 2015.

Mukherjee, Ankhi. *Aesthetic Hysteria: The Great Neurosis in Victorian Melodrama and Contemporary Fiction*. New York: Routledge, 2007.

Mulvey, Laura. '"It Will Be a Magnificent Obsession": The Melodrama's Role in the Development of Contemporary Film Theory'. *Melodrama: Stage, Picture, Screen*. Eds. Jacky Bratton, Jim Cook, and Christine Gledhill. London: British Film Institute, 1994. 121–33.

Neale, Steve. 'Melo Talk: On the Meaning and Use of the Term "Melodrama" in the American Trade Press'. *The Velvet Light Trap*, 32 (1993). 66–89.

'Melodrama and Tears'. *Screen*, 27 (1986). 6–22.

Newey, Katherine. *Women's Theatre Writing in Victorian Britain*. Basingstoke: Palgrave Macmillan, 2005.

Nicoll, Allardyce. *A History of Early Nineteenth-Century Drama, 1800–1850*. 2 vols. Cambridge: Cambridge University Press, 1959.

O'Hara, Glenn. *Britain and the Sea: Since 1600*. Basingstoke: Palgrave Macmillan, 2010.

O'Neill, Norman. 'Music to Stage Plays'. *Proceeding for the Royal Musical Association* (21 March 1911). 85–102.

Pao, Angela C. *The Orient of the Boulevards: Exoticism, Empire, and Nineteenth-Century French Theater*. Philadelphia: University of Pennsylvania Press, 1998.

Pickering, Michael. *Blackface Minstrelsy in Britain*. Aldershot: Ashgate, 2008.

Pisani, Michael V. *Music for the Melodramatic Theatre in Nineteenth-Century London and New York*. Iowa City: University of Iowa Press, 2014.

'*The Corsican Brothers* and the Legacy of Its Tremulous "Ghost Melody"'. *Journal of Film Music*, 5 (2012). 29–39.

'Music for the Theatre: Style and Function in Incidental Music'. *The Cambridge Companion to Victorian and Edwardian Theatre*. Ed. Kerry Powell. Cambridge: Cambridge University Press, 2004. 70–92.

Powell, Kerry (ed.). *The Cambridge Companion to Victorian and Edwardian Theatre*. Cambridge: Cambridge University Press, 2004.

*Women and Victorian Theatre*. Cambridge: Cambridge University Press, 1997.

Preston, Carrie J. *Modernism's Mythic Pose: Gender, Genre, Solo Performance*. Oxford: Oxford University Press, 2011.

Preston, Katherine. 'American Musical Theatre Before the Twentieth Century'. *The Cambridge Companion to the Musical*. Eds. William A. Everett and Paul R. Laird. Third edition. Cambridge: Cambridge University Press, 2017. 21–50.

Rahill, Frank. *The World of Melodrama*. University Park: Pennsylvania State University Press, 1967.

Ranger, Paul. *'Terror and Pity reign in every Breast': Gothic Drama in the London Patent Theatres, 1750–1820*. London: Society for Theatre Research, 1991.

Redmond, James (ed.). *Themes in Drama 14: Melodrama*. Cambridge: Cambridge University Press, 1991.

Reid, Alastair. *Social Classes and Social Relations in Britain, 1850–1914*. Second edition. Cambridge: Cambridge University Press, 1995.

Richards, Kenneth and Peter Thomson (eds.). *Nineteenth Century British Theatre*. London: Methuen, 1971.
Roach, Joseph. *Cities of the Dead: Circum-Atlantic Performance*. New York: Columbia University Press, 1996.
*The Player's Passion: Studies in the Science of Acting*. Newark: University of Delaware Press, 1985.
Rowell, George. *William Terriss and Richard Prince: Two Characters in an Adelphi Melodrama*. London: Society for Theatre Research, 1987.
*The Victorian Theatre, 1792–1914: A Survey*. Oxford: Oxford University Press, 1956.
Roy, Donald and Victor Emeljanow. *Romantic and Revolutionary Theatre, 1789–1860*. Cambridge: Cambridge University Press, 2003.
Russell, Gillian. *The Theatres of War: Performance, Politics and Society, 1793–1815*. Oxford: Clarendon Press, 1995.
Saggini, Francesca. *The Gothic Novel and the Stage: Romantic Appropriations*. London: Pickering & Chatto, 2015.
Saglia, Diego. '"The Frighted Stage": The Sensational Proliferation of Ghost Melodrama in the 1820s'. *Studies in Romanticism*, 54 (2015). 269–93.
'"I Almost Dread to Tell You": Gothic Melodrama and the Aesthetic of Silence in Thomas Holcroft's *A Tale of Mystery*'. *Gothic Studies*, 14 (2012). 93–107.
'The Gothic Stage'. *Romantic Gothic*. Ed. Angela Wright and Dale Townsend. Edinburgh: Edinburgh University Press, 2016. 73–94.
Sala, Emilio. *L'opera senza canto, il mélo romantico e l'invenzione della colonna sonora*. Venice: Marsilio, 1995.
Sala, George Augustus. *Twice Round the Clock*. London: J. & R. Maxwell, 1859.
Schoch, Richard. *Queen Victoria and the Theatre of Her Age*. Basingstoke: Palgrave Macmillan, 2004.
Scott, Clement. *The Drama of Yesterday & To-day*. 2 vols. London: Macmillan and Co. Ltd., 1899.
Sedgwick, Eve Kosofsky. *The Coherence of Gothic Conventions*. Reprint. New York: Methuen, 1986.
Sgroi, Renée. 'Authentic Reality TV Selves: The Case for Melodrama'. *Television, Aesthetics and Reality*. Ed. Anthony Barker. Cambridge: Cambridge University Press, 2006. 225–47.
Shapiro [McLucas], Anne Dhu. 'Action Music in American Pantomime and Melodrama, 1730-1913'. *American Music* 1 (1984). 49–72.
Shaw, George Bernard. *Our Theatres in the Nineties*. 3 vols. London: Constable and Company Ltd., 1932.
Shawn, Ted. *Every Little Movement: A Book about François Delsarte*. Reprint. Princeton: Princeton Book Company Publishers, 1975.
Shepherd, Simon and Peter Womack. *English Drama: A Cultural History*. Oxford: Blackwell, 1996.
'Pauses of Mutual Agitation'. *Melodrama: Stage, Picture, Screen*. Eds. Jacky Bratton, Jim Cook, and Christine Gledhill. London: British Film Institute, 1994. 25–37.
Singer, Ben. *Melodrama and Modernity: Early Sensational Cinema and Its Contexts*. New York: Columbia University Press, 2001.

Skeggs, Beverley and Helen Wood. *Reacting to Reality Television: Performance, Audience and Value*. London: Routledge, 2012.

Slater, Michael. *Douglas Jerrold: 1803–1857*. London: Duckworth, 2002.

Smith, James L. *Melodrama*. London: Methuen, 1973.

Smith, Tiffany Watt. *On Flinching: Theatricality and Scientific Looking from Darwin to Shell Shock*. Oxford: Oxford University Press, 2014.

Sondheim, Stephen 'Larger than Life: Reflections on Melodrama and Sweeney Todd'. *Melodrama*. Ed. Daniel Gerould. New York: New York Literary Forum, 1980, 3–14.

Stephens, John Russell. *The Censorship of English Drama, 1824–1901*. Cambridge: Cambridge University Press, 1980.

Storey, John. *Culture and Power in Cultural Studies: the Politics of Signification*. Edinburgh: Edinburgh University Press, 2010.

Swindells, Julia and David Francis Taylor (eds.). *The Oxford Handbook of the Georgian Theatre, 1737–1832*. Oxford: Oxford University Press, 2014.

*Glorious Causes: The Grand Theatre of Political Change, 1789–1833*. Oxford: Oxford University Press, 2001.

Taylor, George. *The French Revolution and the London Stage, 1798–1805*. Cambridge: Cambridge University Press, 2000.

'François Delsarte: A Codification of Nineteenth-Century Acting'. *Theatre Research International*, 24 (1999). 71–81.

*Players and Performances in the Victorian Theatre*. Manchester: Manchester University Press, 1989.

Thompson, E. P. *The Making of the English Working Class*. London: Gollancz, 1963.

True Brown, Moses. *Philosophy and Expression*. Boston: Houghton Mifflin, 1886.

Trussler, Simon. 'A Chronology of Early Melodrama, 1764–1840'. *Theatre Quarterly*, 1 (1971). 19–21.

Van Kooy, Dana. 'Darkness Visible: The Early Melodrama of British Imperialism and the Commodification of History in Sheridan's *Pizarro*'. *Theatre Journal*, 64 (2012). 179–96.

Van den Akker, Robin and Timotheus Vermeulen. 'Notes on Metamodernism'. *Journal of Aesthetics and Culture*, 2 (2010). 1–14.

Vardac, A. Nicholas. *Stage to Screen: Theatrical Method from Garrick to Griffith*. Cambridge: Harvard University Press, 1949.

Vicinus, Martha. '"Helpless and Unfriended": Nineteenth-Century Domestic Melodrama'. *When They Weren't Doing Shakespeare: Essays on Nineteenth-Century British and American Theatre*. Eds. Judith L. Fisher and Stephen Watt. Athens: University of Georgia Press, 1989. 174–86.

Voskuil, Lynn M. *Acting Naturally: Victorian Theatricality and Authenticity*. Charlottesville: University of Virginia Press, 2004.

Wadsworth, Darryl. '"A Low Born Labourer Like You": Audience and Working-Class Melodrama'. *Varieties of Victorianism: The Uses of a Past*. Ed. Gary Day. London: Macmillan, 1998. 206–19.

Waeber, Jacqueline. *Music and the Melodramatic Hybrid, from Rousseau to Schoenberg*. Trans. Stephen Huebner. Rochester: University of Rochester Press, forthcoming 2018.

Waldman, Harry. *Maurice Tourneur: The Life and Films*. Jefferson, North Carolina: McFarland and Co., 2001.

Wang, Dan. 'Melodrama: Two Ways'. *19th-Century Music*, 36 (2012). 122–35.

Waters, Hazel. *Racism on the Victorian Stage: Representation of Slavery and the Black Character.* Cambridge: Cambridge University Press, 2007.

Waters, Maureen. 'The Stage Irishman'. *The Comic Irishman.* Albany: State University of New York Press, 1984. 41–57.

Wells, H. G. *Anticipations of the Reaction of Mechanical and Scientific Progress upon Human Life and Thought.* London: Chapman & Hall, 1901.

Weltman, Sharon Aronofsky. '"Can a Fellow Be a Villain All His Life?": *Oliver!*, Fagin, and Performing Jewishness'. *Nineteenth-Century Contexts*, 33 (2011). 371–88.

'Theater, Exhibition, and Spectacle in the Nineteenth Century'. *Companion to British Literature.* Eds. Robert DeMaria Jr, Heesok Chang, and Samantha Zacher. London: Wiley Blackwell, 2014. 68–88.

Williams, Carolyn. *Gilbert and Sullivan: Gender, Genre, Parody.* New York: Columbia University Press, 2010.

'Melodrama'. *The New Cambridge History of Victorian Literature.* Ed. Kate Flint. Cambridge: Cambridge University Press, 2012. 193–219.

'Moving Pictures: George Eliot and Melodrama'. *Compassion: The Culture and Politics of an Emotion.* Ed. Lauren Berlant. New York and London: Routledge, 2004. 105–144.

Williams, Linda. 'Mega-Melodrama! Vertical and Horizontal Suspensions of the "Classical"'. *Modern Drama*, 55 (2012). 523–43.

'Melodrama Revisited'. *Refiguring American Film Genres.* Ed. Nick Browne. Berkeley: University of California Press, 1998. 42–82.

*Playing the Race Card: Melodramas of Black and White from Uncle Tom to O. J. Simpson.* Berkeley: University of California Press, 2001.

Wilmore, David (ed.). *Edwin O. Sachs: Architect, Stagehand, Engineer and Fireman.* Northants: Theatresearch, 1998.

Wilson, A. E. *East End Entertainment.* London: Arthur Barker, Ltd., 1954.

Yeandle, Peter. '"Executed with remarkable care and artistic feeling": Music Hall Ballet and Popular Imperialism'. *Politics, Performance and Popular Culture.* Eds. Kate Newey, Jeffrey Richards, and Peter Yeandle. Manchester: Manchester University Press, 2016. 152–73.

Ziter, Edward. *The Orient on the Victorian Stage.* Cambridge: Cambridge University Press, 2003.

Zunshine, Lisa. *Acting Theory and the English Stage, 1700–1830.* 5 vols. London: Pickering & Chatto, 2008.

# INDEX

acting manuals, 116–17, 153
acting, melodramatic, 2, 80, 99, 109, 112–23, 230–1
  'stock' emotions in, 114–17
  in early film, 230–1
  performance conventions of, 99, 112–13, 114–17, 118–19, 121–3
  relation to physiological theories, 115–18, 120–1
  shift to restrained style, 121–3
adaptation, 13, 20–1, 29, 33, 39–45, 49, 51–2, 87, 96, 160, 166–7, 227, 228–9, 232, 239–41, 251, 253, 262–3, 268–73
  novel to stage, 20, 33, 39–40, 43–5, 51–2, 158, 160, 166–7, 268–73
  stage to film, 239–41, 246
Adelphi Theatre, 15, 18, 19, 20, 22, 24, 26, 52, 79, 82, 98, 152, 172, 200
Affect, 2–3, 17, 22, 63, 89, 160, 176, 219
Africa, 177, 179
Aldridge, Ira, 195–6
American Revolution, 52
Anglo-Afghan War, Second, 178
Anglo-Egyptian War, 178
Anglo-Maratha Wars, 181
Anglo-Mysore Wars, 181
Anglo-Zulu War, 178, 183
anti-Semitism, 271–3
  Jewish caricatures in melodrama, 226, 271–3
Armstrong, Lance, 297–301
Astley's Amphitheatre, 18, 86, 230
audiences, melodramatic, 6, 62, 78–90, 170, 266, See also theatres
  age demographics of, 85–6
  class composition of, 78–9, 81–2, 83, 84–9
  early film audiences, 225, 235

Australia, 177, 184
avalanches, 135–6

'bad woman' melodrama, 75, 86, 233, 238
ballet, 263–4
Balzac, Honoré de, 283–6
  Peau de chagin, La (The Fatal Skin), 283–6
Barras, Charles M., 263–4
  Black Crook, The, 262, 263–4
Barrymore, William, 180
  El Hyder; or, The Chief of the Ghaut Mountains, 180–1
Bart, Lionel, 268–9
  Oliver!, 262, 268–73
Bentley, Eric, 112–13, 253, 290, 301
Bernhardt, Sarah, 235
Berthelet, Arthur, 239–40
  Sherlock Holmes (film), 239–40
Biche au Bois, La (The Doe of the Forest), 263–4
Big Brother franchise (television), 291–6
Biograph Company, 227, 232–4, 235
Birmingham, 88–9
Blaché, Alice Guy, 246–7
  Strike, The (film), 246–7
Boaden, James, 34–6
  Fontainville Forest, 35–6
Boer War, 179, 180, 182, 183–4, 186
Booth, Michael, 5, 49, 51, 127, 174, 212, 291, 298
Boucicault, Dion, 75, 80, 82–3, 87, 112, 121–2, 127–9, 134, 186–8, 194, 198–200, 202–3, 221, 253, 265
  Colleen Bawn, The, 75, 76, 82, 87, 98, 122, 128–9, 253
  Corsican Brothers, The, 82, 121–2, 220

# Index

domestic melodrama (cont.)
female characters in, 21, 67–8,
71–2, 150–3
idealized space of 'home' in, 25, 61–2,
65–7, 250–1
marital relations in, 72–3, 152–3,
258–60
oscillation of domestication and
melodramatization in, 61, 64
Donne, W. B., 134–5
*Ashore and Afloat*, 134–5
Drury Lane Theatre, 6, 16, 18, 19, 23, 24,
34–5, 37, 43, 79, 80–1, 83, 139, 176,
182, 237

earthquakes, 130–4
Eastern Orientalist melodrama, 180–1,
*See also* Orientalism
economic distress melodrama, 15, 27–8,
*See also* crime melodrama
Edison Company, 228, 240
Eisenstein, Sergei, 247
Eliot, George, 209, 211, 216, 217, 219
Emeljanow, Victor, 6
emotion, theories of, 115–18, 120–1
Empire, 3, 26, 90, 176–89, 192, 193, *See also*
imperialist melodrama
domestication of empire by melodrama,
184–6
melodramatic spectacle and, 176–7, 178,
181, 182–3
role of melodrama in forging imperial
subjects, 176–9, 182–3, 189
enclosure, 64, 66
equestrian acts, 50, 86, 230
extravaganza, 263–4

facial expression, 114, 116–18, 120–1,
153, 216
family, 3, 21, 28, 48, 61, 65, 67–8, 171–2,
214, 247–51, 258–60
farce, 50
Farley, Charles, 43
*Raymond and Agnes; or, The Castle of
Lindenberg*, 39–40
father, 67–8, 213
relation to daughter in domestic
melodrama, 67–8, 72
*féerie*, 227, 263–4
femininity, 4, 72, 75, 149–50, 152–3, 214,
258–9, *See also* gender
'improper feminine', 149–50
feminist theory, 149–50, 247–51, 257–60

film, 5, 224–43, *See also* moving picture
melodrama
continuities with the stage, 110, 141, 179,
217, 224–5, 230–1
development of early film melodrama,
225–36
explosion of feature-length film
melodramas, 236
outdatedness of 'film melodrama' as a term
today, 245
film studies, 5, 245, 246, 257–60
fires, 134
Fitzball, Edward, 26, 27, 51–2, 65, 87
*Flying Dutchman, The*, 26, 52
*Home Again! or, The Lieutenant's
Daughters*, 65, 69–70, 71, 72
*Inchcape Bell; or, The Dumb Sailor Boy,
The*, 26, 213
*Pilot, The*, 51–2
'fourth wall', 123
France, 13–15, 17, 18, 20, 48, 49–50, 51, 95,
114, 179, 183, 302
French Revolution, 1, 2, 16, 17, 49, 114, 166,
274, 279
Freud, Sigmund, 277–87

Gad, Urban, 233–4
*Afgruden (The Abyss)* (film), 233–4
Gaines, Jane M., 5, 245–60
Gallagher, Catherine, 214–15
Gamer, Michael, 31–45
Garrick, David, 114, 115–16, 119
gender, 3–4, 61, 75, 76, 147–61, 228, 247,
257–60, *See also* masculinity,
femininity
class and, 3, 150, 151–2, 154–5, 160
female protagonists in melodrama, 21,
71–2, 149–53, 236, 259–60
transgender narratives, 296–8
women playwrights, 6, 156–61
Germany, 2, 17, 51, 95, 183
gesture, 112, 113–17, 120–1, 122–3, 153,
161, 216, 229, 230–1, 241, 279–80
Gilbert, W. S., 59, 264, *See also* Sullivan,
Arthur
*H.M.S. Pinafore*, 59
*Pirates of Penzance, The*, 59
Gledhill, Christine, 5, 61–77, 150, 251,
258
Gothic drama, 2, 14, 63, 149–50, *See also*
Gothic melodrama
as containing roots of melodrama, 31, 33,
149–50

318

# Index

# Index

Index

# CAMBRIDGE COMPANIONS TO ...

## AUTHORS

*Edward Albee* edited by Stephen J. Bottoms

*Margaret Atwood* edited by Coral Ann Howells

*W. H. Auden* edited by Stan Smith

*Jane Austen* edited by Edward Copeland and Juliet McMaster (second edition)

*Balzac* edited by Owen Heathcote and Andrew Watts

*Beckett* edited by John Pilling

*Bede* edited by Scott DeGregorio

*Aphra Behn* edited by Derek Hughes and Janet Todd

*Walter Benjamin* edited by David S. Ferris

*William Blake* edited by Morris Eaves

*Boccaccio* edited by Guyda Armstrong, Rhiannon Daniels, and Stephen J. Milner

*Jorge Luis Borges* edited by Edwin Williamson

*Brecht* edited by Peter Thomson and Glendyr Sacks (second edition)

*The Brontës* edited by Heather Glen

*Bunyan* edited by Anne Dunan-Page

*Frances Burney* edited by Peter Sabor

*Byron* edited by Drummond Bone

*Albert Camus* edited by Edward J. Hughes

*Willa Cather* edited by Marilee Lindemann

*Cervantes* edited by Anthony J. Cascardi

*Chaucer* edited by Piero Boitani and Jill Mann (second edition)

*Chekhov* edited by Vera Gottlieb and Paul Allain

*Kate Chopin* edited by Janet Beer

*Caryl Churchill* edited by Elaine Aston and Elin Diamond

*Cicero* edited by Catherine Steel

*Coleridge* edited by Lucy Newlyn

*Wilkie Collins* edited by Jenny Bourne Taylor

*Joseph Conrad* edited by J. H. Stape

*H. D.* edited by Nephie J. Christodoulides and Polina Mackay

*Dante* edited by Rachel Jacoff (second edition)

*Daniel Defoe* edited by John Richetti

*Don DeLillo* edited by John N. Duvall

*Charles Dickens* edited by John O. Jordan

*Emily Dickinson* edited by Wendy Martin

*John Donne* edited by Achsah Guibbory

*Dostoevskii* edited by W. J. Leatherbarrow

*Theodore Dreiser* edited by Leonard Cassuto and Claire Virginia Eby

*John Dryden* edited by Steven N. Zwicker

*W. E. B. Du Bois* edited by Shamoon Zamir

*George Eliot* edited by George Levine

*T. S. Eliot* edited by A. David Moody

*Ralph Ellison* edited by Ross Posnock

*Ralph Waldo Emerson* edited by Joel Porte and Saundra Morris

*William Faulkner* edited by Philip M. Weinstein

*Henry Fielding* edited by Claude Rawson

*F. Scott Fitzgerald* edited by Ruth Prigozy

*Flaubert* edited by Timothy Unwin

*E. M. Forster* edited by David Bradshaw

*Benjamin Franklin* edited by Carla Mulford

*Brian Friel* edited by Anthony Roche

*Robert Frost* edited by Robert Faggen

*Gabriel García Márquez* edited by Philip Swanson

*Elizabeth Gaskell* edited by Jill L. Matus

*Edward Gibbon* edited by Karen O'Brien and Brian Young

*Goethe* edited by Lesley Sharpe

*Günter Grass* edited by Stuart Taberner

*Thomas Hardy* edited by Dale Kramer

*David Hare* edited by Richard Boon

*Nathaniel Hawthorne* edited by Richard Millington

*Seamus Heaney* edited by Bernard O'Donoghue

*Ernest Hemingway* edited by Scott Donaldson

*Homer* edited by Robert Fowler

*Horace* edited by Stephen Harrison

*Ted Hughes* edited by Terry Gifford

*Ibsen* edited by James McFarlane

*Henry James* edited by Jonathan Freedman

*Samuel Johnson* edited by Greg Clingham

*Ben Jonson* edited by Richard Harp and Stanley Stewart

*James Joyce* edited by Derek Attridge (second edition)

*Kafka* edited by Julian Preece

*Keats* edited by Susan J. Wolfson

*Rudyard Kipling* edited by Howard J. Booth

*Lacan* edited by Jean-Michel Rabaté

*D. H. Lawrence* edited by Anne Fernihough

*Primo Levi* edited by Robert Gordon

*Lucretius* edited by Stuart Gillespie and Philip Hardie

*Machiavelli* edited by John M. Najemy

*David Mamet* edited by Christopher Bigsby

*Thomas Mann* edited by Ritchie Robertson

*Christopher Marlowe* edited by Patrick Cheney

*Andrew Marvell* edited by Derek Hirst and Steven N. Zwicker

*Herman Melville* edited by Robert S. Levine

*Arthur Miller* edited by Christopher Bigsby (second edition)

*Milton* edited by Dennis Danielson (second edition)

*Molière* edited by David Bradby and Andrew Calder

*Toni Morrison* edited by Justine Tally

*Alice Munro* edited by David Staines

*Nabokov* edited by Julian W. Connolly

*Eugene O'Neill* edited by Michael Manheim

*George Orwell* edited by John Rodden

*Ovid* edited by Philip Hardie

*Petrarch* edited by Albert Russell Ascoli and Unn Falkeid

*Harold Pinter* edited by Peter Raby (second edition)

*Sylvia Plath* edited by Jo Gill

*Edgar Allan Poe* edited by Kevin J. Hayes

*Alexander Pope* edited by Pat Rogers

*Ezra Pound* edited by Ira B. Nadel

*Proust* edited by Richard Bales

*Pushkin* edited by Andrew Kahn

*Rabelais* edited by John O'Brien

*Rilke* edited by Karen Leeder and Robert Vilain

*Philip Roth* edited by Timothy Parrish

*Salman Rushdie* edited by Abdulrazak Gurnah

*John Ruskin* edited by Francis O'Gorman

*Shakespeare* edited by Margareta de Grazia and Stanley Wells (second edition)

*Shakespearean Comedy* edited by Alexander Leggatt

*Shakespeare and Contemporary Dramatists* edited by Ton Hoenselaars

*Shakespeare and Popular Culture* edited by Robert Shaughnessy

*Shakespearean Tragedy* edited by Claire McEachern (second edition)

*Shakespeare on Film* edited by Russell Jackson (second edition)

*Shakespeare on Stage* edited by Stanley Wells and Sarah Stanton

*Shakespeare's First Folio* edited by Emma Smith

*Shakespeare's History Plays* edited by Michael Hattaway

*Shakespeare's Last Plays* edited by Catherine M. S. Alexander

*Shakespeare's Poetry* edited by Patrick Cheney

*George Bernard Shaw* edited by Christopher Innes

*Shelley* edited by Timothy Morton

*Mary Shelley* edited by Esther Schor

*Sam Shepard* edited by Matthew C. Roudané

*Spenser* edited by Andrew Hadfield

*Laurence Sterne* edited by Thomas Keymer

*Wallace Stevens* edited by John N. Serio

*Tom Stoppard* edited by Katherine E. Kelly

*Harriet Beecher Stowe* edited by Cindy Weinstein

*August Strindberg* edited by Michael Robinson

*Jonathan Swift* edited by Christopher Fox

*J. M. Synge* edited by P. J. Mathews

*Tacitus* edited by A. J. Woodman

*Henry David Thoreau* edited by Joel Myerson

*Tolstoy* edited by Donna Tussing Orwin

*Anthony Trollope* edited by Carolyn Dever and Lisa Niles

*Mark Twain* edited by Forrest G. Robinson

*John Updike* edited by Stacey Olster

*Mario Vargas Llosa* edited by Efrain Kristal and John King

*Virgil* edited by Charles Martindale

*Voltaire* edited by Nicholas Cronk

*David Foster Wallace* edited by Ralph Clare

*Edith Wharton* edited by Millicent Bell

*Walt Whitman* edited by Ezra Greenspan

*Oscar Wilde* edited by Peter Raby

*Tennessee Williams* edited by Matthew C. Roudané

*August Wilson* edited by Christopher Bigsby

*Mary Wollstonecraft* edited by Claudia L. Johnson

*Virginia Woolf* edited by Susan Sellers (second edition)

*Wordsworth* edited by Stephen Gill

*W. B. Yeats* edited by Marjorie Howes and
John Kelly

*Xenophon* edited by Michael A. Flower

*Zola* edited by Brian Nelson

## TOPICS

*The Actress* edited by Maggie B. Gale and
John Stokes

*The African American Novel* edited by
Maryemma Graham

*The African American Slave Narrative* edited by
Audrey A. Fisch

*Theatre History* by David Wiles and
Christine Dymkowski

*African American Theatre* by Harvey
Young

*Allegory* edited by Rita Copeland and
Peter Struck

*American Crime Fiction* edited by Catherine
Ross Nickerson

*American Gothic* edited by Jeffrey
Andrew Weinstock

*American Literature of the 1930s* edited by
William Solomon

*American Modernism* edited by
Walter Kalaidjian

*American Poetry Since 1945* edited by
Jennifer Ashton

*American Realism and Naturalism* edited by
Donald Pizer

*American Travel Writing* edited by
Alfred Bendixen and Judith Hamera

*American Women Playwrights* edited by
Brenda Murphy

*Ancient Rhetoric* edited by Erik Gunderson

*Arthurian Legend* edited by Elizabeth Archibald
and Ad Putter

*Australian Literature* edited by Elizabeth
Webby

*The Beats* edited by Stephen Belletto

*British Black and Asian Literature (1945-2010)*
edited by Deirdre Osborne

*British Literature of the French Revolution*
edited by Pamela Clemit

*British Romanticism* edited by Stuart Curran
(second edition)

*British Romantic Poetry* edited by
James Chandler and Maureen N. McLane

*British Theatre, 1730-1830*, edited by
Jane Moody and Daniel O'Quinn

*Canadian Literature* edited by Eva-Marie Kröller
(second edition)

*Children's Literature* edited by M. O. Grenby
and Andrea Immel

*The Classic Russian Novel* edited by Malcolm
V. Jones and Robin Feuer Miller

*Contemporary Irish Poetry* edited by
Matthew Campbell

*Creative Writing* edited by David Morley and
Philip Neilsen

*Crime Fiction* edited by Martin Priestman

*Dracula* edited by Roger Luckhurst

*Early Modern Women's Writing* edited by Laura
Lunger Knoppers

*The Eighteenth-Century Novel* edited by
John Richetti

*Eighteenth-Century Poetry* edited by John Sitter

*Emma* edited by Peter Sabor

*English Literature, 1500–1600* edited by Arthur
F. Kinney

*English Literature, 1650–1740* edited by Steven
N. Zwicker

*English Literature, 1740-1830* edited by
Thomas Keymer and Jon Mee

*English Literature, 1830-1914* edited by
Joanne Shattock

*English Melodrama* edited by Carolyn
Williams

*English Novelists* edited by Adrian Poole

*English Poetry, Donne to Marvell* edited by
Thomas N. Corns

*English Poets* edited by Claude Rawson

*English Renaissance Drama, second edition* edited by A. R. Braunmuller and Michael Hattaway

*English Renaissance Tragedy* edited by
Emma Smith and Garrett A. Sullivan Jr.

*English Restoration Theatre* edited by Deborah
C. Payne Fisk

*The Epic* edited by Catherine Bates

*Erotic Literature* edited by Bradford Mudge

*European Modernism* edited by Pericles Lewis

*European Novelists* edited by Michael Bell

*Fairy Tales edited* by Maria Tatar

*Fantasy Literature* edited by Edward James and
Farah Mendlesohn

*Feminist Literary Theory* edited by Ellen Rooney